THE BIG BREACH

THE BIG BREACH

From Top Secret to Maximum Security

Richard Tomlinson

First published in Great Britain in 2001 by
CUTTING EDGE PRESS
7 Albany Street, Edinburgh, EH1 3UG

ISBN 1 903813 01 8

A catalogue record for this book is available from the British Library

Typeset in Stone and Typewriter
Printed and bound in Great Britain

CONTENTS

FOREWORD

The fall of the Berlin wall and the end of the Cold War marked the beginning of a period which has seen an unprecedented crisis systematically unfold within the intelligence services of Britain and many other countries. These events – which MI6 and the CIA comprehensively failed to predict – destroyed much of the *raison d'être* of both MI6 and MI5, its domestic counterpart. Organisations which had been created and formed primarily in response to the perceived and actual threats from the Soviet bloc could not easily adapt to the new circumstances. What use now for hundreds of Soviet specialists, of people who had built up a comprehensive expertise on every twist and turn in the Kremlin? Or for those who had spent years building files on subversives and fellow travellers? New conditions require new solutions. But as the world changes and enters a much less certain future, no longer dominated by the two great power blocs, Britain's security services have notably failed to discover a new role for themselves.

Despite moving into new territories, such as anti-proliferation and combating crime, whether it be money laundering or drug smuggling, the evidence is that these activities are seen within the security services as being rather distasteful, like a once well-to-do lady taking in washing. But the world has impinged. The old order no longer exists. Secrecy can no longer be regarded as an absolute in an era of human rights and freedom of information. It is hardly, therefore, surprising that MI5, MI6 and their less well-known sister agencies have all come under increasing scrutiny in the last three or four years. As a journalist, it is hard to think of a time when so much has appeared in print about the security services.

Those seeking reform in Whitehall have, until recently, trodden a lonely path. The security community has amply demonstrated its continuing grip on the levers of power. The British government, no matter of which political hue, has single-mindedly pursued former intelligence officials, journalists and their publications in what has become a vain attempt to stop information reaching the public domain. Richard Tomlinson is not the only person to have been hounded and harassed by the security services and Special Branch. David Shayler and Annie Machon, 'Martin Ingrams', Liam Clarke, Nigel Wylde, Martin Bright, Tony Geraghty, Ed Moloney, Julie-Ann Davies and James Steen have all been subject to injunctions, police raids and threats of imprisonment. This is not a comprehensive list. In court hearings which led to the *Sunday Times* winning the right to publish extracts from this book once it was in the public domain, I found myself in the uncomfortable position of being accused in a witness statement written by an anonymous senior member of MI6. This person produced no evidence other than to say his information came from 'secret sources'. The Master of the Rolls, Lord Phillips, rejected these allegations, referring to them disparagingly as 'speculative possibilities'.

It is clear that Britain's laws are out-of-date. Most democracies around the world have adopted internationally accepted standards of freedom of expression and freedom of access to information. In Britain the level of public accountability of the security services is zero. As Richard Tomlinson spells out in this book, referring to the head of MI6, 'No one can tell the Boss what to do.' The Parliamentary Intelligence and Security Committee, accountable only to the Prime Minister, offers the barest of fig leaves to cover this lack of scrutiny. Compare this to the United States, where several years ago I sat and listened to a potential director of the CIA be examined in public by senators. The use of such procedures has not, as far as I know, weakened democracy.

Richard Tomlinson has been criticised for the suggestion that he may reveal state secrets. There are several points to make in response. First, MI6 has had six years to conduct the most thorough security audit on everything once connected with his work. It is unlikely that they will have left any loose ends. Second, the real objection by MI6 to this book is not what secrets he may have accidentally leaked. His account of his time since leaving MI6 is infinitely more damaging to the service than any possible secrets the book may reveal to a hostile intelligence service. While it may be interesting to read about the latest gizmo developed by Q's real-life equivalent, or derring-do in distant lands, far more can be gleaned about the internal state of affairs within MI6 by the fact that for five years it has been unable to settle what was effectively a personnel issue. Its vindictive pursuit of a former high-flyer throughout the courts of the world – at a cost of millions of pounds to the taxpayer – reveals an organisation which has not got its priorities right.

Despite his experiences, Richard Tomlinson has remained remarkably human. He has shown great resilience, despite numerous arrests, removal of his personal property and off-the-record briefings by his former employers to gullible journalists who have printed extravagant stories about him without bothering to check the facts.

Significantly, this book reveals that MI6 regularly sends its officers into the field under journalistic cover, a practice which is banned in many countries, including the United States. The unhealthy relationship between MI6 and journalists is only one of many issues raised by *The Big Breach*.

Now that the book is out, it cannot be right for MI6 to continue its campaign against Richard Tomlinson. Far better it should put in place the reforms which will ensure such a débâcle never takes place again. No modern democracy can allow a secret organisation spending hundreds of millions of pounds every year to exist free from oversight and oblivious to its public responsibilities.

Nick Fielding
Sunday Times
February 2001

PROLOGUE

In order to protect their identities, the names of all serving MI6 officers have been changed except those of the Chiefs, who have been publicly declared by MI6 themselves. The names of other private individuals have been changed, except where they have been widely reported in the press or have specifically given permission for their real names to be used. Details of the MI6 operations described have also been altered.

1

TARGETING

AUGUST 1976
NORTHERN ENGLAND

There was just enough natural light filtering through the skylight to work. It was quiet, except for the gentle cooing of pigeons and the occasional flit of swallows leaving their nests in the rafters to hunt insects in the evening air. Leaning over the heavily scarred oak workbench, I carefully ground the granulated weed-killer into a fine white powder with a mortar and pestle improvised from an old glass ashtray and a six-inch bolt. A brief visit to the town library had provided the correct stochastic ratio for the explosive reaction between sodium hyper-chlorate and sucrose. With a rusty set of kitchen scales I weighed out the correct amount of sugar and ground that down too. The old one-inch copper pipe was already prepared, one end crimped up using a vice, and a pencil-sized hole drilled into its midpoint and covered with a strip of masking tape. All that remained was to mix the two white powders, tip a few grammes into the pipe and tamp it down with a wooden dowel. When the tube was full, I gingerly crimped down the other end – too much violence could cause the mixture to detonate prematurely. Laying out a couple of feet of two-inch masking tape, sticky side uppermost, I carefully sprinkled out a line of the remaining white powder along its length, then rolled it up like a long cigarette. If thin and loosely packed, the fuse would burn slowly enough to let me reach cover. Rolling up the leg of my jeans, I taped the device to my shin with a couple of strips of masking tape, concealed the fuse in my sock and slipped out of the barn.

Dusk was falling on the village. Most of the population were indoors eating their evening meal and the road through the settlement was empty except for a few old cars parked at the side. There had been no rain for many months and the grass verges were parched white. I hurried past the small post office, carefully scanning the second-floor windows. The net curtains didn't twitch, suggesting that the grumpy postmaster hadn't spotted me.

The handful of middle-aged drinkers in the corner bar, probably farmers judging by their ruddy complexions and outdoor clothing, didn't look up from their drinks as I passed the window. Slipping round the side I hurried down the short hill to the red sandstone bridge across the river. A man was walking his dog towards me, but they paid no attention. Glancing over the parapet to check the river, I saw the normally swift, deep waters were slowed to a trickle between a series of pools, still except for the occasional trout rising for a fly.

Checking once more to ensure no one was watching, I slipped over the parapet and dropped out of sight. There were three arches to the bridge, supported on two small buttressed islands. Under the first arch there was a broad ledge, heavily scoured by the floods which came every winter. I clambered over the barbed wire fence built to prevent sheep from the neighbouring field straying underneath and dropped to my hands and knees to squeeze up to the stonework. I waited for a few minutes, listening – it wasn't too late to abort. Distant wood pigeons cooed gently and a nearby herd of sheep bleated sporadically. A car passed overhead, but that was the only sound of human activity.

Pulling up my trouser leg, I unstrapped the improvised explosive device and scraped at the river gravel under the arch with a piece of driftwood, creating a hole large enough to bury the pipe-bomb against the foundations. A quick tug removed the tape masking the hole in the tube and I inserted the fuse. A last check around confirmed that no one was watching.

With one flick, the Zippo's flame ignited the touchpaper. I watched for a moment, ensuring it was fizzling soundly, and scampered. There was just enough time to reach the cover of a fallen elm trunk before the device blew with a resounding bang that was much louder than expected. A family of ducks quacked away from the cover of some reeds on the muddy bank and the cooing of the wood pigeons abruptly halted.

Gingerly, just as the echo rolled back from the fellsides of the valley, I emerged from my cover to inspect the damage. The dust was still settling, but the bridge was standing. I smiled with excitement. It was easily my best bang of the summer – jolly good fun for a 13-year-old. I set off for home at the double, hoping the grumpy postmaster wouldn't collar me as I passed his house.

Father was from a Lancashire farming family and met my mother while studying agriculture at Newcastle University. In 1962 they emigrated to New Zealand with their son, Matthew, who was then less than a year old. Father got a job with the New Zealand Ministry of Agriculture as a farm adviser in Hamilton, North Island. I was born in 1963 shortly after their arrival; then in 1964 came Jonathan, my younger brother. New Zealand was an idyllic place to bring up a young family – good climate, peaceful, plenty of space – and Father wanted to stay, but my mother wanted us to be educated in England.

On our return in 1968 my father found work as an agricultural adviser in what was then called the county of Cumberland. My parents started house hunting in the area and discovered an old coachhouse that they both liked in a village a few miles north of Penrith. The house was not very large and was in a ramshackle condition, but it had a big garden containing some spacious outbuildings. My mother liked the large garden that would give her three young sons plenty of room to play. My father was keen on DIY and building, and saw plenty of scope for improvement. They scraped together the money they had and mortgaged themselves to the hilt to buy it and we moved in shortly after my fifth birthday. My mother started work as a biology teacher in a comprehensive school in the market town of Penrith.

At first my brothers and I attended local primary schools, but my parents wanted a better education for us than that provided by the secondary schools in the area. Matthew, being the eldest, sat the entrance exams for nearby private schools and won a scholarship to Barnard Castle, an independent boarding school near Durham in north-east England. He started there in 1972 and I followed the year after, also with a scholarship, then Jonathan two years later. Despite free tuition, it was still a considerable financial sacrifice for my parents to pay the school fees every year. It must have been quite an emotional sacrifice for them too, because we all hated the place.

Barnard Castle school was very sport-oriented, particularly towards rugby. I scraped into the school rugby and swimming teams a few times as a junior, but lost interest in later years. The disciplined regime of boarding school was unpleasant. Life was dictated by bells – bells for lessons, meals, prep, bedtime, lights-out and chapel. There were a few good times there, but my strongest memories are of being cold, hungry and slightly bored. The daily chapel services – twice on Sundays – were especially tedious.

The holidays made school bearable, particularly the long summer break. The River Eden ran through the village and many hours were spent with the local boys on the bridge, carving our initials into the parapet and pulling wheelies on our bikes. In the summer we spent long afternoons in the river, swimming and shooting the rapids on old inner tubes. Everything mechanical interested me and many happy hours were spent tinkering in my father's workshop in the big barn next to our house, fiddling with his tools and getting filthy dirty. With my father, I built a go-kart from bits of scrap-metal and an old Briggs & Stratton bail-elevator engine rescued from a nearby farmyard, and used it to tear up my mother's lawn. The go-kart was joined by an old Lambretta scooter, also immediately pulled to bits and rebuilt. There wasn't enough room in the garden to get it beyond third gear, so when my parents were out one day, I took it out on to the village road to see how fast it would go. I nearly crashed it into the grumpy postmaster's car and had to endure years of grudges from him.

Returning to boarding school at the end of the holidays was grim. Unlike my brothers, who both left after O-levels to study at the local comprehensive school, I stuck it out for A-levels. The school didn't much cater for my interests and I was often in trouble for seeking stimulation from unapproved activities. We had a cheerfully irresponsible A-level chemistry teacher, Mr Chadwick, who one organic chemistry lesson demonstrated the stupefying effect of ether by gassing one of my classmates, Villiers, leaving him passed out on the floor of the laboratories. Chadwick turned a blind eye while we stole bottles of the chemical from the labs afterwards and got high sniffing it in the school grounds. He also taught us how to make explosives, whose effects he gleefully demonstrated by blowing up bombs behind the biology labs. Villiers and I stole the ingredients to make our own bombs in the sixth form kitchens. Once we made mercury fulminate, an unstable explosive which involved reacting deadly poisonous mercury and cyanide. We boiled them up in an old saucepan which, to our delight, the school jock used afterwards to make himself scrambled eggs. I bumped into him many years later in London, so it presumably didn't do him permanent harm.

Though school was not always fun, I worked hard and won a scholarship to study engineering at Cambridge University. The gap year was spent working in South Africa for De Beers in a job arranged by my father's brother, a research scientist at the diamond mining and manufacturing firm. The bright blue skies, open spaces of the high veldt, good food and wine were a refreshing contrast to Barnard Castle. One of the prerequisites to study engineering at Cambridge was to learn workshop skills, so the first few months at De Beers were spent learning to lathe, mill and weld. Then the firm gave me a fun project.

Diamonds are created in nature by the intense pressure and temperature deep in the earth's crust metamorphosing raw carbon into diamonds. De Beers theorised that diamonds could be created artificially by the intense but instantaneous temperatures and pressures created in an explosion, and they asked me to investigate. Several happy months were spent designing and making increasingly large bombs of plastic explosive, packed around a core of ground carbon. With the help of demolition experts from the South African Defence Force, we detonated them on ranges just outside Johannesburg, making some huge explosions. It was possible that we managed to make a few diamonds, but we never managed to find them in the huge craters left by the bombs.

It was a wrench to leave that job in the summer of 1981, but I was looking forward to starting at Cambridge.

2

CULTIVATION

FRIDAY, 8 JUNE 1984
GONVILLE & CAIUS COLLEGE, CAMBRIDGE

A sweltering May week was drawing to a close and the rounds of drunken garden parties that undergraduates organised to celebrate the end of final exams were winding down. My engineering tutor had just told me at the Caius College garden party that the faculty had awarded me first class honours in my aeronautical engineering final exams. Too much Pimms and the evening sun slanting into Gonville court were making me drowsy as I returned to my rooms.

'Tomlinson?' an unfamiliar voice called from behind. 'You're Tomlinson, aren't you?' I turned round to see Dr Christopher Pilchard, a tutor in law, leaning out of the open window of his ground-floor study. His face was familiar, but having never met him it was surprising that he knew my name. He was notorious in the college because of his ginger wig, the result of a bicycle accident many years earlier which had caused all his hair to fall out. Slightly tipsy, it was difficult to resist casually examining his hairline for signs of it as he spoke. 'Tomlinson, have you thought about what you're going to do with yourself after you leave?'

'Yes, sir,' I replied cautiously, wondering why he should be interested.

'I'm joining the navy, the fleet air arm.'

Pilchard snorted dismissively, as if he didn't approve of the military. 'Listen, Tomlinson, if you ever change your mind, but would like to try your hand at another form of government service, then let me know.' With that he ducked back into his study, taking care not to catch his wig on the lip of the window sash.

Continuing on to my rooms, it felt flattering to have been approached. For it had been a discreet invitation to join the British Secret Intelligence Service, more commonly referred to by its old wartime name, MI6. Every Oxford and Cambridge college and leading British university has a 'talent spotter' like Pilchard, a don sympathetic to MI6 who looks out for suitable recruits. The majority of MI6 recruits come this way from the two most prestigious universities in Britain, though it is not foolproof – Philby, Maclean and Burgess were all recruited into MI6 the same way.

Pilchard's approach was flattering but, climbing the creaky wooden stairs to my digs at the top of D staircase, I decided not to pursue the offer – for the moment at least. Having read a few John Le Carré novels, I reckoned the job seemed stuffy and desk-bound. Nor did I identify much with the other undergraduates whom Pilchard had approached – conservative, establishment arts students who spent most of their days lolling around drunk in the college bar. For them, getting a tap on the shoulder from Pilchard was a rite of passage, a sign that they had made their mark on college life. If that was the sort of person MI6 wanted then it wasn't the right career for me.

Inspired by the books I had read in my spare time at Cambridge, I wanted a career that offered travel and adventure: Wilfred Thesiger, the desert explorer who crossed the Arabian 'empty quarter' when only in his early 20s; Sir Francis Chichester, who single-handedly circumnavigated the world by sail and almost by light aircraft; Antoine de St Exupéry, the French pioneer aviator whose semi-autobiographical novel *Vol de Nuit*, set in pre-war Argentina, I had so greatly enjoyed; Captain Oates, a former member of the college, who selflessly sacrificed himself on Scott's 1914 Antarctic expedition and whose flag was displayed in the college dining-hall, reminding us of his exploits every evening. It seemed to me that the best way to lead an adventurous life like these role-models, and in a structured and secure career, was to join the armed services, and the navy appealed to me the most.

Pilchard's suggestion, however, was intriguing. Lying back on my narrow bed in the garret room, the evening light slanting in through the open window, I wondered what had marked me out amongst the other undergraduates. On matriculating in the university in 1981, I had been determined to do more than just study. My uncle in South Africa had been a member of the Cambridge University Air Squadron, a flying club sponsored by the Royal Air Force, and he enthused me to join up. The opportunity to learn to fly at the exacting standards of the RAF and even get paid a small stipend was an opportunity too good to miss. The Air Squadron became the focal point of my extracurricular and social activities at the university. We learned to fly in the Bulldog, a robust dual-seat training aircraft. My instructor, Flight Lieutenant Stan Witchall, then one of the oldest still-active officers in the RAF, had been a young Hurricane pilot in the Battle of Britain. Twice a week I bunked out of engineering lectures and cycled up to Marshall's airfield, seven kilometres from the centre of Cambridge, for flying lessons.

Scuba-diving was another activity which enthused me, inspired by the films of Jacques Cousteau. After I had qualified with the university club, Easter holidays were spent in Cornwall diving on the wrecks and reefs of the murky, cold Channel waters, then getting drunk in the evenings on the strong local brews of the old fishing and smuggling villages. It was nothing like the paradises portrayed in Cousteau's films, but was still exhilarating.

The summer holidays of 1982 were spent travelling around Europe on a rail-pass that allowed unlimited travel for a flat fee. My budget was tiny, so nights were spent sleeping on trains and the days sightseeing. Thousands of miles of slumber got me as far afield as Morocco and Turkey. The experience gave me the travel bug, enthusing me to go further afield.

The next year a vacation job in a local bakery yielded enough savings for a trip to the Far East. Two months were spent backpacking around Thailand and Malaysia on a shoestring budget. My return flight was with Aeroflot, the cheapest ticket available, and a brief refuelling stop was scheduled in Moscow. But it was the day after a Russian Air Force Mig 17 had shot down Korean Air Lines Flight 007 over the Sakhalin peninsula, killing all 269 persons aboard the Boeing 747. In reprisal, the Western powers had banned all Aeroflot flights from their airways shortly after my plane arrived at Moscow's Sheremetyevo airport. Along with the other 200 passengers, I was stranded in Moscow for two days, waiting for a British Airways jet to arrive from London to pick us up. Aeroflot put us up in a cheap hotel near the airport, but refused to unload our hold luggage, leaving us with just hand-luggage and the clothes we'd been wearing on leaving sweltering Bangkok. But inappropriate attire wasn't going to spoil my unexpected opportunity to see Moscow. With an equally inappropriately dressed Australian whom I'd met on the plane, I tramped around in the freezing autumnal rain and fog in T-shirts and flipflops, to the bemusement of the dour Muscovites.

It had been a busy three years as an undergraduate, and perhaps my industry and travel was one of the reasons for Pilchard's invitation. Several years later I learned that MI6 was lacking in officers with sufficient technical expertise to understand the increasingly scientific nature of its work and Pilchard, like the other university talent-spotters, had been briefed to look out for science graduates – which was probably another reason he approached me. His invitation was interesting, but I put it to the back of my mind as there were more pressing projects. In a fortnight's time, with five friends, I would be flying to the Philippines for a university-sponsored research expedition to investigate the effects of pollution on the fragile coral reefs of the Philippine archipelago. It was to be a real Cousteau experience, diving in crystal-clear tropical waters.

Three months later, back from the Far East, I made the long trip from Cumbria to the naval town of Portsmouth to take the AIB (Admiralty Interview Board), the entry test for a naval career. After sailing through the exams and practical tests, I assumed the medical exam, held the next day, would be straightforward. I was wrong. Examination of my medical records revealed that I had experienced a mild case of asthma when aged seven, and that was enough to fail me. A Surgeon Lieutenant Commander explained that the expense of training a naval pilot was too great to risk him redeveloping later in life a childhood illness that might jeopardise his operational effectiveness. My aspirations to join the navy were dashed and it was shattering news.

Mooching around London a few days after the AIB, a poster in a Kensington underground station showing a girl wading up to her waist in a tropical swamp caught my eye. It was an advertisement for recruits to join Operation Raleigh, a youth adventure expedition, and it looked just the sort of challenge to get over the disappointment of my rejection. I sent off an application form, was accepted and a few months later was on my way to the Caribbean to join the expedition's square-rigged sailing brig, the *Zebu*, to learn the intricacies of crewing a square-rigger.

Back in the UK three months later, I still could not get enthusiastic about any particular career and so decided to go back to university. I applied for and won a Kennedy Memorial scholarship to study at the Massachusetts Institute of Technology in the USA – a fantastic prize, especially since the scholarship included transatlantic passage to New York on the QE2. I started at MIT in September 1985, but was in for a shock. Whereas life as an undergraduate at Cambridge had been carefree and easygoing, life as a graduate student at MIT was a lot of hard work. But sticking at the task was rewarded with a masters degree in the autumn of 1986. Shortly before the graduation ceremony, the Rotary Foundation wrote to me informing me that they had awarded me a further prize for a year of study in any country of my choice. My only problem was deciding where to go. Inspired by Argentine friends at MIT and their descriptions of Peronism, radicalism, hyper-inflation, military coups and the Malvinas question, I decided to use the prize to experience their country first hand. A few months later in January 1987, a Swissair flight took me to Buenos Aires International Airport.

Gripping my bag hard between my knees I braced myself for the inevitable impact. For the third time, the taxi-driver swerved the battered Renault 12, its worn tyres protesting, around the back of the belching Mercedes bus into the tiniest of gaps in the outer lane of the *autopista*. The journey from the airport to downtown Buenos Aires was proving an uncomfortable baptism. As we passed a huge blue-and-white billboard bearing the slogan 'LAS MALVINAS SON ARGENTINAS' the beetle-browed driver, who had been glaring at me in the rear-view mirror for several kilometres, took a long draw on his cigarette and flicked it out of the window into the darkness. 'De donde es, usted?' he asked, suspiciously.

For a moment it occurred to me to lie. It was only a few years after the Falklands war and I was not sure how a British visitor would be received. But curious to see his reaction, I cautiously answered, 'Soy Britannico.' He glanced in his mirror again, as if he hadn't heard. 'Britannico . . . Inglaterra,' I said, this time a bit louder.

He fixed me with his glare again and I wondered if my answer might have been undiplomatic. 'Señora Thatcher,' he replied, his dark eyes flashing under his eyebrow, 'She is good woman. I wish she come here – make better.' He gesticulated with a sweeping motion of his hand, and broke into a gold-toothed smile.

That was typical of the reaction of many Argentines during the coming year. The bitter memories of the Falklands war were fresh in their minds, but their antipathy was tempered by the long-standing cultural and commercial links with Britain.

That evening, after finding a room in a modest hotel, I met up for dinner with Schuyler, an American student of the same age who had also won a Rotary prize. He had majored in Latin American studies at Stanford and was amusing and laid-back. The next day we rented a flat together in central Buenos Aires.

The main objective of the Rotary prize was to get to know a different culture through travel and friendships, but we were also expected to follow a course of study. Schuyler and I enrolled in a post-graduate political science course, held in evening classes at the

University of Buenos Aires. Our fellow students – senior military officers, left-wing journalists, aspiring politicians and a Peronista Catholic priest – were a microcosm of the powers in Argentine society. Democracy, under Raul Alfonsín's Radical party, was still in fragile infancy after years of tyrannical rule by the discredited military junta. As representatives of the imperialist 'Yanquis' and 'Britannicos', the other students spared us no quarter in the spirited and occasionally fierce classroom debates. Schuyler was soon embroiled in political activity, attending rallies, demonstrations and student meetings. When Alfonsín's government nearly fell to a military coup on Easter Sunday, 1987, we went together to the Casa Rosada to see the passionate Argentine crowds rallying to support democracy.

But most days, I left Schuyler to his own activities. I wanted to start flying again and one of the Air Force officers in my class put me in touch with an instructor, Rodolfo Sieger, who operated out of San Fernando airfield, a couple of hours by 'Colectivo' bus from central Buenos Aires. A German immigrant, Sieger fought in the Luftwaffe during the Second World War, flying Messerschmitt Me109s in the Battle of Britain. After the war, his own family wiped out in the Dresden fireball, he emigrated to Argentina, becoming a civilian pilot, and retired as a senior pilot in Aerolineas Argentinas. Needing to supplement his pension, he bought a 1930s vintage Luscombe Silvaire, a sort of aerial Citroën 2CV, and set up as a flying instructor. It was not the safest machine in which to take the Argentine pilot's licence exam, but it was cheap to hire and it was appealing to learn from a man who may have been one of Flight Lieutenant Witchall's aerial adversaries.

Over the next few weeks, preparing for my practical tests and theory exams, I learned of another aspect of Rodolfo's business. At the time there were very heavy duties on consumer electronics in Argentina, whereas in Paraguay, only a few hundred kilometres away, there were none. There were therefore incentives to smuggle in such goods, though the Argentine customs service naturally did their best to combat this trade. Once a week, Rodolfo flew over the River Plate to a grass airstrip in Paraguay and loaded up the Luscombe with video recorders and televisions. The underpowered aircraft barely staggered into the air and Rodolfo flew back in the dark of night, skimming the waves to avoid detection by Argentine naval radar.

One day we flew out to Mendoza, in the foothills of the Andes. Rodolfo had tracked down a much-needed and rare spare part for the old aeroplane just over the border in Chile and asked me to collect it. The tiny Luscombe was not powerful enough to fly over the Andes, so this stage of the journey would have to be done by bus.

On arrival at the isolated border crossing, nestling in the shadow of Aconcagua, it dawned on me that I had a problem. My New Zealand passport was best for travelling in and out of Argentina as, unlike the British passport, it required no visa. In Chile, however, the British passport was more convenient because, unlike New Zealanders, Brits needed no visa. Rushing to pack for the trip, I had grabbed just my British passport.

The two surly Argentine border police who boarded the bus at the checkpoint might not overlook it, however. Realising that my New Zealand passport with its Argentine entry stamps was in my bedside locker in Buenos Aires, there was no option but to bluff my way over the border. I claimed that my New Zealand passport had been stolen and I was going to Santiago, the only New Zealand embassy in the southern cone, to get a replacement. The elder of the two guards believed my story, but the younger got suspicious and ordered me off the bus to search me. He soon found my unstamped British passport in my rucksack and arrested me on suspicion of having entered the country illegally.

They took me back to Mendoza police station, strip-searched me and dumped me in a dirty cell furnished with a damp mattress and a bucket. After a couple of boring hours they escorted me to an office where two scowling officers sat behind a steel desk. To my bafflement, they were suspicious that I was a spy and interrogated me. Details of my activities, my address, my friends were earnestly noted in little black books. After an hour, their questions seemed absurd. 'What is the name of your dog?' one asked.

'Jesse,' I replied, barely containing my exasperation.

They held me overnight in the dirty cell and in the morning a colonel from the Argentine air force came out from Buenos Aires to interrogate me again. 'What is the name of your dog?' he asked menacingly.

'I told the other bloke that last night,' I replied innocently, wondering why our lakeland terrier puppy was such a threat to Argentine Skyhawks. It later dawned on me that he was testing my cover. If I really was an innocent exchange student, it would be easy to remember inconsequential details like my dog's name. But if I was a spy under cover, spontaneously and correctly answering trivial questions from one day to the next would be harder. The lesson was useful when I did become a spy.

They released me later that day, though not without first making me play an impromptu game of rugby. They reasoned that any genuine New Zealander would be an excellent wing-forward, and my protests to the contrary fell on deaf ears. Mendoza is one of the main rugby-playing provinces of Argentina and some of their players were very good. They made me suffer and on returning to Buenos Aires the following day, my right eye was badly blackened. 'So you met some of my Gestapo friends,' Rodolfo laughed. I wasn't sure whether he was joking.

A few weeks later, a Swiss diplomat friend invited me to a barbecue at the Swiss embassy. Britain and Argentina still had not re-established diplomatic links after the Falklands war, so British interests were looked after by a few British diplomats working inside the Swiss embassy. My Swiss friend introduced me to one of them, a tall, gangly fellow a few years older than myself, who was a second secretary. He was fascinated to hear about my flying and asked eagerly about the range and load-carrying ability of the Luscombe. He seemed a bit disappointed when he learned that it struggled to carry more than a television and a video recorder.

After joining MI6 I discovered that the gangly fellow, Mark Freeman, was from the service. In Buenos Aires he was running what became quite a coup for MI6 against the Argentine navy.

Having failed to predict the invasion of the Falklands Islands in April 1982, the reputation of MI6 in Whitehall nosedived. MI6 set out to avoid repeating the same mistake and threw resources at the region, doubling the size of its station in Buenos Aires, building a chain of listening posts in the Chilean Andes to give early warning of Argentine aircraft movements and opening a new one-man station in Uruguay. Soon a steady stream of intelligence was coming from these efforts.

One piece of intelligence was of particular interest to the DIS (Defence Intelligence Staff) in Whitehall. The Argentines were developing a new and top secret naval mine, made of plastic, rendering it difficult to detect using conventional minesweeping techniques. It contained electronics which enabled it to distinguish the noise-signatures of British and Argentine ships. The DIS regarded the new mine as a dangerous threat and wanted details of its specification. MI6 learned of a French weapons technician who was working on the project in the Rio Gallegos naval base. They successfully recruited him, giving him the codename FORFEIT.

Smuggling the mine out of the Rio Gallegos base was not too difficult as FORFEIT had top-level security clearance and was trusted by the Argentine security guards. He loaded one of the mines into the boot of his car and drove it out of the base, claiming that he was taking it to another naval base in Commodore Rivadavia for sea trials. The hard bit of the operation was smuggling the mine out of Argentina.

Options for getting the mine to the UK were constrained by the need to ensure that the operation was deniable, so MI6 dared not use a submarine to sneak into one of the bays of Argentina's long, unpopulated coastline. MI6 considered recruiting a pilot to fly the mine across the River Plate to Uruguay in a light aircraft, and that was why Freeman had been disappointed to learn of the Luscombe's feeble capacity. In the end, an MI6 officer working under cover as a Danish chemical engineer rendezvoused with FORFEIT at a lockup garage in Buenos Aires, transferred the mine to the boot of his hire car and drove it to the Uruguay border. Prior reconnaissance revealed that the border police rarely searched vehicles but, just in case, the businessman had a cover story that the strange barrel-shaped piece of plastic in the boot of his car was nothing more sinister than a piece of chemical engineering equipment. In the event the cover story was not needed and he drove it without incident to Montevideo. From there it was clandestinely loaded on to a navy ship which was replenishing after a Falklands tour, and shipped to the UK.

Boarding a Swissair flight back to London in December 1987 at the end of an interesting year, I picked up a copy of *La Nación*, Argentina's leading newspaper. Down on page five there was an article about a light aircraft which had crashed while making a night landing at a small grass airfield just outside Buenos Aires, killing the pilot. Police were investigating the wreckage among rumours that the plane was being used for smuggling. The pilot was unnamed but I knew it must be Rodolfo.

Back in London, without money, I needed a job, preferably one that satisfied my sense of adventure and desire to work overseas. I wrote to Pilchard asking if the offer he had made in 1984 was still open. He didn't reply directly, but a couple of weeks later a letter arrived on FCO (Foreign and Commonwealth Office) crested paper signed by a Mr M.A. Halliday inviting me to an interview at 3 Carlton Gardens, London SW1.

Sitting on the low leather sofa in the reception hall of the elegant John Nash-designed house overlooking St James's Park in central London, I was curious and intrigued rather than nervous. The meter ticking next to my battered old BMW parked a block away was more worrying than the impending interview. I checked my watch and hoped it would not last long. Recent editions of *The Economist* and *Financial Times* were scattered in front of me on the low glass-topped table, and I picked one up to pass the time.

I heard soft footsteps descending the stairs from the mezzanine floor above and shortly a tall, pretty girl stepped out on to the marble floor, her high-heels clacking as she approached. I put down *The Economist* and stood. 'Mr Tomlinson?' she asked, smiling. I nodded. 'Mr Halliday will see you now. I'm Kathleen, by the way.' We shook hands and she escorted me up the stairs to the mezzanine floor where she showed me into one of the offices.

A small and slightly built man in a wide-lapelled brown suit with a string vest glimmering through an acrylic shirt awaited behind a desk. We exchanged greetings and shook hands. He urged me to sit down on a low armchair and sat down opposite me, a low table between us. He smiled. 'Do you know what you are doing here?' he asked.

'Haven't a clue,' I replied cautiously.

'Well first, can I ask you to read and sign this?' He handed me a printed sheet of paper and a biro. It was an excerpt from the 1989 OSA (Official Secrets Act), headed 'TOP SECRET' in red ink. He went over to the window and gazed over St James's Park while I read it. I signed it vigorously to signify that I was finished, and he returned with another file. 'Now read this,' he ordered, handing me the green ring-binder.

Halliday returned to the window, leaving me to read the 30 or so plastic-wrapped pages. They explained that MI6 was Britain's overseas intelligence-gathering organisation, administered by the FCO, and that its objective was to gather intelligence from secret human sources on political, military, economic and commercial policies of rival foreign powers. A couple of paragraphs explained the selection procedure – almost identical to the FCO entry procedure, with one extra round of interviews. The positive vetting procedure – an inquisition into a candidate's private life – was described, then it outlined in general terms an MI6 career. Six months of training, a first overseas posting after a couple of years behind a desk in London, then alternate three-year home and overseas postings until compulsory retirement at 55. At the back was the payscale – not generous compared to salaries in the private sector, but still adequate.

I closed the file and put it down on the low table. Halliday got up from his desk and rejoined me. 'What do you think?' he asked eagerly, as though I had just finished inspecting a second-hand car he was trying to sell.

'I'd like to know more,' I replied cautiously.

Halliday asked the usual interview questions with one unusual request. 'One of the jobs we often have to do in MI6 is make a succinct character appraisal of a contact of the service – a pen portrait if you like. Could you describe somebody succinctly who you have come across in your life?' he asked. I thought for a moment, then described Rodolfo. A colourful character, it was not difficult. Halliday made it clear that he was seeking a long-term commitment to the service, in return for which there was a high degree of job security.

'That sounds fine,' I replied. 'I'm looking for just that sort of thing.' The interview ended with Halliday assuring me that he would write to me soon. There were only a few minutes left on the parking meter.

Two weeks later a letter arrived inviting me for a second interview. It was flattering, but my priority was to get overseas quickly and the prospect of having to put in two or three years behind a desk in London first did not appeal. I screwed the letter into a ball and threw it away.

Though keen to go travelling, my debts obliged me to earn some money. Most of my friends from university were settled into steady careers in London in banking or management consultancy. Their lifestyle held no appeal, but pragmatically it offered the best way to save some money. It was the start of the Thatcher boom years and it was easy to get a highly paid job. Booz Allen & Hamilton, a management consultancy in Mayfair, employed me on a salary three times that on offer at MI6. But despite the welcome fat pay cheques, it was clear after a couple of weeks that it wasn't the career for me. Not replying to Halliday's letter was a mistake, and also rude. Writing back, I explained that having taken another job it would be wise to stick it out for a year, but would like to keep in touch. Halliday sent me a polite and understanding reply by return post.

Finding little stimulation in the sedentary consulting job, I needed a more challenging activity to occupy me. When I saw an advert in a newspaper to join the Territorial Army, Britain's reserve army corps, it seemed an ideal avenue in which to channel my spare energy. As it only required attendance at weekends and for two weeks' annual camp per year, joining up would not oblige me to leave the job that paid my bills. Flicking through the glossy recruitment brochure that arrived in the post a few days after my enquiry, I glanced at descriptions of the various reserve units, but the choice was clear: the Special Air Service volunteer regiment. When I rang the recruitment number, a gritty Scottish voice growled the instruction to report to the Duke of York's barracks on King's Road in central London the following Saturday with running shoes and tracksuit for a basic fitness test.

That first test was relatively easy for a fit young man – just five miles around the barracks running track in under 40 minutes. But that was just the start of the demanding selection process. The PT instructor who led the test said that we would need to attend every second weekend for the next year to undertake a series of daunting tests of endurance and stamina, plus a two-week intensive selection camp.

The following weekend just over a hundred other hopeful recruits turned up at the Duke of York's for the first stage of the selection process. Most were former regular army soldiers, or had experience in other parts of the Territorial Army. Some were condescending towards the few recruits, like myself, who had no previous military experience. 'You won't get past the first weekend,' scoffed one shaven-headed former marine. We were briefly interviewed to assess our previous military experience and suitability for the course. Those with criminal convictions and the weirdoes who turned up equipped with black balaclavas or armed with knives were shown the gate. The quartermaster's store issued us with basic army clothing and equipment which we would have to use for the selection course – camouflage trousers, a pair of boots, a couple of hairy woollen shirts, a woolly pullover, webbing, water cans, sleeping bag, a waterproof poncho, a bergen to put it all in and, most importantly, a compass. We were given another running test – this time eight miles in one hour in our new boots. About 20 per cent immediately dropped out and were told to return their newly issued kit.

Soon passing selection became my only goal. My work at Booz Allen & Hamilton was unimportant – just something that had to be done between TA weekends to pay the rent. Every second weekend for the next five months, along with the other surviving candidates, I reported to the Duke of York's at 1930 on Friday evening after a boring but tiring day in the office. We were issued rations and our kit was checked by the DS (Directing Staff) to ensure that we were using only the original equipment issued to us. Anybody who tried to make the selection process easier by purchasing better-quality boots or goretex waterproofs was immediately 'binned', the terminology for ejection from the course. At about 2130, we crammed into the back of a leaking canvas-roofed four-ton lorry and drove down the King's Road, past its thronging pubs, out of London and down the M4 motorway towards Wales.

We would arrive in the early hours of the morning at a remote forest location somewhere in the bleak Brecon Beacon mountains, often already soaked if it was raining. Using our standard army issue sleeping bag and poncho to make a bivouac, we slept for a few hours in a copse or by a mosquito-infested reservoir. Reveille would be at 0600 and the DS gave us an hour to eat a breakfast of dehydrated porridge, canned meat and boiled sweets, make a mug of tea, then pack away all our kit into our bergens. At 0700, the DS gave us a grid reference, usually a hilltop six or seven kilometres away. We set off at the double *en masse*, navigating to the control-point with our waterproofed ordnance-survey map and precious compass. The field rapidly strung out as the fittest and best navigators got to the front. On arrival at the checkpoint, another member of the DS, enviably curled up in his tent with a hot brew on, called out a new grid reference another ten kilometres or so away across difficult terrain. On arrival there, we would be given another grid reference, then another, and so on, never really knowing where or when the march would end.

At around 1800 the fastest runners reached the final checkpoint where we cooked some of the rations that we had been carrying all day and got some rest. The other runners would straggle in over the next few hours. The really slow candidates, or those who could not complete the course through exhaustion or injury, were binned. At about 2100 the DS would brief us on the night march, done in pairs, as the risk of navigating through the craggy mountain ranges in darkness was too great – candidates had occasionally died of exposure or made navigational errors and walked off cliffs. We normally finished this shorter march at about 0400, caught about two hours' sleep before reveille and breakfasted, then there followed an hour or so of hard PT, known as 'beasting'. A 'warmup' run of about four kilometres in our boots, with badly blistered and cut feet from the previous marches, half-killed us and and then a gruelling routine of press-ups and sit-ups finished us off. At about 1100, the torment was over and we collapsed into the lorry for the five-hour drive back to London.

Every weekend, the ratchet was tightened a bit more and the field of remaining candidates got smaller. The marches increased in length and difficulty of navigation and we had increasingly heavy loads to carry in our bergens. I was secretly pleased to see the marine who had sneered at me drop out of one of the harder marches, moaning about badly blistered feet.

The final and most dreaded selection weekend was the infamous 'long drag'. We had navigated all over the Brecon Beacons and knew them too well, so long drag was held in unfamiliar territory in the Peak District of northern England. The goal was to cover a total of 65 kilometres cross-country in under 20 hours, carrying full webbing, a 50lb bergen containing all our gear and rations, and an old FN rifle from which the sling had been removed. At the end of that test only 19 of the 125 who started the course remained of which I, proudly, was one.

Although the long drag endurance test was a major hurdle, there was still a long way to go before those of us who remained would be 'badged' with SAS berets bearing the famous 'Who Dares Wins' motto and accepted into the regiment. Every second weekend for the next six months was taken with 'continuation' training, learning the basic military skills required of an SAS soldier. We were still under scrutiny, however, and any recruit who was deemed by the DS not to have the right attitude or aptitude was binned. Having had no previous experience of the army, even the most basic infantry skills were new to me: field survival, escape and evasion, long-range reconnaissance patrol techniques, dog evasion, abseiling from helicopters, foreign weapon familiarisation. The final two week selection took place at Sennybridge camp in Wales where these skills were put to the test in a long and arduous field exercise.

At the end of the exercise we were 'captured' by the enemy – role-played by paratroopers – blindfolded, roughed up a bit, then taken in the back of a cattle truck to an old disused farm in the Welsh hills. There, still blindfolded, we were stripped and forced into 'stress' positions – either hands spread against a wall, feet kicked back a metre or so and spread wide apart, or else squatting on the floor with back arched and fingers on our heads. After a few minutes either position became uncomfortable, and after 20 minutes cramps and muscle spasms set in. The discomfort was relieved every few hours when we were taken to be 'interrogated' by officers from the Joint Services Interrogation Wing. We were only allowed to give away the 'big four' permitted by the Geneva Convention – name, rank, date of birth and service number – and the interrogators used every ploy they knew to trick us into giving away more. Anybody who gave away the smallest extra detail, even merely admitting that they were thirsty, was immediately binned. After 20 minutes of that we were lead back to the cattle pen and put into a different stress position. Those who endured were finally released after 20 hours.

Finally, because we would shortly learn to parachute, we had to pass P-company, a brutal fitness test taken by the Parachute Regiment as a test of suitability for parachute training. It required explosive strength and power rather than the stamina of SAS selection and I was sorry to see that after going so far a couple of guys failed this last hurdle. The handful of us who remained were 'badged' in a simple ceremony by the CO (Commanding Officer), a colonel in 22 SAS, and accepted into the regiment. It was a proud moment for me, but it needed to be kept in perspective. Our selection process was a stroll in the park compared to the far more arduous and drawn out selection of the regular army's 22 SAS regiment, and our standards of soldiering were much lower. We were awarded an identical beret, but that was about the only thing that was equal between the two regiments.

Between TA weekends, my first priority was to get fit enough to pass SAS selection. Most mornings I arrived at Booz Allen & Hamilton after running twice around Hyde Park, then clock-watched until the evening when I could escape to the nearby Lansdowne sports club for a couple of kilometres of swimming. My lifestyle priorities were very different from my colleagues', who dedicated their spare time to eating and drinking, and I felt little sense of identity with them, exacerbated by the sense of achievement in getting badged. Every morning at my desk I wondered what motivated them in their daily struggle to climb the corporate ladder. Ernst Goldstein was particularly inscrutable. He only had a few more years to wait to receive a fortune that was held in a trust fund until his 30th birthday and although he earned a hefty salary as a management consultant, he lived as if he had already inherited big money, borrowing heavily to support a lavish and extravagant lifestyle. He spent hours on the phone, mostly chatting to friends organising expensive parties and occasionally to clients whom he oleaginously addressed as 'Sir'. Whenever his trimphone rang, his hand shot out like a striking cobra, reaching the receiver before the first 'tring' had finished, and he answered 'Goldstein speaking' with irritating eagerness. While the whole office was working late one night on a 'vitally important' project, I sneaked over to his cubicle while he was absent and glued down his trimphone receiver with a couple of blobs of superglue. When he returned a few minutes later with the managing director and started enthusiastically discussing a cashflow spreadsheet, I rang him on the internal line. As usual, his hand shot out like a frog's tongue for the receiver, but this time it came back with the phone attached, clattering into the side of his head. Worse, because the cradle had not been tripped, the telephone would not stop ringing. Goldstein went berserk, waving the still-ringing phone around as if he were trying to shake a mad dog off his arm. At last, with a manic desperate yank, he ripped the receiver away – only it came away with the top half of the telephone, spilling wires and bells on to the desk. The office was in uproar by now, but Goldstein was oblivious. He put the receiver to his ear and, oleaginous as ever, replied, 'Goldstein speaking.' The managing director stalked off, trying not to lose his dignity by bursting into laughter.

Shortly afterwards, I resigned. The writing was on the wall even before the trimphone incident. The managing director realised that I was not interested in the job and started playing games to make life unpleasant. One evening he arranged a meeting with me at 0730 the following day, forcing me to get into the office unusually early. Then he rang in to tell me that his train had been 'delayed'. It was a relief to get out of the oppressive company, and besides it gave me more time for courses with the Territorial Army.

We were obliged to learn to parachute, and I signed up for the next available basic course at RAF Brize Norton. Two weeks and twelve jumps later, the RAF awarded me my coveted SAS parachute wings. I also got myself on a signals course, learning how to operate the encrypted PRC319 radios and high-speed morse, and completed a basic German course.

I had also just passed my motorcycle test and bought a battered old 800cc BMW trail bike. Inspired by Thesiger's adventures, I wanted to experience the vast emptiness of the deserts for myself. I got a Michelin map of the Sahara from Stanfords map shop, strapped a few jerry cans to the side of the bike, packed up some camping gear and set off on a freezing April morning for Africa.

The trip went smoothly until the end of the tarmac road at Tamanrasset, about halfway down Algeria. The soft sand exposed the inadequacies of the heavily laden motorbike, my inappropriate tyres and lack of off-road motorcycling experience. I covered only five miles on the first day, continuously bogged down in the soft sand or heaving the heavy bike upright after crashing. After one severe fall the forks bent backwards so far that the front wheel rubbed on the engine casings. There was no option but to dismantle them and turn the stanchions through 180 degrees in order to get going again. The wheel no longer fouled the engine but the bike was even harder to handle. Luckily the next morning another big crash straightened the forks out so that the bike handled properly again.

Just south of the dusty and derelict Algerian village of In-Guezzam, I reached the Niger border, marked by a dilapidated wooden hut flying a faded Niger flag and housing a small army detachment. A handful of saffron-robed Tuareg desert traders waited outside, their camels snorting in a patch of shade provided by a sun-bleached awning. The Niger border guards, supervised by a hefty-looking captain dressed in khaki and sporting a set of sunshades, were poking through the Tuaregs' bundles. On the other side of the hut three immaculate BMW motorcycles bearing German number plates were neatly parked. Their owners were camped out alongside, lounging under a flysheet with a few books and magazines, cooking a meal. They looked bored, as if they had been there for some time, and were not much interested when I rode over to greet them. 'How long have you been here?' I asked.

'Three days,' answered a tall, crew-cut Aryan type, dressed in expensive-looking motocross gear. 'That bastard,' he nodded at the fat Captain, 'vill not let us through,' he spat.

I tried to lighten his mood with some small talk. 'Good trip down?' I asked cheerfully.

The German looked at me, then my bike, examining its damage. 'Jah,' he paused for emphasis. 'We have not fallen off once.' I left them to get back to their magazines and went over to introduce myself to the fat captain.

Glaring at me through his dark glasses as I approached, he bristled with animosity. The Germans must have had a few slanging matches with him and perhaps he expected trouble from me. 'Attendez-là,' he snapped, indicating me to go back and wait with the other motorcyclists.

I didn't protest, but in my bad French asked how long I should prepare to wait. His anger abated as he realised that I was not seeking a confrontation. Approaching a bit closer, I noticed that he wore French army parachute wings on the breast pocket of his shirt. 'Ah, vous êtes parachutiste,' I said, affecting a tone of respect.

His anger subsided like a spoilt child presented with a lolly. He drew himself to attention, puffed out his chest and proudly announced, 'I am the most experienced parachutist in the Niger army,' and told me the alarming stories of his eight jumps.

The simple piece of childish flattery was enough. After half an hour, the captain stamped my passport and waved me through. Riding away southwards, in the one wing-mirror that remained intact, I could see the Germans remonstrating angrily with the captain that he had let me through before them.

Stopping a few days later in Agades, the first town on the southern side of the Sahara, I was drinking a beer at a small outdoor bar when another motorcyclist approached. His front wheel was buckled and the forks badly twisted, so the bike lolloped like an old horse. He dismounted painfully, dropped the bike on the ground rather than putting it on its sidestand, came into the bar and ordered a large beer. He turned out to be an orange-packer from Mallorca called Pedro and over our beers we laughed at our various crashes. He spoke no French, so the next day I translated while the local blacksmith straightened out his bike, then we rode together down to Lomé, the main port and capital of Togo. There my trip was over and I put my battered bike on a Sabena cargo plane back to Europe, but Pedro continued his tour of West Africa. A few years later I visited him in Mallorca, and he told me what happened next. Whilst waiting on his bike at some traffic-lights in the lawless town of Libreville in Sierra Leone, two men had pulled him down and robbed him. Gratuitously, one had also bitten him hard on the cheek, leaving not only a vicious scar but also infecting him with the HIV virus.

I arrived back from the Sahara just in time to go on a NATO-organised LRRP (Long Range Reconnaissance Patrol) exercise in Belgium. All NATO countries were invited to send their LRRP troops to the exercise: there were American Rangers, German Fernspähtruppen, Danish Jaeger troops, a reconnaissance troop from the French Foreign Legion, Spanish special forces bizarrely carrying umbrellas as part of their field kit, Greek special forces with bright green camouflage cream applied like a clown's mask, unhappy-looking Dutch conscript special forces, Portuguese, Canadians and Turks. We were there as the British representatives. Ian, a former Royal Tank Regiment sergeant was our PC (Patrol Commander). Mac, a scouser, was lead scout and Jock, with a barely comprehensible Scottish highland accent was the fourth member of our patrol. Ian appointed me signaller, meaning I would have to carry the PRC319 VHF radio, DMHD (Digital Message Handling Device), code books and OTPs (One Time Pads), an SA80 5.68mm rifle, SUSAT telescopic day-sight, image-intensifying night-sight and all my personal survival kit. With a static-line parachute on my back, a reserve parachute on my chest and all this equipment bundled up and hanging off the front of the parachute harness, it was nearly impossible to walk to the Transall transport aircraft for the flight to the DZ (Drop Zone).

As dawn was breaking, we were parachuted in our patrols into the flat farmland of northern Belgium. The Belgian army were out in force with helicopters, ground troops and search dogs acting as the 'enemy' to track us down. We had to get off the DZ and into cover fast to avoid capture. We got ourselves into a small copse by a pond and I set up the radio while the others mounted stags (look-out) and got a brew on. Within minutes the DMHD had received a string of 40 numbers. After decyphering it with the OTPs and decoding it with the code-book, we had the order to set up an OP (Observation Post) on a road about ten kilometres from our existing location, in order to report on 'enemy' traffic movements. To avoid detection, we had to make the distance straight away in the few hours that remained before daybreak.

That would be the pattern for the next four days. A long walk at night, sometimes as far as 40 kilometres, then a lay-up during the day in an OP where we signalled back to the UK command centre our observations of traffic movements of the Belgian army. Between shifts on stag or manning the radio, we grabbed a few hours' sleep.

By the end of the first week, we were all filthy dirty and dishevelled. Camouflage cream and mud was ground into our beards, our fingernails were clogged and our clothing was stinking and soaked with the ceaseless rain. We had also run out of food. Given time, finding food and water would not be much of a problem – there were turnips and potatoes in the fields, water in ditches and ponds. But the DS were piling the pressure on us and we had no time to foray.

The exercise was drawing to a close but the hardest part was still to come. That night we were supposed to make an RV with a 'partisan' friendly agent on the other side of the heavily guarded Albert canal. All the bridges would certainly be guarded and there would be foot patrols along the towpaths. We'd heard endless shooting during the night as the Dutch and German patrols, who had started the exercise the day before us, ran into trouble. All we had eaten for the past two days was a few boiled sweets and biscuits that we had got from one of the buried caches, whose locations had been signalled through to us. Our maps showed a pond in the midst of our copse but it was dried up to nothing more than a foul-smelling, mosquito-filled swamp, meaning we also had no safe water.

'We need some food, badly,' announced Ian, to grunts of approval from the others. 'Tomlinson, you speak French, don't you?' he said. 'Get your civvies on and see if you can get us some food.' At the bottom of my bergen there were some training shoes for use on river crossings, lightweight dark grey Tenson trousers which could double as tactical trousers and a blue Helly Hansen thermal shirt. While I changed into them Jock got some of the foul-smelling swamp water on the boil, picking out the the mosquito larvae, so that I could have a wash and a shave. An hour or so later, I almost looked like part of the human race again. With a handful of Belgian francs in my pocket, I set out for the nearest village.

It was early lunchtime when I got to Zittart. As I strolled into a bar, trying my best to appear casual, one old fellow cradling a glass of Stella Artois glanced up at me and a couple of crew-cut youths sporting downy moustaches were playing pool. At the side of the bar was a small fast-food counter, displaying backlit photographs of chips and hamburgers. I ordered eight portions of hamburgers and chips for the patrol and, while they were frying, got myself a glass of Stella. On an empty stomach my head was soon humming and I found myself chatting to the barman. 'Where are you from?' he asked, noting my bad French. The presence of the exercise in the region had been announced in the local press, and any civilian who helped capture a soldier was given a reward, so some imaginative lying was required. 'Sweden,' I replied. It was the first non-NATO country that came into my head. I padded out the story, inventing answers to his questions on the hoof. 'Yeah, my name is Rickard. I'm an engineer at the SAAB factory in Gothenburg. I'm driving down to Paris with a few friends for a holiday. The car's broken down just outside the village, radiator's boiled over.'

The cover story flowed easily and the two lads finished their game of pool and came over to meet the foreigner. 'What's life like in Sweden then?' asked one. 'Do you get well paid?'

I replied with invented figures, and he seemed impressed. 'Do you have to do military service?' asked the other.

'Yeah, two years,' I replied, knowing from Swedish friends in London that it was the correct answer. 'What about you?' I asked.

'We have to do two years "mili" here,' sniffed the younger of the two. 'We've only got six months till we get out. What a waste of time it is. There is some stupid NATO exercise on around here at the moment.'

'Yeah, I've seen a few convoys and helicopters,' I interjected, trying to sound casual.

The elder joined in. 'We spent the whole of last night trudging up and down the Albert canal, down by Strelen, firing blanks at stupid German soldiers trying to swim across. We're supposed to be down there again tonight but our Lieutenant fell over and cracked a rib last night. The tosser thinks we are going to carry on without him tonight.' They laughed sarcastically.

I left 20 minutes later with a bag of hamburgers for my 'Swedish friends' and five litres of water for the 'car radiator'. After I told Ian what I'd heard in the bar, we swam the canal uneventfully at Strelen that night and were one of three patrols to make it to the final RV without capture. At the end of the exercise all the patrols were graded on their performance and we were in the top ten, only behind the four Danish Jaeger patrols, a Portuguese patrol and a few American Ranger patrols. Considering we were only part-timers and the rest were all the full-time elite of their professional armies, it was not a bad performance.

A couple of weeks later, back at my parents' home, I wrote again to 'Mr Halliday' to reapply to join MI6. The Territorial Army was a lot of fun, but it was no career and at 27 I was too old to join the regular army. MI6 offered the satisfaction of public service, plus it was a structured and secure career with plenty of variety, good pay and perks, and it promised an intriguing lifestyle. The little incident extracting intelligence from the Belgian soldiers had been satisfying and if that was a taste of what MI6 would be like, it would be the right career for me. A couple of days after writing to Halliday, he wrote back inviting me for another interview in Carlton Gardens.

As I rang the doorbell for the second time, I wondered if Halliday would remember my face. As before, Kathleen showed me up to his office on the mezzanine floor. Halliday had changed a lot since our meeting, gaining about six inches in height, losing his beard and acquiring a better wardrobe. 'Please, take a seat.' He ushered me into the same low chair as at the first interview. 'I expect you have already guessed,' he said, 'that I am not the same Halliday you met on your last visit here. Halliday is an alias we use in the recruitment process.'

'Oh yes, I knew that, of course,' I blustered.

Halliday smiled sagely, seeing through my feeble bluff. The rest of the interview was much as before – the same OSA flyer to sign, the same plasti-wrapped folder to read. The new Halliday though, asked more searching questions than the first. 'Often in MI6,' he said, 'we must use charm, guile and our wits to persuade somebody to do something they may not want to do, or to get them to tell us information which perhaps they should not. Are there any examples from your own life where you have had to do that?' I thought for a moment then told him about flattering the Niger army captain into letting me cross the border during my Sahara trip and about my 'undercover' intelligence gathering from the Belgian soldiers in the bar. Halliday seemed to like both those stories.

Halliday wrote to me a few weeks later, inviting me to attend a further round of tests and interviews in Whitehall. MI6 is part of the civil service, so to join the 'Intelligence Branch' candidates have to first pass exactly the same exams which fast-stream candidates for other parts of the civil service must take, whether they are joining the FCO, Treasury or Department of Trade and Industry. MI6 candidates sit the exams separately from other candidates, however, because even at this early stage of the selection process their identities are regarded as secret.

Five other candidates sat with me in the waiting-room before the first exam. One was the son of a serving MI6 officer, one a Metropolitan Police SB (Special Branch) officer, another in the DIS, one a merchant banker and the last worked for a political consultancy in Oxford. The multi-choice tests were like something out of a 1960s 'know your own IQ' book – lots of weird shapes from which we had to choose the odd one out, or dominoes in which we had to guess the next in the series. There was a simple test of numeracy, then a longish but straightforward written paper in which we had to compose a couple of essays. In the afternoon we had to discuss a couple of current affairs topics individually with one of the serving MI6 officers who were supervising the tests. Finally, there was a group discussion exercise. We were asked to plan what advice we would give to a notional high-tech British company which had caught a couple of Chinese exchange engineers spying. The policeman was loud and outspoken, adamantly maintaining that the Chinese spies should be arrested immediately. He dismissed as utterly wet the political consultant's pleas for lenient treatment to safeguard Anglo-Chinese relationships. The discussion exercise broke down in acrimony, despite the diplomatic intervention of the merchant banker.

Having no benchmark, I had no idea if I had done well or badly so after the exams were over a few of us went for a drink to the Admiral Nelson pub across the road and discussed the day's events. The bespectacled and mild-mannered political consultant told me that he would not pursue his application, whether or not he passed the test, if they accepted applicants like the aggressive policeman.

The final stage of the selection process, a lengthy interview before a panel of serving MI6 officers, took place a few days later in Carlton Gardens. The interview got underway late because one of the three had got a puncture on his bike, but eventually they lined up behind the table with 'Halliday' observing from behind. They grilled me with detailed questions on current affairs, my reasons for joining MI6, my long-term ambitions and whether I was genuinely committed to a lifelong career. When I didn't know an answer, I admitted my ignorance rather than bluff. I left Carlton Gardens an hour later convinced that they would fail me.

I was delighted to receive a letter to the contrary a few weeks later. Subject to a successful background security check, I had a job in MI6.

The security vetting procedure was the last hurdle. Many government employees are 'positively vetted', which means that perfunctory checks are made that an individual does not have a criminal record, extreme political views, drug or alcohol dependence or financial problems. Candidates for MI6 must undergo more stringent examination leading, if successful, to an EPV (Enhanced Positive Vetted) certificate. It is a labour-intensive process and MI6 has a staff of about a dozen officers in the vetting department. First, my name was checked with MI6's database, showing up my brief meeting with Freeman in Buenos Aires which he had recorded. The search of MI5's databases and police SB records drew a blank. My creditworthiness was also investigated. My moderate debts were acceptable, as I had not been long out of university, but any records of defaulting on loan repayments or very substantial debts would have disqualified me. Still on a green light after this first round, I was invited to an interview with the vetting officer assigned to my case. He was an avuncular former head of the East European controllerate in MI6 and delved into my personal life. He wanted to know about my political views, any contact with extremist organisations of the left or right, friendships with foreign nationals, any problems with alcohol and contact with drugs. MI6 has loosened up considerably in recent years. Not so long ago, former membership of an organisation such as the Campaign for Nuclear Disarmament would have excluded a candidate, but is acceptable nowadays, and casual experimentation with drugs is ignored. The vetting officer did not take my answers at face value, though. He asked me to nominate eight referees who knew me well, covering all periods of my life since schooldays. These referees were all interviewed by him to check the veracity of my statements. Honesty pays – if it is discovered that a candidate has tried to hide some misdemeanour, he or she is unlikely to be awarded an EPV. There were no skeletons in my cupboard and two months later a photocopied letter in a plain envelope arrived announcing the award of an EPV certificate and confirming the job offer. There were no clues about what my new career would involve. The FCO crested notepaper simply stated to 'arrive promptly at Century House, 100 Westminster Bridge Road, at 10 a.m. on Monday, 2 September 1991. You should bring your passport'.

3.

RECRUITMENT

Nervous and excited at the prospect of my first day in MI6, I had not slept well the previous night and drank too much coffee in an attempt to compensate. My palms were sweating slightly from anticipation as well as the caffeine as I walked the couple of miles from my temporary lodgings in south London to Century House, situated in the run-down borough of Lambeth in South London. The 20-storey concrete office block, grubby from traffic and pigeons, but discreet and anonymous, did not look like a glamorous place to work and was a world away from the swanky Mayfair offices of Booz Allen & Hamilton. Glancing up at the mirrored windows, I tried to imagine what might go on behind them. What decisions were taken, what arguments were made, what secrets were hidden from those of us on the outside? It was exciting to think of soon being permitted inside.

There was little overt security around the building. A couple of CCTV cameras peered at passers-by, anti-bomb net curtains blanked the windows on the first few floors, but there was little else to distinguish Century House from any other mid-rent London office block. Staff were filing into the building, some with umbrellas and newspapers tucked under their arms, others more casually with their hands in their pockets or a sports bag slung over their shoulder.

I pushed open the first heavy glass door, paused to wipe my feet on the mats in the porch, then pushed open the second heavy door to enter a gloomy lobby. The mushroom-brown walls and grey lino floor reminded me of the dingy Aeroflot hotel that I stayed in during my brief stopover in Moscow. Directly opposite the entrance was a reception kiosk, glassed in up to the ceiling, with a small counter opening towards the door. Two security guards sat behind it, manning old-fashioned Bakelite telephones. Either side of the kiosk were a couple of lifts, around which the incoming staff congregated, impatiently jabbing the call buttons. A large plastic plant with dust-covered leaves stood in the corner, mildly alleviating the gloom.

A blue-suited security guard stepped forward from the reception desk. Rotund and avuncular, he had a friendly bearing. 'Pass, please, sir,' he asked briskly. I hesitated and he detected my indecision. 'You must be on the IONEC, are you, sir?' he asked.

'IONEC? What's that?' I asked.

The guard's smile broadened. 'That's the name of the course you're about to spend the next six months on, the Intelligence Officer's New Entry Course,' he replied patiently. 'What's your name?'

'Tomlinson,' I replied. 'That's T-O . . .'

'Yes, yes,' he cut me off, as if ticking me on a memorised list. 'Have you brought your passport?' I handed it over to him, one of the old-fashioned blue hard-covered passports, battered and dog-eared. He flicked it open, checking my name and photograph, then handed it back. 'Welcome to the service, sir.' He pointed to the waiting-room to the right, containing a low table scattered with newspapers.

Two other suited young men waited, talking politely and quietly to each other. I presumed that they were also new candidates, and they eyed me up in a friendly, curious way. The youngest stepped forward confidently, grinning. 'Hi, my name's Markham, Andrew Markham.'

Markham introduced me to the other, who was familiar. Terry Forton was the political consultant who had taken the civil service entrance exams with me. 'I thought you would get in,' Terry said, grinning. 'Remember that ex-special branch guy who wanted to arrest everybody?' he asked. 'He was a fascist bastard. Thankfully he's not here,' he laughed.

'We're the first course for years without any women on it, apparently,' chirped Markham, breaking into our conversation. 'There's nine of us in total. One of them was at Oxford with me, got a double first in Physics, but I couldn't believe it when I heard he was joining this outfit.' They didn't like each other, I guessed. 'Two are ex-army officers, one of them was in the Scots Guards,' he added, impressed that one of them should be from such a respected and smart regiment.

The next student to arrive looked like he was the ex-Scots Guard. He stepped confidently towards us with a rigidly straight back, immaculate Brylcreemed hair, pinstriped suit, expensive shirt and highly polished Oxford shoes, and introduced himself as Ian Castle. He was followed a few minutes later by another young man, wearing the sort of flashy suit and brassy tie favoured by the money traders in the city, which Castle examined disdainfully. Markham reluctantly shook hands with him, grunting an acknowledgement as he introduced himself as Chris Bart. The other newcomers drifted in over the next ten minutes and we chatted with amiable small talk.

The wall clock above the guard's desk showed five past ten, later than the hour that we had been asked to present ourselves. Markham impatiently checked his watch. 'There's still one more to arrive,' he clucked, 'What sort of person turns up late for his first day in MI6?' he tutted.

At that moment a tall, stooped fair-haired figure shuffled in, glancing shiftily towards us. The guard grabbed him by the arm. 'Name, please, sir?' he asked.

'Spencer,' replied the newcomer suspiciously.

'Can I see your passport?' the guard asked.

Spencer looked surprised and hesitant. 'Why? This is still England, isn't it?'

The guard sceptically raised an eyebrow. 'I would like to check your ID, sir.'

Spencer shifted uncomfortably. 'Well, I've kind of forgotten it,' he replied sheepishly. Spencer was eventually allowed to join us some ten minutes later, once the guard had carefully checked his biographical details against the records.

Two others joined us shortly afterwards, as if they had been observing from the wings. Their confident bearing suggested that they were in charge. 'Welcome to IONEC 89, the 89th Intelligence Officers New Entry Course since the Second World War,' announced the elder of the two. Jonathan Ball, a chain-smoking veteran from the cold war, would be the principal teacher on the six-month course, known in MI6 parlance by the designation TD7. In his late 40s, a heavy drinker judging by his florid features, his rounded, chubby face and peculiar tottering walk reminded me of an oversized toddler. The second of the two introduced himself with a slight lisp as Nick Long. In his mid-30s, dressed in a smart suit, heavily padded at the shoulders, with a handkerchief lushly arranged in the breast pocket, Long was Ball's eager assistant, designated TD8. Ball announced that we were to be welcomed into the service by the Chief, in his office suite on the 18th floor, and ushered us towards the lift.

It took forever to arrive and when it did there were too many of us to fit in. Long volunteered to take the stairs while the rest of us crushed in. The 18th floor of Century House was as lugubrious as the lobby. The walls appeared not to have been been painted for years and the grubby linoleum was worn through in parts. As we filed down the corridor to the conference room an old man dressed in a crumpled blue suit like the security guard, collar and tie askew, lurked in one of the small offices. Stealthily he ducked behind a desk, as though he was embarrassed to be seen by us. Presumably one of the porters, who had perhaps just delivered the biscuits and tea which were laid out on the large formica table in the centre of the room. Long arrived, a bit flush from the run up the stairs, just as we were taking our seats around the table.

Before we were all settled, Bart spied the plate of biscuits in the middle of the table and helped himself to a couple of custard creams. Castle glared at him. 'Anyone like a biscuit?' asked Long quickly. Bart munched on, oblivious to Long's diplomacy. Forton smirked.

As we sipped lukewarm tea from the civil service crockery, Ball told us about the Chief's background. 'Colin McColl has put in the legwork on the ground, working at the coalface as an operational officer. He is not just a Whitehall mandarin, like some of the previous Chiefs,' Ball sniffed. 'He holds a lot of respect from all of us.' McColl, the son of a Shropshire GP, was appointed Chief in April 1989. He joined the service in 1950 and spent his first two postings in Laos and Vietnam, where he gained a reputation as a keen amateur dramatist and musician. He spent the mid-'60s in Warsaw, where he forged a reputation as a far-sighted and competent officer, and his last overseas posting was to Geneva in 1973 as head of station. Long told a story about how, when he was in Laos, McColl broke the ice with the visiting Royal family with an impromptu display on his flute. Ball added, 'We're not normally a particularly formal service, but we should always show due respect to the Chief. When he walks in, we should all stand.'

We had finished the tea and biscuits and were starting to relax, chatting amongst ourselves, when the dishevelled old man who was lurking in the corridor returned. Nobody paid him any attention, presuming that he had come to clear the table. Long coughed discreetly and Castle sprang to his feet, his back rigid as if on a parade ground, as he realised quicker than most that the scruffy old man in the crumpled blue suit was not a porter but Sir Colin McColl. The rest of us scrambled to our feet and there was a clatter as Bart's chair fell over backwards behind him.

'Please,' the Chief murmured, indicating to us to sit down with a small hand movement. McColl looked us over, blinking like an owl struck by a light, but it was evident that a razor intellect gleamed behind his steady gaze. 'Congratulations to you all on being selected for this service. You are about to take the first step on what I hope will be for you all a long and rewarding career.' His voice had a sonorous authority to it, as though he could be a solid church baritone. 'We are still one of the leading intelligence services in the world and we play a major role in maintaining Britain's position at the forefront of the international community. You can be assured that, despite all the changes that are happening in the world today – the crumbling of the iron curtain, the increasing closeness of Britain to our European partners, the problems in the Middle East – MI6 has a bright, certain and exciting future.' It struck me as odd that McColl should underline the security of the future of MI6. It had never occurred to me that it could be to the contrary; perhaps McColl knew things we didn't. 'The Government's commitment to MI6 is such that we will shortly be moving to splendid new headquarters, a modern purpose-built building to replace this ageing but fondly regarded edifice. It will become, unlike Century House, a conspicuous part of the London skyline. I see it as a symbol of the move of MI6 from a shadowy, secret organisation into a body more accountable to the public and to Parliament.' McColl went on to outline new legislation, at that very moment being prepared for debate in Parliament, which would formally acknowledge the existence of MI6. 'You will therefore see wide-ranging changes in the administration and running of this service during your career here.' I didn't suspect at the time those changes would have such dramatic consequences for me just four years later.

McColl elaborated his vision of how the priorities of the service would change. 'The cold war is now over and the former Soviet Union is crumbling into chaotic republics. That by no means, however, should suggest that we drop our guard for a moment. Russia remains, and will remain, a potent military threat.' McColl blinked as he paused to let the words sink in. 'Though their military intentions may no longer be belligerent, their capability remains. The unpredictability and instability of the new regime could make them all the more dangerous. MI6 will, for many years to come, have an important role in warning this country of danger signs on their long road to democracy.' McColl sounded convincing and authoritative as he drove home the importance of our future careers. 'Our greatest allies will continue to be our American cousins,' he continued. 'The relationship between MI6 and the CIA is central to the special relationship between our countries. We endanger that relationship at our peril.' McColl explained the mechanics of how the relationship was maintained and the level of cooperation between the two services. 'The Americans have fabulous technical resources which we cannot match. To tap into that, we need to be a valued partner to them by playing on our strengths of guile and native cunning to gather first-rate human intelligence.' McColl beamed and I reflected on what a fascinating life this unassuming man must have had. 'There are a number of areas in which the requirements put upon us for intelligence gathering are rapidly increasing. We have long had interests in the Middle East, but to the usual concerns about political instability and state sponsored terrorism we now must add a third threat, that of the pariah nations acquiring nuclear, chemical and biological weapons. There is a real danger that, as the former Soviet Union collapses, technology, personnel and materials relating to these weapons of mass destruction may leak out and fall into the hands of countries such as Iran and Iraq. The consequences would be deadly and we must strive to prevent this happening.' McColl paused again briefly, as he let his words sink in. 'There will also be an increasing emphasis on commercial espionage. We are under pressure from the Treasury to justify our budget, and commercial espionage is one way of making a direct contribution to the nation's balance of payments.'

McColl pursed his hands and leaned back in his chair, signalling that the speech was over. Ball stood up to take his turn. 'Thank you, sir, for that fascinating and revealing speech. I am sure that the students must be burning to ask questions.' He turned to us, expectantly, his eyes appealing that nobody just asked for more biscuits.

Forton fidgeted awkwardly. Spencer stared sheepishly at the ceiling. It was the garrulous and pushy Markham who, predictably, spoke up first. 'Sir, as Britain aligns itself more closely with Europe, will this weaken the special relationship between MI6 and the CIA?'

'No,' McColl replied firmly. 'Our relationship with the Americans will always be more important than that with the various European intelligence services.'

Castle, displaying the sharp mind with which we were to become more familiar, shrewdly detected that there was more to that answer. 'Does that mean, sir, that we spy on other European countries?'

McColl balked, briefly floored, before deciding to answer honestly. 'Yes, we do. There are always important requirements for intelligence on the economic intentions of our European partners, particularly regarding their negotiating positions on the Maastricht treaty.'

Forton pushed his spectacles back up the bridge of his nose and, with a trace of a nervous stammer, posed a daring one. 'Sir, why do we have an intelligence service at all?' The other students glanced nervously at Forton as he continued with his audacious question. 'There are countries more important on the world stage, with much more powerful economies, who have only small or non-existent external intelligence gathering operations. Japan or Germany for example. Could the money Britain spends on MI6 not be spent better elsewhere, on healthcare or education?'

A flicker of a smile crossed McColl's lips. 'Ah, young man, you overlook the fact that we are still on the United Nations Security Council, unlike Germany and Japan. Britain has international responsibilities much greater than its economic wealth might suggest.' McColl beamed at us avuncularly, thanked us for our attention, wished us well for our future careers and we stood as he got up and left.

Ball and Long glowed with relief. We had acquitted ourselves well before the Chief – nobody had asked him a dumb question. The progress of an IONEC was closely followed by senior officers, and its success or otherwise was reflected on the subsequent careers of the DS. Ball and Long knew they had a good class. Ball resumed. 'You will all have plenty of time to get to know us and each other over the next six months, and you will no doubt form a bond which will last throughout your careers,' he smiled as he shifted his weight from foot to foot. 'But to break the ice, get the ball rolling, so to speak, we'd like you to go round the table, just giving your name and saying a few words about what you did before joining.' He surveyed us and I hoped that he would not pick me out first. 'Let's start with you, Terry,' he finally said, pointing to Forton.

Forton, 24 years old, was the most thoughtful student on the course. He came from a liberal, academic family and was deeply interested in politics. He read Politics, Philosophy and Economics at Oxford University and would probably have got a first if he had spent less time in the college bar. After graduation, he worked for a couple of years for Oxford Analytica, a political consultancy, before applying to join the FCO. During the application process one of the FCO recruiters suggested that he consider joining MI6 instead. Forton accepted the invitation very much against the wishes of his father, a vehement opponent of secrecy in government.

Andrew Markham was the youngest on the course at 23 years old. He studied French and Spanish at Oxford. An energetic undergraduate, he had been involved in amateur dramatics and had also been a bit of a star on the sports field.

Andy Hare, 34, graduated from Durham University, joined the army and served as an intelligence officer. He looked familiar to me as he spoke. 'I finished my army career seconded as the Adjutant to one of the Territorial Army Special Air Service regiments where the young man opposite me . . .' – he nodded at me – '. . . was one of my troopers.' I remembered him now, giving me a dressing-down on the Brecon Beacons one drizzly winter night for talking on parade. He explained how an army officer at Sandhurst had put him in touch with the service. MI6 has a permanent army 'talent spotter' based at Sandhurst Royal Military College, codenamed ASSUMPTION. Another talent spotter, also based at Sandhurst and known by the codename PACKET, looks at the college's foreign cadets and provides MI6 with tips as to which might be suitable informers. Famously, in the 1960s the then PACKET tried to recruit a young Libyan cadet called Mohammar Gadaffi.

James Barking, 26, read law at Oxford and received a second-class degree. He was articled to a city law firm for a few years but didn't find the work stimulating. A casual remark at a drinks evening from another guest, a retired MI6 officer, led to his recruitment.

Bart was next to speak. He had only just graduated from Oxford with a first-class physics degree and had not much other experience, but spoke at length about himself. Like me, he had been recruited as part of MI6's drive to attract more officers with scientific and technical degrees to work in weapons counter-proliferation.

Martin Richards was the eldest on the course, in his mid-40s. He was talent-spotted while an undergraduate at Oxford but declined to join the service immediately. Instead, he joined Shell Oil and spent most of his career working in the Middle East. Like many other Shell employees, he remained in contact with MI6, and 22 years after his first approach he took up the offer to start a second career. Because of his age he would not have the same opportunities as us, and had been earmarked to become a specialist officer concentrating on the Middle East oil industry.

Castle was next. Speaking concisely in an upper class accent, he described his education at Eton, then Magdalen College, Oxford. Twenty-eight and recently married, Castle had worked in the city for a few years where he was a successful merchant banker and took a hefty pay cut to join MI6. He later made no secret of his intention to only in the service for only a few years because he regarded the salary as inadequate stay. Based on his militaristic bearing and spotless pinstripe suit, it seemed he must be the former Scots Guard. Since Castle made no mention of a military career I assumed he was too modest to mention it.

We turned expectantly to Spencer, the next student in line. He was staring dreamily out of the window, paying little attention to the proceedings. 'Sorry, where were we?' he laughed, only mildly embarrassed to be caught napping. He stood up and began telling us his background. 'Yeah, I flunked around at St Andrews University, Scotland, couldn't make my mind up what subject to read and took a long time to graduate. When I left, still wasn't sure what to do, so

I sort of drifted into the army, hoping it would sort me out. It didn't really, so I ended up here.' We laughed at his self-deprecation.

Hare couldn't imagine Spencer serving in the army. 'Which regiment were you in?' he asked, sceptically.

'Oh, I was in the Scots Guards for a few years,' Spencer replied. Spencer was actually a fairly adventurous sort despite his muddled dreaminess. He was an accomplished climber and mountaineer and had worked for a while in Afghanistan with a mine-clearing charity called the Halo Trust, clearing Russian minefields. He was recruited by an MI6 officer then serving in Kabul who had contacts with the Halo Trust.

The DS spoke briefly about themselves. Ball had been posted to both Czechoslovakia and East Germany in the 1970s but became disillusioned with the service in the early 1980s and left to spend ten years in Control Risks, a private security company. That career ground to a halt, so he rejoined MI6 in the mid-'80s. At the time, redundancy or dismissal from MI6 was unheard of and it was not difficult or unusual to rejoin MI6 after a lengthy gap in another career. Long explained how he joined the service directly from Oxford, had been posted to Uruguay shortly after the outbreak of the Falklands war, then went to New York to work in the British mission to the United Nations.

Looking around the table, I realised the new recruits were all from similar backgrounds. All were white, male, conventional and middle class. All of us were university graduates, mostly from Oxford or Cambridge. It was pretty much the background of all MI6 officers. The service's recruitment figures refute its claims to be an equal opportunity employer: only about 10 per cent of the officers were female, there were no black officers whatsoever, only one of mixed Asian parentage, and there were no disabled officers, even though there were plenty of suitable opportunities. These issues gave me no concern at the time, though. I was deeply enthusiastic about my new career and could hardly wait to get started on the training.

4

INDOCTRINATION

MONDAY, 9 DECEMBER 1991
PORTSMOUTH, ENGLAND

The nine of us, crammed into the Bedford minibus, were silent and tense as we drove through the darkness and driving rain towards the centre of Portsmouth. It was 8.30 p.m. and the streets were almost empty. Only a few stragglers, huddled under umbrellas, were scurrying to the pubs. Ball drove, with Long silently alongside. One by one, they dropped us off in dark side streets or deserted parking lots to merge into the night. Castle went first, striding confidently towards his target, dressed in his suit with a Barbour jacket to protect himself against the elements. Spencer followed, sheepishly scuttling into the darkness under a Burberry umbrella. My turn was next and Markham wished me luck as I slipped out of the back door of the minibus and orientated myself towards my target.

The IONEC was designed to train a recruit to a level of proficiency to step into a junior desk job in MI6. Approximately half of the course was spent in the classroom, learning the administration of the service, the theory of how to cultivate, recruit, handle and debrief agents, listening to case histories and receiving presentations from the different sections of the service. The remainder was spent in exercises, and we were on PERFECT STRANGER, the first of many increasingly complicated tests that were to form the backbone of the course.

Our brief was simple but a little nerve-racking for novice spies. We were each assigned a pub in downtown Portsmouth in which we had to approach a member of the public and, using whatever cunning ruse we could invent, extract their name, address, date of birth, occupation and passport number. We were given an alias, but had to use our initiative to invent the rest of our fictional personality.

Ball explained that the purpose of the exercise was three-fold.

First, it was a gentle introduction to using and maintaining an alias identity in a live situation, an essential skill for an intelligence officer. Second, it would test our initiative and cunning in devising a credible plan to achieve the objective. Third, it would illustrate the workings and immense size of MI6's central computer index, or CCI. This is a mammoth computerised databank containing records of everybody with whom any member of MI6 has come into contact operationally since the start of record-keeping in 1945. The biographical details of our random victims were to be fed into this computer to see what, if anything, would be unearthed. The size of the database was such, Ball explained, that it was rare for an IONEC not to chance upon at least one individual with a mention in the CCI on a random trawl of the pubs of Portsmouth,

Pushing open the heavy mock-Victorian door of my designated pub, the Hole In The Wall on Great Southsea Street, I felt apprehensive. Although a simple exercise, it was our first test and I wanted to get off to a good start. We'd been given an £8.50 advance to buy ourselves and targets a couple of drinks, so I made for the bar intending to make the most of it. Scanning the room for potential targets I was alarmed to find the pub empty. Ordering a pint of Guinness, I dismissed the barman as a potential prey. Old, fat and surly, there was little chance of getting him to talk. I sat down in a red-velveted alcove with a view of the entrance and waited for better prospects.

Time slipped by with the Guinness. I was starting on my second pint before the first customers, a smooching couple, straggled in. They would not welcome the approach of a stranger. Then a rowdy bunch of youths marched in to play pool. It would be difficult to mix with them and single one out for inquisition. A glance at my watch showed only 20 minutes before the minibus would return to pick me up. The exercise was getting awkward.

At last my luck changed as two girls wandered in. I watched as they bought drinks and settled into an alcove. In their 20s, they were casually dressed, one pretty, the other less so and a bit overweight. Probably flatmates out for a quiet drink. I had to act quickly – not only because time was running out, but also because the pool players had noticed the girls and were egging each other on to make a move.

Swearing I would never do this again, I picked up my Guinness, walked over and asked if I could join them. To my relief they agreed. 'You're not from round here, are you?' the fat one asked as soon as I was seated.

'What makes you think that?' I asked.

'Your accent. You're from up north,' she volunteered. 'What are you doing here?'

Her curiosity was encouraging and an opportunity to implement my plan. 'I'm a yacht skipper and I'm delivering a Contessa down from Scotland to Cherbourg.' The girls listened with interest to my brazen lying. 'But my mate just got ill and went home. I've called in to Portsmouth to find a new hand and restock.'

We chatted about the boat, the voyage, my apocryphal crewman, how I had got into the job. I fabricated everything on the spot, drawing on my limited sailing experience. Just like talking to the soldiers in the bar in Belgium, it was alarming that the art of deception came so easily and surprising how gullible strangers could be. They told me they were nurses and had only recently moved to Portsmouth. Encouragingly, they had done some sailing and were keen to continue now that they were living on the coast.

'Do you know anybody who might be interested in helping this weekend?' I asked. The girls glanced at each other, checking whether the other was thinking the same. 'Perhaps yourselves?' I pressed home.

'Sure,' the pretty one replied hesitantly, then turned to her flatmate as if to speak for her. 'Sure, we're free this weekend.'

It was easy once they were baited. In order to get in touch with them again, I asked for their names, addresses and telephone numbers, which they neatly printed in my notebook. On the false pretext that I needed to clear them with Customs in advance of our departure, I asked if they had their passport numbers handy. That too was no problem: the pretty one got up and phoned home to another flatmate and asked her to read the numbers. With only a few minutes to go, all the details required by Ball and Long were in my notebook. With my mission accomplished, I bade the unfortunate pair goodbye, promising that I would soon be in touch.

I climbed into the minibus a few minutes later. It was bursting with animated chatter. The others, some a bit tipsy, were elatedly describing how they conned innocent pub-goers into providing personal details. Markham had affected a silly French accent and pretending to be a student from Paris, claimed that his mother, who worked in the French passport agency, had told him that all British passport numbers ended with the numbers '666'. The incredulous victim rubbished the boast, so Markham bet him five pounds that it was true. The target hurried home to collect his passport, chuffed to be making some easy money out of a stupid Frenchman. Markham noted down the number, equally chuffed.

Castle, reflective of his background in the city, posed as a marketing consultant and distributed to each drinker a questionnaire that he had prepared in advance. The form enquired about the clients' drinking habits, purportedly on behalf of a major brewing company, and at the bottom were spaces to fill in name, address and passport number. Castle sipped orange juice on his own for an hour, pleased that he could pocket the cash advance, and then collected the completed questionnaires.

Hare found an old man drinking on his own, wearing the wartime maroon beret of the Parachute Regiment. The lonely veteran was happy to talk to somebody interested in his army career, and he readily volunteered his army number, as good as a passport number for the CCI.

'Is everyone accounted for?' called Ball from the driving seat, turning to check the rabble behind him. Long read out the roll call, with difficulty against the chatter. Bart, much the worse for drink, replied with a loud belch. All were present except Spencer. We waited a few more minutes before Ball decided that we would have to look for him and drove round to Spencer's watering hole, the Coach & Horses on the London Road, a notably boisterous pub. Spencer was not waiting outside, so Long went to look for him. The MI6 trainee was found, very much the worse for drink, in the midst of a lively party. He had not devised a plan, and unsure what to do with himself, had started playing the fruit machine. On the third pull, accompanied by the clanging of bells, the machine disgorged its contents. A crowd gathered round to witness this good fortune and the easy-going Spencer bought everybody a round. They returned the compliment, one thing lead to another and a party ensued. Spencer became hopelessly drunk and forgot about the boring task of extracting personal details – until Long turned up to drag him back to the minibus.

All were in high spirits that night as we returned to our training base. A strong sense of camaraderie was already developing amongst us, a feeling of being up against a common foe. For a moment, sitting quietly at the back of the bus, I pondered the morality of my actions. The girls might spend the whole week looking forward to a sailing trip that would never happen. Was it right to dupe members of the public so casually? As we drove through the portcullis entry to the 'Fort', MI6's discreet training establishment in Portsmouth and our main base for the IONEC, I dismissed such concerns. We were lying for Britain and that was sufficient justification. Unwittingly, I took the first step down the long path of indoctrination towards becoming an MI6 officer.

The largest and best kept of the four coastal forts built by Henry VIII in 1545 to defend the strategically important naval harbour of Portsmouth against the French Navy, Fort Monckton, as it is marked on Ordnance Survey maps, is a dramatic and atmospheric training base for MI6. Situated on the bleak and windswept southern tip of the Gosport peninsula, it is approached by a short, winding track across the tee of the first hole of the Gosport and Stokes Bay golf course. Officially known as 'No.1 Military Training Establishment', the Fort was a training base for the Royal Engineer Regiment of the army until 1956. When the Royal Engineers no longer needed it, MI6 discreetly took it over. The takeover was so discreet, in fact, that the Ministry of Defence supply branch continued to pay for its upkeep, unaware that it no longer belonged to them.

The only access through the thick grey stone walls is across a drawbridge over an empty moat, through a guarded gatehouse into the central courtyard. Directly above the gatehouse is a luxury suite of rooms, reserved for the Chief on his frequent visits. Set around the courtyard are three main blocks, east wing, main wing and west wing. Each wing is self-contained and has its own complex of bedroom accommodation, kitchens, dining-rooms and bars. Spread amongst the wings are the other training facilities needed to prepare trainees for a career in the secret service – a gymnasium, an indoor pistol range, photographic studios, technical workshops, laboratories and lecture rooms. There is even a small museum, containing mementoes from the SOE (Special Operations Executive) of the Second World War and obsolete Cold War spying equipment. At the extremity of east wing is a helicopter landing pad and an outdoor pistol and sub-machine gun range. Recreation is not forgotten and there is an outdoor tennis court and croquet pitch to the west, as well as an indoor squash court just beyond the outer wall.

Main wing, directly opposite the entrance, was our home for the IONEC. We disgorged ourselves from the minibus and headed into the in-house bar for another drink. Alcohol plays a prominent part in MI6 life and Ball and Long encouraged us to drink every night. The main wing bar, decorated with military emblems and souvenirs from Second World War SOE operations, soon became the focus for relaxation during the IONEC.

That evening Ball and Young entered the results of our work into the CCI computer. Three individuals turned up with records. Hare's old paratrooper turned out to be a Walter Mitty with no military service, one of Castle's finds had a long criminal record and the pretty girl that I had interviewed turned out to be the younger sister of an MI5 secretary.

Officially, the drab, nondescript yellow-brick building just opposite the police station on Borough High Street in Southwark, London, was a government stationery store. In reality, until recently it housed another MI6 training school. During the IONEC we spent alternate weeks at 'Boro' and at the Fort. Training at Boro was oriented towards the administrative and theoretical aspects of the work and it was here that Ball and Long initiated us into the service's history, purpose and modus operandi.

MI6's roots were in the Bureau of Secret Service, founded partly in response to the Boer War which took Britain by surprise, and partly in response to an increasingly belligerent Germany. On Tuesday, 30 March 1909, a sub-committee of the Committee of Imperial Defence met in a closed session in Whitehall. Colonel James Edmonds was the first speaker. He was head of MO5, the forerunner of today's MI5, whose job was to uncover foreign spies in Britain with his staff of two and budget of £200 per year. Edmonds had ambitious plans and wanted to extend his service to spy abroad, primarily in Russia and Germany. But Lord Esher, the chairman of the committee, disbelieved Edmonds's tales of German spying successes in England and insisted that Edmonds prepare a detailed list of cases to back his arguments.

Rather than back down, Edmonds resorted to a tactic which was used successfully by many of his successors in MI6 – he fabricated evidence to support his case. He provided Esher with a fictional list of spies drawn from a contemporary best-selling novel, *Spies of the Kaiser* by William Le Queux. When Esher asked for corroboration of his evidence, Edmonds claimed that such revelations would compromise the security of his informants – an excuse that was copied many times by his successors to extricate themselves from awkward inquisitions by government. It was enough for Edmonds to win his argument and with it the budget to expand MO5 to form the Secret Service Bureau. In 1911, the Official Secrets Act gave Edmonds sweeping and draconian powers to imprison anybody suspected of helping the 'enemy', which at the time was Germany. That same primitive act is still on the statute books in Britain and even today there are people serving lengthy jail sentences under its auspices. Through both world wars, the Secret Service Bureau survived and thrived, eventually being named MI6 in 1948.

In the company of America's CIA and Russia's newly revamped intelligence service, MI6 has one of the few genuinely global intelligence networks, but with a staff of approximately 2,300 it is the smallest of the three by a long way. About 350 of the staff are intelligence branch or 'IB' officers, the fast stream which we were being trained to join. About 800 are general service or 'GS' officers, who mostly do technical and administrative work. The remainder of the staff are secretaries, clerks, guards, cooks, drivers, cleaners and mechanics.

About half of the IB and most of the support staff are based in London. Their main task is to support those in the field, plan operations, liaise with foreign intelligence services and distribute intelligence to decision-makers in Whitehall. MI6's intelligence 'product' is known as CX, an anachronism from the earliest days of MI6 when the Chief, 'C' in popular fiction, was Mansfield Cummings. Then the service was so secret that intelligence reports were not distributed outside MI6 and so were marked 'Cummings Exclusively', abbreviated to CX. Intelligence is worthless if it is not passed on to decision-makers, and nowadays CX reports are disseminated far more widely to 'customers'. The FCO and the MOD are the most important, but any government department can receive CX if the material is relevant to them. Even some large British companies, such as British Aerospace, BP and British Airways, have MI6 liaison officers who receive relevant CX.

IB officers working in British embassies overseas under cover as diplomats gather the majority of CX. These officers normally work in a small, discreet cell within the embassy, known as the 'station'. The station has its own highly secure communications with Head Office and only MI6 staff are allowed access to its rooms. These rooms are frequently swept for listening devices and in many stations there is a special 'safe-speech' room where important meetings are held.

There are about 50 stations around the world. The size of the station reflects the importance of the host country to Britain's interests. Those in the spy capitals of the world – Geneva, Moscow, Vienna, New York and Hong Kong – may contain up to five IB, three or four GS and perhaps half a dozen secretaries. Most stations in Western Europe are two- or three-man stations, while third world stations usually consist of only one officer and a secretary. However there are exceptions. Jakarta, for example, has a three-man station because Indonesia is a good customer for Britain's weapons industry, and Lagos is a three-man station by virtue of British interests in its oil industry. The head of station, usually a senior officer in his 40s working under cover as an FCO Counsellor, is normally 'declared' to the secret service of the host country, and much of his work is in liaison. The other officers are mostly 'undeclared' and may spend part of their time spying against the host country.

Certain stations exist primarily to spy against the host country – Moscow and Beijing, for example. Others do not spy against the host at all. Austria has no secrets of interest to Britain, but MI6 maintains a large Vienna station to spy on the Iranian and Russian communities, the arms trade and the International Atomic Energy Agency which is based in the outskirts of the city. Likewise, the New York station exists entirely to run agents in the United Nations.

The stations are administered and serviced from Head Office in London. Each has its own 'Production' or 'P' officer who determines the station's strategy and targets, oversees and plans operations, and administers the budget. 'Requirements' or 'R' officers distribute the intelligence production to customers. These P and R officers are organised in pyramidal structures into 'controllerates', which have either a regional or functional focus.

When I joined, there were seven controllerates, the largest and most powerful being the East European and Western Europe controllerates. The Middle East and Far East controllerates were assuming more prominence, while the African and Western Hemisphere (Latin America and the Caribbean) controllerates were shrinking. The Global controllerate was responsible for issues such as weapons counter-proliferation, large-scale drugs trafficking and international money laundering.

The controllerates formed the 'teeth' of the service, grouped in the Directorate of Requirements and Production. Alongside this directorate were two further large and unwieldy directorates responsible for administering the service and providing technical back up. Four directors form the 'Board' and control the overall strategy and administration of the directorates, and they are presided over by the Chief.

One of our first lectures at Boro, given by Ball, was on maintaining our 'cover' as members of the diplomatic service. We were permitted to tell immediate family about our true occupation after obtaining written permission from personnel department, but we were forbidden to tell casual acquaintances that we worked for MI6. Ball explained that to them we were to claim that we worked for the FCO in King Charles Street, Whitehall. To defend this cover, we needed to know how to behave and talk intelligently about the life and career of a genuine diplomat.

Ball assigned each of us to a cover department in the FCO. Over the next few days, we went along to Whitehall, met our 'colleagues', learned about their work and memorised details about the room where they worked, bus and underground routes from our homes into Whitehall and the names of the best local pubs.

One evening, after a further lecture on cover, Ball invited us to his house for a party. 'It's my wife's birthday,' he said, 'and I am so pleased with how this course is gelling together that I'd like her to have the opportunity to meet you all.' In MI6 socialisation amongst officers and their spouses is not unusual, and particularly so on the IONEC, so Ball's invitation did not strike us as odd. 'My wife is inviting a few of her friends around too, and since none of them are conscious as to MI6, it will be an opportunity for you to defend your cover in a social situation,' Ball added.

On the evening of the party, we trooped round to Ball's comfortable Islington house, clutching birthday cards and flowers for his wife. A long and bibulous evening ensued. His wife's friends were an eclectic, lively and interesting bunch. I spent much of the evening chatting to a commercial diver, who had now set up a marine engineering business. Hare discovered a fellow former army intelligence officer. Markham, who was fond of good wine, found a kindred spirit in one guest who was a wine merchant. It was flattering to find that all the guests were so interested in our careers as diplomats. Armed with Ball's lessons, however, it was easy to fend off their questions and maintain cover.

One guest was an attractive blonde and Spencer, his courage fortified by a few cans of Younger's lager, was soon in animated conversation with her. She was a lingerie saleswoman and model and was delighting Spencer with descriptions of some of her range of goods. They were soon swapping telephone numbers, promising to meet up.

The following morning we assembled at Boro as usual at 10 a.m., some of us nursing hangovers. The chatter was all about the previous evening. The former army officer didn't impress Hare. 'He was talking bullshit. No way was he in the green slime.' Markham too spoke sceptically about the ignorance that the alleged wine merchant had displayed. But glowing with pride, Spencer related his conversation with the blonde and beamed when he revealed his success in snagging a dinner date with her.

A few minutes after ten, Ball shuffled to the front of the class and wished us good morning. He didn't look as cheerful as normal and the classroom fell silent. 'I hope you had a good time last night,' Ball said, shifting awkwardly, as if he had something to hide. Spencer looked smug. 'But I have an apology to make,' he paused for a moment. 'The guests at the party last night were not really friends of my wife, but were MI5 officers. The purpose of the exercise was to ensure that you had all learnt your lessons about cover.' There was a stony silence as it sunk in that we had been so easily duped. It was exhilarating to con unsuspecting members of the public in PERFECT STRANGER, but we didn't like having the tables turned.

Hare was most annoyed at being fooled. 'In my experience from the army,' he spoke out indignantly 'if you con students they quickly lose faith in the DS.'

Only Forton found something to lighten the mood. With a chuckle, he gleefully pointed to Spencer. 'Feeling alright, Alex?' he asked mockingly. 'Still going on that date?' Poor Spencer was staring at the floor, ashen-faced.

Thereafter, whenever friends or relatives asked us about work, it was easy to fend off their curiosity. At first it was exhilarating to 'lie in the interests of national security', but it brought changes in my relationships with friends. Carl Jung's statement that the 'maintenance of secrets acts like a psychic poison, which alienates their possessor from the community' rang true.

The bread and butter of the work of an intelligence officer is targeting, cultivating, recruiting, then running informers who are prepared to give or sell secrets about their country to MI6. During the first weeks of the IONEC we practised these skills in a series of small exercises. Experienced officers would come down from Century House to role-play the agent, pretending to be Brazilian Generals, Russian scientists, Iranian revolutionaries, or whatever the exercise required. We would play the case officer and practise the art of getting alongside them, cultivating them, recruiting them and extracting intelligence. We then wrote up a contact report recording the circumstances of the meeting and issued a mock CX report containing the intelligence. Afterwards the role-player debriefed us and Ball and Long graded us on how well we had performed. Some of the exercises were done in public, so to a casual eavesdropper the conversations must have appeared odd, particularly as the more colourful role-players would affect the accents and dress of their role.

One such was PERFECT PASSENGER, which was intended to take the lessons learnt in PERFECT STRANGER a step further and test our ability to cultivate a target. Often MI6 use the confines of public transport – especially aeroplanes – to cultivate a target, because he or she cannot escape. In this exercise we were told that MI6 had intelligence that a South African diplomat, who was vulnerable because of financial problems, was returning from Portsmouth to London one Friday evening by train. Our assignment was to take the same train, find him amongst the other passengers, engage him in conversation and cultivate him so that he would agree to have a drink on arrival at Waterloo station. Ball showed us a surveillance shot of our target, but our only other information was that he had radical pro-apartheid views and that he always carried *The Economist*, which would help us identify him in the crowded train.

I was lucky and found my target alone in a compartment. The 'South African diplomat' was easy-going and affable, and I arranged a follow-up drink at Waterloo without problem. For Barking the exercise was less straightforward. He found his target without much difficulty and engaged him in conversation. Talk soon turned to apartheid politics when Barking, posing as a politics student, 'discovered' that the role-player was a South African diplomat. Barking decided that the best way to persuade the target to come for a drink was to appear amenable and politically like-minded so he pretended to be a racist apartheid apologist. Soon the two were enthusiastically discussing the merits of racially segregated education, the unacceptability of mixed marriages and the impossibility of allowing non-whites to vote. Concentrating on the assignment and enjoying the sympathetic response his extremist views were eliciting from the play-acting South African, Barking paid little attention when two other men sporting beards and tweed jackets entered the compartment, and didn't notice that his conversation agitated them. Eventually the two men, left-wing politics lecturers at Portsmouth Polytechnic, could no longer stomach Barking's racist bluster and they furiously joined in the argument. Unfortunately, Barking, mindful of the 'party' a few weeks earlier, presumed that they were MI5 role-players sent to see how he would handle the situation and grade his performance. He refused to back down and the exercise degenerated from a quiet attempt to gain the supposed diplomat's confidence into a four-way shouting match that ended only when the train arrived at Waterloo.

We had a busy schedule down at the Fort the following fortnight learning the 'tradecraft' of spying. Tradecraft is the term used to describe the practical skills that enable a spy to meet or communicate with an agent without arousing the suspicion of the counter-intelligence opposition. It covers such skills as surveillance, anti-surveillance, counter-surveillance, brush contacts and loading and clearing dead letter boxes. All require guile, cunning, a degree of acting ability, but most of all, careful planning and preparation.

An intelligence officer cannot go to a clandestine meeting with an informer without first ensuring that he is not being followed by counter-surveillance; but he must not make it obvious that he is looking out for watchers. Nervous glances over the shoulder or frequent stops to tie shoelaces would clearly signal to the surveillance that the target was up to mischief. The skill in anti-surveillance is therefore to appear an innocent diplomat, yet still identify any followers. This involves walking or driving, under the guise of an innocuous cover activity such as a shopping trip, a planned route which contains 'surveillance traps'. For example, the escalators in many department stores are arranged in a switchback cascade, so from the second escalator it is often possible to check the first without appearing suspicious. A full anti-surveillance route may have dozens of such surveillance traps and may take many hours to complete. At every one of the surveillance traps the officer must make a mental note of everybody who is behind. Most of them will be innocent shoppers, but amongst them may be surveillance operatives. Ball taught us that in order to firmly identify surveillance, we must note the same face at least three times.

Surveillance teams try to make themselves difficult to positively identify, in part by using nondescript 'grey men' as watchers – not too tall, not too short, unremarkable clothes – so that there is nothing that draws attention to them in a crowd. The more sophisticated surveillance teams like the Russians use tricks like reversible clothing and disguise, making repeat sightings difficult. In Moscow, strict rules about anti-surveillance drills are followed and 'dry-cleaning' may mean spending a whole day 'shopping' with wife and kids in tow. 'Moscow rules' are also used in Iran and in South Africa because their counter-intelligence services are skilful. In contrast, in most South American countries, anti-surveillance is easy as the watchers seem to have learnt their trade from *Starsky and Hutch* and sport leather jackets, large moustaches and dark glasses.

Sometimes the only means to communicate with an agent may be by 'brush contact' or a 'dead letter box'. A brush contact is a fleeting meeting with the agent, transferring information or instructions in the process. It relies on careful co-ordination ensuring that both parties arrive at the same place at the same time so that it is possible to carry out a brush contact even when under surveillance. The followers cannot get too close, otherwise they make themselves too obvious. This gives an opportunity to brush an agent in 'dead ground', for example a dogleg in a corridor or passage. We were taught to watch the agent approach the dead ground from an observation post, say a table in a café. Having previously timed to the second how long it would take him to reach the dead ground and knowing how long our own trip would be, it was in theory possible to meet at the correct point, unobserved by surveillance. In reality, brush contacts are difficult to pull off reliably and we practised them assiduously.

Most of the exercises took place in Portsmouth and we took turns playing the roles of officer or agent. The 'officer' found a suitable brush-contact site and then, back at the Fort, wrote instructions for the 'agent' on its location. We were usually under surveillance from teams from MI5, the Portsmouth SB, Customs and Excise, or the army Intelligence Corps, so we would have to 'dry-clean' before attempting the brush – sometimes identifying the surveillance, sometimes not. On one exercise, it was Spencer's turn to play the agent and I carefully planned a brush contact with him on the back stairs coming down from the public library in Portsmouth town hall. I spotted surveillance on my way to the library, but calculating that they would not follow me closely enough on the deserted stairs to see the brush contact, I did not abort. However, instead of the usual film canister or brown envelope, Spencer handed me an extravagant ice-cream, complete with chocolate flake, just before I emerged from the stairs into the street below, on a cold December's day. The surveillance team noted my bizarre acquisition and reported it to the DS.

Every evening after a day of lectures or foot-slogging around Portsmouth practising our anti-surveillance skills, we listened to a lecture from a guest speaker, usually a member of the service, who would describe a real-life operation in which they had taken part so that we could see how our new skills could be applied. One evening, Ball announced that we had a special guest who should be treated with the utmost respect. Oleg Gordievsky, the so-called 'jewel in the crown' of MI6's Russian defectors, told us the story of his defection to Britain, as he does to every IONEC, providing a dramatic account of tradecraft in action.

Gordievsky first made contact with MI6 in 1974 while working as a KGB officer in Copenhagen under cover as the press attaché in the Russian embassy. He was cultivated over a series of badminton games and was eventually recruited by Colin Figures, who later became Chief. For the next 11 years Gordievsky provided MI6 with a treasure trove of information from the heart of the KGB. Gordievsky was run with such secrecy that only a handful of officers knew of his existence and, rather than risk widening the indoctrination circle, many non-indoctrinated officers were allowed to pursue futile operations which were known from Gordievsky to be compromised. But despite the care taken to keep his existence secret, it was inevitable that Gordievsky would eventually fall under suspicion from his masters in Moscow. During a period of home leave, he was arrested and interrogated. He was eventually released, but was suspended from work and his passport confiscated while the KGB conducted further enquiries. He managed to get word of his plight to the station in Moscow, where a mid-career officer, the Honourable Raymond Horner, was the number two. Every station has on its standing orders at least one plan for exfiltration of defectors in such emergencies. The exfiltration plan in Moscow was to smuggle the agent over the Russian border into neutral Finland. A route from Moscow had already been reconnoitred, and Horner had a Saab 90 as his official car, which in 1985 was the only car with a large enough boot to comfortably hold a grown man. This upmarket foreign car had caused some resentment amongst Horner's FCO colleagues, as they were forced to drive inferior British models and assumed that the Honourable Horner had been exempted from this rule because he held a title. Every evening Gordievsky took a stroll in Gorky Park, followed closely by his round-the-clock surveillance team. Horner identified a patch of dead ground where Gordievsky would be momentarily out of sight of his followers, meaning the pickup had to be made with split second precision, and spent the day driving around Moscow ostensibly on 'errands', in reality doing thorough anti-surveillance. With military precision, he arrived at the designated spot at exactly the same time as Gordievsky, who leaped into the Saab's capacious boot, under the soon-to-be-disjointed noses of his surveillance. Horner drove out of Moscow and started the long and nerve-jangling ride to the Finnish border. Horner could not be sure that his car was not bugged, so dared not communicate with his hidden passenger. Even when over the border, it was too risky to speak out, though he must have been stifling a shout of jubilation. To let his passenger know he was safe, he played Gordievsky's favourite piece of music over the car stereo. To this day, Gordievsky is referred to in MI6 by the code name OVATION, a reference to this piece of music.

Another common tradecraft technique we learned was the 'dead letter box' or DLB. This technique involves clandestinely hiding a message where it can later be picked up by the other party. Usually the message is put in a small container such as a film canister and the hiding spot is chosen so that it can be posted or cleared even when under surveillance. DLB sites are much easier to find than brush contact sites – and we were expected to find one in less than an hour in an unfamiliar environment – behind a loose brick in a wall, in an old tree stump, tucked into a crevice of a prominent rock. The disadvantage of DLBs is that they are occasionally discovered accidentally by the public – usually by small children – who may inform the local police. It is thus risky clearing a DLB, as the opposition may be lying in wait.

I got my revenge on Spencer a few days later on a DLB exercise. In Winchester Cathedral there is a small statue of St Jude next to the fourth pew from the back on the west wall. Sitting in the pew, on the pretence of praying or meditating, it is possible for one to grope round the back of the legs of the statue without being observed. I chose it as a DLB site, but instead of a film canister I left a loaded mouse-trap for him. Poor Hare fared even worse. Against Ball's advice, Barking loaded a DLB for him in the toilet cistern of the gents in the Mr Pickwick pub in Portsmouth. The cistern was set high on the wall and Hare had to climb up on the toilet seat to reach it. Unfortunately, the gentleman in the next door cubicle took exception to Hare's activities and, in a rage, called the police. Hare was interviewed and, unable to explain the truth, he was forced to admit to cottaging and was fortunate to be let off with only a caution.

The requirement for these old-fashioned tradecraft skills is not as great for the modern spy as in the days of the Cold War. These days, electronics and computers have simplified agent communications and it is often easier to communicate with encrypted e-mail. Traditional tradecraft was emphasised on our course partly because Ball was an enthusiast and deeply inured with the techniques, but partly because the discipline and nerve required to plan and execute such operations was greater than simply clicking the 'send' button on a computer, instilling better tradecraft discipline. Practising these old-fashioned techniques was also better for morale and team-bonding than sitting in front of a computer screen, and we thoroughly enjoyed the exercises. One exception, however, was Martin Richards, the eldest student on the course. A quiet, academic man, he found the exercises rather silly. One afternoon, he failed to return to the Fort and eventually rang the DS to say that he could go on no longer. He was forced to resign from MI6 and they resettled him with Shell Oil, his old company.

Secret Writing (SW), the grown-ups' term for schoolboys' 'invisible ink', still plays a role in spying, but modern techniques are more sophisticated than the lemon-juice-in-a-fountain-pen familiar from *Boys' Own* magazine. There is a three-man joint MI5/MI6 section known as TS/SW which is responsible for research and training in the latest SW techniques. TS/SW has several different SW techniques, but the method we were taught on the IONEC and which is used ubiquitously by MI6 oficers in the field is the miraculously simple 'offset' method. Like many great inventions, it was discovered by accident.

The problem with early invisible inks was that the writer could not see what he had just written. A visible ink which faded shortly after it dried was developed but that was not perfect because the indentation made by the pen could be detected and the possession of the peculiar ink itself could be compromising.

The solution came one day in the mid-1980s, when a TS/SW technician was developing a conventional SW message sent by an agent in Russia. The secret message had been written on the back of an envelope with an innocuous 'cover' letter inside and posted from Moscow. As the technician swabbed the back of the envelope with developing fluid, as expected the secret message began to emerge. But to his surprise, other writing – in a different hand and mirror-written – also started to develop. Close inspection of the writing showed that it was an address in Kiev. But who was the addressee and how had it appeared over the top of the message?

There was only one logical explanation for the mysterious writing. When the agent posted his letter, the back of the envelope must have fallen to rest in the postbox on top of another envelope. That envelope must have been addressed with an ink which possessed the property of transferring an invisible chemical to paper in contact with it. The technician realised that the Kiev address must have been written with a commercially available pen. If that pen could be identified, it would be a superbly elegant, simple and deniable SW implement. MI6 mounted a systematic worldwide search for the magic pen and every MI6 station was asked to send a secretary to the local stationery store to buy every make available. TS/SW were soon at work testing them. Each was used to write a few characters, a piece of paper was pressed over the top, then swabbed with developer. It took many weeks to identify the magic pen – the Pentel rollerball. The 'offset' technique has the dual advantages that the agent or officer can see what he is writing before taking the offset copy and because the pen is commercially available it is deniable and uncompromising. Offset is now used routinely by MI6 officers in the field for writing up intelligence notes after debriefing agents. It is also issued to a few highly trusted agents, but is considered too secret to be shared even with liaison services such as the CIA.

Many other technical means are used for clandestine communication between agents, officers and Head Office. Development and issue of these systems was the responsibility of the section known as TOS/AC (Technical and Operations Support, Agent Comms). One morning they brought along their latest gadgets to demonstrate to us.

The essential feature of these gadgets is that they are non-compromising, that is, they are identical or virtually indistinguishable from commercially available equipment. PETTLE recorders were particularly ingenious. Any normal audio cassette has two tracks running parallel to each other, one for each 'side' of the cassette. PETTLE recorders exploited the unused part of the magnetic tape which lies between the two strips. TOS/AC demonstrated an ordinary personal stereo which played and recorded on both sides of the tape like a standard machine. But turning it upside down tripped a microswitch so that pressing the 'stop' and 'record' buttons together made the machine record over the central track. Pressing 'stop' and 'play' together played back the recording. They also demonstrated modified laptop computers. The removable floppy discs used in ordinary computers have a hidden space which is just big enough to hide a simple word processing system and file retrieval system. Typing in a simple command at the DOS prompt started up the special word processor system, allowing notes to be secretly recorded. Exiting the software, the computer reverted to normal mode, leaving the secret files invisible even to an accomplished computer specialist.

We also learned how to use SRAC (Short Range Agent Communication). This system is only issued to long-established and highly trusted agents in countries such as Russia and South Africa. The agent writes a message on a laptop computer, then downloads it into the SRAC transmitter, a small box the size of a cigarette packet. The receiver is usually mounted in the British embassy and continually sends out a low-power interrogation signal. When the agent is close enough, in his car or on foot, his transmitter is triggered and transmits the message in a high-speed burst of VHF. The transmitter is disguised as an innocuous object and for many years 'Garfield Cat' stuffed animals were popular as their sucker feet allowed the agent to stick the transmitter on the side window of his car, giving an extra clear signal as he drove past the embassy.

Photography is another important skill for an intelligence officer, whether to snap a surveillance shot of a target or to photograph secret documents. We were taught photography by an instructor from the service's technical support division, TOS/PH. He showed us how to take long-range snaps of targets using huge telephoto lenses and how to take clear close-ups of documents. MI6 uses commercially available photographic equipment where possible because anything specially made could be compromising. We did, however, practise with gadgets such as midget cameras and specially made collapsible document-copying cameras. Best fun, though, were the lessons on covert photography during which we secretly photographed members of the public with a variety of still and video cameras mounted in briefcases or shoulder bags. Back in an underground cellar below the Fort we were taught how to develop our shots as every overseas MI6 station has a darkroom which we were expected to know how to use.

Twice a week, we were given instruction in self-defence in the Fort's small gymnasium. Our instructor, Bill, was a former sergeant in the Royal Marines Special Boat Service who had also worked for a few years for the Las Vegas police force. Although only a little over five feet tall and dwarfed by all of us, he could put any of us on the floor or in an agonising thumb-lock within seconds. Over the weeks, we were taught how to judo-throw would-be attackers, fend off knife attacks, escape from headlocks and armlocks, and disarm a gunman. Self-defence is taught more for fun and morale building than for any real purpose – a traffic warden has more need of it than an MI6 officer and physical violence is never deliberately used. Bill could only recall one incident when a former student put the teaching into practice. A female officer was receiving unwanted attention from a drunken lout on a train during her evening commute. While the yob pestered her, the other male passengers buried their noses deeper into their newspapers. Eventually she could take no more and, just as Bill had taught her, she tightly rolled up her copy of *The Economist* and jabbed it into her assailant's eye, quickly silencing him.

We were also taught weapons-handling but, like self-defence, it was more for fun and fostering of team spirit than for any practical purpose. It was virtually unknown for MI6 officers to carry a weapon and no officer has ever used one in anger. Our instructor, Tom Nixon, a former sergeant in the Special Air Service, participated in the May 1980 Iranian Embassy siege at Prince's Gate. Under his expert supervision, we practised twice weekly at the outdoor range at the western edge of the Fort and in the small indoor range, modelled on the famous 'killing house' range at the SAS barracks in Hereford. We mostly used the Browning 9mm pistol, standard issue to the British armed forces, but also trained on foreign weapons like the Israeli Uzi and German Heckler & Koch sub-machine guns.

The DS and lecturers taught us how to plan and mount bugging operations, even though this is not the job of the IB. TOS has about a hundred officers trained in the specialist skills to carry out these tasks: locksmiths, clandestine entry specialists, sound engineers, electricians. We just required an understanding of their skills and abilities. Ball gave us an exercise, PERFECT NEIGHBOUR, in which we had to plan such an operation. Briefing us on the scenario, Ball said to imagine that the IRA had acquired a 'safe house' in Gosport, near the Fort, and that intelligence showed that the house was to be used to plan a bombing campaign. Over the next two weeks, we had to draw up a detailed portfolio of the house, its layout, its occupants and their movements, then make recommendations on how and when the house should be entered to place covert listening devices. All of us were given a different house to recce. These belonged to innocent members of the public. 'Are there any restrictions on what we can do?' asked Hare at the end of the briefing.

'No – you can do whatever you want,' replied Ball. 'Just don't get caught.'

That evening I borrowed a covert shoulder-bag mounted camera from the photographic laboratories and strolled round to my target, a medium-sized family home set in a small garden and fronting on Gomer Lane. To the rear was a small garden, backing on to the grounds of Stanley Park and Bay House School. Squeezing the bag to activate the Pentax SLR inside, I covertly photographed the house, shooting a roll of film which I developed that evening. The following morning, a visit to Gosport Town Hall on Walpole Road yielded a copy of the electoral roll, giving the names and occupations of the occupants. Posing as an architectural student, I borrowed the plans of their house from the building regulations department on the fourth floor on the pretext that it was for a design project at the polytechnic. The clerk would not release photocopies but allowed me to study them in the waiting-room. As soon as he was out of sight, an SLR with close-up lenses was used to photographed them. Just as I finished, Castle walked in. He too had thought of the same ruse. He got away with it but Spencer, who turned up an hour or so later, was not so lucky. The clerk was by now wary of the rush of odd requests for plans of Fareham town houses. He called his superior, who refused to believe Spencer's protests that he was a builder's jobber.

Thereafter every spare half-hour from the classroom was spent observing the house to build up a detailed picture of the daily movements of the occupants. The best place for the listening device would be in the kitchen, where the family socialised. But more detailed information was needed. One evening I jogged round to the house and found that it was empty. This was my chance. After checking that nobody was watching, I climbed the fence bordering

Stanley Park, scrambled through the shrubbery and up to the hedge at the back of the house. Nobody was at home next door either, so I scuttled the few metres of open ground into the cover of the lean-to at the back of the house, sending a startled cat shooting through my feet and under the windsurfer lying nearby. Crouching in the shadows for a few minutes, I listened for any sign of compromise. There was silence, so I stood up and peered through the kitchen window. After my eyes adjusted to the gloom, I sketched the kitchen layout in a notebook. Just as I turned to make my exit I noticed that the key had been left in the door. Recalling Ball's words – 'just don't get caught' – I turned it and pushed the door open. My intrusion into a stranger's house was amoral and illegal but in the euphoria of the IONEC it seemed totally justified. Ball rewarded my efforts with full marks on the exercise.

We worked long hours down at the Fort. Training started at 9 a.m. and a typical day would involve several lectures, small-arms drill or self-defence classes, an exercise in the afternoon, more lectures, then dinner, perhaps another evening exercise and then we had to write up the exercises going into the middle of the evening. Socialising in the bar afterwards was obligatory, so often we would not get to bed until the early hours. To compensate for the long weekday hours, we finished just after lunch on Friday afternoons and were not expected back at the Fort until mid-morning the following Monday. All of us lived in central London, so we normally shared lifts back into town. For the first few weeks of the IONEC I rented a room from an old Cambridge friend, but realising early in the course that MI6 would be a lifetime career, getting on the property ladder became imperative. I found a one-bedroom garden flat on Richborne Terrace in the pleasant but slightly dilapidated Victorian suburb of Kennington. It was in poor decorative order and the garden was sorely neglected, but it was as much as I could afford and I was very proud of it. Every weekend was spent digging, planting, painting and sawing.

I was enjoying the social life in London too. One day Julian, an English friend I met in Argentina, invited me to an evening of indoor go-kart racing in London to celebrate his birthday. Having spent so many hours tearing up my mother's garden in my home-made go-kart, I fancied my chances in a race and so was looking forward to the event.

The track was built in an old bus depot in Clapham. Julian had invited 30 or so other friends and amongst them were some very pretty girls. One in particular I noticed imediately. As we milled around sorting out helmets and awaiting our heats, I could hardly keep my eyes off her. She was tall, almost five foot ten inches, and had blue eyes and long shiny dark hair which she often caressed and pushed back from her face whenever she laughed. She had cinched-in the waist of the baggy overalls issued to us with an old school tie, accentuating her slender waist. I watched her race in one of her heats. She drove like an old granny popping down to the supermarket for a tin of Whiskas and soon the leaders were bearing down on her to lap her and the race marshalls pulled out the blue flag to show that she should give way. But it was to no avail. Lap after lap, the leaders sat on her bumper, trying to get past. Being lighter than the men behind her, she could accelerate more quickly on the straights, but tiptoed around the corners. The marshalls waved their flags more vigorously, but it was in vain. She just took one hand off the steering wheel and waved back at them. I found out from Julian that she was called Sarah.

After the karting we went for dinner at a nearby Italian restaurant. In the mêlée as we waited to be seated, to my surprise I found that she seemed to be trying to get a seat near me. We chatted all evening and ended up going out to dinner again two days later.

Although the core activity of MI6 is agent-running, its charter, known as the 'Order Book', requires it to maintain a capability to plan and mount 'Special Operations' of a quasi-military nature. MI6 officers do not have the necessary military skills to carry out such operations themselves. Their role is to set the objectives of the operation and obtain political clearance for it from the Foreign Secretary. Thereafter the operation is executed by specially trained officers and men from the three branches of the armed forces.

The Royal Air Force provides a small detachment of around ten pilots known as the 'S&D flight'. They are selected by the RAF for their outstanding skills and most arrive with prior experience in the special forces flights which service the SAS and SBS. They operate a Hercules C-130 transport aircraft and a Puma helicopter, are trained on many other military aircraft, and because they may be required to fly commercial aircraft the lucky selectees also obtain civilian commercial pilot's licences. The C-130 is mostly used for delivering or recovering equipment at overseas stations which are too big or dangerous to travel in a diplomatic bag, and the Puma is used for ferrying MI6 personnel and VIPs around the UK, particularly on the shuttle run between Head Office and the Fort. It can frequently be seen at Battersea Heliport or over London on such journeys, distinguishable from normal RAF Pumas by the large undercarriage containing long-range fuel tanks.

The army provides a detachment from the SAS regiment, called Revolutionary Warfare Wing in Hereford, and the navy provides a small detachment from their Special Boat Service in Poole. Both have similar roles as far as MI6 is concerned and are known collectively within the service as the 'increment'. To qualify for the increment, SAS and SBS personnel must have served for at least five years and have reached the rank of sergeant. They are security vetted by MI6 and given a short induction course into the function and objectives of the service. If they have not already learnt surveillance skills, they take a three-week course at the Fort. Back at their bases in Hereford and Poole, their already substantial military skills are fine-tuned. They learn how to use improvised explosives and sabotage techniques, as well as advanced VIP protection skills, study guerilla warfare organisation and practise advanced insertion techniques – for example high-altitude parachuting from commercial aircraft or covert landings from submarines. Advanced civilian qualifications are acquired: several of the SBS Increment have commercial ship's skipper's tickets in their alias name, enabling them legally to hire, say, a fishing trawler.

On the IONEC, a week of the course is dedicated to familiarisation with the increment and the S&D flight and 'military week' was eagerly anticipated by most of us.

After being issued with a set of military fatigues and boots so outdated they looked like they were SOE relics, we set off from the Fort helipad in the S&D Puma. It was just after nightfall and the cabin of the helicopter was lit by the dim, red emergency exit lights. Using infra-red night sights, the two pilots showed off their impressive low-altitude skills by flying at high speed over the rolling west country farmland, often below the normal military legal limit of 50-feet, a privilege given only to the S&D flight. Every few minutes, one of the pilots cheerfully called out over the intercom, 'Everyone OK back there? Just sing if you feel sick.' Nobody replied, though Bart was looking pale. Half an hour later, the Puma hovered to a standstill a couple of feet off the ground in the corner of a dark field. 'Jump,' screamed the loadie, pushing us out into the darkness, and the Puma roared off into the night. As my eyes adjusted, I realised that we were in the SAS's Pontrilas training area in Wales. 'What are we supposed to do now?' asked Hare to nobody in particular, 'Pretend to be sheep?' Bart groaned and threw up, splashing Castle's boots, but before we had time to laugh an authoritative voice rang out from behind a nearby hedge, 'Over here, lads.'

We shuffled over to where two shadowy figures waited. One was no more than five foot six inches tall and of slight build. The other sported the sort of moustache favoured by soldiers. He spoke first, in a strong Brummie accent. 'I'm Barry, the 2IC of RWW. The purpose of tonight's exercise is to give you a little insight into some of our work, so that when you're back at your comfortable desks, you'll have an idea what it is like for us out in the field.' With that, he turned away, expecting us to follow. Barry's smaller companion was more amiable and trotting alongside us, introduced himself as 'Tiny'.

Tiny was also a sergeant in RWW and was one of its longest-serving members. It was easy to see why he would be useful – his diminutive frame and modesty were advantages in undercover work. As Tiny himself explained, 'I once spent a whole evening trying to convince my mum I was in the SAS, but even she wouldn't believe me.' It was difficult to imagine how he could have passed SAS selection, but all members of RWW must do so. The only exemptions are the few female officers who are occasionally seconded to RWW from the army intelligence corps.

We trudged in silence in the drizzle for ten minutes or so until Barry called a halt. Tiny pulled out a folding spade from his small backpack and started digging. In a minute or so he uncovered a plastic screwtop container, about the size of a beer keg. It was a cache, just like the ones I had dug up in Belgium, and it contained survival rations, water, maps, compass and money. 'We often bury several of these overseas to support emergency exfiltration contingency plans for you guys,' Tiny explained. He then showed us how to bury it, leaving no sign of disturbance, and gave us tips on how to record its location succinctly and unambiguously. Tiny finished his demonstration and lead us back to the field we had come from. From his backpack he fished out eight NATO issue torches complete with infra-red filters, handed them out to us and arranged us in a 'T' shape, the standard pattern used in NATO for guiding down helicopters. We pointed our torches skyward and in seconds the Puma roared into view out of the darkness. We piled into the back, keeping well clear of Bart.

We were dropped off at a small military airfield a few minutes away. It was just past midnight, cold, and the drizzle had thickened into driving rain. Forton was getting fed up and Castle looked disinterested. We followed Tiny out of the wet into a small classroom just below the airfield control tower. A woman in her late 20s, dressed in outdoor casual clothes, waited by the blackboard. She introduced herself as Mags, a captain from the Army's shady agent-handling Force Reaction Unit, on attachment to the RWW, and gave us a lecture on the next stage of the exercise, a simulated agent emergency exfiltration using the S&D Hercules. She explained how we would have to spread out in a set pattern along the runway and use our infra-red torches to guide in the aircraft, and then she numbered us off, assigning us each a position in the pattern. Turning to Barry, who was standing at the back of the class, she snapped, 'Hand out the comms, sergeant.' Barry glowered back and gave each of us a Motorola walkie-talkie. Mags assigned Forton and me to opposite sides of the far end of the landing pattern and we trudged off down the runway together. 'Troll-bitch from hell, isn't she?' Forton laughed.

As we reached our assigned positions, Mags's voice crackled over the Motorolas. 'Alpha one, confirm position, over.' I turned to face her at the far end of the runway and, as she had instructed, flashed the letter A in morse on the torch. 'Bravo one, confirm position, over,' she called for Forton, but he was still chatting besides me and just turned to wave his torch like a child with a sparkler. 'Bravo one, get in position immediately, over,' snapped Mags. Forton sauntered over the runway and Mags continued checking off the rest of the pattern. She got as far as Barking when her instructions were blotted out by Forton singing into his Motorola, turned on full power, his best rendition of 'Strangers in the Night'.

Forton reached the fourth verse before the Hercules screamed into view and drowned him out. With its props on full reverse thrust and its tyres screaching in protest, it halted in an astonishing short space. The rear ramp dropped and a Range Rover burst out and tore off down the runway towards the control tower. As briefed by Mags, we ran to the aircraft and clambered into the spacious hold. The aircraft executed a sharp U-turn and accelerated back down the runway as we clung to the webbing seats inside, took off, flew a tight circuit and landed again. The rear ramp was already half-open as the plane touched down, giving a view of the Range Rover hurtling down the runway after us. With the aircraft still rolling, the Range Rover hurtled up the ramp at alarming speed, the RWW crew strapped it down and only seconds after touching down we were airborne again. 'That was an example of how we do hot exfiltrations,' Barry shouted over the roaring engines.

We spent the night at Stirling Lines, the SAS's headquarters in Hereford, dining in the officer's mess. It was an honour, because normally only SAS personnel are allowed to set foot in the building. After dinner, Barry stood up and spoke. 'I've arranged an interesting talk. I'm sure it will be a humbling experience for all of you.' He glowered at Forton and lead us into a meeting room by the mess. A stocky, dark-haired soldier was waiting, standing by an overhead projector. As we settled into our seats he stared blankly at the wall behind us and waited until there was silence before he spoke. Quietly he introduced himself and for the next hour he told how in the Gulf War his eight-man Scud-hunting patrol, Bravo Two Zero, was compromised and ambushed, and how he was captured and tortured by the Iraqis for several months. He spoke with no trace of boastfulness, emotion or humour, as if he was telling us about a trip to buy a bit of wood from B&Q. When he finished, he thanked us for our attention and left.

We trooped back to the bar in silence. It was some minutes before Spencer spoke up. 'It would make a cracking book, that would.' For once, Spencer was right. Andy McNab published his story a year later and it became a worldwide best-seller.

The next morning, the Puma picked us up and took us down to the Special Boat Service's base in Poole, Dorset. The SBS contribution to the increment is much smaller than RWW, only about 15 men. As one would expect, given its naval roots, the SBS increment is oriented towards marine operations and its men are expert frogmen and underwater demolitions experts. Many have served also in Commachio troop, the Royal Marines' maritime counter-terrorist unit, or in their Mountain and Arctic Warfare cadre. The SBS increment is primarily employed by MI6 to place tracking beacons on ships whilst they are anchored in harbour.

The beacon is about the size of a house brick and to work effectively it must be placed high up on the ship's superstructure. We were given a demonstration in the indoor swimming pool by an SBS sergeant of the lightweight drysuit, recycling breathing apparatus and compact collapsible ladder used to covertly approach and board a ship in harbour.

The SBS increment also operates MI6's mini-submarine, about the length of two cars. The pilot and navigator sit astride the cylindrical forward hull dressed in drysuits and breathing apparatus. The rear half of the craft flattens into a passenger compartment which is just large enough to carry four persons, packed together like sardines. The compartment is flooded during a dive and the drysuited passengers breathe air piped from the craft's onboard supply. The mini-sub is used for infiltrating specialist agents into a hostile country and for exfiltrating compromised agents.

The SAS and SBS increments are complemented by another specialist cadre who occasionally participate in increment operations and we were also introduced to their skills during military week. These 20 or so men and women, known collectively as UKN, encompass a diverse range of specialist skills. Only the small 'core' who are on call full-time draw a modest salary from MI6. The rest work unpaid and take time off from their real jobs to participate in MI6 operations. Their core skill is surveillance and counter-surveillance. To blend into foreign streets, some are drawn from ethnic minorities and many have a good command of foreign languages. Other skills are diverse: one is a pilot who, though working full-time for an air-taxi company, is prepared to drop everything to help out in an MI6 operation when required. Another is a yachtmaster who provides his boat when required. UKN have an odd status in the office because they are regarded as agents rather than staff, so we dealt with them under alias. They are also deniable assets – if an increment soldier were captured in an operation, MI6 would initiate diplomatic efforts to secure their release, but UKN have no such reassurance. They would be denied and their only hope of securing release would be through private legal action. As they clearly cannot get insurance on the commercial market, they take enormous personal risks every time they go abroad.

Although Ball and Long kept us under continuous assessment on the IONEC, most emphasis was placed on our performance in the final exercise, known as EXERCISE SOLO. Traditionally SOLO took place in Norway with the cooperation of its secret service. But our SOLO was to be hosted for the first time by SISMI, the Italian secret service.

The decision to base SOLO in Italy was taken for political reasons at a high level in both countries. MI6 had been in liaison with SISMI before, but the relationship was tetchy and weak. MI6 regarded southern European liaison services as unprofessional and insecure and SISMI preferred to work with the CIA and the BND (the German external intelligence service). Recent developments, however, had brought MI6 and SISMI closer. SISMI was doing some good work against its recalcitrant southern neighbour, Libya, and MI6 wanted access to this intelligence. SISMI's relationship with the BND was also going through a difficult patch, so they regarded bolstering links with MI6 as a useful insurance policy. MI6 proposed to SISMI that they cooperate on training exercises as a means of cementing the relationship, so the Italian-based SOLO was born. In return, MI6 offered to host training on its home turf for SISMI's new recruits.

Because of the political background to the decision, it was important that the exercise was a success. Ball and Long spent a month in Italy prior to the start of the IONEC, planning the exercise with the help of SISMI and Rome station.

Ball briefed us that we were to imagine that we were employed in

UKB, the section which works against IRA operations outside the UK. An intelligence report from GCHQ had revealed that the IRA were cooperating with the Italian mafia to smuggle Chinese-made SA-14 hand-held anti-aircraft missiles into Sicily where they would be clandestinely shipped to Northern Ireland for use against British army helicopters. Our imaginary mission was to go to Italy and debrief APOCALYPSE, a mole within the IRA. We were to write up the CX, then pass it in a brush contact to 'Eric', a courier who would hand us 'further instructions'. We were issued with Pentels for secret-writing and developer fluid disguised as aftershave, but had to plan the rest of the operation ourselves over the next fortnight. We were all now wise to the trickery of the DS and did not expect an easy time.

5

FIRST SOLO

SUNDAY, 23 FEBRUARY 1992
HEATHROW AIRPORT

'Just my luck,' I thought, as the tall, well-dressed blonde sat down in the aisle seat. For the first time in my life I get to sit next to somebody interesting on the plane, and I'm stuck with an alias name and fictional background. Probably a trick anyway – Ball and Long had no doubt arranged for attractive undercover women to sit next to all of us on our flights, hoping that one of us would accidentally drop our cover and let something about our real lives slip out. Ball warned us in the SOLO briefing that one trainee once fell for such a trick. He was at Manchester airport, waiting in the departure lounge for his flight to Amsterdam, when an attractive woman sat down next to him. She started chatting to him and he responded, at first sticking to his cover story; but, becoming increasingly attracted, he wanted to get in touch after the exercise and crassly told her that he was an undercover MI6 officer and gave her his real home phone number. At the post-exercise debrief, his newly acquired 'girlfriend' strolled in and revealed that she was an undercover customs officer. Needless to say, he was never allowed to undertake any real natural cover work. There was no way that Ball was going to dupe me into the same error during our two-hour flight from Heathrow to Rome's Fiumicino airport.

The girl turned towards me, smiling. 'Hi, I'm Rebecca. Are you staying long in Rome?'

The DS would expect me at least to give out part of my cover story. I was posing as a nerdy academic, so hopefully it would put her off. 'I'm Dan. I'm just off to Velletri for a week.'

'Oh really?' she replied. 'What are you doing there?'

'I'm a historian, writing a post-doctoral thesis on the contrasting approaches to urban reconstruction after the Second World War in the UK and Italy.' To my relief, her friendly smile waned. Pulling out a weighty academic book on post-war urban redevelopment in Italy, borrowed from London University library, I started to study earnestly. With a shrug of her shoulders, she reached into her shoulder bag and pulled out *Hello* magazine. We sat in silence for the rest of the flight.

Velletri in February was not an enticing place and it had not been easy to devise a plausible cover story for visiting such an unremarkable town in the depths of winter. It had no industry of note, ruling out business cover. Journalism, the other mainstay cover for MI6 officers, was also not easy as I discovered in my research through the library archives that little of note ever happened in Velletri. Indeed, the only reference to the town in the Italian tourist office in London was that it had been heavily bombed by the American air force during the last days of the Second World War as they drove the retreating German army northwards. In the absence of anything more plausible, this bombing campaign would have to form the basis of my cover for the visit.

In my spare time in the fortnight preceding EXERCISE SOLO I carefully built up a thick file of notes, photocopies and cuttings about Velletri. The archives of the Imperial War Museum, fortuitously only a stone's throw from Century House, furnished a wealth of detail on the wartime events in the town. Noticing one day an advertisement in the education supplement of *The Guardian* for a vacant post-doctoral urban-redevelopment teaching post at University College, London, I applied using an alias and false academic qualifications, forged by TOS. An invitation to interview arrived shortly afterwards. I would not attend, of course, but the letter slipped into my briefcase would add credibility. Every other piece of paper in my briefcase, every dry-cleaning slip or receipt in my wallet, every item of clothing, would have to match the legend that I was a Daniel Noonan, a post-doctoral history student.

Arriving at Velletri's small railway station on a cool Monday morning, I felt comfortable in my alias identity and well prepared for the exercise. After checking into the Pensione Arena, a tiny bed and breakfast tucked away on the Via Cannetoli, I spent the rest of the evening exploring the narrow cobbled streets and winding alleys of the hilltop medieval town. First I recced the Café Leoni on the Corso della Repubblica, just off Piazza Cairoli, where a meeting was scheduled with Eric, and then found the Bar Venezia on Via Lata where I was to meet APOCALYPSE.

Ball told us that we would be under surveillance throughout the exercise by Italian teams. He was probably bluffing, as the Italians would probably not divert their limited surveillance resources to our exercise, but taking no chances I mentally noted useful anti-surveillance traps. At the same time, I tried to immerse myself completely in my false identity, mentally rehearsing every small detail of my cover, trying to think and act just like a real historian would do on a research trip. I stopped to examine and photograph any buildings which were of pre-war origin – all the churches, the town halls – and my research had revealed where some of the USAF bombs had landed, so I inspected the repairs and reconstruction. Everything was noted in copious detail in notebooks, building up documentation to support my cover story.

That evening was spent eating a simple meal of pizza and chianti at the Bar Centrale on the main town piazza. There did not seem to be much nightlife in Velletri, so I went to bed early in the low budget pensione. There was a long day ahead of me on the morrow, and I would need a good night's sleep.

On Tuesday I arrived at Bar Venezia at 10.50 a.m., ten minutes before APOCALYPSE was due, ordered a cappuccino, and sat down at the table furthest from the bar, my back to the wall so that the quiet street outside was visible. The five or six other tables were deserted; the only other customer, an old man, sipped a brandy at the bar. He wore a faded black beret and a padded jacket with one pocket nearly torn off. Two fingers were missing from his calloused right hand and an old sheepdog lay dozing under his stool. Not the sort that even the Italians would use for surveillance. I pulled out a copy of *The Economist* from my shoulder bag and laid it on the table in front of me. It was the all-clear sign for APOCALYPSE.

I spotted him out on the street just before he entered the café. In his mid-40s, thickset, neat short hair, dressed in fleece jacket, jeans and Timberland boots – the clothing gave him away as a Brit. He didn't acknowledge me but went straight to the counter and ordered an expresso. The sheepdog sniffed the air, growled softly and went back to sleep.

APOCALYPSE brought his coffee over to my table. 'Do you mind if I take a seat?' he greeted me cautiously.

I didn't stand up to greet him – that would disclose to an observer that we were expecting each other – but indicated for him to sit down and, following Ball's briefing introduced myself as successor to 'Peter', APOCALYPSE's former case officer. I established a cover story for our meeting as quickly as possible, as we had been trained. 'If anybody should ask how we met, you should simply say that you walked into the café, saw me reading *The Economist*, and went up to speak to me as a fellow Brit.' APOCALYPSE nodded, but he still seemed cautious. Ball had trained us on the IONEC to build a rapport with an agent to ease nerves or suspicion. 'Nice boots,' I commented, nodding at his new Timberlands. 'Did you buy them here?'

Soldiers love talking about boots and APOCALYPSE was no exception. 'Aye, excellent piece of kit, these, can't fault 'em.' APOCALYPSE started to open up and once the rapport was established it was time to start the debrief. APOCALYPSE briefed me that he was in Italy to meet a contact in the Italian mafia who had access to Soviet weaponry by virtue of their links with the Libyan government. APOCALYPSE had negotiated the purchase of 20 SA-14 anti-aircraft missiles. The consignment would be shipped from Tripoli in a tramp steamer to the Irish coast, where, under cover of darkness, it would be unloaded into rigid hull inflatables. Once landed, the missiles would be driven overnight to an IRA safe house near the border.

It was important information, but APOCALYPSE didn't know the sort of detail which would enable Head Office to act on the intelligence. They would want the name of the tramp steamer, its departure date, the exact date it would arrive in Ireland. APOCALYPSE promised that he could get the answers from his fictional contact. We arranged to meet again two days later, this time in a different café, the Bar di Poniente on the west side of the town. I reminded APOCALYPSE of our cover story for the meeting and left.

I scurried back to the Pensione Arena, locked the door of the simple room and, using the Pentel pen provided by TOS/SW, wrote up the intelligence in block capitals in the standard format of a CX report. At the top, a brief one-line summary of the intelligence. Next, the date of the meeting at which the information had been acquired. Then a brief description of the source – 'An excellent source with direct access, who has reported reliably in the past,' I wrote. Then the text of the intelligence. It all fitted on to one page of A4 paper from my pad of water-soluble paper. Putting the sheet face-up on the bedside locker, I laid a sheet of ordinary A4 over it, then on top of them both *The Theory of Postwar Urban Redevelopment.* Five minutes was enough for the imprint transfer to the ordinary A4. The sheet of water soluble paper went into the toilet bowl and in seconds all that was left was a translucent scum on the surface of the water which was flushed away. Back in the bedroom I took the sheet of A4, folded it into a brown manilla envelope and taped it into the inside of a copy of the *Gazzetta dello Sport.* I had to work quickly because there wasn't much time before the 2 p.m. meeting with the Eric.

He was sitting at the Café Leoni's crowded bar, milling with office workers on their lunchbreak. His dark jacket and red tie, recognition features which Ball had briefed us to look out for, were easy to pick out. In front of him was a nearly finished glass of beer and a folded copy of the *Gazzetta dello Sport*. Squeezing into a gap between him and another customer, I placed my own copy next to his and ordered a coffee. Wordlessly, Eric picked up my paper and left. I enjoyed my coffee, leaving 15 minutes later with Eric's newspaper under my arm. Even if surveillance were watching me, only the most acute observer would have noticed the brush contact.

There was not another meeting scheduled with Eric until the following morning, but there was plenty to keep me occupied for the rest of the afternoon. Ball had told us to do a house recce, as we had learnt on PERFECT NEIGHBOUR. The scenario was the same – it was a suspected IRA safe house and we were to help TOS plan a bugging operation. Number 41 Via Antonio Gruinaci was on the east side of the town. That afternoon, a casual stroll past gave me a first look. A detached three-storey house, probably of post-war construction, it was stuccoed in a creamy colour and set just off the road with a small iron gate leading into the front garden. There was a new and expensive Lancia parked in the drive. I strained to get a better look at the small plaque hanging from the side gate: 'Studio di Architectura, M di Rossi, Pietrangelo Di Vito, M Caracci.' I memorised as much detail as I could but no amount of written detail can beat a good photograph. We had not been issued with covert cameras – that would be far too compromising if we were arrested – so I took a photograph openly with my Pentax SLR. If questioned, I would claim that it was part of my research. It would be enough to make a good report for the DS – not as good as on PERFECT NEIGHBOUR, but good enough given the limited time. I stashed the camera away and hurried back to the pension.

The rest of the afternoon was spent doing the work a real academic on a research visit might do. Maria Vialli, a pretty assistant clerk in the town hall planning department, provided me with maps of the town before and after the war and photocopies of town records. 'You're in luck,' she told me in good English, 'the local priest who has lived here all his life is displaying his collection of sketches of the town from 1945 to present – you should go and have a chat with him.' She gave me her business card in case I needed to contact her again. At the gallery, just underneath the town hall, the priest, Monsignor Berlingieri, was hosting the exhibition, humbly showing visitors around his pictures. He was delighted to escort me around the collection and two hours later, the tour finished, I pressed a calling card into his hand to ensure that he would remember my name.

Eric was waiting for me the following morning in a third café, just off the town square. The *Gazzetta dello Sport* swap was two-way this time. My copy contained the write-up of the house recce and a canister containing the undeveloped film and there was a message for me in Eric's copy.

Back in my room at the Arena, the brown envelope inside the paper contained a plain sheet of A4 paper. Surprisingly, there was also a thick wadge of £50 notes, amounting to £1,000 in total. Eager for an explanation, I moistened a ball of cotton wool with the doctored Polo aftershave and applied it to the blank sheet and waited. Nothing happened. I reversed the sheet and tried again. This time typed script gradually appeared, faint pink at first, then darkening to a deep purple. It was a message from the Rome station:

> MESSAGE BEGINS
> 1. CONGRATULATIONS ON YOUR SUCCESSFUL FIRST MEETING WITH APOCALYPSE. THE INTELLIGENCE WAS EXCELLENT BUT, AS YOU POINT OUT, WE NEED FURTHER DETAIL. UNFORTUNATELY APOCALYPSE CONTACTED ROME STATION YESTERDAY AT 1900 HOURS ON HIS EMERGENCY CONTACT NUMBER. HIS MAFIA CONTACT HAS REQUESTED A MEETING IN MILAN AT 2100 TODAY. IT IS IMPORTANT THAT YOU DEBRIEF APOCALYPSE IMMEDIATELY AFTER THE MEETING. WE FEAR HE MAY BE IN TROUBLE. WE ENCLOSE £1,000 STERLING TO PAY HIM IF REQUIRED.
> 2. YOU SHOULD MAKE YOUR WAY TO MILAN THIS EVENING. ROM/1 SEC WILL MEET YOU IN THE LOBBY OF THE HOTEL TREVISO AT 2130. APOCALYPSE IS DRIVING TO MILAN FROM YOUR LOCATION AFTER YOUR MEETING. WE SUGGEST YOU ACCOMPANY HIM.
> GRS0000
> ENDS

I didn't like the last line. We'd been trained not to let an agent take control of a meeting and getting in his car would put APOCALYPSE literally in the driving seat. If the scenario were real, I would hire my own vehicle and make my own way to Milan. But this was an exercise and perhaps there was another agenda. Were Ball and Long testing my initiative with a little ploy? Did they expect me to refuse the order to get in APOCALYPSE's car and make my own way? Or did they want me to accept a lift from APOCALYPSE so that my arrest could be engineered more easily? Evading the inevitable arrest would not be well received by the DS – much of the training value of the exercise lay in the interrogation phase. Against my instinct, I reluctantly decided to go with APOCALYPSE.

There was no smoke alarm in the room, but nevertheless I took the sheet of paper bearing the instructions and carefully folded it, concertina fashion, into four and stood it in the empty bathroom sink. Lit at the top, it would burn downwards and make much less smoke than when lit from the bottom. The Zippo's flame touched the paper and, accelerated by the alcohol-based aftershave, quickly consumed it. I swilled the ashes down the plughole, taking care that no trace of soot was left in the sink.

I met APOCALYPSE again later that afternoon in a small café just behind the town church. He had arrived early and was sitting on his own in the corner table. The school day had just finished and the other tables were crowded with giggling adolescents. APOCALYPSE didn't look too comfortable. 'Shall we go somewhere else?' I offered.

'We'll only be a minute or so. I've got you lots more information,' APOCALYPSE whispered. He delved into his small backpack and handed me three photocopies. They were the specifications for the SA-14s. 'I've also got you lots more detail on the tramp steamer and the shipment. You'll need pen and paper to write it down,' he said firmly. I fished out my notebook and he dictated the name of the fictitious ship, sailing date, expected rendezvous date in Ireland, cargo bill-of-loading number and the number of the end-user certificate which the Libyans had used to acquire the weaponry.

I guessed that APOCALYPSE was loading me up with documentation so that when I came to be arrested, there would be plenty of incriminating material on me for my interrogators. But I couldn't throw the papers away. The exercise scenario was that I should give them to H/ROM SEC in the Hotel Treviso that evening, and the DS wouldn't be too happy if I jettisoned them. While APOCALYPSE excused himself to visit the bathroom, I slipped the scrap of paper down the inside of my sock. Dealing with the other papers would have to wait.

APOCALYPSE returned to his seat. 'Listen, I've got to go to Milan tonight to meet the mafia guys. I don't know what they want. I want you to come up with me in case there's trouble.'

APOCALYPSE's invitation reeked of a trap, but the DS wanted me to fall for it. 'Yes, I got the same message last night,' I replied. 'I've got my bag. Let's go.'

Minutes later, we were speeding up the S7 *superstrada* towards Rome in APOCALYPSE's hired Fiat Panda. APOCALYPSE drove in silence, deep in thought. We were nearing the centre of the capital before he turned to me. 'I've got to make a phone call to my girlfriend. I'll just be a minute.' He pulled into an AGIP petrol station on the Via 20 Settembre, and left the car to make the call. I guessed that he would probably be calling the DS, alerting them that we would soon be arriving at the arrest site.

Using a 500-lire coin, I partially unscrewed the trim panel from the side of the passenger footwell, stuffed the three sheets of information on the SA-14s down the gap and had just finished screwing it back together when APOCALYPSE returned. 'OK, everything's in order,' he announced, 'Let's get on our way to Milan.'

We navigated northwards through the busy Rome traffic and were approaching the entry to the A1 *autostrada* when we came upon a carabinieri roadblock controlling the traffic flowing on to the motorway. Four uniformed officers were questioning the driver of a battered Fiat 500, their dark-blue Alfa-Romeos parked alongside. As we drew closer, one raised a white gloved hand, indicating for us to pull in. 'Shit' exclaimed APOCALYPSE, a little too vehemently. We drew to a halt just as the little Fiat accelerated away in a cloud of blue exhaust smoke.

One of the carabinieri strutted over to APOCALYPSE's window, dark glasses hiding his eyes. 'Documenti,' he snapped, clicking his fingers.

APOCALYPSE looked at me, bemused. 'He wants your driving licence and insurance details,' I urged.

'I haven't got them,' replied APOCALYPSE with a shrug of his shoulders.

The carabinieri glared back. 'Documenti,' he repeated, then in accented English, 'Passport.'

APOCALYPSE shrugged his shoulders, 'I left it in my hotel,' he replied, speaking slowly and deliberately.

The carabinieri beckoned to his boss who strutted over and barked out a few orders. 'Chiavi,' he demanded impatiently, while the first carabinieri went round to the front of our car to send the registration number through to their control centre. The officer reached through the window, grabbed the ignition keys and ordered us out of the car. Two other carabinieri started searching the boot. 'Whose car is this?' the senior officer asked in heavily accented English.

'It's a Hertz rental car' answered APOCALYPSE.

The officer conferred on his radio again and ordered us to wait. I had expected to be arrested but still was not sure if this was a mock arrest or whether we had genuinely stumbled into one of the many random traffic controls on Italian roads. Surely the DS would not plan a mock arrest to this level of detail? That smoking Fiat 500 pulling away as we arrived was so plausible. Could this be a real road block? Was the exercise was about to go spectacularly wrong?

The senior officer came back and snapped a few orders to his subordinates, then turned to us. 'There are some irregularities in the paperwork of your car. You must come with us to the station while we investigate further.'

They bundled us into the back of separate Alfa-Romeos, carabinieri clambering in either side of me, SMGs cradled in their laps. Two other officers took charge of APOCALYPSE's Fiat. With sirens blaring and blue lights flashing, we hurtled down the *autostrada*, traffic parting in front of us.

We turned off ten kilometres later and pulled into a carabinieri station in the shadows of the flyover. My captors wordlessly dragged me out of the Alfa-Romeo, escorted me into a large room and pushed me into a chair in front of a substantial steel desk. Four armed guards stood over me. Another officer walked in, causing the guards to spring to attention. He was dressed in civilian clothes and spoke impeccable English. 'I'm sorry to treat you like this, but we have had intelligence that two mafia contacts were making their way up to Milan in a car like yours. We need to eliminate you from our enquiries.'

He handed me some forms and ordered me to fill in details of name, address, occupation and date of birth. The DS would check that we had remembered all the basic details of our alias cover story. I handed back the paper and the civilian cross-examined me on them. I answered confidently, determined not to let him catch me out so easily.

One of the carabinieri who made the original arrest entered and interrupted proceedings. 'Capitano, ho trovato niente nella macchina.' It was close enough to Spanish for me to understand that they had failed to find anything incriminating in the hire car. The captain glared at his subordinate and irritably ordered him to go back and continue searching. Eventually they would find the papers hidden in the door panel, but hopefully it would take them a while. Meanwhile, I rehearsed in my head a cover story to explain their existence.

The captain questioned me politely for the next hour, checking through the minutiae of my cover story. It reminded me of the Mendoza police interrogation in Argentina. I did not diverge from my cover story and he was starting to run out of justification for holding me when the carabinieri returned, triumphantly clutching the photocopies. The captain studied them for a few minutes, then turned to me. 'So, Dr Noonan, if you really are a historian as you claim, how do you explain these papers in your car?' He shuffled through them in front of me. 'They appear to be detailed descriptions of a shoulder-launched anti-helicopter weapon, which we know the mafia have just acquired from Libya.'

I faked an innocent expression. 'I've never seen them before,' I replied, shrugging my shoulders. 'They must have been left in the car by the previous hirer.'

It was a plausible explanation. The captain had not uncovered even a tiny chink in my cover story, but I knew he would not release me yet as the DS would want to hold me until my cover was broken. The captain got up and left.

Half an hour later, he returned. His mood was more hostile. 'Dr Noonan, I do not believe your story. I am arresting you under Italian anti-terrorist laws. You do not have the right to call a lawyer.' He snapped his fingers. Two of the four guards handcuffed me and frogmarched me back outside. Their grip on me was vice-like. If these guys were acting, they were doing a good job. As they pushed me towards the two Alfa-Romeo patrol cars, I caught a glimpse of the Fiat. The wheels were off, both front seats and all the carpets were stripped out and the bonnet insulation had been pulled away. Foolishly, I couldn't hold back a smirk. One of the guards noticed and, as he bundled me into the back of the Alfa, he gave my head a stealthy bash against the door pillar. Armed carabinieri climbed in on either side. One of them blindfolded me, then thrust my head down between my knees, viciously tightening the handcuffs a couple of notches so they bit into my wrists.

They dragged me from the car, stiff, aching and still blindfolded some 40 minutes later, and escorted me indoors. I didn't know it, but I was at the main carabinieri HQ just outside Rome. The blindfold was pulled away and I found myself in a small cell, no more than ten feet by ten feet, furnished with a simple iron bed with a mattress and one pillow. In the corner was a continental-style hole-in-the-floor toilet, with a shower rose above it.

One of the guards released the handcuffs, letting blood flow back into my numbed hands, and ordered me to strip. As I removed each garment, he shook them and examined them carefully for hidden objects. The scrap of paper bearing the details of the ship and end user certificates was still in my right sock. Steadying myself by leaning on the mattress, I pulled off the sock, secreting the wedge of paper between thumb and palm. Handing the sock to him with my left hand, I steadied myself with my right hand as I pulled off my left sock. As he examined and shook it, I slipped the incriminating evidence under the pillow.

My clothes were stuffed into a black bin liner and the carabinieri handed me a pair of grey overalls a size too small, blindfolded me again, then handcuffed me face downwards to the bed. The heavy door clanged shut so probably the guards were gone, but I waited for five minutes, listening carefully, before moving. There wasn't much slack on the chain of the handcuffs but by sliding them along the rail of the bedstead I groped for the scrap of paper under the pillow, transferred it to my mouth and swallowed it.

Lying chained to the bed felt isolated and slightly humiliating, but it was just an exercise. I tried to imagine what it would really be like to be caught working under natural cover. Ball told us that it had happened only once to an MI6 officer. He was working in Geneva when, unbeknown to him, a fellow guest in his hotel was murdered. One of the staff had noticed the officer chatting – wholly innocently – to the guest earlier in the evening, so he became a key suspect. At 4 a.m., the police burst into his room and arrested him. His cover story was solid, however, and he survived the police interrogation. He was eventually released.

It seemed like hours before the door opened again. The guards unlocked me from the bed, handcuffed my wrists, hauled me to my feet and man-handled me down a corridor and out into welcome fresh air. It must have been just after nightfall because the still air was laden with dew. The guards forced me up some stairs and into another building. I heard the guards whispering something in Italian to a third person and then got a whiff of the strong, unmistakable smell of stale cigarettes and whisky, indicating that Ball was nearby. The guards pushed me onwards for a few more yards, forced me into a chair, handcuffed my wrists behind me and pulled the blindfold away.

I was in a large high-ceilinged room, big enough to be a school dining-hall or army drill-hall. Twenty feet or so in front of me three interrogators sat behind a long desk on a low stage. In the middle was an athletic-looking man in his early 40s, whose groomed jet-black hair and perfectly symmetrical handlebar moustache suggested that he spent a lot of time in front of a mirror. To his right sat the captain who had interviewed me earlier in the carabinieri station. To his left sat a dark-haired woman, whose heavy wrinkles on a once-attractive face were explained by the foul-smelling cigarette she was holding. The three stared at me impassively and disdainfully and it felt like several minutes before the moustache spoke.

'So, Dr Noonan,' he began imperiously. 'I understand from my colleague that you are a historian, visiting our town of Velletri.' He paused for effect. 'Let me tell you. We don't believe your story. We have intelligence that you are involved in an operation to smuggle weapons from Sicily to the IRA. What have you got to say for yourself?'

'Rubbish!' I replied with convincing irritation. 'Your intelligence is wrong and you've arrested the wrong person.'

The moustache questioned me for 20 minutes or so, cross-examining me on details of my cover – my fictitious date of birth, address, where I worked, how long I had worked there, names of members of my family. The only thing he didn't ask was the name of my dog.

Then it was the wrinkly's turn to question me. 'Who is this woman, Maria Vialli? Where did you meet her?' she asked cattily, holding her business card.

'Why not ring her up and ask her,' I replied. 'Better still,' I added, 'why not ring Monsignor Berlingieri, the priest at the church of Mary Magdalene?' My interrogators looked at each other, seeking inspiration. It was not going well for them.

The moustache snapped his fingers and the guards behind me sprung forward, blindfolded me and dragged me back to my cell. They gave me a glass of water and slice of bread before shackling me on to the bed again. It seemed like four or five hours before they took me back before my interrogators where they asked me the same questions again, only this time more impatiently. 'We have interviewed your companion, with whom you were arrested,' snapped the moustache. 'So tell me, Dr Noonan, where did you meet him?' Hoping that APOCALYPSE had stuck to the agreed cover story, I explained that he had seen me reading *The Economist* in a café and had introduced himself as a fellow Brit. APOCALYPSE must have remembered, because the moustache seemed satisfied with my explanation. He changed tack. 'Do you know who I am?' Without waiting for a reply, he continued. 'I am Major Claudio Pagalucca, of the airborne carabinieri.' He puffed out his chest with pride. 'I have three medals, won for bravery. Do you know what that means?'

I was tempted to reply flippantly but bit my lip. 'No, I've not a clue. I'm just an academic – that sort of thing's got nothing to do with me.'

Pagalucca looked deflated. The airborne carabinieri are Italy's equivalent of the SAS. Their role is to work against the mafia and they are parachute-trained in order to launch surprise attacks against mafia hideouts in Sicilian valleys. When asked the same question in his interrogation, Hare had been unable to resist a jibe at Pagalucca's vanity. 'Some sort of parachuting aerial traffic warden, is it?' he replied flippantly. Pagalucca held him in detention for four hours longer than the rest of us.

Between interrogation sessions, the only discomfort was boredom, and there was no physical hardship. The resistance to interrogation exercise I had done in the TA was tougher physically. But whereas on the SAS exercise the actual interrogation interview was easy – we just had to ensure that we did not give away any more than our name, rank, date of birth and army number – here the difficulty was keeping every detail of our cover story entirely consistent between interrogation sessions. One little slip would be spotted and exploited ruthlessly and once the cover story started unravelling, it would be very difficult to retract the damage. But by my third session, some four or five hours later, my interrogators had not prised open my story. Pagalucca gave up and only the wrinkly asked a few easy questions. The session lasted less than ten minutes, so I guessed that they were close to releasing me.

I had not been in my cell for long when the door opened again. The guards pulled off my blindfold, released my handcuffs and handed over the bag containing my clothes. I fumbled for my watch. It showed 5 p.m., just over 24 hours since the arrest. Once I was dressed, the guards led me out into the evening darkness over to another building up a short flight of steps and, with a friendly smile and a handshake, indicated that I should go inside.

Ball, Long, Eric and APOCALYPSE were all waiting to shake my hand inside the room. 'Congratulations,' said Ball. 'We had to let you out early. We just couldn't pin anything on you – you did an excellent job.' He ushered me over to a trestle table laden with food, beer and wine. 'We'll debrief you properly later. For the moment, get yourself a drink.' Over a beer, Ball explained what was going on. 'Some of the others should be along in a while, but they've still got a bit of explaining to do . . .'

One by one, the other students emerged from their captivity to join us around the buffet table and to tell their stories. Spencer was the next to be released, an hour or so later. He had pretended to be a priest and although the cover story held for a while, it unravelled when he was asked to say a few prayers and had been unable to even recite the Lord's prayer in full. Markham panicked when he saw the roadblock and threw the papers and the thousand pounds out of the window of the moving car, causing chaos on the *autostrada*. Bart had done well. His cover as a scientist was too complicated for Pagalucca to probe with any authority and his prodigious memory had enabled him to maintain a consistent cover story. Castle's suit and business cover was not plausible in his small market town and his story folded. Forton's cover was as a chorister on a tour of churches in Rome and when Pagalucca asked him to prove his singing prowess, Forton started and did not stop, to Pagalucca's irritation.

But there was something else that was still puzzling me about the exercise. Ball was standing on his own in the corner, as ever with a cigarette in one hand and a whisky in the other, rocking gently backwards and forwards with a satisfied smile on his face. 'Jonathan,' I asked, 'where's that pretty blonde you put next to me on the plane? Is she not coming tonight?'

'What girl?' Ball replied, genuinely bemused.

'Oh come on,' I replied, 'the girl you put next to me on the plane to test my cover story.'

'Nothing to do with us!' Ball assured me. 'You missed an opportunity there,' he laughed.

––––––––––

We flew back from Rome to Southampton the next morning on the S&D Hercules C-130 at spectacularly low level over the Alps. Arriving back at the Fort that evening we were demob happy. We had spent an intensive six months in each other's company and had got to know each other well. Even Bart and Markham were now mates. Officers on the same IONEC tend to keep in touch throughout their subsequent careers and no doubt we would too, but for the moment we were all keen to get into our new jobs. Our IONEC scores and first Head Office postings were to be announced the following day.

There is a formal performance appraisal system in MI6. Approximately every six months line managers summarise a subordinate's performance on a 'Staff Appraisal Form' or SAF. The most important part of the SAF is the overall grading or 'box number'. A 'Box 3', signifying a satisfactory performance, is the median and the grade most commonly awarded. 'Box 1' is outstanding, 'Box 2' above average, 'Box 4' substandard; 'Box 5' indicates a seriously deficient performance and can lead to a rapid exit from the service. Each SAF is sent to personnel department where they play an important role in determining the career structure of each officer, deciding postings and seniority. Ball and Long were responsible for preparing our SAFs on the IONEC and the following day they gave us the morning off while they considered our grades.

While they deliberated, Nixon kept us busy with a shooting competition down on the Fort's outdoor range. We were now moderately proficient and could handle a Browning 9mm safely, which was an improvement on when we started. Most of the time most of us managed to hit the centre of the figure 12 (half-size man) target from ten metres on a fast draw with the Browning, and we were accurate at that range within a few centimetres with the Heckler and Koch MP5. Hare ironically reckoned that he had personally shot more rounds of 9mm during the IONEC than during his entire eight-year army career. Our training was a wasteful extravagance, but one that we all enjoyed. Even the mild-mannered and liberal Forton, who initially regarded guns with distaste, now approached the lessons with relish. One round of Nixon's competition was to knock down empty beer cans against the clock with the Heckler & Koch set on its single-shot setting. Forton won by flicking the sub-machine gun into automatic mode and spraying the row of cans with a full magazine, grinning wildly like a raver on ecstasy.

As the competition progressed, one by one we were called away to see the DS in main wing. Bart went first – he was awarded a Box 2 and was posted to counter-proliferation section, a job I was disappointed not to get myself. Castle got a Box 2 and became a junior R officer in the Middle East controllerate. Markham was posted to a junior P desk in the West European controllerate with a Box 2. Hare was assigned to a joint section with MI5 to work against Middle East terrorists, also with a Box 2. Spencer was relieved to get a Box 2 and went to work as a targeting officer in the East European controllerate. Forton was badly criticised for his performance on Exercise Solo and for annoying the SAS with his Frank Sinatra impression. He was marked down to a Box 3 and posted to an R desk in the Africa controllerate, much to his disappointment. I was called away from the shooting competition just as Forton, chuckling maniacally, was about to demolish an old safe with a Remington Wingmaster repeat-action shotgun, and walked over to see Ball in the west wing.

'Congratulations,' Ball announced, shaking my hand. 'Your performance throughout the course was outstanding. You never put a foot wrong and we feel we had no other alternative but to award you a Box 1 for your outstanding performance.' Long beamed in the background, as Ball continued. 'It is a remarkable achievement. We've checked through personnel department records, and nobody has ever before received a Box 1 on the IONEC.' Ball handed me my SAF and let me read it for a few minutes. It was filled with glowing praise, and I felt justifiably proud. 'In view of your grade, we've decided to post you to SOV/OPS department,' Ball announced.

'That's a great post,' Long added, 'you'll get lots of travel and will get to work on some really interesting operations. H/SOV/OPS asked for you especially.'

6

TOP SECRET

MONDAY, 30 MARCH 1992
CENTURY HOUSE, LONDON

'Interesting, if true.' The biro had run out of ink at the 'f' and the anonymous author had not bothered to get a new pen, scratching the remaining letters into the paper. I was looking at the 'customer comments' box at the bottom of my first CX report, which had just come back to my in-tray. I issued it a week earlier after debriefing a small-time British businessman who had just returned from a business trip to the Ural mountains. He'd been shown some industrial diamonds that his Russian contact said were made in a controlled explosion, the same method which I had experimented with unsuccessfully in South Africa. Back in Century House, I mentioned it to H/SOV/OPS. 'I'd write that up as a CX report,' he said, holding his head slightly to one side in affected sincerity. I didn't greatly trust Fowlecrooke and suspected that his advice was more to make me feel useful than for any genuine need for such minor intelligence.

I wrote it up as a CX report, classified 'TOP SECRET, UK EYES A', and sent it off to R/CEE/D, the requirements officer responsible for issuing technical reports from the East European controllerate. He graded it 'two star' and forwarded it to the relevant desk in the DIS. A two-star grading meant that the information was only of minor interest and would be seen only by a junior desk officer; a three-star might influence the thinking of a head of a Foreign Office or Ministry of Defence department; a four-star would perhaps be seen by a permanent secretary of a Whitehall department, and a five-star grading would be seen by the government at cabinet level. Most of MI6's CX output got two-star gradings, and the reports were usually returned by sceptical and largely disinterested customers bearing the 'interesting, if true' dismissal. Considerable store was placed on an officer's ability to extract high-grade CX from a source, and every overseas station and head office UK station was given annual CX production targets. Setting targets in this way was open to abuse, since MI6 itself judged the star-grading of each report and its accuracy was dependent on the integrity of the officer who drafted it. As in any walk of life, the scruples of MI6 officers varied. Some had reputations as 'CX embellishers' and others pressured R officers to increase the grading of their reports. The problem was widespread, but few cheats were exposed. One who was went down in MI6 folklore.

During the '70s, when Britain was negotiating its entry to the European Common Agricultural Policy, the tactics and negotiating position of the French government were an important requirement. The head of the Paris station, H/PAR, made his number two, PAR/1, responsible for this intelligence and he successfully recruited an agent in the French agricultural ministry. Soon a steady stream of two- and three-star CX started flowing. A few eyebrows were raised in Century House at the financial demands of PAR/1's new informant, but his productivity gave good value for money. Over the next 18 months, this agent became the mainstay of intelligence production by the Paris station. When PAR/1's two-year tour in Paris came to an end, the handover to his successor at first went smoothly. But every time a meeting was arranged to introduce the star agent, PAR/1 would announce some excuse to cancel it. Eventually Head Office became suspicious and an SBO (Security Branch Officer) was sent out to Paris to interview PAR/1. He cracked and confessed to what his colleagues had started to fear. Like Graham Greene's agent in *Our Man In Havana*, he had invented the agent and all the meetings, fabricated the CX and pocketed the agent's salary. He was dismissed from the service, though no charges were brought. Fearing adverse publicity if the fraud was exposed, MI6 bought his silence with a pay-out and used its contacts to arrange a job for him in the Midland Bank. Eventually he rose to become one of the most prominent figures in the City of London.

I got up to see if Anna, in the office next door, wanted some tea. She was typing up a YZ (highly classified) telegram for Fowlecrooke, which she covered discreetly as I entered – being a probationer, I could not be privy to such information. Anna had followed her brother and sister into the service; MI6 likes to recruit from the same family as it simplifies the vetting process.

'Has that telegram to Moscow gone off?' I asked.

'You only gave it a ROUTINE status – it'll go this afternoon,' she replied without taking her eyes off the computer screen. 'I've got something more important to do for Mr Fowlecrooke, he'll be furious if I don't get it done immediately,' she added. Rick Fowlecrooke, a former army officer who had no work experience outside the military and MI6, had specially requested me for SOV/OPS, rather naïvely imagining that the few hated months I had spent in management consultancy would give me invaluable insight into the Russian economy. Luckily he was soon moving to a new posting and Anna and I would have another line manager.

I made the tea, sat down at my desk and looked out from my perch on the 13th floor at the panoramic view of London, from Canary Wharf in the east to the Oval cricket ground in the south. The spectacular view contrasted with the otherwise dingy office. The walls were covered with maps of the Soviet Union, pinned above grey, chest-high steel safes, the only colour provided by a sickly spider plant. The battered safes were plastered with peeling stickers exhorting us to ensure that they were securely locked. The need for security had been drummed into us on the IONEC and every evening before leaving the office we had to ensure all our documents and every scrap of paper – no matter how innocuous – were securely locked away. The security guards diligently inspected each room every night and if they found even the slightest lapse the miscreant was issued a written 'Security Breach Warning'. Paul, a GS clerk who shared my office, got 'breached' one evening for leaving a monogrammed shirt on the coat hook after an evening football match. Three 'breaches' in a year incurred a formal reprimand by personnel department which could mean being ruled out of consideration for overseas posts.

I switched on my ATHS (Automatic Telegram Handling System) terminal and waited for the cogs to start turning. ATHS was a neolithic internal networked computer system, designed especially for MI6 at great expense. Its development fell so far behind schedule that it was out of date when it eventually came into service in early 1990. It was supposed to allow officers to send and receive telegrams directly from their desks without the inefficiency of using a secretary and paper-based system. Unfortunately the word processing system was so cumbersome that only computer-literate junior officers used it, and the message handling system was so slow and unreliable that it was often quicker to resort to old-fashioned pen and paper. After what seemed like an eternity, the screen warmed up and I flicked through to see if there were any telegrams for me. There were none, so I would have to find something else to do. Such were the early days in SOV/OPS. The novelty was interesting but the slow routine was anticlimactic after the hurly-burly of the IONEC. Every few days I would debrief an agent – mostly British businessmen with interests in Russia – then spend the next day writing up the ensuing paperwork. So far, I had produced only the one rather obscure CX report. My contribution did not feel as if it was vital to the execution of British foreign policy – unless we were trying to do some paper-exporting nation a favour.

I joined the East European controllerate in changing times in both the controllerate and the geographical area that we covered. The Berlin wall had recently fallen and news bulletins were filled every day with the political break-up of the Soviet Union and the realignment of the former Sovbloc countries with the West. Changes swept through the old Soviet administrative machine and even the KGB had not escaped. Under the leadership of Yevgenniy Primakov the old directorates were reorganised into two new organisations. The SVR was responsible for gathering oveseas intelligence, roughly equivalent to MI6. The FSB was responsible for counter-intelligence, the approximate analogue of the British MI5.

In Century House this news was received with satisfaction at having defeated the old enemy, tempered with caution. MI6 had to reorganise its strategy in response and one of the first changes was to enter into liaison relationships with the SVR and FSB, something that would have been unthinkable only a few years earlier. Both sides recognised that dialogue would be mutually beneficial, so H/MOS, John Redd, was 'declared' to the SVR and a programme of regular liaison meetings started. There were still more requirements for intelligence on Russia than on any other country, but their scope changed. The greater political openness brought by 'Glasnost' meant that information which would once have been regarded as intelligence was now openly available. It was now fairly easy to find out from public sources what a particular factory in, say, the Ural mountains manufactured. What MI6 remained interested in was at a higher level; in intelligence parlance, the CX 'threshold' was higher.

As a probationer in the service, I would not be indoctrinated into the most sensitive Russian casework, known as 'YZ' cases, which were the source of most of this high-grade intelligence. I had to start at the bottom, with the consolation that even the most productive cases sometimes had the most humble and unlikely beginnings.

It was with this in mind that Stuart Russel, who had just replaced Fowlecrooke, developed my first serious task. Russel had served in Lisbon, Stockholm and most recently Moscow, and was now at the crucial stage of his career where he had to mark himself out to be a high-flyer (otherwise his career could peter out in a series of unimportant Head Office jobs or postings to sleepy stations in Africa and the Far East until compulsory retirement at 55). He had his eye on heading the Vienna station. It was one of the biggest and most important MI6 stations and would be an opportunity to prove his potential as a high-flyer. But first, he had to sort out SOV/OPS after the departure of the ineffective Fowlecrooke.

Russel called me into his office. He had enlivened the grim civil service decor with oil paintings and souvenirs acquired on his overseas postings, and from his desk he enjoyed a splendid view over Lambeth Palace and up the Thames. The new SOV/OPS chief was reading a telegram from John Redd, recording the first liaison meeting with his FSB counterpart. The first task in a fresh liaison relationship is to establish mutual trust, and Redd and his counterpart had done this by swapping details of suspect intelligence officers which each side had identified over the past decade. 'They identified me while I was there and nicknamed me the "Silver Fox",' giggled Russel. Partly the nickname was attributable to his thick, smooth silver-grey hair, but partly it was because of his cunning tradecraft while under surveillance.

Discarding the telegram into his out-tray, Russel outlined my assignment. 'I want you to devise an operation to sift through Russian defence journalists, and recruit one with good access to military secrets,' he explained. 'As you know, journalists do not normally make good agents because their inclination is to publish what they know which instantly makes it unusable as CX, but they sometimes have good relationships with key decision makers which occasionally gives them access to confidential information.' Russel's objective was for me to track down such a journalist and cultivate him. 'I suggest that you set up a fake newsagency in London, use that to make the initial contact, then see where that takes you,' Russel advised. 'And go and see NORTHSTAR – he'll have lots of ideas for you, I am sure,' he added as an afterthought.

NORTHSTAR was the codename for Mikhael Butkhov, a former KGB officer who had defected to MI6 a year earlier. He had worked under cover in Norway as a TASS journalist, so knew many of the genuine Russian journalists. Hopefully he would be able to provide a long list of names to get the operation kicking.

I borrowed a maroon Ford Sierra from Century House's

underground garage, one of a fleet of similarly uninspiring models in inconspicuous colours, falsely registered so they could not be traced to MI6. It was a two-hour drive to the pleasant commuter village of Pangbourne, just outside Reading. NORTHSTAR had certainly benefited materially from his defection. His modern four-bedroom detached house was set in a spacious garden, and parked in the drive were a new Rover Sterling and his girlfriend Maria's sporty red Citroën BX19 Gti, its dents and scrapes suggesting she had not mastered driving on Britain's clogged roads.

'Come on in,' called NORTHSTAR in impeccable English with only a distant trace of a Russian accent. He ushered me into the living-room and bade me sit down on a black leather sofa. The room was dominated by an expensive television and hi-fi system and was sparsely furnished with brand new, soulless pieces from a soft-furnishing chain.

NORTHSTAR recognised me from a brief meeting on the IONEC. Trips to the Fort were important to his morale, as he was now suffering from post-usefulness syndrome. Every tiny detail of his training, his KGB colleagues and his career had been sucked from him, and the heady days of VIP treatment, champagne receptions and all-expenses-paid trips to visit friendly intelligence services in Washington, Paris and Sydney were now over. His value to the West, and the sense of importance that this had bought, was now gone and he was bored and demoralised. MI6 had tried to find him a new career, but without success. Work experience as an intelligence officer is not very marketable, and besides there are few careers which can match the fascination and intrigue. So although MI6 set him up with a nice house and a lifelong pension and persuaded the Russians to let his girlfriend and daughter join him, he was restless.

He made coffee and took me through to his study where we could discuss the plan in private. A half-finished model of a Sea Harrier jump-jet and a tube of glue lay on the desk with his computer and a few manuals. I sat down in a black leather chair and outlined Russel's idea. 'Why not let me run it?' NORTHSTAR asked before I had finished. 'I have worked as a journalist with TASS, am a trained intelligence officer and Russian is my native language – I have the perfect background.' NORTHSTAR's arguments were persuasive, but the Russians were still smarting over his defection and if they found out that we were using him in operations against them it might damage the fledgling liaison relationship. 'I'll have to ask if it is OK,' I replied. 'But no promises.'

Back in Century House, I wrote up the proposal in the form of a minute and popped it in my out-tray. First Russel, as my immediate line-manager, would want to pass comment. Next P5, the production officer for Moscow station, would want to check that there were no implications for other operations under his control. SBO/1, the security officer for Russian operations, would need to comment on operational security. R/CEE, the requirement officer, would want to comment on whether it was likely to yield any worthwhile intelligence. Finally, the controller of the East European controllerate, C/CEE, would want to be kept informed about what was going on beneath him. Such a circulation list was typical and it could often take many weeks for all the decision makers to have their say. This decision-making process would be impossibly cumbersome in a commercial organisation, but its advantage is that it usually avoids coming to the wrong conclusion. The disadvantage is that when the decision is obviously wrong, it is very difficult to reverse. Too many officers have laid down their reputation on paper and so stubbornly defend the decision, no matter how foolish it seems in hindsight.

Fortunately, this decision was quick. Only a few days later, the minute was returned to my in-tray by one of the messenger clerks. The hand-written scrawl by the various addresses added to the bottom boiled down to an agreement to allow NORTHSTAR to be involved in the operation, but on no account could he be allowed to run it alone. I would have to stay closely involved and monitor all his activities.

Setting up the operation was straightforward. The only equipment I needed was an ordinary fax machine, which TOS supplied. I called my newsagency 'Trufax', alluding to the true facts that I hoped would be received by the facsimile machine, and attractively close to the name of the Russian newsagency 'Interfax'. Normally operations of this sort would be run out of Century House, using an out-of-area telephone number and call diverter provided by British Telecom. But NORTHSTAR, like other defectors, was not allowed in the building so I rented a small office, hardly big enough for a desk, on the top floor of a rabbit-warren of an office block in Conduit Street. TOS manufactured a small brass plaque bearing the Trufax name, which the building's caretaker added to the other plaques on the outside door of the building, and G/REP, the printing and forging department, ran off some smart Trufax stationery. I got myself a fresh alias, Ben Presley, with matching passport and driving licence from CF (Central Facilities) department, but getting NORTHSTAR sorted out with an alias identity required a bit more imagination. Any Russian journalist on speaking to him would almost certainly enquire about his background and how he arrived in the West. The wisdom of a more experienced officer was needed to come up with a suitable legend, so I went to see SBO/1, John Bidde.

SBOs are in charge of overseeing operational security in each controllerate. They are sometimes casually referred to as 'retreads' because they are past the normal MI6 retirement age of 55 and have been rehired for their rich operational experience. Their role is advisory and they have no control over operations, but only a foolish officer would ignore them. Bidde had been East European controller during the Cold War, so his experience was particularly valued.

I found Bidde in his 12th-floor office chuckling to himself. He was analysing a plan proposed by TOS to bug the penthouse flat of a suspected Russian SVR officer in Lisbon. One of the Lisbon station secretaries had rented the flat three storeys below in the same ancient, rickety apartment block and TOS proposed to use this as a base for the recording equipment. They had identified a means of breaking into the loft above the target's flat, and reckoned that it would be easy to find a suitable place to mount and hide a small microphone. Unfortunately, for technical reasons, it would not be possible to link the microphone and recording equipment with the normal radiolink and they would need to be physically connected with a fine wire, running from the loft to the secretary's flat below. The only means of hiding it from view was to thread it down a convoluted drain-pipe which wound its way down the building. After experimenting with various mechanical crawling devices which had all proved unable to work their way down the pipes, TOS had hit upon the idea of using a mouse. They reckoned that by leaning out of one of the loft skylights under cover of darkness, using a fishing rod, they could dangle the mouse, harnessed to the end of the fishing line, into the top end of the drainpipe. They would then lower it down the vertical section of the pipe to the first right-angled bend. From there the mouse could scurry along the horizontal part of the pipe to the next vertical section and so on, down to the bottom of the pipe where it could be recaptured. The wire could then be attached to the fishing line and pulled through the pipe.

Clandestine night-time trials of the murine wire delivery system on the Century House drain-pipes, using three white mice borrowed from the chemical and biological weapons research establishment at Porton Down, proved reasonably successful. One mouse, nicknamed Micky, was a natural and scampered along the pipes enthusiastically. A second, Tricky, occasionally tried to climb back up the fishing line when dangled, but once in the pipe was reasonably competent. The last mouse, christened Thicky, had kept trying to climb back up the pipes and so had been sent back to Porton Down to continue his secret work on chemical-weapons antidotes. Micky and reserve Tricky were to fly covertly to Portugal in the S&D Hercules because they could not be overtly taken out of the country without special export licences. Bidde's dilemma was whether it was ethically correct to recruit animals to use in spying operations. 'Thicky is probably lying bleary-eyed at the bottom of a jamjar by now,' giggled Bidde, 'and the fate of Micky and Tricky is less unpleasant, so I guess it is ethical.' He squiggled an approval at the bottom of the minute and placed it in his burgeoning out-tray. I later learnt that Micky and Tricky carried out their mission successfully, were returned to the UK in the C-130, given an honourable discharge from duties at Porton Down, and went into comfortable retirement in a TOS secretary's London flat. The fate of Thicky remains a state secret.

Still chuckling, Bidde turned his mind to me. 'What can I do for you, young man?' he asked benevolently. Trying to keep a straight face, I explained that his help was needed to devise a suitable cover story for NORTHSTAR's involvement in the Trufax operation. Bidde quickly invented a suitable legend. 'He should claim to be a second-generation descendant of one of the Russo-Germanic families from the German colonies around the lower Volga River basin,' he suggested. 'The Germans have recently given lots of them German passports,' Bidde explained. 'You should get him a Germanic-sounding alias – how about Valery Ruben?' he suggested.

Valery Ruben was at work at the Trufax office in Conduit Street the following day. Within a week he had contacted nearly 20 journalists in Moscow, Leningrad and Kiev and had a steady stream of information flowing to his fax machine. None of it was CX, but it was early days. It would take a while to establish which journalists had good access and which were second-rate.

NORTHSTAR focused his relationship on to one promising Muscovite journalist. Pavel Felgengauer, a 40-year-old freelancer specialising in defence issues, appeared to have some of the characteristics that might just make him a good agent. He had excellent access, being close to Yeltsin's defence minister, Pavel Grachev. The reports that Felgengauer provided after his meetings with Grachev often came tantalisingly close to the CX threshold so we decided to cultivate him.

NORTHSTAR spoke to Felgengauer at length from the Trufax office. Bit by bit, we built up a character profile of his career, lifestyle and aspirations in the hope that we might find a motivation for him to spy for us. But cultivating him over a telephone line was a slow business. To make real progress we needed to meet him face to face, so we tried to persuade him to visit London. Although he would accept payments for his stories – we sent out several substantial lump sums to him by TNT courier – he would always have an excuse to cancel or postpone any tentatively arranged trips out of his country. Eventually, we reluctantly and disappointedly accepted that Felgengauer was most likely playing the line with us, possibly in collaboration with Russian intelligence. We had hooked him, but now he was just teasing us, accepting payments and throwing back morsels of quasi-intelligence to keep us interested. It was a classic disruption tactic, used many times by Russian intelligence to waste MI6 resources. Russel closed down Trufax after three months to NORTHSTAR's intense disappointment. In total, it cost around £40,000 and did not produce a single CX report. Trufax, it would seem, had to be put down to 'experience'.

Russel, meanwhile, was reorganising SOV/OPS. Unlike other natural cover sections which regularly mounted overseas operations into their target countries, SOV/OPS had hitherto limited its operations to Russians travelling outside Russia. Now that the KGB was reformed and weakened, Russel proposed to strengthen his department and start running natural cover operations into the heart of Russia. He renamed the section UKA, bringing its nomenclature in line with other natural cover stations based in Century House. Then he badgered personnel department for reinforcements. One of the first to join was Spencer. He was bored of his job as a targeting officer and wanted to get into natural cover work. Russel allocated him a desk in my office and put him to work running MASTERWORK. Platon Obukov, a Russian diplomat in his 20s, was the son of a former Soviet deputy foreign minister who had worked on the SALT II disarmament talks. MASTERWORK's own direct access at the Russian foreign ministry was not important, but his father was still influential in Moscow and MASTERWORK had indirect access to this. Spencer planned to meet MASTERWORK for debriefing sessions in Tallinn, capital of the new Baltic republic of Estonia. It was a safe location because Estonia was cosying up to the West, yet Russians could still travel there freely without a visa or passport. Spencer chose to travel as a journalist so went down to I/OPS to beef up his credentials. I/OPS looks after MI6's media contacts, not only to provide cover facilities but also to spin MI6 propaganda. For example, during the run-up to the 1992 UN Secretary General elections, they mounted a smear operation against the Egyptian candidate, Boutros Boutros-Ghali, who was regarded as dangerously

Francophile by the CIA. The CIA are constitutionally prevented from manipulating the press so they asked MI6 to help. Using their contacts in the British and American media, I/OPS planted a series of stories to portray Boutros-Ghali as unbalanced, claiming that he was a believer in the existence of UFOs and extra-terrestrial life. The operation was eventually unsuccessful, however, and Boutros-Ghali was elected.

'Flippin' outrageous!' Spencer laughed as he came back from his visit to I/OPS. 'They've got the editor of a magazine on the books. He's called SMALLBROW,' he chuckled. 'He's agreed to let me go out to Tallinn undercover as a freelancer for his magazine – the only condition is that I have to write an article which he'll publish if he likes it. Cheeky bastard wants a story courtesy of the taxpayer!'

Russel's ambition to expand the role of UKA hinged on his ability to convince C/CEE that natural cover operations into Russia were practical and secure. To help persuade them that such operations could be carried out by a VCO (Visiting Case Officer) he asked me to research cover legends suitable for use in Russia. There would be no possibility of me actually using the cover in Russia – being fresh off the IONEC, such responsibility would not be entrusted to me. My job was just to do the groundwork for somebody else to take over later. Nevertheless, it was an interesting assignment.

No natural cover is unbreakable as no matter how carefully it is researched, it can never be as rich and varied as a real life. To plug every hole would be futile and expensive, so I needed to tailor the cover to match the likely inquisition by the Russian defences. This entailed first examining the sort of jobs that could be done in Russia under natural cover. The most likely would be one of the simple tasks which were time-consuming for a station officer to undertake, such as letter-posting. Posting an SW letter to an agent is fraught with risk because even after dry-cleaning for several hours, perhaps even a whole day, it cannot be guaranteed that surveillance has not observed the posting and dropped a marker letter on top. When the postbox is emptied, the letters immediately beneath the marker would be scrutinised, the addressees noted and traced, and any holding jobs with access to secrets would come under suspicion. Letter-posting is thus not a popular job with members of the station. But if a VCO could enter Russia without attracting surveillance, letter-posting would be simple and relatively cheap. We knew from defectors such as NORTHSTAR and OVATION that even the FSB did not have the surveillance resources to watch every British businessman visiting their country.

The FSB relied heavily on visa applications to screen visitors to their country, examining every detail against their records for discrepancies. The easiest to check was the birthdate because in the UK every birth is registered in a legend at St Katherine's House, which is open to public inspection. Each birth is entered consecutively when the child is born, so it is impossible to enter back-dated births and MI6 do not use 'dead baby' aliases, as described in Frederick Forsyth's book *The Day of the Jackal*, for fear of legal action by angry relatives if the operation should go wrong and be publicly exposed. For most operations, this lack of birth registration is not a problem because the resources of the opposing counter-intelligence service were not that inquisitive, but to fool the enquiries of the FSB visa inspections a workaround was required.

The solution was simple. My own birth was not registered in St Katherine's House because, although a UK citizen, I was born overseas in New Zealand. Enquiries by the Buenos Aires station revealed that in Argentina they had no verifiable register of births, so if I claimed to have been born of British parents in Argentina, it would be difficult for the FSB to check its veracity.

I asked G/REP to forge me an Argentine birth certificate, based on a genuine one that they held in their files. Then through their liaison with the passport office, CF obtained me a British passport in the name of Alex Huntley, born in Buenos Aires on 13 January 1963. From the DVLA they got me a driving licence and then provided a robust ACA (alias cover address) keeper. ACA keepers are agents who act as a cover landlord for VCOs, providing a checkable home address. With an address, CF arranged a bank account and credit card with the Natwest Bank.

All DSS (Department of Social Security) files of Britain's 54 million inhabitants are computerised and held in Newcastle. CF occasionally used these records to obtain information on people of interest to us. But what if the FSB were able to hack into the DSS computer? It wouldn't be difficult as it was linked to every high street DSS office and the log-on procedure was not complicated. The only way to make my alias stand up to hacking was to falsely enter the details in the DSS central computer. This had not previously been done but, after a few weeks' negotiation with the DSS, Alex Huntley had a full DSS record with national insurance number and registration card.

The next task was to research a legend for my alias life. Every element would need to be plausible but uncheckable. A check through the *Public School Handbook* revealed that Scorton Grammar School in Richmond, North Yorkshire, had gone into liquidation in the late '80s, leaving no publicly available records of its ex-pupils, so I could safely claim to have studied there. The records of the

University of Buenos Aires were hopelessly disorganised, so this is where Anglo-Argentine Alex Huntley claimed his economics degree, proved with a G/REP forged certificate. From my experience at MIT, I knew a small university in Boston, the Massachusetts Community College, which had gone out of business, and so awarded Huntley a MBA from there. Thereafter, drawing on records from Companies House, I invented a CV in a series of small companies and consultancies which all went bankrupt shortly after Huntley supposedly left, then fudged tax records in the DSS computer to match his career. Huntley needed a plausible current occupation. The usual practice is to front the BCA (business cover address) in a high-street business-answering service; a modest subscription secures a mailing address and a receptionist to answer incoming calls. Their disadvantage is that they could be too easily checked by the FSB. For my purpose, a more robust BCA was needed.

CF maintained a list of small companies whose managing director was prepared to vouch that an MI6 officer was a bona-fide employee, and they suggested a small Sussex investment company, East European Investment, which worked in Czechoslovakia, Poland and Hungary, but not Russia. This gave perfect cover; they had no track record in Russia that I could be quizzed about, but it would be plausible if Alex Huntley were to start exploring business opportunities there. I went to see the managing director and he took me on as a consultant.

The bones of my false life were in place, but they needed fleshing out. Regularly using my Huntley credit card built up a realistic spending pattern on the bills, and consultancy 'payments' from East European Investment into my bank account ensured that it would appear realistic to inspection. My alias documentation was beefed up with miscellaneous 'wallet litter', forged à la carte by G/REP. I chose membership cards to Tramps and Annabel's nighclubs, and Sarah and I spent some enjoyable evenings ensuring that Alex Huntley was familiar to the doormen.

My file on Huntley was now bulging with plausible information, but some genuine Argentine documents would be useful. MI6 often obtains and uses genuine documentation from friendly liaison services such as the Danes and Austrians for 'false flag operations'. The station in Buenos Aires had just entered into a tetchy liaison relationship with the Argentine security service, so I fired off an ATHS telegram asking whether SIDE might provide Huntley with documentation. I expected a swift and curt response ridiculing my idea, but H/BUE, an enthusiastic officer, asked at the next liaison meeting. SIDE agreed and sent a genuine Argentine passport, driving licence and identity card in the name Huntley. The documents arrived on my desk a fortnight later and I promptly lent them to G/REP so that they could examine and photograph them for their files in case it became necessary in the future to forge similar documents.

It took just over two months to make the Huntley cover strong enough to satisfy the scrutiny of Russel and Bidde, and I submitted the dossier for examination by C/CEE. He wrote at the bottom of the report, 'An excellent piece of work. This will be a solid foundation for future VCO operations into Russia.' It was glowing praise and I was pleased with my contribution.

Meanwhile, Spencer was back from his own natural cover trip to Estonia. 'MASTERWORK's a nutter!' he announced as he chucked his hand-luggage on to his desk. 'Completely off his rocker! So much for that crap that Ball taught us on the IONEC about only recruiting agents who are mentally stable,' he chuckled. Spencer explained how MASTERWORK had turned up at the meeting wearing a Mickey Mouse hat, clutching the manuscript of a manic and twisted book he was writing. 'The guy should be getting pyschiatric help, there's no way we should be running him as an agent,' Spencer concluded. But his judgement was over-ruled by P5 because MASTERWORK helped meet the controllerate CX targets, and Spencer was ordered to continue the bi-monthly meetings in Tallinn. The relationship was later taken over by the Moscow station and they ran MASTERWORK until one clandestine meeting in a Moscow restaurant in April 1996 was rudely interrupted by FSB. They arrested MASTERWORK, charging him with 'broadcasting classified information of a political and strategic defence nature to a foreign intelligence service'. The female case officer at the meeting and three other officers from the Moscow station were expelled from Russia. In July 2000, after four years in a pyschiatric detention hospital, MASTERWORK was sentenced to 11 years in a top security prison. The Russians were alerted to MASTERWORK by his rambling boastings that he was a spy, but the real fault lay with MI6 who should never have continued to run an agent so manifestly unstable.

As a probationer, I was expected to take every opportunity to learn from the work of senior colleagues. An objective of UKA was to acquire advanced Russian weaponry, and one operation had been very successful. Russel told me to read the file, adding, 'It's a classic operation, you'll learn a lot from studying it.'

BATTLE was one of the arms dealers that MI6 had on its books. Arms dealers are useful sources of intelligence on international arms deals and can be influential in swinging the deals to British companies. BATTLE, a multi-millionaire Anglo-Iranian, earned a salary of around £100,000 per year from MI6. In late 1991, the United Arab Emirates (UAE) asked BATTLE to buy them a consignment of new BMP-3 armoured personnel carriers. The BMP-3, then the most advanced APC in the Russian armoury, was a heavily armed tracked amphibious vehicle, capable of carrying seven infantry and its three-man crew. The MOD heard rumours that its performance was better than western equivalents and asked MI6 for intelligence.

BATTLE set to work on the deal, flying regularly between the BMP design bureau in Kurgan and Abu Dhabi, and he eventually sealed a deal for the Russians to sell a batch of the lower-specification export variant BMP-3s to the Gulf state. He did not omit to see his MI6 handler every time he passed through London, however, and on one visit mentioned that he had been shown around the advanced variant of the BMP-3 on his last trip to Kurgan. MI6 persuaded him to try to acquire one. On his next trip, with a £500,000 backhander and forged end-user certificate provided by MI6, BATTLE persuaded his Russian contact to hide one of the advanced specification BMP-3s amongst the first batch of 20 export variants which were shipped to the UAE.

The consignment of BMP-3s went by train from Kurgan to the Polish port of Gdansk. There the 20 UAE vehicles were offloaded into a container ship and sent on their way to Abu Dhabi. The remaining vehicle, under the cover of darkness and with the assistance of Polish liaison, was loaded into a specially chartered tramp steamer and shipped to the army port of Marchwood in Southampton. From there it was transferred to the RARDE (Royal Armaments Research and Development Establishment) for detailed examination and field trials.

The RARDE technicians were highly impressed by their new toy and established that the BMP-3's firepower was substantially higher than anything in the UK's armory. Field trials on army ranges in Scotland – with the vehicle disguised under a fibreglass shell to prevent being spotted by Russian satellites – revealed that its manoeuvrability, cross-country ability and speed were also better than western equivalents. The complicated and expensive operation was a great success and they invited most of the East European controllerate to their establishment near Camberley to thank us for the operation.

While reading BATTLE's file, I came across something that, though just mildly interesting at the time, became significant five years later. Some of the meetings that were described took place at the Ritz hotel in Paris, and intelligence on the whos, whats and wheres of these meetings was provided by an informant in the hotel. The informant did not have a codename and was just addressed by a P-number, referring to the number of his personal file. The P-number was mentioned several times in BATTLE's file so, curious to get a better fix of his access, I called up central registry and asked for the file. Flicking through, it was no surprise to learn that he was a security manager at the Ritz and was being paid cash by his MI6 handler for his reporting. Hotel security managers are useful informers for intelligence services because they have access to the hotel guestlist and can be helpful in bugging operations. What was a surprise was that the informer's nationality was French, for we had been told on the IONEC how difficult it was to recruit Frenchmen to work for MI6 and for this reason he stuck in my mind. Although he was only a small cog in the operation and his name was unimportant to me at the time, I have no doubt with the benefit of hindsight that this was Henri Paul, who was killed five years later on 30 August 1997 in the same car crash that killed Diana, Princess of Wales and Dodi Al Fayed.

Most breakthroughs in espionage come after a lot of methodical research and tedious sifting of leads and contacts, but occasionally a worthwhile lead came out of the blue. Such was the case when one morning in June 1992 a former colleague in the TA called me asking for some advice. The sergeant, a keen long-distance runner, had recently gone to Moscow to run in the city marathon. A spectator who spoke English approached him at the finish line and it emerged that he was a colonel in the Russian strategic rocket forces. The two men became friendly and the sergeant invited the colonel to visit him if ever he were in England, not really expecting that it would be taken up. But the colonel did take him up and he was due to arrive at Gatwick airport the following week. 'Would we be interested in meeting him?' my former colleague asked. Russel agreed that the story was worth checking out. The following day I took the train out to Clacton-on-Sea, a couple of hours east of London, to visit the sergeant in his home.

Terry Ryman greeted me at the front door and ushered me into the pin-clean front-room of a small terraced house where his wife served tea. Ryman was in his 40s, greying with milk-bottle glasses, but took pride in his fitness. He worked as a black cab-driver in London to earn his living.

Ryman verified the story that I'd heard over the telephone. When a friend suggested that they enter the Moscow marathon together, Ryman didn't hesitate. He had spent many years training for war against the Soviets, learning to recognise their tanks and armoured cars, studying their fighting tactics and shooting snarling images of them on the rifle range, and he wanted to experience the country and its people first-hand. When a real-life Russian introduced himself at the end of the race, speaking good English, Ryman was thrilled.

Colonel Alexander Simakov had invited Ryman around to his flat in a distant northern suburb of Moscow which he shared with his wife, daughter and mother-in-law. Ryman was fascinated and appalled at the cramped living conditions of such a relatively senior officer. Simakov moaned about his pay and conditions and said how much he envied the English lifestyle. 'He says he wants to come to England just to see Stratford, Oxford and Cambridge,' Ryman explained. 'But,' he added, lowering his voice conspiratorially, 'I think he wants to, you know what I mean, defect, to Britain.'

'OK, when he comes next week, we'll find out if he knows anything useful,' I replied.

Simakov would have to offer some spectacular CX to be accepted as a defector. As their world crumbled with the Berlin wall, several Sovblock intelligence officers offered their services to MI6, and most were turned away. MI6 only had the budget to accept high-level defectors such as OVATION and NORTHSTAR, and even they had to work for several years *en poste* before being allowed into Britain. Even the likes of Viktor Oshchenko, a KGB officer specialising in science and technology who offered his services in July 1992, did not have an easy time persuading MI6 that he was worth a resettlement package. His revelation that, while serving in London in the mid-'80s, he had recruited a GEC-Marconi sales engineer was regarded as only mildly important and I saw an MI5 report which concluded that the engineer, Michael John Smith, did not pass damaging secrets. (This did not stop MI5 having Smith arrested in an entrapment operation, and this paper was not made available to Smith's defence at his trial. He was sentenced to 25 years' imprisonment, the judge summing up with the outlandish claim that Smith had done incalculable damage to Britain's national security.)

Given Oshchenko's difficulty in winning defector status, I would most likely have to persuade Simakov to return to his job in Russia and then earn defector status by providing regular intelligence to the Moscow station. If his intelligence was valuable then he might earn a reasonable salary, paid into a UK account so that his new found wealth would not attract suspicion. Perhaps on his retirement he could be allowed to come to the UK to enjoy his money, but even then MI6 would probably try to persuade him that retirement in his homeland would be more enjoyable. My task on meeting Simakov would be to assess his access and motivation, recruit him if suitable, then persuade him that this was his best option.

Ryman looked grim when he answered the door the following week. He took me through to the living-room, dark because the curtains were drawn against the afternoon sun. A bulky, pallid and unshaven man, dressed in tight polyester T-shirt and jeans, struggled to his bare feet from the sofa. Ryman icily introduced me to his guest, jerked open the curtains and made an excuse to leave. Simakov glared after him as the door slammed shut. Next to the sofa were two large red plastic suitcases, straining against the string which held them together. Beside them was a battered cardboard box, filled with books and journals. He had been reading some of them and they lay opened, scattered on the low coffee-table along with several unwashed mugs and biscuit wrappers.

'I have defected,' he announced triumphantly in a thick Russian accent. He paused for a moment, then realising that I was not about to give him an ecstatic bearhug, he adjusted the cushions and sat back down on the sofa.

'Tell me a bit about yourself, first,' I asked, putting off discussion of defection until later. In good English, Simakov related his life story. He had been born into a poor family in a village north of Kiev in the Ukraine. His father was killed in a mining accident when he was five and his mother died of tuberculosis when he was seven, so he and his two younger sisters were bought up by his maternal grandmother. The young Simakov would probably have followed his father into the mines but from an early age showed a talent for mathematics. He got the best grades of his class in every term except one, when he had broken his leg and couldn't walk the three miles to school. Simakov was still proud of this achievement and rummaged in the cardboard box to dig out the certificates to prove it. His mathematical prowess was his only hope of getting out of a life of poverty.

Simakov won a scholarship for secondary education at a military school in Kiev. Finishing there with high grades, he was selected to join the Soviet Strategic Rocket Force as a research scientist. After basic military training, he studied for a degree and a doctorate in Leningrad. Compulsory English lessons there fuelled a lifelong interest in England and particularly its literature – he knew far more about Shakespeare's plays than I would ever be likely to know. On completion of his studies he was posted to the Soviet ballistic missile test ranges in the far eastern peninsula of Kamchatka and spent his entire career working there as a flight-test engineer. After compulsory retirement from the military in his mid-40s, he had been unable to get another job and he, his wife and eight-year-old daughter were forced to move into the one-bedroomed Moscow flat of his ageing mother-in-law. Life soon became intolerable; his military pension was decimated by inflation, his daughter started to suffer from asthma and his wife was desperately unhappy.

The final straw came when Simakov emerged from his flat one morning to find his Lada on bricks, with all four wheels missing. He vowed to move to England where, he fondly believed, such things never happened. He set about scouring the streets of Moscow to find an Englishman who could help him accomplish his plan and he stumbled across Ryman. The two of them made an unlikely couple. Fate had transpired to bring them together and produce the tragedy which I could see was about to unfold.

Simakov's aspirations were wildly starry-eyed. In return for defecting, he wanted 'a house with a straw roof and a garden full of flowers for his wife, £100,000 cash and a Ford Orion Gti with Executive pack'. He produced a copy of *Autocar* magazine from his cardboard box and jabbed his finger at a picture of the car of his dreams.

It was not going to be an easy task to let him down. Far from being able to waltz into the country, he would probably be hard pressed to persuade the Home Office to give him leave to remain. Only if he had some spectacular CX could MI6 ask the Home Secretary to make an exception of him. Depending on how much CX he produced, he might receive a few thousand pounds in a one-time payment. Thereafter, he would have to rely on DSS housing and income support. Simakov's surly nature wasn't going to make things any easier either. He had quickly outstayed Ryman's welcome, but being used to the cramped quarters of his mother-in-law's flat he couldn't understand why Ryman was fed up with him living on the sofa. 'I don't understand Terry,' Simakov said, scratching his stomach. 'When we were in Moscow, he was like a long-lost brother. Now he doesn't want to know me.'

Ryman was just as unhappy with the situation. He thought he had done his duty and expected me to take Simakov off his hands. 'My wife is going spare,' he explained out of earshot of Simakov. 'He can't stay here much longer.' It was a mess that I couldn't sort out immediately. Everything would depend on how much CX Simakov could produce but, as his knowledge was too complicated for me to assess, it would require the expertise of one of the technical specialists in the office. I bade goodbye to the odd couple in Clacton and returned to Century House.

There were around 15 specialist officers in MI6 who provided expertise which the IB, with their broader career paths, could not master. They covered technical disciplines such as chemical, nuclear and biological weapons and ballistic missiles, or had expert knowledge in areas of particular interest such as the Middle Eastern oil industry. Martin Richards, who dropped out of our IONEC, was earmarked for this branch.

Malcolm Knightley, R/CEE/D, was the missile specialist in the East European controllerate. A physicist by training, he developed his expertise in Soviet missiles in the DIS. Knightley was on secondment to MI6 for two years but was hoping for a permanent transfer judging by the way he laboured fearsomely long hours behind a huge in-tray. I arranged for Knightley to meet Simakov the next day in 'Room 14', the suite of MI6 interview rooms in the Old Admiralty Buildings in Whitehall.

'The guy's a goldmine,' Knightley told me afterwards. 'We've got to get him residency here.' Knightley explained that Simakov had worked in mission control for every ballistic missile test the Soviets had done between 1984 and 1990. His information would be invaluable to the DIS, GCHQ and, more importantly, to the Americans. Knightley booked Room 14 for a series of weekly debrief meetings.

'We've decided to recommend to the Foreign Secretary that we accept him as a full defector,' Russel advised me once the first reports had filtered up to him. 'You'll need to get him a codename, write the submission to the Foreign Secretary and sort out his resettlement with AR.'

AR (Agent Resettlement) were responsible for easing defectors into a new life once their usefulness to MI6 had expired. OVATION, NORTHSTAR and other important defectors all had their own dedicated AR officer who was responsible for helping them find a house, adjust to British life, administer their pensions and, hopefully, find a decent job. AR got in touch with Clacton DSS and found a small cottage for Simakov, so at least he was off Ryman's hands. A few weeks later, his wife and daughter flew out to join him and AR sorted the family out with DSS payments and schooling.

I wrote the 'submission' to the Foreign Secretary arguing that there was justification for allowing SOU, the codename now allocated to Simakov, to remain in the UK. MI6 does not need any authorisation to mount small operations such as Trufax. But operations which might have embarrassing consequences or, as in this case, affected the interests of another part of the civil service, required the authorisation of the Foreign Secretary. Douglas Hurd was notoriously diligent about examining submissions, so my arguments had to be carefully drafted.

Meanwhile, Knightley finished another long debriefing session with SOU. He stuck his head into my office late one afternoon, clutching a thick sheaf of notes from the four-hour session. 'We've hit the jackpot with this guy,' he enthused. 'He's just given us the location of the Russian MOD's new strategic command headquarters.' Knightley produced a sketch map showing the location and layout of a new, top secret command bunker set deep inside a mountain in the Urals. It was a Russian equivalent to the American NORAD complex in the Colorado mountains. 'I'll be issuing this as a five-star CX. It will go up to the PM,' Knightley said. He later told me that it eventually reached President George Bush's office. 'But there's loads more to come,' he added. 'Apparently he left a notebook filled with notes from the missile tests in his mother-in-law's sewing-box in Moscow. If we can get that notebook, we'll really be in business.'

Knightley explained that the notebook described perturbations in the flight paths of every ballistic missile fired from the Soviet missile test range in Kamchatcka between late 1987 and early 1990. SOU had obsessively and illicitly noted all the numbers in a couple of school exercise books after each test flight. Such detail would aid the DIS's understanding of the accuracy and range of the Soviet missile armory. More importantly, Knightley would pass the intelligence to the Americans who could use it to improve their anti-ballistic missile defences. It would bring considerable kudos for MI6. 'We've got to get that notebook out of Moscow,' concluded Knightley.

7

NOTED FRIEND

WEDNESDAY, 11 NOVEMBER 1992
MIRROR ROOM, HOTEL METROPOL, MOSCOW

I saw Goldstein over in the opposite corner of the crowded conference room just before he spotted me. A bit plumper round the waist, his collar-size maybe an inch bigger, but still fond of Hermes ties, Gucci shoes and expensive Italian suits – flamboyant tastes even by the diverse standards of the eclectic throng of delegates mingling in the elegantly mirrored room. I had not seen him for over five years, since shortly after the trimphone incident, but it was certainly him. Worse, the lift of one eyebrow and the hint of a friendly smile showed that, to my unease, he still remembered me.

I was displeased to see Goldstein not because I disliked him, far from it, but the last thing I needed at the moment was to meet someone who knew me as Richard Tomlinson. This accidental encounter might mean that I would have to call off the operation and return embarrassingly empty-handed to London. Russel, Bidde, P5 and C/CEE had taken a lot of persuading that I was the right person to go to Moscow to exfiltrate SOU's notebook. Eventually they had been swayed by my argument that as I had researched the Huntley cover for just such a job, I was the best person to take it on. They reluctantly allowed me, a relatively inexperienced officer, to make the trip that was not without risks – risks that Goldstein, intentionally or inadvertently, could make very real.

The first day of the '1992 Conference on Doing Business in the New Russia', organised by the *Financial Times*, and held in the opulent surroundings of the recently refurbished Hotel Metropol in central Moscow, was a roaring success. Registering as Alex Huntley of East European Investment, I fitted in smoothly with the mixture of foreign businessmen, diplomats and civil servants who paid £1,500 to attend the three-day symposium. The opening day's lectures having just finished, we retired to the elegant Mirror Room to relax and socialise over a few glasses of champagne. Siberian industrialists chatted with officers from the World Bank and the IMF, angling for capital investment to rebuild their out-dated factories. Newly wealthy oil barons from Kazakhstan rubbed shoulders with representatives of British Petroleum, Shell and Amoco, discussing the terms of joint ventures to exploit their oil and gas reserves. Armenian and Georgian commodity traders ingratiated themselves with British diplomats and trade officials, anxious to get their hands on the cheap credit and expertise available through the British government-financed 'Know How Fund'. Russian politicians flitted about with interpreters, earnestly persuading anybody who would listen that their country was a safe investment, despite the continuing political uncertainty. Journalists hovered on the edges of the conversations, anxious for a titbit that might constitute a story.

Only a few years earlier under the old Soviet communist system, such freedom of trade, information and friendship would have been unthinkable. Now in the new proto-capitalist Russia, the pace of change was so fast that it verged on chaotic. For the clever, entrepreneurial, dishonest or greedy, fortunes could be made overnight. For the careless, unlucky or unfortunate, they could be lost just as quickly. Inflation was rampant, destroying the salaries, savings, pensions and lives of the millions of state workers who did not have the skills or wit to move with the times. Manufacturing and engineering jobs in the formerly state-funded military-industrial complex were being lost by the tens of thousands. In their place were springing up new professions intrinsic to capitalism and commerce – banking, management consultancy, import-export businesses, accountancy and, unfortunately, organised crime on a large scale.

Through this chaos, however, some things remained constant. The world's two oldest professions were still steadily pedalling their wares. The previous evening the mini-skirted representatives of the first had perched at the stools of the Metropol's Artists bar, preying on the assembled delegates. Representatives of the second were also mingling more discreetly amongst the delegates, and I was probably not the only spy present. The CIA would be attracted to the collection of movers and shakers of the new Russia and probably some of the American 'diplomats' sipping the sweet, sickly Georgian champagne chatting innocuously about anodyne commercial and diplomatic affairs actually reported to Langley, not the State Department's headquarters in Foggy Bottom. Beneath the pleasant and agreeable questioning they would be weighing up every Russian they met. Did he have access to any secrets? Did he have the sort of psychological make-up that might make a good spy? Did he need money and might he be prepared to sell secrets?

I had no doubt that agents from the FSB were also present. Working undercover as journalists, businessmen, or perhaps even as one of the dinner-jacketed waiters, they would be keeping an eye on the delegates, particularly any diplomats. They would already know the faces, character, hobbies, biographical details, even favourite restaurants, of all the suspected intelligence officers. Surveillance teams would have covertly followed them from their homes as they drove to the Metropol. Their every move in the conference would be watched. If they spoke a bit too long and animatedly to any Russian, the identity of that Russian would be established and noted, a file opened, and their job, financial status, access to any secrets would all be established. If the diplomat again contacted the same Russian, alarm bells would start ringing. Nothing would be left to chance. If one of the so-called 'diplomats' excused himself to go to the bathroom, the toilet would be carefully checked afterwards – it was just possible that he had filled a DLB for later collection by an agent.

I could see Guy Wheeler, MOS/2, lurking around amongst the delegates under his cover of commercial secretary in the British embassy. I had met him only once before, when he briefly returned to London on leave, but I had communicated at great length with him by enciphered telegram, coordinating every detail of the operation. Wheeler fell into the classic mould of a British spy. He read Greats at Oxford, then worked briefly for one of the old family merchant banks in the city. He fitted easily into his diplomatic cover. Courteous, well-bred, slightly stuffy, he took his job very seriously and frowned disapprovingly at any joke or flippant remark about the spying business. Like many officers who had experience of working in Moscow, he had acquired the irritating habit of speaking barely audibly, even when there was no possibility of eavesdroppers.

Wheeler glanced towards me and as quickly looked away. He could not come over and greet me – that might be enough to alert his FSB watchers that we were acquainted and so bring me to their attention. Nevertheless, the flash of recognition in his eyes gave me a reassuring feeling that I was not totally alone. At least somebody appreciated what I was doing.

Operating under diplomatic cover, like Wheeler, is the normal, acceptable, gentlemanly way of spying. Those caught undertaking 'duties incompatible with diplomatic status' are just declared *persona non grata* and put on the first aeroplane home. There might be a bit of a diplomatic row and a tit-for-tat expulsion from the other side, but no further action would be taken against the officer, who would be protected by diplomatic immunity. Working undercover as a businessman, journalist or whatever, is more complicated and risky because there would be no diplomatic immunity if discovered.

The instant that Goldstein spotted me, therefore, I had to act quickly. He knew me as Richard Tomlinson and obviously still remembered me; a few words would be enough to blow my cover. Images of my name and face on the front pages of newspapers around the world, headlines announcing the arrest of a Britsh spy, flashed into my imagination. Even if I could keep my cover story intact, the Russians would not believe it. In theory, under their laws, I could face life imprisonment or even a firing squad if found guilty of espionage. In practice, they would not carry out such draconian reprisals, but they would milk the incident to maximise the embarrassment to Britain.

It would be ridiculous to ignore or pretend not to know Goldstein – he knew me too well and it would just make him suspicious. I decided to grab the bull by the horns, take him into my confidence and hope that he would prove discreet.

Politely disengaging from Monsieur Poitiers, the French water and sanitation engineer from Lille who had been telling me, in animated soliloquy, about the opportunities for investment in the soon-to-be privatised sewerage system of Moscow, I steered for Goldstein. He saw me coming and also eased out of a pack of businessmen.

'Hi Ernst, its good to see you again. My name's Alex, you might remember we worked together a few years ago.' I introduced myself under alias, in the hope that Goldstein might be temporarily thrown off balance.

'Yes, I remember you. But what did you say your name was again?' he asked, confused.

I didn't want to explain anything in the crowded conference room. ' Ernst, let's get a breath of fresh air, a quick walk round the block. There's something important I need to tell you.'

Goldstein agreed, a bit reluctantly, and we slipped out through a side exit, down the steps into the damp evening air of Prospect Marx Street. An old woman, huddled in a filthy blanket on the last of the steps, looked up at us imploringly. Holding out a battered tin can, she muttered something unintelligible in Russian. There was no disguising, however, the desperation in her voice. It was a graphic contrast to the opulence we had just left and a poignant reminder of how the less fortunate suffered in the new Russia. I felt a momentary sense of shame. I was here to exploit this chaos, to spy. It was just a game compared to the reality which this old woman was living. Reaching into my suit pocket, I dropped all my loose roubles into her tin.

Goldstein and I walked in silence for a few yards. We both knew that our own little problems and responsibilities were trivial compared to the old babushka's. I eventually broke the silence. 'Ernst, sorry about this bit of drama, but you obviously want an explanation.'

'Yes, what's going on? I remember you as Richard. What's this Alex business?'

I explained how I'd ended up working in Moscow under cover with a false identity and Goldstein tried to hide his surprise, but he was obviously intrigued and a little impressed. I went on. 'I'm sure you'll understand that it would cause a right stink back home if any of this gets out, but I am confident that you'll keep this little encounter to yourself.' Hopefully Goldstein would respond positively to the simple bit of flattery. 'We'd best not associate too much for the rest of the conference. Acknowledge each other of course, but there's no need for us to talk at any length. When we're back in London, I'll get you lunch, and we can talk properly then.' We had now walked round the hotel back to the main entrance. There might be FSB surveillance around, waiting for Wheeler and other suspected intelligence officers to leave. Goldstein wanted to rejoin the reception, so after some small talk we shook hands and I went back up to my room to think a few things through.

This operation had taken months of planning and preparation and had already cost a substantial amount of money. All the effort would be wasted if I aborted now. On the other hand, could I completely trust Goldstein? He'd told me that he was dining with some of Yeltsin's personal staff that night, hoping to clinch a big business deal. An indiscreet word, perhaps after a few too many glasses of vodka, might land me in Lefortovo prison. Although I felt nervous about continuing it was too late to abort. I would recover the notebook, as planned, the next day. My mind made up, I got up from the bed, grabbed my sports gear and went down to the hotel gym.

The gym was moderately equipped – a few rowing machines, exercise bikes and a bench press. A tall, rangy fellow occupied one of the running machines. He was in his 50s but fit for his age, and I recognised him as one of the delegates in the conference. I started warming up on the machine adjacent to his. 'How are you doing?' he asked, in the friendly but condescending way army officers address their soldiers. We swapped introductions – he worked for Control Risks, a corporate security company that was preparing a consultancy report for clients who wished to invest in Russia. 'Damned pleased to be here,' he continued. 'My first trip to Russia, fascinating. Don't know how I managed to get a visa though.'

'Why's that?' I asked.

'I was in the army, you see, a colonel. They've been following me everywhere.' He nodded over to a young man working out on one of the rowing machines. 'It's OK. We can talk here. He's a Brit, works for Morgan Grenfell. Checked him out earlier,' he whispered conspiratorially. I tried not to laugh at the colonel's fanciful imagination, and carried on with my work-out. I saw him again the following morning on Prospect Marx Street in front of the hotel, scrutinising the faces around him as if looking for a hooligan in a football crowd. Fifty metres down the road, he stopped and bent down to tie his shoelaces, checking behind him studiously for his imaginary surveillance.

That morning I attended the last lectures at the Metropol. Future Prime Minister, Victor Chernomyrdin, then head of Gazprom, was the star speaker. Several members of the British embassy came to listen, including Wheeler, whose cover job provided a good excuse to attend the lectures. I scribbled a few jottings in my notebook to keep up my cover, but didn't pay too much attention to the content of the lectures. My mind was on the job ahead.

After a quick lunch, I hurried to my room, locked the door firmly and removed a WH Smith pad of A4 notepaper from my briefcase. The first 20 pages or so were filled with the notes I had taken from the conference – junk which would be discarded in London. At the back of the pad, I carefully ripped out the fifth-to-last page, took it to the bathroom, placed it on the plastic lid of the toilet seat and removed a bottle of Ralph Lauren Polo Sport aftershave from my spongebag. Moistening a small wad of cotton wool with the doctored aftershave, I slowly and methodically wiped it over the surface of the paper. In a matter of seconds, the large Russian script of SOU's handwriting started to show, slowly darkening to a deep pink. Using the hotel hair dryer I carefully dried the damp sheet, trying not to wrinkle it too much and driving away the strong smell of perfume. It now looked like a normal handwritten letter, though in a slightly peculiar dark red ink. Reaching into the back of my TOS supplied briefcase, I pulled on the soft calfskin lining, ripping apart the Velcro fastening it to the outer casing, slipped the paper into the small gap and resealed it. It would take a very diligent search to find the hidden pocket.

P5, who was a former H/MOS, had warned me that there would be no point in an inexperienced officer like myself attempting anti-surveillance in the Russian capital. 'Their watchers are just too good,' he had told me. 'Even officers with good anti-surveillance experience struggle in Moscow. Normally we reckon on six months before a new officer can reliably pick them up. There's just no point in you looking,' he had advised me. Nevertheless, as I stepped out of the hotel lobby on the walk to the Ploschad Revolutsii Metro station, I couldn't help but take advantage of the natural anti-surveillance traps that presented themselves – staircases that switched back on themselves, subways under the busy main roads, shopping malls. It gave some assurance there wasn't any obvious surveillance.

The journey out to the Zelenograd suburb, one of Moscow's poorest and most run-down 'sleeping districts', was long, tedious and tricky. P5 had ordered me to use public tranport because the risk of a Metropol taxi-driver reporting a westerner making such an unusual journey was too great. The rickety but easy-to-use Moscow subway system only went part of the way; thereafter I would have to use buses. SOU gave clear instructions – out to Metro Rechnoy Vokzal, the last station on the green line, then the 400 bus to Zelenograd, changing to a local bus for the final leg – but his information was over a year old. Moscow station had been unable to verify the details because any of their staff, even one of the secretaries who weren't always under surveillance, making such a journey would have appeared suspicious. I would just have to hope that the bus routes had not been changed or, if they had, that it would be possible to navigate my way by reading the Cyrillic information panels on the front of the buses.

It was 3 p.m. by the time the bus arrived at the small, run-down park near SOU's flat that he had suggested was the best place to disembark. The housing estate was a soulless, depressing place, made worse by the dull skies above. All around were the grey, monstrous, nearly identical residential blocks that dominate much of Moscow. The lack of colour was striking – the grass was worn away, the trees were bare and even the few battered Ladas parked around were dull greys and browns. One was on bricks with all its wheels missing and I wondered if it was SOU's old car. Apart from a couple of small children playing on the only unbroken swing in the park, there was nobody around. I orientated myself, recalling the details of SOU's sketch map. Exactly as he had promised, looking down the broad street which stretched in front of me, the corner of a dark green apartment block, in which his mother-in-law's flat was situated, protruded from behind another identical block. The short walk took me across a pedestrian crossing, providing a final chance to check up and down for surveillance.

The rubbish-strewn entrance lobby stank of piss and vomit and was covered in graffiti. I pushed the button to call the lift – more out of hope than expectation. SOU had told me it hadn't worked for years. There was no sign of movement so I began the trudge to the eighth floor, thinking it was understandable that his elderly mother-in-law hardly ever left home.

Knocking gently on the peeling metal door of appartment 82a, there was no reply. I knocked again, this time more firmly, but still no response. Increasingly anxious that my visit coincided with one of the few occasions when she was out, I banged harder. Finally, a nervous female voice answered, 'Kto tam?'

In carefully memorised and practised Russian I replied, 'My name is Alex, I am a friend of your daughter and son-in-law from England. I have a letter for you.' Her reply was well beyond the range of the few Russian words I'd learned, so I repeated once more the phrase. There was no letter-slot through which the letter could be posted, so there was no alternative but to gain her confidence sufficiently that she would open the door. After I had repeated myself three times, hoping the neighbours weren't taking note, the heavy doorbolts slid back and the door opened a few inches on a chain. I pushed the letter through the gap and just caught a glimpse of wizened hands grasping it. The door closed and was wordlessly re-bolted.

I waited outside for about five minutes, watching the street below through a narrow and dirty window, before knocking again. The door was opened without delay and a tiny old lady beckoned me into the gloomy flat, smiling toothlessly, and indicated me to sit down on the sofa. It was the only piece of furniture in reasonable condition in the tidy but sparsely furnished and drab room. The old lady mumbled something that I presumed was an offer of hospitality, so I nodded enthusiastically and she disappeared into the kitchen. SOU had told me that his mother-in-law was fairly well-off by Russian standards – she had a flat all to herself and a small pension from her late husband. But looking around the cramped quarters, it was understandable why SOU and his family fled. Just as SOU had promised, in the corner of the room stood a sewing-box, which if he was right, would still contain the two blue exercise books containing the notes.

The old lady returned a few minutes later with a cup of strong, heavily sugared black tea, which I sipped out of politeness rather than thirst. SOU had listed in his letter a few of his personal belongings and their collection was my ostensible reason for the visit. The old lady pottered around the flat, adding to the growing pile of books, clothes and knick-knacks accumulated in the middle of the floor, ticking each off against the list. Awaiting my opportunity to sieze the notebooks, I reflected that it was typical of SOU to take advantage of the offer and expect me to carry back his entire worldly possessions.

When the old lady popped back into the kitchen again, I bolted from the sofa and delved in the sewing-box. Just as SOU had assured me, the two light-blue school exercise books were still there. I sneaked a quick look inside them to be sure and they were filled with row upon row of numbers – meaningless to anybody except an expert. I slipped them into one of the part-filled cardboard boxes.

Glancing at the wind-up clock ticking on the sideboard, I saw that it was 4 p.m., only half an hour before dusk. I wanted daylight to navigate on unfamiliar public transport back to central Moscow, so it was time to extract myself. When she added two pairs of SOU's bright red Y-fronts to the pile, it was the last straw. Using sign language, I made her understand that I would carry only one cardboard box. She understood and started prioritising the items and I was out of the dingy flat five minutes later.

Struggling back into the Metropol, briefcase in one hand, the heavy box containing the precious notebooks under the other arm, it was sorely tempting to dump the excess baggage. There had been a fierce debate in Head Office about the merits of bringing back SOU's belongings. P5 had been vehemently against it, arguing that they were an incumbrance and a hostage to fortune. But SBO/1 had argued that they gave me cover for visiting SOU's mother-in-law. If apprehended on my way back to the hotel, I could feign innocence, claim that SOU was a friend in England who had asked me to bring back some of his clothes and deny any knowledge of the significance of the notebooks. In the end, SBO/1's wisdom won out, so I was lumbered with the heavy load back to the Metropol.

The following morning, after a leisurely breakfast in the Metropol's Boyarsky dining-room, I rang the British embassy and made an appointment to visit the commercial section's library, ostensibly to obtain information for East European Investment. The MI6 secretary who answered the phone asked, as arranged, if I would like to make an appointment with the commercial secretary. I accepted a meeting for 11.30 a.m. and started on the short walk from the Metropol through Red Square then over the Moskva river to the British embassy, directly opposite the Kremlin. P5 and SBO/1 concurred that I needed to get rid of the notebooks as soon as possible, hence they had to be dropped off at the embassy from where they could be returned to London in the diplomatic bag. Even that option was not entirely straightforward. The station staff worked under the assumption that every room in the embassy was bugged, except the station's secure safe-speech room that was electronically swept on a regular basis. Like most foreign embassies, the embassy also employed a small number of locally engaged staff such as clerks, drivers and cleaners, and these were also all assumed to be reporting back to the FSB. My telephone conversation to the MI6 secretary would have been intercepted and the watchers in the clandestine FSB observation post opposite the embassy would have already been briefed to expect a businessman to call in at 11.30 a.m.

I proferred my Huntley passport to the receptionist behind the desk in the entrance lobby and she showed me through to the commercial section. To my satisfaction, Wheeler was at his desk, just as he had promised. 'Ah, Mr Huntley, I presume?' he stood to greet me. We shook hands, pretending never to have met. 'Take a seat, Mr Huntley.'

'Sorry?' I replied.

Wheeler repeated the instruction more audibly and courteously indicated me to sit down. 'What can I do for you?'

Ten minutes later, I was on my way back to the hotel, my briefcase stuffed with leaflets produced by the embassy and the Department of Trade and Industry about business opportunities in Russia. More importantly, SOU's notebooks were now off my hands. As planned, my copy of the *Financial Times* had been accidentally left on Wheeler's desk with the notebooks inside. They would now be in the hands of the station secretary who would be preparing them for the next diplomatic bag. It left for London that night, so they would be back in Century House before me. I flew back to London the next day along with many of the other delegates, including the colonel who was still checking over his shoulder for his surveillance as we boarded the British Airways 757.

After the debrief from the successful Moscow trip, Russel asked me to become the UKA representative on MI6's natural cover committee. This think-tank committee had been set up so that all the UK natural cover stations – UKA (Eastern Europe), UKB (Western Europe), UKC (Africa, primarily Republic of South Africa), UKD (Middle East, excluding Iran), UKJ (Japan), UKO (India and Pakistan) and UKP (Iran) could share their ideas and expertise on natural cover operation. It consisted of representatives from each of the stations, plus most of the SBO officers and representatives from CF. Different stations were always coming up with innovative covers, and attending the meetings gave fascinating insights into imaginative operations. For example Kenneth Roberts, a former officer of the Black Watch regiment and a *Times* journalist, now working in UKO, had persuaded a prominent Tory Lord to allow him to be his personal emissary in India where he had extensive business contacts. This gave Roberts unparalleled access to the upper echelons of Indian society and he had amassed some worthwhile CX on the Indian nuclear weapons programme. Nick Long, TD7 on the IONEC, was now working in UKC and was travelling around South Africa as a Zimbabwean chicken-feed salesman, which gave him cover to meet ANC and Inkatha agents in remote rural locations. Another officer, who had qualified as a veterinary surgeon before joining MI6, had just returned from an ODA (Overseas Development Administration) sponsored tour of Iran to teach Iranian vets how to immunise their cattle and sheep against various illnesses. As the tour passed through most of the veterinary research sites which were suspected to hide biological weapon production plants, MI6 had slipped a suitably qualified officer into the training team.

At one meeting, conversation turned to the feasibility of inserting 'illegals' into hostile countries. Illegals are officers so carefully trained in natural cover that they can live in the target country for extended periods without arousing suspicion. The Soviet Union used them widely against the West until about 1970. Indeed, three Russian illegals were caught actively spying in Britain during this period. The first, a KGB officer called Konan Trofimovich Molodi, assumed the identity of a long-dead Finnish Canadian named Gordon Lonsdale and ran a juke-box hire business in London as cover for his spying activities from 1955 until his discovery and arrest in 1960. The other two, Morris and Lona Cohen, were actually American citizens, but had been recruited by the KGB and given false New Zealand identities and spied in London under cover as second-hand book-dealers Peter and Helen Kruger.

But MI6's recent KGB defectors NORTHSTAR and OVATION told us that the practice of running illegals had been stopped. Even the KGB realised that the investment in training is rarely paid back by the intelligence yield. The natural cover committee quickly reached the same conclusion. It would only be worthwhile training an officer up to the required level, they argued, to run one or perhaps two very productive agents whose public position was so prominent that it would be too risky for members of the local station to run them. Russia was the only country where the intelligence requirements were high enough – and the counter-intelligence services formidable enough – to make the investment worthwhile, though UKC also made a case for South Africa. Even post-apartheid, Britain's interests in the southern cone of Africa were such that MI6 was very active there. Also, they had been very successful in recruiting a network of informers under the apartheid regime and a lot of these agents were now high up in the ANC. As Nick Long explained to me with a touch of sarcasm, 'It's amazing how many of them, having spied for years for 'ideological reasons', are now happy to carry on pocketing their agent salaries post-apartheid.'

Back at my desk a few days later, thinking over the question of illegals, it occurred to me that we had been looking at the problem the wrong way round. Instead of labouriously building a false identity and cover legend for an existing MI6 officer, why not find somebody outside the service with the right professional and personal qualities, secretly put him through the IONEC under a false name and identity, then post him under his real name to work in his former occupation in the target country?

Russel liked the idea and encouraged me to draft a paper outlining the plan in detail. I did so, and was even able to suggest a suitable candidate. Leslie Milton, a friend since we'd studied engineering together at Cambridge, had drifted from job to job in the city, got an MBA and was now working as an independent investment consultant in London. He was not married, so it would be easy for him to move overseas and set up some form of business. Moreover, he was born in New York and so held an American passport in addition to his British one, allowing him further to distance himself from MI6.

My ideas were accepted and Milton was recruited into MI6 and started the IONEC in March 1993. His real identity and destiny were kept secret from most of the office, including his IONEC colleagues. He was given the alias Charles Derry and was entered in the diplomatic list, the official record of FCO officials, under this name. A few months after he completed the course, word was spread around the office that his father had fallen seriously ill, forcing him to leave MI6 to take over the family business. 'Derry' bade a sad goodbye to his new colleagues, and disappeared.

A month or so later he re-emerged in Johannesburg under his real name, working as an American investment consultant. He rented a small two-bedroom detached house with swimming pool in the affluent suburb of Parkview and set himself up as a consultant in investment opportunities in the emerging economy of post-apartheid South Africa. His house was conveniently close to the homes of MI6's two most important agents in South Africa, a senior army officer and a senior government official. Both had been recruited early in their careers but had risen to such prominence that no member of the MI6 station in Pretoria could safely contact them. Milton met these two agents twice a month at his home or sometimes overtly in bars and restaurants in the plusher parts of Johannesburg. Their meetings would most probably pass unnoticed but if anybody asked they would have been told perfectly plausibly that Milton was merely offering investment advice. Indeed, Milton genuinely invested their considerable agent salaries for them, so that their added wealth would not be noticed by colleagues or even their wives and family. The CX Milton gathered from the meetings was encrypted using highly secure but commercially available PGP encryption software, then sent to London over the internet.

The system was simple, cheap and completely secure. Even had the South African security services become suspicious of Milton, they would never have found a shred of evidence to prosecute him or his agents.

As well as Russia, UKA was responsible for mounting natural cover operations into the rest of Eastern Europe. From the end of the Cold War until early 1992, Russia had been the only country of any substantial interest. But a new concern was rising rapidly in prominence. Yugoslavia was breaking up and Croatia and Slovenia had already been recognised by the European Community as independent states. MI6's coverage of the region was increasingly stretched because each newly independent state needed a station.

Apart from the two officers already in the Belgrade station, MI6 had only one other competent Serbo-Croat speaker, but he had just finished a lengthy Finnish course in preparation for a three-year posting to Helsinki. Personnel department were reluctant to waste this investment by reassigning him to the Balkans, so several other officers were thrown into intensive Serbo-Croat courses, but it would take at least nine months before they would be competent enough to take up overseas postings. In the meantime, the efforts of the stretched Belgrade station would have to be augmented by UKA. Since none of us spoke any Serbo-Croat, there was a limit to what we could do. At best, we could perhaps take over some of the English-speaking agents of the station. Russel sent me down to the floor below to see P4, the desk officer in charge of Balkan operations.

P4 took up the post when it had been a quiet backwater job before the problems in Yugoslavia had started in earnest. Prior to that, he had worked for a spell in Northern Ireland before MI5 took over responsibility for the province, then served without distinction in various quiet European liaison posts and briefly as 'Mr Halliday' – where I had first come across him. P4 had made a mark in the office only with his dress sense, which would have made a Bulgarian taxi-driver wince. He was known ubiquitously in the office as 'String Vest', though 'Flapping Flannels' or 'Woolly Tie' would have suited him equally. The spotlight that had now fallen on the P4 job was his chance to make a more positive mark on the office hierarchy and he attacked the job with scattergun enthusiasm.

'Sure, I've just the job for you,' he said, peering from behind his mountainous in-tray and disorganised desk. 'We've got a lead that a Serbian journalist, Zoran Obradovich, might be worth an approach.' String Vest dug around on his desk and pulled out the relevant file. 'He's in his mid-30s, war correspondent for the independent newspaper *Vreme* and regular contributor to the anti-government B-92 radio station,' String Vest continued. 'He's made several liberal and anti-war remarks both publicly and to BEAVER.' BEAVER was a trusted British defence journalist run by I/OPS and he had given the office several useful leads in the past. String Vest passed me Obradovich's file, taking care to remove and sign the tag, meaning that the safekeeping of the file was now my responsibility. 'Get yourself a new alias, a cover story and get yourself out to Belgrade. You'll have to make your way overland from a neighbouring country – there are no direct flights because of the UN sanctions.'

8

WELL TRAINED

WEDNESDAY, 2 JUNE 1993
DANUBE CAFÉ, BELGRADE

'You know, Ben, I've had you checked out, ' Obradovich dropped his eye contact and continued in a softer voice, 'with some friends . . . contacts . . . of mine in the police.' He reached for his packet of Marlboro Lights, lost in the debris of a long and drunken lunch scattered over the stiff tablecloth, and lit one ceremoniously. He exhaled slowly, took another drag, exhaled melodramatically, then fixed me in the eye again. 'It took a while, but your credentials, your press accreditation . . . well, they check out OK.' Obradovich drew again on his cigarette, studying my reaction. I reached for a glass of water as calmly as I could, realising that he was definitely playing games with me. I needed to get out of the hotel dining-room fast – if Obradovich had really checked me out with the Serbian secret police, he would have found that my credentials as a freelance journalist didn't add up at all.

It was my second meeting with Zoran Obradovich. Two weeks earlier I had made the trip from London to meet him in the same downtown Belgrade café. UN sanctions against Serbia, imposed on 1 June 1992, were in full swing and there were no direct flights to Belgrade. The only route was to fly to Budapest and then travel the 370 kilometres to Belgrade by overnight bus. At our first meeting, Obradovich seemed promising agent material. A freelancer in his 30s, of mixed Serbian and Croatian parentage, he professed to have neutral views on the civil war and stubbornly proclaimed his nationality to be 'Yugoslav'. His views were anti-war but he had access to senior military officers and politicians in both Serbia and Croatia. He took my 'consultancy fee', some 500 Deutschmarks, with scarcely disguised alacrity. His podgy features betrayed a taste for imported wine, good food and western cigarettes, all of which were prohibitively expensive under the sanctions, but which I could easily provide. All the characteristics were there – access, suitability, motivation – suggesting he might make a good agent.

Back in Century House after the first trip, String Vest enthusiastically recommended that I return as soon as possible to continue the cultivation. Obradovich looked like he could fill a few gaps in the intelligence from the Belgrade station.

The second trip started uneventfully. I flew to Budapest as Ben Presley, a freelance journalist. In my wallet was a forged NUJ (National Union of Journalists) identity card and a Royal Bank of Scotland chequebook and credit card, but not much else to substantiate my cover. The coach journey – packed with Serbs carrying huge suitcases bulging with sanction-busting supplies – was quiet and gave me the opportunity to grab a few hours' sleep.

The juddering of the bus as the engine was cut brought me gently out of my slumber. A glance at my watch showed that it was 4 a.m. I rubbed the steam from the window. Dim fluorescent lights barely penetrated the mist and darkness, but I could see that we were at the Hungarian–Yugoslav border. Every available parking space was filled with tiny but overladen Zastava cars or flatbed lorries loaded high with goods bought in Hungary, and despite the late hour there were long queues of Serbs waiting their turn to have their passports stamped. The coach-driver stood up and made a surly announcement, then handed round a sheet of paper on a clipboard, presumably for the border police. When my turn came, a glance showed that my name and passport number were required on the manifesto. Still only half-awake, I almost signed in my real name. Hastily scribbling over the error, I re-signed in my alias. Nobody noticed and no harm was done, but it jolted me awake.

A few minutes later, a Serbian border guard clambered on to the coach, sub-machine gun strapped across the chest of his heavy, dark-blue great-coat, and inspected the manifesto. He grunted an order, presumably to produce our passports, and started working his way down the bus. Sitting near the front, my turn soon came. He glanced quickly at my passport, saw that it was British and unapologetically put it in his coat pocket. Having worked his way to the end of the aisle, he disembarked, taking my document. I wanted to protest, but having not a word of the language there was not much option but to remain silent and patient. The bus-driver glared at me and said something in Serbian that sounded caustic, so presumably he'd been told to wait until my passport was returned. The other passengers grumbled impatiently while the minutes ticked away, but eventually the border guard returned and gave back my passport. A quick inspection revealed that it had not been stamped, but my details would certainly be logged in the police computer.

The remainder of the trip to Belgrade went without hitch and after checking into the Intercontinental Hotel there was time for a shower and breakfast before ringing Obradovich. He wanted to meet for lunch at 2 p.m., so my free morning was a good time to check for surveillance. String Vest told me that the station officers in Belgrade rarely came under surveillance, but it was not a reason to be lazy. Sarah had asked me to buy her a handbag, so a shopping trip would provide good cover for my anti-surveillance drills – I could traipse slowly around the leather goods stalls, idly stare at the displays, flit in and out of the shops, back-track and use the usual tradecraft tricks without looking suspicious.

Despite the sanctions, the shopping centres in Belgrade were thronging. Imported high-tech goods were unavailable or hugely expensive, but domestic production of consumer goods – particularly leather goods and clothing – was booming. There was no shortage of shops displaying a wide selection of handbags.

Standing on a busy street, studying a shop window display, I cursed gently to myself that I had agreed to buy Sarah a handbag – she could be so fickle and it was difficult to know which to choose. Turning away in exasperation, I noticed a young man a couple of shopfronts away also move off. He was of medium height, moon-faced, clean-shaven and with his head covered with a grey cap. He was a grey man – perhaps a bit too grey.

An hour later, drinking a coffee at a pavement café, I noticed the grey cap reading a book at a café opposite. It was by no means conclusive proof of surveillance. For that, I would need multiple confirmed sightings or two sightings of different watchers. The double sighting of one person could just be coincidence. Nonetheless, I decided to be very careful.

There was no question of aborting the meeting with Obradovich after just one dubious surveillance sighting. But it would be prudent to change my plans slightly. I had planned to leave for Budapest by bus the following morning, giving me the whole day for the meeting. But given the real possibility of surveillance and the ease of penetrating the thin crust of cover protecting my identity, it would be tempting fate to risk an overnight stay. I decided to leave by the train that departed Belgrade's central station at 1625. It would not leave much time for my lunch meeting, but that was now a lesser concern. I jumped into a taxi – a few were running despite the fuel shortage – and returned to the hotel to pack.

My concern mounted when Obradovich pulled up to the meeting

an hour late in a new red Fiat Bravo with diplomatic plates, parking it ostentatiously on the pavement. 'That's a smart little car,' I commented as soon as we had shaken hands. 'You must have some powerful contacts to get that.'

'How else do you think I get petrol here, and am able to travel all over Serbia, Bosnia and Croatia?' he replied a little boastfully. Only those with diplomatic plates were excused petrol rationing and the lengthy queues, and only with neutral CD plates could he travel to Croatia. But how had he obtained such privileges? He had to be very well connected – too well connected.

At our lengthy, expensive lunch, Obradovich spoke animatedly and knowledgeably about the war and the situation in Bosnia but nowhere did he breach the CX threshold and give me anything that was not already in the public domain. Nor did he give any more indications of recruitability. My optimism that he could become a good agent was now starting to look ill-founded and my priority shifted to ending the meeting and getting safely back to the UK. It was 1605 before he moved on to cognac and I could get the bill. A few minutes later, as I anxiously checked my watch again, he casually dropped the bombshell that he had 'checked me out'.

We shook hands outside the restaurant, next to his car which had miraculously escaped parking fines. 'Thank you for the meal, Ben,' Obradovich said without much sincerity.

'I'll be in touch soon,' I replied, with equal insincerity.

Obradovich half-turned to his car, then called over his shoulder, 'Good luck.' He sounded as sincere as a bishop in a brothel. I smiled, clenched my bag and ducked out of sight around the corner.

With only nine minutes before the train was due to depart, I threw my shoulder bag on to the back seat of a dirty black Fiat and leapt in after it. 'Station,' I yelled at the taxi-driver. He looked at me blankly through the rearview mirror. I cursed myself for not having learnt the correct Serbo-Croat word before leaving. 'Bahnhoff,' I shouted, hoping that like most Serbs he would understand some German. There was no sign of comprehension. I cursed again, struggling but failing to remember the Russian word which I had once learnt – Serbian was a close linguistic relative. 'Chuff, Chuff, Chuff,' I pumped my arm, pulling an imaginary whistle, Casey Jones style. The taxi-driver broke into a smile, clunked down the arm of the mechanical meter, and engaged gear. Seven minutes to go – I should just make it.

The driver jerked the hand-brake back on the moment he released it, as a tram, four carriages bursting with shoppers and commuters, clanked in from behind. We were cut off. We couldn't move forward because the lead carriage and a half of the tram were blocking us. To the rear, passengers were embarking and disembarking from the rear carriages, flooding across the gap to the pavement. I cursed again, aloud this time, as valuable minutes slipped away. The wait for the passengers to sort themselves out seemed interminable. The last was an old lady, weighed down with hessian shopping bags. A couple of guys disembarked from the carriage to let her on, then squeezed back on to the last step themselves. At last the tram drew away, its brakes hissing as the compressed air was released.

The taxi-driver sensed my urgency and put his foot down as we weaved between the thankfully sparse traffic, but even so it was 1625 as we drew up alongside the station. I shoved a fistful of Deutschmarks into his grateful hands, grabbed my bag and sprinted into the station. There was no time to buy a ticket. A quick glance at the departures board – thankfully the destinations were still written in Latin script rather than the now obligatory Cyrillic – showed that my train left from platform eight. Like a character in a poorly scripted film, I sprinted down the platform and jumped on to the footstep of the nearest carriage as the train lazily pulled away.

For the next 45 minutes I stood by the open window of the door, watching the grim suburbs of Belgrade gradually give way to featureless agricultural land, letting the breeze cool my face. Despite Obradovich's ominous words and the problem of crossing the border ahead, my thoughts were with Sarah. I had not bought her a present – not through lack of trying, but because I couldn't find anything that she would like. I knew she wouldn't be angry. At the worst, she would pull a funny face and make a jestful, mocking comment, but she would be disappointed. Resolving to find her something in Budapest, I set off down the rocking corridor to find a seat.

Four hours remained until the train reached the Hungarian border and my fate was out of my hands. Would Obradovich have reported me to the Serbian authorities? Probably. But having told him that I was leaving Belgrade by bus the following morning, he might not have rushed to report me, meaning that the Serb border police would not yet be notified. There was a slight possibility that surveillance might have followed me throughout my trip and that my rush to the station may have been seen. But even if my cover was blown, would the Serbs order an arrest? That would depend if it would serve any political purpose. They were under UN sanctions and catching a British spy would give them some leverage in the UN HQ in New York, but on the other hand they might not want to antagonise the West any further. The risk of arrest was slight, but that did not stop me carefully rehearsing every detail of my cover story as we approached the border. What was my date of birth? Where was I born? Address? What was my profession? Where did I work? I chastised myself for not having worked harder on my cover. Having rattled off natural cover trips to Madrid, Geneva, Paris and Brussels since Moscow, I was becoming blasé. It had become as routine to me as jumping on a bus, and I vowed then never to take the responsibility so lightly again.

The train slowed to a crawl as we clanked into Subotica station just before 9 p.m. The Serbian border police had checked my passport here on my first uneventful trip, so presumably they would do so again. I left snoring Serbs in the compartment and stood in the corridor, pulling down the window to let the damp summer air spill into the musty corridor. Outside, only a few lights twinkled in the deserted-looking town.

The train lurched to a halt, its brakes squealing unpleasantly. Doors slammed as a couple of passengers disembarked. Most, like me, were continuing. A child ran up to my window, thrusting a tray of unappetising, sweating pastries. Her brown eyes met mine for a second or two before she registered my disinterest and ran to another window. Two border guards, sweating under the weight of thick coats and sub-machine guns, climbed into the front carriage and began methodically working their way through the train, examining each passenger. Were they looking for me, or was this just their usual nightly routine?

For a fleeting moment, I considered jumping and legging it across the sidings and junctions into town and onwards to the unpatrolled border. It was a moonless night, but the sky was clear and it would be easy to navigate by the stars the ten kilometres to Kelebia, the nearest Hungarian village. A hike like that would have been regarded as a stroll when I was in the TA.

But such ideas were frivolous. This was an MI6 operation, not a military exercise, and I should stick to my training and bluff it out. I went back to the compartment. A few minutes later, the guards arrived. The elder of the two, barrel-chested and sweating in his heavy coat, examined another passenger's Yugoslav passport while the younger guard, pale and baby-faced with a downy moustache, prodded his voluminous baggage on the rails above us with a stick, as if he were checking for people illegally hidden in the cases. The elder then turned to me and with a snap of his fingers demanded my documents. He flicked open the back page of the new-style EEC passport, checked the photograph, then examined my face against it, his eyes staring blankly at me as if he were reading a train timetable. He pocketed it and left the compartment with no word of explanation, his young colleague trailing behind like a faithful dog.

There was nothing to do except await my fate. The guards hadn't confiscated my documents on the way out on my first trip, so it was an anxious moment. I went back out into the corridor and stuck my head out of the open slide-down window. Outside on the platform, at the far extremity of the long train, another two guards were patrolling towards me. They walked side by side, inspecting the passengers carefully in each compartment through the windows, as if they were looking for somebody. When they were three carriages away, looking back the other way up the inside of the train, I saw the first two guards walking back towards me from the other direction. I was caught between the two sets of soldiers and there was no chance of making a dash.

The connecting door slammed as the first pair re-entered my carriage. I waited until they were a few paces from me, then turned to face them. The corridor was too narrow for them to walk alongside each other, and the elder lead. He flicked the stub of an acrid Serbian cigarette out the window as he approached. The younger, a step behind him, was chewing gum urgently. The sickly smell of the sweet gum, mingling unpleasantly with their body odour, wafted towards me on the heavy evening air. They stopped menacingly in front of me and the elder reached into the breast pocket of his heavy tunic, exposing his sweat-speckled shirt underneath, and pulled out my passport. His dark eyes flickered as he held it out in front of me, growling something unintelligible in Serbian. I shrugged, my pulse racing. He growled something again, then realising it meant nothing to me, switched to German. 'Fahrkarte,' he snapped. The meaning swam from some recess of my mind where it had lain dormant since my TA German course years earlier, and a smile of relief flickered across my face. Reaching into my breastpocket, I pulled out a fistful of Deutschmarks to pay for the ticket that I had omitted to buy at Belgrade station. The guard handed me my passport and the pair strutted off.

The train rolled into Budapest station in the early hours of dawn, and after a night in a cheap hotel by the station I flew back to London. It took a day or so to finish all the paperwork and debriefings at Century House. Afterwards Bidde called me up to his office. Looking over his bifocal glasses, he gently admonished me. 'You won't be using the Presley alias again, I trust.'

The work in MI6 was endlessly fascinating. It was not just the natural cover trips abroad: almost everyday some snippet of information came my way from friends in sections that, if it were in the public domain, would be on the front pages of the newspapers. One day Forton invited me for lunch in the restaurant on the top floor of Century House. He was still in his job as R/AF/C, the junior requirements officer for the Africa controllerate, and had just come back from a three-week trip to Ethiopia and Eritrea. Over the surprisingly good MI6 canteen food he enthusiastically described bush-wacking by Land Rover around Eritrea and Ethiopia on reconnaissance with his increment guide, an ex-SBS sergeant, and a UKN photographer, whose other 'normal' job was as a paparazzo photographer of the Royal family. In addition to the Horn, Forton's other important area of responsibility was South Africa. He had been processing South African intelligence that morning, and the conversation soon turned to the politics of the region. 'Yeah, I got a great CX report today,' Forton casually boasted. 'Apparently the AWB (*Afrikaaner Weerstandsbeweging*) are planning to assassinate Mandela next month. They're gonna blow him up at an open-air rally or a boxing match or something. They've just acquired a pile of PE from the South African army for the job.'

'Are you sure?' I asked sceptically. 'What's the source on that?'

Forton sniffed and casually chewed on his salad. 'It's good CX all right. UKC have an agent in the AWB who has reported reliably in the past. H/PRETORIA is going to give the report directly to Mandela – it would be too risky just to give it to South African liaison. Too many of those bastards would like to see Mandela dead themselves and the message might never reach him.'

The assassination plot was averted and MI6's stock with President Nelson Mandela no doubt rose.

Shortly after returning from my Belgrade trip, Nick Fish, P4/OPS/A, the targeting officer for P4 section and assistant to String Vest, called me into his office. 'How'd you like to work on my plan to assassinate Slobodan Milosevic then?' he asked casually, as if seeking my views on the weekend cricket scores.

'Oh come off it, I'm not falling for your little games,' I replied dismissively, believing that Fish was just trying to wind me up.

'Why not?' continued Fish, indignantly. 'We colluded with the Yanks to knock off Saddam in the Gulf War, and the SOE tried to take out Hitler in the Second World War.'

'Yes, but they were legitimate military targets in wartime,' I replied. 'We are not at war with Serbia, and Milosevic is a civilian leader. You can't top him.'

Fish was undaunted. 'Yes we can, and we've done it before. I checked with Santa Claus upstairs,' he said, flicking his head disparagingly towards Bidde's office on the tenth floor. Fish was perpetually at war with everybody, even the jovial, silver-haired SBO1. 'He told me that we tried to slot Lenin back in 1911, but some pinko coughed at the last minute and the Prime Minister, it was Asquith then, binned the plan.' Fish's disappointment was plain. 'Santa Claus has got the papers in his locker, but he wouldn't show them to me. They're still more secret than the Pope's Y-fronts, apparently.'

Has MI6 ever assassinated a peacetime target? It was a question that a few of us sometimes discussed on the IONEC but nobody quite dared to ask one of the DS in class. It was a taboo subject, left unsaid by the DS and unasked by the students. One evening down at the Fort bar, when nobody else was listening and after several pints of beer, I asked Ball about it. 'Absolutely not, never,' he replied, his face puckered with sincerity. I was not very sure, however, as he had already proved himself a convincing liar. In any case, if an assassination were plotted, only a tiny handful of officers would know about it and even if Ball were one he would not make a lowly IONEC student privy to such sensitive information.

I did not take Fish's proposal too seriously but a few days later, in his office again to sort out expenses from the Belgrade trip, he casually threw over a couple of sheets of A4. 'Here, take a butcher's at this.' It was a two-page minute entitled 'A proposal to assassinate Serbian President Slobodan Milosevic'. A yellow minute card was attached to the back, showing that it was a formal document rather than just a draft, and the right margin showed a distribution list of String Vest, C/CEE, MODA/SO (an SAS Major, seconded to MI6 as a liaison officer with the increment) and H/SECT, the assistant to the Chief himself. I checked the date on the top-left corner, established that it was not 1 April, then sat down at the visitor's chair beside his cluttered desk to read it. Fish's first page was a justification for the assassination, citing Milosevic's destabilising plans for a Greater Serbia, his illegal covert support for Radovan Karadzic and his genocidal plans for the Albanian population of Kosovo. The second page outlined the execution of the assassination.

Fish proposed three alternative plans for the attempt and gave advantages and disadvantages for each. His first proposal was to use the increment to train and equip a dissident Serbian paramilitary faction to assassinate Milosevic in Serbia. Fish argued that the advantage of this plan was its deniability, the disadvantage that it would be difficult to control. His second plan was to use an increment team to infiltrate Serbia and kill Milosevic with a bomb or sniper ambush. He argued that this plan would have a high chance of success but would not be deniable if it went wrong. The third proposal was to arrange a car 'accident' to kill Milosevic, possibly while attending the ICFY (International Conference on the Former Yugoslavia) peace talks in Geneva. Fish proposed using a bright flashing strobe gun to disorientate Milosevic's chauffeur while the cavalcade passed through a tunnel. The advantage of a tunnel crash was that there would be fewer incidental witnesses and a greater chance that the ensuing accident would be fatal.

'You're off your trolley,' I muttered and passed it back to him. The audacity and ruthlessness of the plan was astonishing. Fish was serious about his career in MI6 and he would not send a suggestion like this up to senior officers out of frivolity. 'This will never get accepted,' I added.

'What do you know?' Fish retorted, looking at me disparagingly as if I was an innocent schoolboy learning for the first time the facts of life.

I never heard anything more about the plan, but then I would not have expected to. An indoctrination list would have been formed, probably consisting only of the Chief, C/CEE, P4 and MODA/SO. Even Fish himself would probably have been excluded from detailed planning at an early stage. A submission would have been put up to the Foreign Secretary to seek political clearance, then MODA/SO and the increment would have taken over the detail of the operational planning. If the plan was developed further, it clearly did not come to fruition, as Milosevic remained very much alive and in power for many years.

As the war in Bosnia intensified and threatened to destabilise south-eastern Europe, urgent demands were placed on MI6 for more intelligence. In mid-1992, the only officers in the FRY (Former Republic of Yugoslavia) were a one-man station in Zagreb, and two officers in Belgrade. A few other stations, notably Athens and Geneva, were producing some reasonable CX on the region from refugees and visitors, but there were still gaping holes in the intelligence coverage. MI6 urgently needed many more officers on the ground, but was hampered by lack of financial and personnel resources and by cover considerations. The FCO had no embassies in Bosnia, Montenegro, Kosovo or Macedonia, so officers could not be inserted there under diplomatic cover. A more flexible approach was needed.

Colin McColl came up with an imaginative solution to fill quickly the holes in intelligence coverage, that was at first met sniffily by most senior officers. He proposed setting up, in each newly independent region of the disintegrating Yugoslavia, 'shoe-box' stations of one officer armed with a laptop computer, encryption software and a briefcase-sized portable satellite facsimile machine. The shoe-box officer would be declared to the local secret police and would rely on this liaison for protection rather than the physical security of an embassy and diplomatic immunity. The shoe-box officers would not have the usual benefits of comfortable, free housing, car allowance or home leave of normal postings, so they would serve only for six months and be paid a generous hardship allowance.

The first shoe-box officer was sent to Tirana, the Albanian capital, in September 1992. Rupert Boxton was an ageing former parachute regiment officer who had just returned from a three-year posting in the backwater of Namibia. He was regarded as 'a bit thick' and wasn't suited to administrative Head Office jobs. His task in Tirana was neither easy nor pleasant. Though the Albanian leader, President Berisha, was keen to improve relations with MI6, his secret police were stuck in the closed mind-set of the days of Albanian communist isolationism. They did not trust Boxton, did not want him in Tirana and refused to give him any worthwhile intelligence or targeting leads. In any case, the German BND (*Bundesnachtrichtdienst*) had got in first and built a strong relationship with the Albanians. MI6's attempts to belatedly muscle in went nowhere. Boxton was withdrawn after just a few months and forced into early retirement by personnel department.

The Tirana fiasco convinced the service that a shoe-box would only survive and prosper if the local liaison service were dependent on MI6 for money, training help and intelligence. Prospects for a shoe-box station in Skopje, the capital of the newly formed republic of Macedonia, seemed more promising. The Macedonian economy was in tatters. Trade with Serbia on its northern border had been stopped by the UN sanctions. To the south the Greeks had closed the border and access to the port of Thessaloniki over fears that the re-emergence of the Macedonian nation would cause unrest in their own province of Macedonia; and communications with Albania to the west were poor because of the mountainous terrain. Relations with Bulgaria to the east were better, but even they were tempered by mistrust for the expansionist ideas of some Bulgarian factions. Macedonia was thus all but cut off from the outside world and urgently needed powerful allies.

The Macedonian secret police were underfunded, and so were vulnerable to financial inducement. MI6 saw the opportunity and stepped in before the BND or the CIA. After some paper shuffling in Whitehall, an emergency aid package was negotiated by FCO and ODA officials. Britain would supply urgently needed medical equipment and drugs; in return Macedonia would harbour an MI6 officer. The Macedonian secret police were further sweetened by a week-long training course at the Fort. All stops were pulled out to impress them. They were very taken by a demonstration of some advanced surveillance communication equipment, and MI6 reluctantly acceded to their requests for the system, even though they had no possible need for it.

Jonathan Small, an energetic and competent GS officer, was sent to Skopje to open the Macedonia shoe-box in December 1992. He had previous experience in one-man stations such as Valletta in Malta, so was well qualified for the job. He was declared to the Macedonian secret police, so there was no need for any cover story for them, but to stave off the curiosity of casual acquaintances he set himself up as a charity worker with credentials supplied by CF contacts. With his satellite dish on the balcony of his one-bedroom flat in central Skopje, Small was soon sending back a stream of reports, mostly on President Gligorov's dealings with Milosevic.

MI6 also set up two more shoe-box stations in the Balkans. One senior officer was sent to Kosovo for three months under cover as an OSCE (Organisation for Security and Co-operation in Europe) observer, but this was not a great success as the ruthless and omni-present Serbian secret police made it too dangerous to attempt any agent-running. To cover Bosnia, MI6 drew on experience gained during OPERATION SAFE HAVEN, the allied operation to protect the Kurds from Iraqi reprisals in the aftermath of the 1990 Gulf War. Clive Mansell, a mid-career officer and Kurdish speaker, was attached to the Royal Marines in Kurdistan as their mysteriously entitled 'civil adviser', mingling with the refugee population to obtain intelligence on the nascent Kurdish nationalist movement. MI6 decided to try the same tactic in Bosnia and sent Mansell to Split with the British UNPROFOR (United Nations Protection Force) contribution to set up a shoe-box station under the designation H/BAP.

By early 1993, all of these assets were in place and MI6's coverage of the Balkans was starting to meet some of the demands placed upon it. Meanwhile, String Vest assigned me to a role supporting Small in Skopje. Small's close liaison with the Macedonian secret police meant that he had no access to one of the main local intelligence requirements, the ethnic Albanian PRI party. The PRI, and the Albanian population in general, were deeply mistrusted by the Macedonian secret police. The intelligence on the PRI which they fed to Small was biased, so MI6 needed independent penetration. String Vest asked me to get together a cover to visit Skopje and cultivate the targets in the PRI leadership.

Now that Ben Presley had retired, CF issued a new alias name, Thomas Paine, and I got myself documented again as a freelance journalist. After my nerve-jangling Belgrade visit, SBO1 insisted I acquire better credentials: 'Get yourself down to I/OPS section and see if they have got any contacts who can help.' I/OPS provided me with a letter of introduction from SMALLBROW, commissioning me to write an article for *The Spectator* on the effects of UN sanctions on Macedonia. 'If anybody from the PRI rings to check you out, he'll vouch for you,' I/OPS/1 assured me. I was ready for my first trip to Skopje within a couple of days.

It was dusk as a tattered taxi with a single working headlight drove me the ten kilometres from Skopje airport to the capital, but I could still see the scars of the 1963 earthquake that destroyed most of the city. The clock on the central railway station was still stuck at ten to five, the time when the first tremors started, and even 30 years later there were swathes of open ground in the town centre where buildings had once stood. Though the war to the north had not directly touched Skopje, the signs of economic hardship were clear. Refuse lay uncollected in the streets, men hung around idle on corners and ragged Kosovo refugees kicked footballs outside the abandoned buildings they now occupied in the run-down Albanian quarter.

The relatively wealthy Macedonian-Bulgar quarter where Small lived was better, but I did not envy his lot. His flat was owned by the Macedonian secret police and lay in a grim concrete block a short distance from the Grand Hotel where I had a reservation. After checking in, I made my way over – Small had invited me for a drink to discuss the operational plan. Strictly I ought not to have been associating with him for security reasons. Skopje was not large and being seen together by officers of other intelligence services could conceivably compromise either or both of us. But String Vest and SBO1 had relented on this occasion. They decided that the risk was small and Small's posting was lonely and boring so an occasional visitor would be good for his morale. Besides, he had been *en poste* for nearly three months and his knowledge would be useful for me.

'Hi, come on up to the third floor,' Small greeted me enthusiastically on the intercom, which was still working. Stepping over the piles of human excrement which littered the floor, I made my way up the stairs. Small greeted me like a long-lost friend on his doorstep. 'Welcome to sunny Skopje.' It didn't take him long to show me around the small, sparsely furnished flat and soon he cracked open a bottle of Scotch and we sat down and got to work. Small had a quick mind and was an excellent operational officer. His ability was wasted in the GS branch, but personnel department would not let him transfer to the IB. There was no point: keeping him in the GS meant that he could be posted to slots like Skopje which most of the IB did not want, and they could still pay him a GS salary. Small briefed me expertly on the various Albanian factions and personalities. Occasionally, when the conversation turned to more sensitive areas, he would sweep his hand through the air, reminding me that his hosts might have bugged his flat. As the evening drew to a satisfying close, he scribbled a note on a scrap of paper and slipped it over to me. It was an invitation to accompany him the next day on a trip to the countryside to check out the station exfiltration plan.

'Sure, I'd love to come,' I answered, careful not to reveal more than was necessary to possible listeners.

The Skopje exfiltration plan differed from usual station plans in that its purpose was to not to smuggle out compromised agents, but to get Small out in case the Macedonian liaison turned against him. They were a brutish lot and the political situation was not stable enough to wholly trust them. If it suited their purpose to kidnap or imprison Small, he could not claim diplomatic immunity as officially he was not there. He would hope to get enough warning of the deterioration in the relationship to be able to get out of the country legally but, just in case, he had an escape route. Two members of the increment visited him earlier in the year to design and rehearse the plan. But then the winter snow lay thick on the ground, and Small wanted to check that he could still find the route now that spring had changed the landscape.

We left early the next morning in Small's Land Rover Discovery and drove out into the countryside. It was early May and the hedgerows were ablaze with the fierce yellow of wild forsythia. The exfiltration plan called for Small to hide out in the countryside until rescue arrived. In a small copse on a hillside a few miles south of Skopje, the location of which Small had carefully memorised, the increment had buried a cache which contained enough materials for Small to survive for a few days out in the open – food, water, clothing, a couple of torches with infra-red filters, materials to make a lightweight bivouac and sleeping bag, a set of false identification papers and passport, a moderate sum of Deutschmarks, a few gold sovereigns and a military EPIRB (Emergency Position Indicating Radio Beacon). We trudged a few hundred yards into the woods and, using a compass to get a bearing from a prominent tree stump, paced out a few yards and found the cache without too much problem. After carefully digging it up to check that it had not been tampered with, we reburied it making sure there was no sign of disturbance.

From the top of the hill behind the copse, Small pointed out a small disused airstrip. 'That's where the plane will come in to pick me up,' he explained. 'It used to be used by crop-spraying aircraft but they've all been grounded through lack of spares now.' We took the Discovery over to the runway to check that it was still serviceable. 'It's just long enough for UKN to get their Piper Aztec on the ground,' Small explained. 'They would come at night, wearing IR goggles, so I'd have to mark out the landing strip with the IR torches.' Flying below radar height, the plane would then make its way under cover of darkness across Albania and the southern Adriatic to the safety of Italy.

Small dropped me off outside the Grand Hotel after the enjoyable morning. It would be an unnecessary risk to spend much more time with him. Besides, later that evening I was to have my first meeting with the deputy leader of the PRI and the afternoon could be better spent preparing for the meeting. I went back up to my room, fished out my laptop computer from my briefcase and waited for it to graunch into life. The hard disk had been modified by TOS to carry invisible files which they guaranteed could not be detected by even the most capable expert. I typed in the password, the hard-disk graunched some more, and magically all my briefing notes were revealed on the screen. I read through them, reminding myself about the key CX requirements and shaping in my mind the sort of questions I would ask at the meeting.

The first meeting went smoothly and my contact in the PRI was delighted to find a western journalist so interested in him. He agreed to further meetings and over the next couple of months I made repeated trips to Skopje, building up the relationship, gaining his confidence and edging him closer to the CX threshold. It was slow work, made all the more irksome because air links to Skopje were few and far between, meaning that each trip required three or four days. The meetings yielded some intelligence but eventually it became obvious that my contact was holding back, afraid for his personal security. His concern was that the Macedonian secret police would make life difficult for him if they discovered that he was talking too regularly to a foreign journalist. Back in Century House, both Bidde and String Vest agreed that the only way forward was to drop my journalistic cover and make the relationship completely clandestine. On my next trip out to Skopje, I used the line that we had practised so diligently on exercise on the IONEC. 'I expect that you've already guessed that I am not really a journalist, but an officer from British Intelligence.' To my relief, my contact did not get up and run. Instead, he accepted my assurance that as he was dealing with a professional intelligence officer rather than a flaky journalist, the Macedonian secret police would never discover his contact with me. He thus became my first recruited agent, and I won my spurs in the office. Thereafter, with the relationship on a more secure and stable footing, he became a productive CX producing agent.

Back in London, between trips to Skopke, Fish was keeping me busy with a series of small but interesting tasks related to the Bosnian War. His job was to coordinate targeting leads to possible informers from other stations or UK-based assets such as BEAVER, and he was an energetic worker. Under various covers, I made trips to Strasbourg, Hamburg, Lisbon and Brussels to meet Bosnian and Serb journalists, dissidents and politicians. Every time I put my head into Fish's office he would offer another interesting task. 'How'd you like to run BEETROOT?' he asked one day.

'OK,' I replied. 'But who is BEETROOT?'

'He's a right-wing vegetable,' replied Fish. 'A Tory MP, but surprisingly he's OK,' he added. 'Here's his file – go and read it.'

BEETROOT had tried to join MI5 after university, but had been rather unfairly turned down on security grounds. After his rejection he went into business, making frequent trips to the Soviet Union, and was soon picked up by MI6 as a provider of low-level economic CX. He then joined the Conservative Party, which proposed him as a candidate. To everybody's surprise, he was elected after a large swing in favour of the Tories. Normally, MI6 are not allowed to run MPs as informers but in this case Prime Minister John Major personally granted MI6 permission to continue running BEETROOT. He was making frequent trips to Bosnia as part of the parliamentary working group on the war, and String Vest and Fish had decided that his access to leading actors in the region made him a worthwhile agent.

My first meeting with him was at the Grapes pub on Shepherd Market which he chose as it was only a short walk from Parliament, and no other MPs went there because the prostitutes in Shepherd Market could potentially bring embarrassing publicity. After shaking hands we ordered a pint of Ruddles each and bags of pork scratchings. 'I'm glad you've got in touch with me,' he said once we were seated at one of the large oak tables. 'There's something that's been worrying me for a while, but I have not known what channel to report it on.'

'Please explain,' I asked, mystified.

He went on to tell me about a young prospective Tory parliamentary candidate. Although a British citizen, the subject was from a Serb family, spoke fluent Serbo-Croat and had changed his name by deed poll. He was a passionate supporter of the Bosnian-Serb cause and Karadzic appointed him as his unofficial spokesperson in London. Fish had a FLORIDA warrant to keep his telephone and fax machine under intercept, and this had produced some useful CX.

'Well, it seems that he has arranged for the Bosnian-Serbs to make a financial donation to the Conservative Party,' explained BEETROOT. 'He's channelling the money through a Serb bank to make it look legitimate, but basically the money is coming straight from Karadzic. He boasted to me about it only yesterday – he's hoping that getting some funds for the party will help his chances of becoming an MP.'

The Tory Party was deeply in debt after emptying their coffers in the 1992 general election campaign. Accepting money from any foreign government would be controversial enough, but Britain had soldiers attached to UNPROFOR in Bosnia who were regularly shot at and sometimes killed by Karadzic's forces. If this news was leaked to the press, it would cause a huge scandal and it explained why BEETROOT had not known where to turn with this information – he could hardly report it to the Tory Party chairman, the normal chain of command, because the party chairman himself was accepting the money. I thanked him for his information and promised to be in touch, BEETROOT honourably insisting on paying for the beer and pork scratchings, concerned that otherwise he would have to register my hospitality in the Parliamentary Register of Members' Interests.

'Christ, you could sell that story to the *Mirror* for 15 grand!' exclaimed Fish when I told him the news back in Century House. 'And it makes sense, too. I saw on the FLORIDA that there was discussion of some form of money transfer with Karadzic, but I couldn't make out what for,' Fish added. 'Now it is all clear. You'd better write that up as CX fast.'

I scurried upstairs to my office, clutching the FLORIDA transcripts, already putting the report together in my head. Half an hour later, the finished CX report was on its way to R/CEE and would be on the desks of Whitehall customers the next morning. Thereafter, there would be a hell of a storm. The Tory Party were already reeling from a series of funding scandals, fuelled by a vitriolic press campaign, and there was no doubt that this report would be leaked by a Whitehall official. It might even bring the government down, forcing another general election. But half an hour later such thoughts were interrupted by the PAX (internal phone system) ringing on my desk. 'Hello, Richard, R/CEE here. I'm afraid that CX of yours has been spiked. And H/SECT wants to see you about it – go up and see him right now.' I dropped the phone and urgently made for the lift to take me up to the 18th floor. H/SECT was the personal secretary to the Chief, and if he wanted to see me it must be about something very important indeed.

Alan Judd carried a lot of clout in the office hierarchy. He had been largely responsible for drafting the new 'avowal' legislation that was due to come into effect the next year and which would allow the government formally to acknowledge the existence of MI6 for the first time. He was also well known in the office for the series of lighthearted novels that he had written about spying, his powerful contacts in Whitehall allowing him to side-step the normally strict rules that prevent MI6 officers from writing books about their experiences. He even had the nerve to put in a flyleaf dedication to Nick Long, the inspiration for *Tango*, a spy-caper set in Latin America.

'Take a seat, UKA/7.' Judd addressed me formally by my job designation rather than first name, perhaps to underline his status. 'That CX report you wrote about Tory Party funding' – Judd nodded to my report lying on his desk – 'I'm afraid we can't possibly issue it. If it leaked out, it could bring down the government.'

'So?' I replied. 'It's not MI6's job to interfere with the governance of the country, is it?'

'Well,' replied Judd lugubriously, 'there are other channels to report this sort of information.'

'Such as?' I asked. We'd never had any other channel explained to us on the IONEC.

'The Chief has decided to issue it as a "hot potato", meaning that it will go only to the Prime Minister. I want that CX report destroyed.' Judd handed over the paperwork that I was required to sign in order to have the report officially struck off the records. There was no choice but to sign, though I knew it was wrong. 'And you're to talk to nobody about this report or this incident,' Judd threatened ominously as I was getting up to leave.

Perhaps it was no coincidence that I got a phone call from the head of personnel department's secretary a few days later, informing me that they were removing me from UKA. 'We've got an interesting overseas posting for you,' the secretary said. 'PD/1 will give you the details at the meeting.' The good news of my first overseas posting was exciting, but it was tempered by the fact that I would have to deal again with Fowlecrooke, who had been appointed PD/1 after finishing as my line manager in SOV/OPS.

'We've decided to post you to Bosnia, as H/BAP,' announced Fowlecrooke at the meeting. 'We think that you have the ideal blend of experience for the job – your time in the Territorial Army will be useful experience in a war zone, and you have worked enthusiastically on the conflict for the past six months. You'll be taking over from Kenneth Roberts in two weeks. It's not a lot of time to prepare for the post, but I am sure that you will cope.'

9

DEEP WATER

FRIDAY, 26 NOVEMBER 1993
CENTRAL SARAJEVO

I heard the screaming shriek of the shell cutting through the air a split second before the shock wave of the detonation crushed me to the ground, so I knew I was going to live. Harris, a 12-year-old street urchin, petty crook and veteran of the three-year Serbian siege of Sarajevo, gave me the tip only a few days earlier. He made a living hanging around the Sarajevo Holiday Inn and 'guarding' the vehicles of the journalists and aid workers – if they chose not to acquire his services, windscreen wipers, aerials and anything else removable would disappear overnight. Clapping his grubby hands and whistling through broken teeth to provide the sound effects, he cheerfully explained in his pidgin English that if an incoming shell whistled, then it would land far enough away to be harmless. His words of wisdom were the first cogent thoughts that entered my mind as my senses returned and the awareness of where I was drifted back into my consciousness.

Angus, the dour, moustached NCO (Non-Commissioned Officer) of the British army detachment in Sarajevo, had dropped me off on a quiet street corner in central Sarjevo just a few minutes before the shellburst, promising to return to the RV in three hours time, then again the following hour if I failed to show up for the first. Gruffly, he had wished me luck, then drove off into the mist of an early winter's evening.

As the red tail-lights of the kevlar-armoured UNPROFOR Land Rover disappeared into the murk, I slipped into a shadowy doorway to let my eyes adjust to the falling light before beginning the ten-minute walk to the home of DONNE, MI6's most important agent in Sarajevo. Unshaven, shabbily dressed and with a woollen hat pulled low over my head, I looked like any of the other Sarajevans employed by UNPROFOR being dropped off by a friendly soldier after a day's work. To further the disguise, in my left hand I lugged a half-full 25-litre polythene jerry can of the sort carried ubiquitously by Sarajevans in their daily toil to fetch water from the public spigots. Over my right shoulder was slung a canvas bag containing a notebook and pencil, a PETTLE recorder and presents for DONNE – a bottle of Johnny Walker Black Label whisky and 400 Marlboro cigarettes.

Despite my innocuous appearance, there was a risk of a routine ID check by one of the Bosnian police officers who lurked on street corners. I felt nervously in my breast pocket for my G/REP forged ID card and the grubby, cellophane-wrapped card bearing the words 'Ja sam gluh i nijem' – 'I am deaf and dumb' in the local language. It was a worn and clichéd ruse, but perhaps it would be enough to deflect further interest from a bored and tired policeman. My cover would not withstand further scrutiny – stuffed into a holster in my trouser band was a loaded 9mm Browning and in the poacher's pocket of my grubby overcoat a vial of morphine and two Joint Services standard issue shell dressings. All were hostages to fortune, but the benefits of carrying them outweighed the risks of their discovery. The pistol would also counter the threat from the armed muggers (usually hungry and drunken off-duty Bosnian soldiers) who lurked in the unlit alleys. The morphine and shell dressings were to counter the biggest threat in central Sarajevo – the deadly, calculated sniper's bullet or the indiscriminate and random shelling which killed everyday and blanketed every Sarajevan with the constant fear of imminent death.

Stepping from the shadowy, stinking doorway I reflected that at least I would only face these hazards for a few hours until Angus returned with the sanctuary of the armoured Land Rover. Sarajevans, like the woman scurrying home half a block in front of me, had to put up with it day in, day out. I wondered what sort of a life she led. It was impossible to gauge her age. Head down, shuffling wearily but urgently with a heavy bundle of firewood, wrapped in heavy clothes against the damp cold, she could have been a teenager, a mother or a grandmother. For sure, she would have lost at least one member of her family or a close friend to the shelling and sniping siege. No one had escaped that grief.

I must have blacked out for a second when the shell exploded, and regained consciousness gasping to refill my lungs, emptied by the crushing blast. My heart was racing so fast I could feel its every beat in the throb of my head and my ears howled with white noise. An excruciating pain shot through me from my right leg, stabbing into me as my chest moved to suck in air. Gingerly, as my breathing stabilised, I opened my eyes and it took a moment to work out what had happened. Whether it was the shock wave from the exploding shell or my instinctive leap for cover, I had been thrown back into the doorway and was lying in a contorted, twisted heap, wedged head uppermost into the corner. Still too shocked to move, I looked down at my right leg, the source of my agony. There was nothing from the knee down. I closed my eyes and swallowed hard, trying not to throw up. Shifting my weight eased the pain slightly and slowly, with my right hand, I explored my lower body, dreading the worst. My hand brushed against leather, perhaps my boot. Glancing down, alarmed and apprehensive, it was indeed my Timberland, with my lower right leg still inside it. Still scarcely able to breathe, head throbbing, I felt along its length and realised with ecstatic relief that it was still attached to my upper leg. I hadn't lost it, it was just twisted at an excruciating angle underneath my crumpled body. Gingerly, I rolled further to my left. The pain eased a bit more. A bit further and there was an excruciating twang as the ligaments at the back of the twisted knee uncrossed themselves. Groaning and panting for breath, I straightened my leg, relieved that I was in one piece. Little Harris was right – I'd heard the shell coming in and it had landed far enough from me not to cause serious injury.

Lying still for a few minutes, I calmed my breathing. White noise still rang in my ears, though it was subsiding. Suspecting that my eardrums must have been blown out, I put my hands to my ears to check for blood. There was none. I checked for the Browning. It would be difficult and embarrassing to explain losing that to the office, whatever the circumstances. It was still there. I sat upright, then struggled to my feet, trying not to put weight my right leg. My body had now started shaking and shivering involuntarily. Shock was setting in and I needed fluids. My jerry can was lying on the pavement, split, and leaking slightly. I limped over, picked it up, and squeezed it, drinking eagerly from the crack. My shakes were uncontrollable and the cold water spilt down the front of my shirt, sending spasmodic shivers down me. I desperately wanted to lie down somewhere warm and be anywhere but where I was.

I heard the plaintive wailing for a few seconds before realising from what, or from where, it was coming. It sounded inhuman, high-pitched and tremulous, like a mortally injured dog that knows it is about to die. I looked up the street to where the swaddled woman had been scurrying only minutes earlier. Darkness was falling, but at the limit of vision lay the dark silhouette of a prone body. I dropped the jerry can and semi-hopped, semi-limped towards her.

She must have taken virtually the full blast of the explosion. There was a fresh detonation scar in the pavement just a few feet in front of her, and a smell of cordite lingered. The blast had blown away all her clothes except part of the heavy woollen overcoat which still clung to her upper body, exposing all that was left of her below. Her stomach was split with a vicious gash and her groin and thighs were shredded by shrapnel. Her lower right leg was almost unmarked, but her left leg was blown off just below the knee. The shattered bone was exposed and blood pulsed from the torn artery, squirting into the pool on the pavement. At that rate of blood loss, she would not live long. My hands were on autopilot, driven by the first-aid training I had received in the TA. ABC – airways, breathing, circulation. There was no need for the AB – she was wailing piercingly and her chest was moving. The priority was C – to stop blood loss and to keep her circulation going. Kneeling beside her, I scrabbled in my overcoat for the shell dressings. Hastily pulling them out, I dropped the morphine vial into the pool of blood. Hands still shaking, I tore off the brown waterproof outer layer of the dressing, ripped off the sterile inner layer, unfolded the thick pad of absorbent lint and rammed it up against the stub of her leg. Jamming it in place with my knee, I fumbled to open the second dressing. Despite binding the two dressings in place tightly using the attached bandages, it barely stemmed the bleeding.

She was still wailing weakly, more in fear than in pain, and presumably she was losing consciousness. I scrabbled for the morphine vial and cleaned it off, intending to give her a shot. Grabbing her right arm, I twisted the palm towards me, exposing her lower inner arm to find a vein. She had already lost so much blood that even after squeezing and massaging none stood out. I was about to jab in the syringe, thinking that it was better than nothing, when from my TA training came a distant recollection – check for head wounds before administering morphine. I fumbled for the mini-maglite torch in my jacket pocket and shifted to see her face. Grabbing a handful of her long, dark hair to hold her head steady, I shone the beam into her eyes. The pupils were pinpricks. As I pushed back her hair to expose her ears, a trickle of straw-yellow fluid ran from her left ear. It would be dangerous to give her morphine. Apart from vainly attempting to stem the blood flow, there was nothing more I could do. I had exhausted the limits of my medical training and the equipment with me and resignedly slipped the vial back into my pocket.

As I bowed my head, questioning the fate that brought me here to watch this girl die, I became aware of other people around me. An old man knelt beside me, mumbling something incomprehensible in Bosanski. A Bosnian soldier stood overlooking us, his back pressed against the wall, wary of another salvo of shells. It was time for me to go. Standing up, my twisted knee reminded me about itself and I winced. The old man grabbed me by the arm and murmured something but I twisted free and stepped back into the shadows. I still had a job to do.

I limped back to the cover of my doorway. Looking back up the road to where the girl still lay, I saw that a car had pulled up – a few still ran in Sarajevo despite the siege, fuelled by black-market petrol. The bystanders were loading her limp corpse into the back seat, arguing incomprehensibly. Another shell whistled overhead, sending them and me ducking for cover. It landed perhaps a few streets away, perhaps harmlessly, perhaps not. The car carrying the dying girl pulled away and sped past, a white Volkswagen Golf splattered with rusting shrapnel pockmarks and with an improvised windscreen from another make. I hoped they were on their way to the Kosovo Hospital rather than straight to the morgue.

Sheltering in the corner of the doorway to take stock, I glanced at my watch showed that only ten minutes had passed since Angus had dropped me off. There remained two hours and fifty minutes before he would return. I was in shock from the incident, I felt cold, and my hands and trousers were stained in the girl's blood. This was no fit state for a meeting with DONNE. I removed my boots and took off my trousers. The water that remained in my split water-carrier was sufficient to rinse out the worst of the blood. After being wrung out, the damp trousers were a bit uncomfortable, but the modern lightweight material would dry quickly. Nevertheless, I hoped that DONNE's flat would be warm.

The route to DONNE's took me past the spot where the girl had been hit. As I limped by, a mongrel bitch, probably an abandoned pet, trotted out of the shadows, her long teats swinging, and cautiously sniffed the congealing blood on the pavement. She whimpered approvingly and a puppy scampered out of the shadows to join her. Eagerly, they started lapping up the blood and scraps of flesh. It was a repulsive, hellish vision, but I did not chase them off. They were only doing what came naturally. At least a couple of starving dogs would benefit from the tragedy.

Normally when an IB officer is posted overseas, he or she spends up to two years in pre-posting preparation. The most time-consuming element is the language training. Even if an agent speaks good English, it is preferable to speak to him in his mother tongue – that way his real character is more exposed. For a difficult language such as Chinese or Arabic, it takes two years to reach the required level of fluency, even if the officer is a talented linguist. For an easy language like Spanish or French the training is shorter, usually about six months. The other important element of pre-posting training is to build a thorough understanding of the political issues, intelligence requirements and agent assets of the host country. An officer therefore usually spends a few months on attachment to the relevant P desk and might even do the job full-time for a year or so. He will read in detail the files of all the station agents – CX agents, OCP keepers, liaison officers, facilities agents – and will learn the administrative background of the station – its budget, its targets for the year ahead, the CX requirements. He will meet the relevant desk officers in the FCO to get up to speed with the political situation in the country and usually takes advanced FCO courses in politics and economics. The result is that he is already thoroughly familiar with the station's work and the host country before he even packs his bags.

Shortly before leaving for the station, the officer also undertakes 'refresher' training down at the Fort. The course consists of further tradecraft instruction, especially in anti-surveillance; more instruction in photography; and a brush-up in small-arms and self-defence training. There is also a course in defensive driving techniques given by Royal Military Police instructors on the runway of the HMS *Daedalus* naval airfield near the Fort, encompassing fast-driving techniques such as hand-brake turns and J-turns. (Hire cars, rather than the Fort's pool cars are used, because it is not unheard of for over-enthusiastic novices to rip tyres off them or even overturn them.) Officer's spouses are also invited to attend a week-long course at the Fort, as it is useful to have a trained second pair of eyes during anti-surveillance runs. The course also allows partners to understand the profession better – the divorce rate in MI6 is high because of the demanding and secretive work.

For some postings, even more specialised training is required. For example, Andrew Markham, my IONEC colleague, was selected for the ORCADA slot in Bonn. This was a deep cover job, running MI6's most important agent in Germany, a high-ranking official in the ministry of finance. In return for a substantial salary, ORCADA provided five-star CX on the German economy and interest rate movements, enabling the Chancellor of the Exchequer and the Governor of the Bank of England to adjust Britain's interest rates and economy to best advantage. The ORCADA posting was so sensitive that only the ambassador in Bonn and H/BON were briefed and no one else in the embassy was even aware that Markham was from the 'friends' (FCO-speak for MI6). Markham thus had to learn to become a thoroughly convincing diplomat to fool his FCO colleagues, so he attended the FCO pre-posting training courses in addition to all his MI6 courses, and in order to debrief ORCADA effectively he also attended advanced lectures at the London School of Economics and did an extended attachment with the Treasury.

It was thus highly unusual when Fowlecrooke told me that he would give me only two weeks to prepare for the posting in Bosnia. There would be no time for any language instruction or any of the normal courses. It was just enough time to read the station files, have a couple of meetings with String Vest and take a one-day refresher course on the Browning down at the Fort.

String Vest explained that my cover was not in the usual diplomatic slot in an embassy, the scenario for which we trained on the IONEC, but as the mysteriously entitled 'civil adviser' to Brigadier John Reith, the commander of the British UNPROFOR contribution in Split on the Dalmatian coast. It was a flimsy, ill-considered cover-story which fooled nobody. As I was to find out, every one of my contacts in Bosnia assumed immediately that I was from British intelligence and even the greenest of army privates in the Divulje barracks was smart enough to guess. The only people naïve enough to be duped by the fig-leaf were, it seemed, back in Head Office.

The files revealed that Clive Mansell, profiting from his experience on SAFE HAVEN, set up the BAP station. He equipped a small office in the Divulje barracks with a computer and satellite dish and found a suitable flat in a fishing village a few kilometres from the barracks. But Mansell left after a few months on promotion to an administrative job in Century House and Kenneth Roberts, the former Black Watch officer who had been in UKO, took his place. Roberts was in post for eight months, and changed the scope of the job. Not content to restrict himself to networking in the Divulje barracks and the safety of the Dalmatian coast, he travelled extensively around central and northern Bosnia. Roberts's efforts paid dividends: he successfully recruited two useful agents and had the cultivation of three more well advanced. STEENBOX was an official in the northern town of Tuzla who provided CX on the activities and intentions of the Bosnian militia unit based there, which stubbornly refused to fall wholly under the control of Sarajevo. DONNE, his most important recruit, was an official in the Bosnian government in Sarajevo and provided key information on the tactics of the Bosnian delegation in the ICFY peace talks in Geneva.

Roberts also brought in a four-man detachment of soldiers from 602 Troop to beef up his communications and provide physical protection on forays into central Bosnia – 602 Troop are an 80-strong detachment from the Royal Signals Regiment whose permanent home is in Banbury, Oxfordshire. In peacetime, they man MI6's overseas high-frequency radio relay stations and rotate between postings in Kowandi, northern Australia (until it was closed in March 1993), Ascension Island, Northern Ireland and the Falklands where they support the chain of listening stations in Chile. In wartime, they are responsible for providing field communications for MI6 operations, such as during SAFE HAVEN, the Gulf War, and now in Bosnia. The four-man BAP detachment installed HF radio sets, known as KALEX, which were faster and easier to use than the satellite communications used by Mansell. One was set up in the top floor of the Divulje barracks in Roberts's office, the other mounted in the back of a long-wheelbase Land Rover to provide mobile communications.

As if the flimsiness of my cover was not enough of a handicap, the H/BAP job would be a challenging enough post for an experienced officer to take on at such short notice. The unusual cover, complexity of the communication arrangements, logistical difficulties and physical risks all made it a daunting prospect for an inexperienced probationer like me. There was a lot to cram in during the fortnight before flying out to Split.

———————————

The scheduled British Airways flight touched down at Split airport on the morning of the 8 November 1993. The apron of the small provincial airport was heaving with Hercules C-130s and Ilyushin 72 transport aircraft that were flying supplies to the besieged city of Sarajevo, and the terminal was teeming with transiting soldiers from the multinational UNPROFOR force, journalists, TV crews and refugees. It was not easy for Roberts to identify me in the arrivals hall. 'Sorry old boy,' Roberts announced in his slightly plummy public school accent as we threaded our way through the soldiers' bergens and weapons that littered the arrivals hall, 'but I've had to cut the handover down to four days. I'm desperate for some leave and personnel want me on a course in London on the twenty-second.' The station handover was scheduled for two weeks, but by now I was used to being shortchanged. It was not Roberts's fault. He was quite reasonably in dire need of a break and was expected to report in ten days for pre-posting training for his new job in the British mission to the UNHQ in New York. Personnel department screwing up again, I thought.

In the few days available for the handover, our priority was to meet DONNE, so Sarajevo was to be our first port of call. 'I've booked ourselves on an Arizona Air National Guard C-130 that's flying some beans up to Sarajevo this afternoon,' Roberts told me cheerfully. There's just time to dump your stuff in the flat and then we'll pop into Divulje and meet the lads from 602 Troop.' The small flat Roberts had rented for me, a ten-minute drive in the station's Land Rover Discovery, was comfortable enough and it had views over the Adriatic. 'You'll need your woolies when the snow comes, though,' Roberts grinned. 'There's no heating.'

After dropping off my baggage we rushed back to the Divulje barracks for a whistlestop tour. The office, tucked away on the top floor of the main HQ building, contained a metal desk, filing cabinet, hefty safe for classified material and large wall maps of Bosnia and Sarajevo. 'Here, have a look at my souvenirs,' Roberts grinned, opening the bottom drawer of the desk. Inside were a Yugoslav-made pistol, several clips of 7.65mm ammunition for it and a hand-grenade. 'I got them off a stiff I found near Tuzla,' Roberts laughed gleefully. 'Here, take a look at this, one of Karadzic's bodyguards gave it to me.' Roberts handed me a small implement that had been disguised as a fountain pen, but which contained a 7.65mm bullet. 'Turn the cap and it fires. Real James Bond stuff, huh?' Roberts laughed.

'Are you taking this stuff back with you?' I asked, not too happy about having a small armoury in my desk.

'Sorry old boy, I was hoping to send it back in the dip bag and donate it to the museum at the Fort, but I never got around to it.' Roberts slammed the drawer shut and we continued the tour.

Alongside the office was another small room housing the KALEX communications gear. The detachment lived in a small dormitory opposite that they had fitted out with satellite television and a few sofas. Roberts introduced me briefly to the troops. Jon, a bright and efficient young sergeant, was the detachment's leader. Baz, a caustic Geordie corporal, was dedicated and hard-working, but liked to affect a devil-may-care attitude. Jim, a cheerful lance-corporal, was full of initiative and drive, and was overdue for promotion. Finally Tosh, a Londoner, was a bit of a jack-the-lad, forever ready with a cheeky quip. 'They're a good bunch,' Roberts later told me 'They work hard and you won't have any trouble with them.'

Ominous grey clouds were gathering outside as we squeezed into the C-130 alongside the dusty pallets of flour and beans and strapped ourselves, bloated by our obligatory flak-jackets and helmets, into the webbing seats which stretched down the sides of the aircraft. A cheerful National Guard loadie handed us flight rations, a small, white cardboard box filled with crisps, an apple and a cheese sandwich. 'Here, have some gum, it'll save your ears popping,' the grinning loadie shouted against the throbbing roar of the turboprop engines as he thrust a small box at us. I reached in and put the yellow tabs where they were supposed to be, in my ears. The loadie smiled ruefully, perhaps hoping he'd be able to catch out his next civilian passenger.

Ten bumpy minutes into the hour-long flight, the dark hold was suddenly illuminated with a blinding flash that raced the length of the fuselage and a whip-like crack audible even above the engine roar. 'Fuck, we've been hit!' shouted Roberts. The Hercules lurched into a steep nosedive, forcing me to grip the webbing seating to stop myself falling into Roberts's lap and making my ears pop ferociously. The dive lasted a few heart-pumping seconds before the pilot pulled some g's to level out. 'What was that?' shouted Roberts to the loadie when we were straight and level. 'Was that a sniper bullet?' A few C-130s had taken sniper shots, but normally only on the approach to Sarajevo airport. We were a long way from the risky zone and so it was unlikely.

'I'll go find out,' shouted back the loadie, unstrapping himself to make his way forward to the cockpit. He returned a minute later. 'Lightning strike,' he announced. 'Pilot says it hit the tail, came down the fuselage, and punched a fist-sized hole out the nose, smashing up some avionics. We've got to divert to Frankfurt.' Roberts and I looked at each other in resignation. It would take another day out of our already tight schedule.

The USAF put us up in their comfortable officer's quarters in their sprawling Ramstein base and we took the first available flight to Sarajevo the next morning. This time we got within ten minutes of Sarajevo and the C-130 had just started its anti-sniper dive towards the runway when the flight was again aborted. A burst of Serbian artillery on the runway shut the airport and we had to retreat again, this time to Zagreb in Croatia.

We finally made it into Sarajevo the next day on board a Russian Ilyushin 72, their pilots taking a more robust view of bombs and bullets than the Americans, and touched down on the heavily guarded Sarajevo runway on a fine autumnal day. We were met on the apron by the affable commander of the four-man British detachment in Sarajevo, Major Ken Lindsay, with his armoured Land Rover. 'You've picked a fine day for a visit,' he greeted us. 'The sun's shining, we're flush with Fosters and the Serbs have only lobbed five shells at us today.' Originally a truckie in the Australian army, he married the daughter of a senior British cavalry officer, who arranged for his new son-in-law to transfer to the smart King's Royal Hussars cavalry regiment. Lindsay's official job was to ensure that the UNHCR relief deliveries were fairly shared amongst the various distribution stations in Sarajevo. But unofficially he and his team provided transport and lodging for us while in town. 'Chuck your kit in the back of the wagon. We'll go for a tour of Sarajevo, then have a few tinnies in the PTT building,' Lindsay ordered cheerfully.

As we drove through the Serb–Muslim front lines into town, past the burnt-out shell of an old T-55 tank, Lindsay pointed out the Sarajevo landmarks. The pock-marked PTT building, the former telecommunications centre which had been commandeered by the UN, was where he and his contingent were based in two cramped rooms. 'Ken normally lets me sleep on the floor of his room if I'm staying in Sarajevo,' explained Roberts. 'He'll do the same for you as long as you don't snore.'

'And as long as you bring a slab,' added Ken.

'That's the Holiday Inn on the left,' Roberts pointed out a heavily bombed 15-storey building. 'I stay there sometimes, but CNN have commandeered all the best rooms, and most of the time there is no water, so it's better to stay in the PTT.' We drove down sniper-alley, the long dual-carriageway linking the airport and PTT building to downtown Sarajevo, and took a whistlestop tour of the main Bosnian government building, the impressive but sadly bombed-out library and the Kosovo hospital.

There was little point in gratuitously risking Serbian snipers' bullets and shells so once Roberts had orientated me, we returned to the safety of the sturdy PTT building. But once dusk had fallen, Angus, Lindsay's NCO, drove us back the three kilometres into town for the handover with DONNE. There was only time for a half-hour meeting, but it was enough for Roberts to introduce me as his successor, extract a CX report and hand over a large carton of Marlboros that DONNE could trade on the burgeoning Sarajevo black market.

'Right, let's get back to the PTT building for some beers with Ken,' Roberts urged eagerly as soon as the debrief was over. 'That'll be Angus there.' Sure enough, two headlights were coming towards us and Angus pulled up at the RV bang on time. Roberts climbed into the passenger seat, leaving me to clamber into the back of the vehicle over assorted flak-jackets, helmets and tools. Before pulling the heavy door shut, I had a last glance round; my next trip would be alone and I hoped I would remember the route.

We spent the evening drinking heavily with Lindsay and his detachment, and arose early the next morning, hungover, to take the first flight back to Split. Roberts was due to fly home to London the next afternoon, leaving me in charge. 'No time to meet STEENBOX, I'm afraid,' grinned Roberts as we shivered in the dark airport waiting room, 'but I'll explain how you get to Tuzla and where to find her.' Roberts was understandably demob happy and I would have to pick up the pieces from scratch after the heavily curtailed handover.

Peering through the rain-spattered windscreen into the darkness, I tried to pick out physical features weakly illuminated by the Discovery headlights and relate them to the map spread on my knee. Silently, I cursed Fowlecrooke for leaving so little time for the handover. Meeting STEENBOX required navigating to Tuzla, 360 km north-east of Split along forest tracks and through two war fronts. It would not have been a straightforward task in daylight, but we had been badly held up by an aid convoy earlier on the route and now darkness and rain were both falling. The narrow, potholed lane traversed a steep valley side. The hillside to the right, densely packed with trees, rose to the clouded skyline. Down to the left, I could just pick out through the trees the glint of the stream on the valley bottom. It could have been any one of hundreds of similar valleys in rugged central Bosnia, but there was something not quite right about it. The road was narrower and the valley contours steeper than those on the map. 'Jim, are you sure this is the right road?'

'Yeah,' Jim replied casually from behind the wheel. 'Know it like me own bell-end.' Jim was grinning like a kid on a bouncy castle. Nothing ever bothered him. He was a big chunky guy, but serious about his fitness. Down at Divulje he was out running and lifting weights every day. But I wasn't too sure he knew his body parts as well as he thought he did.

Jim lifted on the throttle and changed down a gear, the V8 engine growling as it slowed the heavily laden vehicle. The headlights had picked up a tree trunk, the size of a telegraph pole, which had fallen across the narrow road and we drew to a stop in front of it. 'Must have been the storm last night,' Jim announced cheerfully. Without further ado he hopped down from the vehicle and, as if he was trying out for a 'world's strongest man' competition, picked up the trunk, staggered with it in his arms for a few yards up the road and threw it in the ditch.

I glanced in the mirror to see the familiar lights of Jon and Baz's underpowered Land Rover crawling up the hill behind us. Reaching down to the stereo I flicked off Jim's tape and grabbed the Motorola from behind the instrument binnacle. 'Baz, do you reckon this is the right road?' I asked.

There was a pause while he consulted Jon, before the Motorola hissed back. 'Keep yer keks on. Just round the next corner we should come to that burnt-out Scroat village.' Baz sounded confident and as he had done the trip three times with Roberts I trusted his judgement. I put the Motorola down just as Jim clambered back into the vehicle, slapping his hands together to brush away the bark and leaves adhering to them. He clunked the vehicle into first gear and pulled away.

Round the next corner there was no burnt-out Croatian village, just another fallen tree, much bigger than the first. Beyond that, I could see another, then another. Undaunted, Jim prepared to jump out of the vehicle to move them, but I grabbed his arm. 'No, this isn't right,' I said. This was not the work of a storm. The trees had been laid across the road for a purpose. 'Baz, Jon, turn round immediately, we've taken a wrong turn,' I ordered down the Motorola.

Jim detected the urgency in my voice, and had already launched the Discovery into a three point turn. He'd just got it pointing the other way when Baz squawked on the Motorola 'Hey Rich, we've got trouble.'

The comms-wagon was about 100 metres down the road, halfway through the three-point turn. With no power steering Jon must have been cursing trying to get the heavy vehicle turned round, and he'd been too slow to get away from the militiamen. Two were standing over the bonnet, pointing their AK47s directly through the windscreen at Baz. Two more were at the driver's door, perhaps talking to Jon or, worse, trying to force it open. More were at the rear door, peering in through the window at the computers and communication equipment and pulling at the handle. Other shadowy figures were emerging from the woods, making purposefully towards the vehicle, weapons held out menacingly.

There was no time to reply to Baz before our vehicle was also surrounded. The barrels of two AK47s loomed at me through the windscreen, their owners just dark shadows. There was a sharp tap on my side window and, looking round, a pistol gesticulated for me to open up. Trying not to make a sudden movement, I slipped my hand round to feel for the button on the top edge of the door – Jim would have tripped out the central locking when he got out to move the tree. I pushed it down, praying that the unreliable system would work. There was a satisfying clunk as all five doors locked up.

The pistol crashed threateningly against the window in response.

The situation was awkward rather than desperate. Thankfully most of the soldiers were clean shaven, so they were not from the Afghan Mujahideen group that was known to be operating in the area and who would not hesitate to execute infidels. Our lives were probably not in danger – even the worst Bosnian militia groups were unlikely to murder UNPROFOR soldiers as it would lead to severe retribution. But I was worried about the vehicles and equipment. Only a few weeks earlier a group of French journalists had been ambushed a few kilometres from this spot, ordered out of their Land Cruiser at gunpoint and left at the side of the road as their ambushers drove away in the new vehicle. It would be a disaster if the same thing happened to us. Losing the Discovery and comms-wagon would be bad enough but the KALEX HF comms equipment, though outdated, was still classified 'TOP SECRET'. Still, I thought to myself with a weak smile, they would be in for a nasty surprise if they tried opening my briefcase. The metal box that contained the encryption OTPs and other classified material had an inbuilt incendiary device that would destroy the contents with a satisfying bang if it were opened incorrectly. I hoped that they would not get that far.

Grabbing the Motorola I got on to Baz. 'Don't get out of the vehicle at all costs,' I shouted.

'Gotcha,' Baz replied, not as cockily as before.

The pistol banged against the side window again and an order was barked in Bosanski. Stooping slightly so that the pistol owner's blackened face was visible, I shrugged and held up my hands. 'I don't understand. Ich verstehe nicht. Je ne comprends pas,' I replied, cursing for the umpteenth time how ridiculous it was for personnel to send me on a posting of this nature lacking even rudimentary language training. The voice barked out again and a rifle butt smashed into the right headlight, breaking the lens. I got the message and reached for the steering column stalk to flick out the remaining light.

The voice barked out again, so I dropped the window a crack, hoping that it would be taken as a gesture of conciliation. 'How can I help?' I asked feebly in English. The voice screamed again, more aggressively this time, and the vehicle rocked as he pulled hard on the door handle. Other soldiers tried to force open the rear door too. Winding down the window another half-inch, I tried to identify myself. 'UNPROFOR, UNPROFOR. British soldiers,' I said, holding my United Nations ID card up against the window.

Meanwhile, I could hear that Jim was also getting an interview, though his inquisitor spoke a few words of English, and I glanced across. 'Manchester United,' the face uttered proudly, grinning into Jim's window. 'Bryan Robson,' the face beamed even more broadly, giving a thumbs up.

Jim, a fan of Liverpool, swallowed his pride. 'Yeah. Man United. Very good, best team in the world.' He gave a thumbs-up sign and the face grinned with appreciation.

But the voice in my window, which I took to be the commander's, snapped out another order and I turned away from Jim as the soldiers milling around the front of the vehicle sprung forward, the windscreen bristling menacingly with AK47s. My eyes were getting accustomed to the dark now that the headlights were out and I could make out the faces peering down the barrels at us. They looked tired and pissed off. The commander barked another order and the sound of 7.62mm rounds slotting into the AK47's breaches sent my stomach churning. The young soldier in front of me slipped the safety catch down on to the first notch – automatic fire on the AK47. His face was no longer pissed off, but tense and frightened. I resigned myself to losing the vehicles and turned to Jim to give the signal to get out.

But Jim had other ideas. Smiling like a teddy bear on a grand day out, he reached down the side of the transmission tunnel and pulled his Browning from its holster. Like John Wayne in the OK Corral preparing for a final showdown, he pointed it skywards, paused for a second, then with his left hand pulled back the slider, driving a round into the barrel. 'What the fuck are you doing? Put that down!' I gasped.

'Nah, they're just bluffing,' Jim replied. 'Watch . . .' The Manchester United supporter's weary face cracked into a smile, then a smirk, then an infectious giggle, as Jim waved the pistol at him. 'See, they're more scared than we are.' One by one, the tension in the other faces ranged against us lifted and the barrels drooped as the laughter spread at Jim's grossly disproportionate response. The commander alongside me shouted something in Bosanski as he sensed the mirth on the other side of the vehicle, but nobody paid any attention. A moment later he realised that he'd lost face amongst his undisciplined rabble and, turning away angrily from me, skulked off back up the road.

I watched for a second through the rear-view mirror. 'You are a crazy bastard,' I said to Jim, as soon as I was sure that he was gone. 'What the fuck possessed you to do that?' I said, trying to hide my admiration for his coolness.

'That Man U supporter told me not to worry,' Jim replied. 'Apparently that O/C's a right cunt and his bark's worse than his bite.' Jim tucked the pistol back into the holster as most of the soldiers drifted away, leaving just a couple hung around our vehicle, now relaxed and friendly. The Manchester United supporter grinned at the window and Jim lowered it.

'You go now,' the Bosnian smiled. 'You lucky. You nearly cross front line. Serbs . . .' He gesticulated to the next corner, his English failing him. 'That captain . . .' He gestured up the road, made an O with thumb and forefinger, and pumped it up and down in an internationally recognised sign – 'Fuck him, nobody like him.' I reached over with a pack of Marlboros – we always carried them for such occasions though none of us smoked. He took one and lit it up and I thrust the rest of the packet at him as soon as he had put away his lighter. 'Follow me,' he urged. 'Mines, that's why trees.' He set off the way we had come, occasionally indicating us to keep well away from one verge or the other. Only then did we realise that we had had more than one lucky escape. After our guide had tapped the window to signify the all-clear, we continued down the road in silence, reflecting on our good fortune.

Thereafter, we ensured that we made no further navigational mistakes by avoiding driving on unfamiliar roads after dusk. Others who made similar mistakes in Bosnia were not as lucky. A few weeks later, a British captain took the same wrong turn as us but ran over one of the anti-tank mines and was killed instantly. In March, a group of ODA workers were ambushed by a Mujahideen group just outside the town of Zenica in central Bosnia. They were driven to woodlands a few miles away, forced from their vehicles and made to kneel at the side of the road. Their captors shot one victim dead with a bullet to the back of the head. The others ran for their lives, diving into a freezing river to avoid a hail of lead, and were lucky to escape with only minor wounds.

We were able to establish contact with STEENBOX in Tuzla later on that first trip and thereafter we made the three-day trip to see her every two weeks. The logistics of each trip were in the capable hands of Jon, who loaded up our two vehicles with the comms equipment, supplies, a small armory of an SA-80 rifle and Browning 9mm pistol for each of us, flak-jackets, helmets and spare parts for the vehicles. We took camping gear in case we had to rough it, but slept whenever we could in the mess halls of the various UNPROFOR bases that dotted Bosnia, or in the few hotels that remained open, catering to aid workers and journalists. Jon plus two others accompanied me on every trip, the fourth member taking it in turn to stay at Divulje barracks to operate the fixed KALEX. They always looked forward enthusiastically to the trips up country, the highlight being the traverse of the front line between the Bosnian-Croat forces and the Bosnian-Muslim militia at Gornji Vakuf. Both sides liked to snipe at UNPROFOR vehicles passing through the bombed out town, then to milk the propoganda points by blaming the other. Soft-skinned vehicles such as ours were obliged to travel through the town in convoy under the protection of two Warrior APCs, which returned fire enthusiastically and spectacularly at any suspected sniper position. In the dozen or so traverses of Gornji Vakuf that we made, we were lucky that neither of our vehicles were hit, though we regularly came under fire.

STEENBOX proved a problematic agent to debrief. The information she gave about the intentions of the local militia was not CX but merely the official propaganda of the Bosnian VIth army in Tuzla. At one meeting, just after dusk in a small café in Tuzla, a group of senior Bosnian militiamen walked in and ordered coffee at the bar. As they had not yet noticed us at a small table in the corner, I whispered to STEENBOX 'I'd better get out of here – it'll be dangerous if they see us together. I'll meet you in 20 minutes in the café opposite the town hall.'

'No, no, it's OK,' STEENBOX casually replied. 'They're friends of mine and they already know that you are Kenneth's successor.'

There was clearly no point in pretending to Whitehall officials that information from STEENBOX was CX, as it was being passed to me with the blessing of the VIth army command. They were just using her and me as a direct route to disseminate their propaganda into Whitehall. I sent a series of telegrams to String Vest arguing my case, but he would have none of it.

'We are convinced that STEENBOX is reporting without the knowledge and approval of her superiors,' String Vest wrote in one telegram, without substantiating his position with evidence, 'and her information is valuable CX.' String Vest's intransigence was due to new obligations he was under as the P officer for the Balkans. A year earlier, under pressure from the Treasury, MI6 had admitted a team of specially vetted management consultants to look at productivity. They treated CX and agents as widgets and introduced an 'internal market' system. P4 was given targets for how much CX his section had to produce per month and how many agents it had to cultivate and recruit per quarter. In the last six months of 1993, he had to have CX-producing agents in the Serb, Croat and Muslim factions of Bosnia, and one under cultivation in each. If STEENBOX was written off through my argument, then he would be behind on this target. Rather than do that, he preferred to distribute her propaganda as CX.

String Vest was equally adamant that I should attempt to recruit

John Vucic, a young Australian-Croat who was working in the headquarters of the Bosnian-Croat faction in the town of Posusje. Vucic was a 26-year-old second-generation Croat accountant from Sydney, who worked as a clerk in the headquarters. Vucic had good access and would be a useful source if he could be recruited. String Vest was adamant that I should try. 'As an Australian national, you should play on his Anglophilian interest in cricket to pursue a recruitment,' he wrote in one telegram. String Vest ignored my protests that Vucic was more extreme than Attila the Hun, resolutely defending human rights abuses by his beloved Croatian people. String Vest was blatantly ignoring my judgement as the officer on the ground so as to satisfy targets imposed by faceless management consultants.

'Slow down a bit, Tosh,' I urged. 'Baz'll be effin' and blindin' at you, trying to keep up on these roads.' Tosh lifted off slightly, but I knew that I'd have to remind him again ten minutes later. The heavily laden comms-wagon with its underpowered diesel engine struggled at the best of times to keep up with the powerful V8 Discovery, but with the impetuous Tosh at the wheel Baz and Jon's job would be harder. We were hurrying into Sarajevo with a busy few days ahead of us. I'd been unable to get into the city for the past ten days through a combination of circumstances. The Serb besiegers had shut down completely the sporadically open land route into the city after a tizz with the French UNPROFOR contingent; then the airfield had been shut through heavy fog, and when that lifted, the Hercules that I was about to board at Split went unserviceable on the runway.

DONNE was long overdue for a debrief and String Vest had been sending increasingly irate telegrams of complaint. Also, two senior FCO diplomats from the Balkans desk wanted a meeting with Karadzic in his headquarters in the village of Pale just outside Sarajevo to understand better his negotiating position in the ongoing ICFY talks. As there was no other British diplomatic representation nearby, String Vest asked me to organise the trip. Getting permission to travel from Sarajevo to Pale was not easy, as it meant negotiating a safe passage through the Bosnian-Muslim and Bosnian-Serb front lines, not to mention clearing the trip with the obstreperous French UNPROFOR contingent in Sarajevo. I'd arranged a meeting with them at 1800 that evening, but we'd been held up when a Spanish UNPROFOR APC crashed in front of us, blocking the road.

'We'll never get there unless we leg it,' Tosh answered back.

'Listen, Tosh, this is your last warning, if you don't lift off a bit, I'll have to drive,' I slapped down the sun visor against the low winter sun which was reflecting from the day-old snow that covered the abandoned fields and returned to my briefing notes.

'Shit, Jon's lost it!' shouted Tosh urgently, slamming on the brakes of the Discovery.

I spun round in the seat to see the comms-wagon completing a somersault on to its roof, 50 metres behind us. Tosh brought the Discovery to a juddering halt on the ABS and gunned it into a three-point turn to get back to the accident scene. As we skidded to a halt alongside, Jon and Baz were crawling out of the wreckage, dazed and shaken, but thankfully not hurt. 'Yer bastard,' muttered Baz as he got to his feet and surveyed the remains of the comms-wagon. 'We'd better call the AA.' The vehicle had rolled twice before ending on its roof in a ditch, and even if it could be repaired it would be off the road for several weeks.

'Black ice, there was nothing Baz could do,' Jon apologised to me.

We now had to replan the next few days. 'Tosh, set the HF up,' ordered Jon, 'We'll have to get Jim to fly the spare comms-wagon up from Split.' There was no way that the French would give us permission to travel from Sarajevo to Pale for the Karadzic meeting in a single vehicle, so it was imperative that Jim acted fast. I left Jon and Baz to guard the crippled vehicle against scavengers until the REME (Royal Electrical and Mechanical Engineers) recovery unit arrived, and set off with Tosh in the Discovery for the meeting with the French.

The 48 hours were a whirlwind of meetings to debrief DONNE and sort out the Pale trip. The recalcitrant French commander eventually agreed to allow the diplomatic visit, but not until his decision was eased by two bottles of Scotch. Multiple meetings with the Bosnian-Muslim militia and several cartons of cigarettes eventually secured a safe passage through their lines, though they were deeply opposed to British diplomatic contact with the Serbs. Finally, Major Indic, the temperamental Bosnian-Serb liaison officer in the PTT building, agreed to give us permission to travel onwards through Serbian-held territory to Pale, though, to show who was boss, he made me wait in his office for six hours before he would agree.

602 troop were working just as hard. Jim managed to get the spare comms-wagon on to a Hercules arriving in Sarajevo the evening before the arrival of the two VIPs, a considerable accomplishment because all the incoming flights were supposedly only for humanitarian aid. Baz and Tosh got the Discovery gleaming clean for the visitors, no mean feat given the sparsity of running water at the airfield and its filthy

state from the overland journey up from Split. They'd also got their uniforms cleaned up and boots polished and I too had changed into a clean shirt and jacket and tie. I was in the French operations centre at the airfield, checking with the ops officer that there were no last minute hitches on the route up to Pale, when Jon called me up on the Motorola. 'Rich, if you've got a spare moment, could you come down to the loading bay and give us a hand dealing with the Frogs? I want to get the damaged comms-wagon on the flight back to Split, but I can't understand what they are saying.'

Down at the loading bay, our sad-looking vehicle was waiting to be loaded on the next Hercules, and was in the custody of a French loadmaster sergeant. 'C'est quoi le problème?' I asked. The sergeant explained that only vehicles that could move under their own power were allowed on to the runway, to minimise the time that the aircraft were stationary and thus vulnerable to sniper fire.

'OK, I'll see if the REME can get it running again,' Jon replied as soon as I had translated.

Although the vehicle's bodywork was badly damaged, the running gear was mostly untouched and, with some attention, it might be got moving again. 'It's piston locked,' announced the grubby REME mechanic after a cursory inspection. 'When she went over on her back, oil from the sump leaked past the rings into the combustion chambers. I'll have to blow the oil out.' He removed the gloplugs from each cylinder, then asked Jon to crank the engine on the starter motor. But more oil had leaked past than even the mechanic had imagined and as the starter-motor engaged an angry geyser of black oil shot out of the cylinder head, catching him square in the face. I was not quick enough to duck either and my jacket, tie and shirt were splattered. 'Sorry about that, sir,' grinned the REME grease-monkey, wiping his face on an old rag. No doubt he would have a laugh with his mates over a beer that evening.

There was only an hour and a half until the visitors arrived, and I was far from presentable. Baz dashed back to the PTT building in the Discovery to try to find me a change of clothing, but a frantic search yielded nothing. The worst of the oil scrubbed out of my shirt with swarfega and tissue paper, but my silk tie was beyond redemption. Later that morning I was forced to meet the VIPs with my shirt open at the neck. It was not appropriate dress for a diplomatic meeting but the more important objective was to get the two VIPs to Pale safely and back for their return flight that evening.

The meeting with Karadzic and his henchmen went smoothly enough, and that evening with the VIPs dispatched back to Zagreb, I typed out a telegram to P4 on the portable PC. The KALEX HF radio had not yet been swapped from the damaged comms-wagon into the replacement vehicle, so John manually encrypted the telegram and beamed it back to MI6's Poundon communication centre using the satellite transmitter. An hour later, String Vest, who must have been working at his desk late that evening, sent me a return telegram. 'Congratulations on setting up a difficult meeting under what must have been very trying circumstances,' he wrote.

In February 1994 an uneasy ceasefire was brokered by UNPROFOR between the warring factions and the Bosnian Serbs paused their indiscriminate shelling and sniping of the city. Sarajevo was temporarily more or less safe and, coincidentally, I had a rush of requests to visit me, amongst them String Vest. 'I'd love to have come out earlier, and accompanied you on one of your up-country trips,' he told me over dinner in a comfortable Split restaurant, 'but I was just far too busy.'

Shortly after String Vest had returned to London, Head Office took the decision to close BAP. Now that Bosnia had been recognised as an independent state and Sarajevo was returning to some semblance of normality, the FCO opened an embassy, incongruously over a mafia-run casino, and had established diplomatic relations. It was the right time to run MI6 operations out of the embassy under diplomatic cover and end the charade of my 'civil adviser' fig-leaf. Personnel had already selected a suitable H/SAR, and she was nearing the end of her language training.

I was relieved when the telegram arrived in mid-April 1994 announcing that the new H/SAR would be flying out to Sarajevo in early May. SBO/1 recommended that her diplomatic cover not be tainted through direct contact with me, as he rightly suspected that I was well-blown to the Bosnian secret police, so I was not required to show her around her new patch.

My only task therefore was to oversee with Jon the closure of the station in the Divulje barracks in the first week of May. String Vest suggested that I drive the Discovery and small station items back to London overland rather than incur the expense of sending out the S&D C-130 to pick it up; 602 troop stayed behind for a few more days to pack up the two remaining vehicles, the original comms-wagon now repaired, and they followed with the KALEX's and other gear.

Although I enjoyed aspects of the posting, particularly working with 602 troop, the lack of guidance from a more experienced hand made it frustrating. I needed a break from the constant proximity of bombs, bullets and blood, and I was looking forward to a holiday with Sarah. She had had a cancer scare a few months earlier, though fortunately she was by now out of hospital.

Driving up the spectacular cliff-top road that runs up the Dalmation coast from Split to Trieste on the first leg of my return home, I stopped off at the top of one of the highest cliffs just as the sun was spectacularly setting over the sea. There was still one more task remaining to complete the station closure; reaching into the back of the Discovery, I pulled out Roberts's gun collection and hand-grenade and threw them as far as possible into the deep water of the Adriatic.

10.

CHEMICAL THERAPY

On my return the office had moved from the dim and anonymous Century House to spectacular new premises on the Albert Embankment. The state-of-the-art Terry Farrell-designed office block occupied a prime site in central London on the south bank of the Thames, facing Westminster Palace and Whitehall, and its siting and architecture presented a radically revamped image for the service. Gigantic shoulders towering over a glowering head in the form of its central gazebo, it was like a Terminator, belligerently daring anybody to challenge its authority. It was supposedly built to an official budget of £85 million, but everybody in the office knew that in reality it had cost nearly three times as much. We were warned in the weekly newsletter that discussion of the cost over-run would be considered a serious breach of the OSA and would be dealt with accordingly.

The aggressive facade was appropriate, for MI6 was facing the most serious threats to its hitherto unchallenged autonomy since its inception. It had recently been 'avowed', or publicly acknowledged to exist, by the Queen at her speech opening the new session of Parliament in October 1993. New legislation came into effect in December 1994 bringing a modicum of accountability to the service. A select group of MPs won limited powers to scrutinise the budget and objectives of the service, but were not allowed to investigate MI6 operations, examine paperwork or cross-examine officers. The changes yielded a token of public accountability to the reluctant service, but nothing like the oversight exercised by the US Congress over American intelligence agenices, or even by the Russian parliament over their services. The Treasury was also for the first time allowed to make basic investigations into the service's efficiency and had wielded its knife, forcing the service to make hitherto unheard-of redundancies.

Many familiar faces departed the service during my absence. Even the Chief, Sir Colin McColl was ejected, along with the clubbable but lethargic old-guard directors. They had been jostling for the top job and the office rumour was that one had burst into tears when he learned that he would not inherit the post. Instead, a new, younger breed of managers was appointed, headed by David Spedding as Chief. A pushy Middle East specialist, at 49 he was the youngest-ever officer to reach the top. He forged his reputation during the Gulf War which broke out when he was deputy head of the Middle East controllerate. The controller refused to return from holiday when the war started, and Spedding siezed the opportunity to grab the reins of power, leaving an indelible impression on Whitehall. He promoted an equally thrusting bunch to senior management positions.

The new leadership reflected the new building – younger, meaner, more aggressive. Perhaps it was a necessary change to combat the financial challenges and intensified public scrutiny of the new service, but would it be wise in the people-business of spying? It was with a mixture of curiosity and trepidation that I walked the mile from my home to Vauxhall Cross to start my first day in the new building on a drizzly June morning.

Personnel department gave me ten days off after returning from Bosnia, happily spent sorting out my garden which had fallen into bedraggled despair during my absence. The experience in Bosnia left me feeling remote from the egotistical and brazen hurly-burly of London and I had not felt inclined to socialise much except with Sarah. My solitude was disturbed only by a brief visit from Fowlecrooke to inform me of my next job. He offered me an undercover slot with the UN weapon inspection teams in Iraq, but I wanted my next overseas post to be a normal one, so until something came up he offered me a Head Office slot in the PTCP (Production-Targeting Counter-Proliferation) department. The section gathered intelligence on and disrupted the attempts of pariah nations – mainly Iran, Iraq, Libya and Pakistan – to obtain biological, chemical and nuclear weapons of mass destruction. I wanted to go to the department immediately after the IONEC, but the job had gone to Bart. It was pleasing to now get an opportunity there, and to get out of the East European controllerate.

There was no friendly guard waiting in the entry lobby to greet staff and check photo IDs as in Century House. Security checking was done electronically and to enter the main building, we had to pass through a row of six perspex, time-locked security doors, stacked like the eggs of a giant insect. A small queue stretched behind them. When my turn came, a swipe of my card through the slot and the entry of my personal code, six-nine-two-one, illuminated a small green light by the slot, and the perspex door slid open with a *Star Trek*-like swish. I stepped into the narrow capsule, my shoulders brushing the sides. A pressure pad on the floor established that there was only one occupant, the door swished shut behind me, then the door in front opened, releasing me into the inner lobby.

Like Century House, the interior of the new building felt like a hotel but the shabby Intourist style had been discarded in favour of flashy American Marriott decor. Soft fluorescent light from recessed port-holes in the high ceiling illuminated a hard-wearing ivory marble floor, set off by the matt grey slate of the walls. Two giant columns dominated the hall, containing banks of rapid modern lifts. There would be no more impatient, muttering queues waiting for under-sized lifts in this building. Around the edge of the columns were inset comfortable black leather bench seats. To the right, natural light filtered from a small atrium that opened, by a tall light well, to the sky above. It was filled with large and garish plastic imitations of sub-tropical trees. Several marbled hallways led off from the sides of the central atrium. I was 20 minutes early for the appointment with my new line manager, so I set off to explore.

A few steps down the first hallway revealed the new library. The Century House library was a dismal affair, consisting of metal racks filled with ancient books and ragged filing boxes full of magazines. The new version was much smarter and brighter, with expensive-looking reading tables and swish sliding book racks. Jenny, the cheerful librarian, smiled a welcome from behind her desk. 'How are you?' she greeted me enthusiastically. 'How was Bosnia?' She explained that she had been promoted to chief librarian at the time of the move but Sandra, her older and therefore more expensive superior, was made redundant. 'I felt so sorry for her,' murmured Jenny. 'Twenty years in Century House, and personnel department wouldn't even give her a visitor's pass so that she could see inside the new building. She was dreadfully upset.'

Jenny stamped the distribution list on the morning's newspapers.'And have you seen what they did to the cleaners?' Jenny asked. She showed me a recent article in the *Mirror*. In a cynical attempt to save money, personnel sacked the 47 cleaning staff employed in Century House, then re-employed them on a lower-paid contract basis at Vauxhall Cross. In an unprecedented move, the justifiably furious cleaners took MI6 to an employment tribunal with the help of their local MP, Labour back-bencher Kate Hoey. MI6 used every trick in the book to deny them this basic human right, claiming that even the identities of cleaning staff were too secret to be made public in a court hearing. Eventually, after a long and expensive legal battle, they were granted access to a tribunal, and the *Mirror* showed a comical photograph of the cleaning ladies taking their stand, only a row of sensible shoes visible beneath the screen which they were forced to stand behind. They quickly won the case, compensation and their jobs back. It was an embarrassing setback for the new directors of MI6, not only publicly but also in terms of their standing within the service. They embarked on a damage-limitation exercise, complaining in the internal weekly newsletter and in public comments that the Treasury had forced the cuts 'upon them'. It never crossed their minds to admit that they had simply ignored basic employment law and used the OSA to cover up their mismanagement.

Walking back across the lobby to the lifts, I spied my old IONEC colleague Bart entering the building, carrying a squash racket in one hand and using the other to push the remnants of a bun into his mouth. "Allo, mate,' he grinned, flicking away with the back of his hand a currant which had adhered to the side of his mouth. 'You've been in Bosnia,' he continued, unabashed.

I pointed to his squash racket. 'This exercise business, is this some cover job?'

'Nah, I've really taken up some sport – have you seen the squash court?' Bart showed me through a steel door next to the library exit and through to a small grey-carpeted gymnasium with rowing machines and weights. A portable CD player was thumping out dance music and a large, plump-thighed woman dressed in a too-small, polka-dot leotard was sweating away in time to it on an exercise bike, the seat of which was set several notches too low. 'Phwoar,' murmured Bart, without a trace of sarcasm, 'not bad eh?'

Bart showed me around the rest of the sports complex. The building's architect originally envisaged using the space for a swimming pool, but the directors decided that the extravagance would attract adverse publicity. Some ex-military officers lobbied hard for an indoor pistol range, but eventually commonsense prevailed and the space was used for an indoor five-a-side soccer and badminton sports hall.

I had already spent too long looking around the new facilities and it was time to be getting upstairs to meet my new section. 'So what's PTCP like?' I asked Bart, knowing that he had just departed the section to start pre-posting training for an assignment to Hungary.

'You'll be working for Badger. He likes a few beers.' Bart patted his stomach knowledgeably, his erudite praise reassuring me that I would be joining a happy section. I left Bart to get on with his squash match and made my way over to the lifts.

The refreshingly fast lift sped me up to the fourth floor and the doors opened on to a small lobby with corporate grey carpet tiles and bare white walls, like a 1980s merchant bank. For a second or two I studied the small coloured floor plan conveniently placed by the lift exit, then set off down the labyrinth of corridors to my designated room.

The open-plan PTCP office overlooked the building's spacious open-air terrace and the Thames, and accommodated half a dozen officers and secretaries. A few looked up inquisitively at the newcomer, while others kept their heads down in their files or computer screens. The officer nearest the door stood up and stretched out his hand. 'Hello, you must be Richard Tomlinson,' he said. His tightly curling grey-blond hair was thinning savagely at the temples but still grew thickly on the forehead and at the sides, creating three broad stripes of fur-like hair. I presumed that he must be Badger. 'Sit yourself down. I'll explain what you'll be doing.'

Badger had entered the service later in his career than usual. He obtained a PhD in genetics at Imperial College, worked as a research scientist, then as a management consultant, before joining the service in his mid-30s. He was posted first to to Nigeria, then Costa Rica. Badger's enthusiasm and well-rounded work experience made him an effective officer but he was not destined to be a high-flyer in the office – he was not enough of a back-stabber. 'I want you to take over the running of BELLHOP, the biggest operation in the section,' Badger told me enthusiastically.

After the 1985–89 Iran–Iraq war when Iraqi chemical weapons killed many thousands of Iranian soldiers, the Iranians wanted to build their own arsenal of chemical and biological weapons, but did not have the indigenous capability. They needed to acquire the technology, equipment and precursor chemicals from technically more advanced countries. Prohibitions on the export of such materials under international convention did not deter the Iranians from attempting to acquire the equipment clandestinely. Any Iranian national blatantly attempting to buy banned equipment would instantly attract attention from western intelligence agencies, so they ruled out that option. Instead, they set about recruiting a network of western traders and engineers who would do their dirty work for them, either unaware of what they were getting themselves into or turning a blind eye to its illegality. 'Your task,' Badger explained, 'is to inveigle your way into this network under cover then meet and cultivate the Iranian ringmasters.' From then on, I could take the operation where opportunity led. Badger's hope was to use the infiltration to gather intelligence, perhaps recruiting one of the Iranians if the opportunity arose, then disrupt and delay their programme. He tossed me a hefty pink dossier, labelled P/54248. 'Read that and come back to me when you've got a plan.'

This was going to be fun, I thought to myself. Loads of freedom to design my own operation, a really worthwhile objective and a good boss to work under. I set about reading the file on BELLHOP enthusiastically.

Reading an MI6 file can be a slow and laborious job. The papers are arranged in chronological order but that is the extent of their organisation. They contain a vast jumble of information from many sources. Telegrams, letters, police SB reports, copies of military and DSS records of individuals mentioned in the file, titbits from GCHQ, contact reports, surveillance photographs. Many papers cross-reference to other files, so making sense of them means a trog down to the central registry to pull the file. One document in the file might be only peripherally relevant to the case, the next might be crucially important. It is easy to miss a vital titbit and so lose track of the big picture if not concentrating hard. It took me a week before I had ploughed through the six volumes of files and felt confident to design a plan.

The file opened with the detention at Heathrow airport in the late 1980s of Nahoum Manbar, a Nice-based Israeli businessman whom MI6 suspected had close but thorny links with Mossad. Customs and Excise, in a routine search of his briefcase, found papers and plans that appeared to describe a process to produce mustard gas. Manbar was handed over to police custody,. He claimed in his interview that he was an agricultural engineer and that the formulas related to the production of a new insecticide. Although these protestations of innocence were scarcely credible, there was not enough evidence of wrong-doing to charge him with any crime. He was denied entry to Britain, put on the first plane back to Nice and MI6 asked the DST (*Direction de la Surveillance du Territoire, the French internal intelligence service*) to keep an eye on him.

Through telephone intercepts on Manbar's home and information from other sources, the DST established that in 1988 Manbar obtained the plans for a mustard gas plant which he sold at handsome profit to Dr Tehrani Fahd, a Vienna-based Iranian diplomat, who was in reality a senior Iranian intelligence officer and the ringmaster entrusted with the task of building up Iran's chemical weapons programme. These plans, however, were just the start. Fahd now wanted the bits of specialist equipment and chemicals needed actually to build the plant. He tasked Manbar to help.

Although Manbar was eager for the millions of dollars that completion of the deal would bring, he was initially reluctant to get further involved as he knew that he was getting into murkier and deeper legal waters. While he was considering his options, Mossad discovered Manbar's contacts with Fahd and, according to the DST's telephone transcripts, ordered him to a meeting at the Israeli embassy in Paris. There was no intelligence on what was said at the meeting but the upshot of it was that Manbar embarked on the project with Fahd with mysteriously renewed enthusiasm. He set about finding a cut-out, somebody he could rely upon to carry out unwittingly the possibly illegal work necessary to acquire the equipment requested by the Iranians.

Through one of his business contacts Manbar met Mrs Joyce Kiddie, a British businesswoman who lived in the village of Girton, just outside Cambridge. Kiddie had worked for most of her life as a secretary at a local stationery and office supplies company; but when the managing director, by coincidence a former MI6 agent, retired, he put the small company up for sale. Kiddie, by then in her 40s, twice married with a couple of daughters, daringly used her life savings and a bank loan to buy the company. She proved a natural businesswoman and within a few years started diversifying the business. Kiddie developed contacts in China, initially in the stationery business, but then in chemicals and pharmaceuticals.

Manbar was impressed by her versatility and diligence, and set about cultivating her to become his cut-out. The DST picked up Manbar's increasingly frequent telephone conversations with Kiddie and tipped off MI6. PTCP obtained a FLORIDA warrant to intercept her telephone and an ACANTHA warrant to intercept her mail, and the Cambridgeshire SB were asked to keep an eye on her. Manbar started trusting her with increasingly bizarre jobs. Once he asked her to find and buy a suitable American-Jewish NBA basketball player who would be prepared to emigrate to Israel to bolster the Israeli national team. She passed this and other tests with flying colours. By the middle of 1993 Manbar was confident that she was reliable and trustworthy and was the right person to introduce to Fahd.

Kiddie was delighted with the introduction to a new and lucrative trading partner and flew to meet Fahd in Austria. In the Vienna Hilton, Fahd asked her to buy a couple of tonnes of thionyl chloride, a 'building-block' chemical used in the manufacture of many legitimate products but also an essential basic ingredient for the manufacture of mustard gas and nerve agents such as sarin. There was nothing illegal about the purchase – as long as it did not end up in the wrong hands it was not breaking any international laws.

After six months of research, phone calls and two trips to remote parts of China, Kiddie completed the thionyl chloride shipment to Iran. Fahd was delighted and decided to trust her with a bit more responsibility. Now that he had the plans and a proven source of the main ingredients, he asked her to procure some of the equipment for the plant. This, however, was not as easy as the relatively straightforward acquisition of the chemicals.

Chemical weapons plants are not complicated and need not be particularly large. A nerve gas plant can be built into a space the size of a living-room, or even into the back of a truck. A mustard gas plant requires a bit more space, but a facility the size of a small house could provide a militarily significant production capability. The liquid chemicals used in the recipe are very corrosive and must be contained entirely in glass-lined apparatus – similar to larger versions of the equipment used in school chemistry lessons. Just like in school chemistry apparatus, the glass components – stopcocks, tubes and flasks – clip together, then are physically supported by a scaffold framework. Because of the danger of leaks, the building in which the apparatus is contained must be sealed and force-ventilated with high-volume extractor fans. The extracted air is driven up scrubbers – basically polypropylene chimneys filled with glass marbles down which sodium hydroxide trickles. The gases are absorbed by the sodium hydroxide on the surface of the marbles and form a harmless liquid that can be disposed of safely. The sale of all equipment of this sort is subject to international controls and it is difficult for certain countries, especially Iran, Iraq and Libya, to openly purchase any of it, even if destined for entirely innocent purposes. Fahd gave Kiddie the blueprints for some of the simpler pieces of equipment and asked her to see what she could do.

Kiddie accepted the new assignment with relish but found that she was out of her depth. She had no technical training and was unable to understand the specifications and drawings of the equipment. She needed help from somebody with an engineering background, so she recruited Albert Constantine, a 60-year-old former merchant seaman and engineer and an old friend of her first husband. Constantine was one of life's unfortunate souls whose career seemed to disintegrate around him whichever way he turned. He had started work in the Durham coalmines at 16 but was made redundant when the mining industry started to falter. He obtained an apprenticeship in the Tyneside shipyards, but he'd picked another doomed industry and shortly after he was qualified he was made redundant again. He went to sea with the merchant navy and had just qualified as a First Mate when he was seriously injured in a car crash. As a result of his injuries, Constantine lost his merchant navy medical certificate and that career too. He drifted around doing simple engineering work for many years and then, in his late 50s, washed up as a commodity trader with a import-export trading company in London.

When Kiddie asked Constantine to help, he was delighted. He was struggling to make ends meet from his low-paid job, and the extra cash would come in handy. A few months later, in April 1994, Kiddie and Constantine met up in South Mimms motorway service station, just north of London. Unbeknown to them, their meeting was under surveillance. Two PTCP officers, posing as travelling salesmen, sat at an adjacent table, recording their conversation with a sophisticated directional microphone mounted in a briefcase. From that surveillance and the telephone intercepts of Constantine, it became apparent that he too was unable to understand the technical specifications provided by Fahd. But there was no way that he was going to let on to Kiddie just yet – he badly wanted to be in on the deal.

Normally if MI6 wanted to worm its way into a piece of quasi-criminal activity such as Kiddie's dealings with Fahd, they would try to cultivate and then recruit one of the key individuals, such as Constantine or Kiddie. But Badger was adamant that Kiddie would panic if approached by MI6 and pull out of the deal, denying us the opportunity of disrupting the Iranian operation. He ruled out cultivating Constantine, too. He was more level-headed, but was loyal to his friends and he would probably tell Kiddie. Badger was adamant that the only means to get into the operation was for me to approach Kiddie or Constantine under cover, win their confidence and trust, and hope that they would recommend me to Manbar and Fahd.

It would be difficult to get alongside Kiddie directly. First, she worked alone at home, so was not easily accessible via intermediaries. Secondly, telephone intercepts showed that she was wary of strangers and only trusted them if strongly recommended by somebody she knew. I would have to get alongside Constantine first, then hope that he would introduce me to Kiddie.

Delving into the files turned up Constantine's home address in Southampton on the south coast of England. A quick recce trip on my motorbike revealed that the house next door to his terraced cottage was vacant. 'Why don't you rent it and get to know him as a neighbour?' Badger suggested. Returning to Southampton to visit the estate agent the next week, I found it was already too late; a young couple had just moved in. I had to find another plan.

Tracing Constantine's employer through the CCI computer fortunately threw up a positive lead – there was already a file on Bari Trading, a trading company in the posh London area of Mayfair. The managing director was being run by H/UKP, the head of the Iranian natural cover section. A quick call on the PAX and at their next debrief the managing director agreed to take me on temporarily in Bari Trading. He would be the only person in the company conscious to the operation, so I would have to get together a cover story which would deceive the other employees.

SB05, the operational security officer for the PTCP section, agreed to let me use the Huntley alias that was developed for my trip to Russia. Strictly, a fresh alias should be used for every operation but this rule was relaxed to save time and money. SB05 thought the Huntley alias was unlikely to have been compromised in Russia and the operations were geographically unrelated. Besides, Huntley already had a national insurance card, simplifying the paperwork for Bari Trading. SB05 insisted that I put up a submission to the new Foreign Secretary, Malcolm Rifkind, as the operation could be embarrassing if uncovered. Submissions were supposed to ensure that potentially sensitive operations were legally accountable, but there was no independent scrutiny and so the only check on the judgement and honesty of the drafting officer was the diligence of the Foreign Secretary. Writing submissions for Douglas Hurd was a time-consuming task, requiring flawless reasoning and perfect prose, but Rifkind was already renowned for looking favourably on whatever MI6 put in front of him.

Even back in my familiar Huntley skin, there was still a lot of preparatory work needed. From study of the telephone transcripts, we knew that Kiddie and Constantine needed a qualified chemical engineer, somebody who could easily interpret the technical drawings they had in their possession, and who would know where to source the components. Two weeks later, after a lot of study in Imperial University's chemical engineering library, I was working alongside Constantine in Bari Trading, just a stone's throw from the Hyde Park Hilton Hotel, with the cover that I was an Anglo-Argentine chemical engineer who wished to start a new career in chemical commodity dealing. My fictional father was allegedly the manager of a Bauer plant in Buenos Aires and friend of the Bari managing director, who had agreed to give me a six-week secondment so that I could learn the business of import-export trading. The story seemed to satisfy Constantine and the other occupants of the dingy, cluttered second-floor office: Patricia, a pretty young Guyanese-born Anglo-Indian and Fazad, a chain-smoking Iranian in his 60s. Constantine, a friendly and helpful character, loaded me down with books and papers on 'Bills of Lading' and 'Import Export Duties'. The work was tedious but I was not there for fun. My objective was to befriend Constantine and so, without going suspiciously over the top, whenever an opportunity arose for a chat, a tea break or an evening pint of beer with him, I would take it up.

Meanwhile Badger and his crew were continuing to work on other aspects of the case. One morning Debbie, a buxom transcriber, rushed into the office carrying a pink FLORIDA report. Normally she would put transcripts into the internal mail system so they would arrive on our desks a day or so later. But this transcript needed Badger's urgent attention. It was Kiddie ringing from her home in Girton to Fahd in Vienna to arrange an urgent meeting to discuss details of the contract. They arranged to meet two days later in the lobby of the Hilton in central Amsterdam. The transcript showed that Fahd intended to give her some more documentation concerning the components for the plant.

Badger leaped at the opportunity. If we could eavesdrop on the conversation, we could learn about Fahd's intentions and the state of the Iranian chemical weapons programme. More important, though, were the documents. A detailed look at the plans for the plant would be invaluable. Badger ordered the whole PTCP section to drop whatever else they were doing and get cracking on this urgent task.

Kiddie planned to fly in and out of Stansted airport, near her home in Cambridgeshire, to Schipol airport. Badger got on to Customs and Excise at Stansted and arranged for her to be searched on her return to the UK. To avoid arousing her suspicion, Customs suggested searching all the other passengers and placing an undercover officer in the queue to plant a rumour that they were looking for drugs.

Listening into the meeting in the hotel lobby would be more difficult and would require the cooperation of the Dutch secret service. Fortunately, the BVD (*Binnenlands Villigheidsdienst*) is one of MI6's closest allies overseas. They are regarded as reliable and efficient, and will usually drop everything to help MI6 on an urgent job. MI6 is still a powerful player in the hierarchy of world intelligence services, so smaller services scurry to help out where they can, knowing that it will give them leverage to request a returned favour at a later date. Badger sent a FLASH high-priority telegram to the MI6 station in The Hague and got the wheels turning immediately.

The junior MI6 officer in The Hague station, HAG/2, drove over to

Amsterdam with the BVD liaison officer to check out the possibilities of bugging the meeting. Walking into the Hilton lobby, they found a large fountain in the centre of a number of tables, chairs and sofas and HAG/2 realised that it would be difficult to get a good-quality audible 'take' of the meeting. There was no way to predict which table Kiddie and Fahd would sit at, bugging every table would be expensive and time-consuming, and the sound from the fountain was just the sort of gentle white noise which is excellent for swamping microphones tuned to pick up distant conversations. These problems did not daunt the energetic BVD, however. They pulled out all the stops to put into place a complicated and labour-intensive operational plan.

Any guest of the Amsterdam Hilton hoping to enjoy a nice lunch in the lobby on Tuesday, 7 February 1995 was in for a disappointment. The attractive fountain was turned off, a prominent sign announcing that it was shut down 'for maintenance', and most of the lobby was closed down with rope barriers for 'essential cleaning'. As with most Hiltons worldwide, the hotel security manager was an agent of the local secret service. The BVD asked him to temporarily rearrange the lobby, where a single vacant table was wired for sound. A couple of 'businessmen' occupied it to stop it being taken by incidental passers-by and all the remaining tables were filled with other businessmen, all BVD and MI6 officers, amongst them Badger, HAG/2 and a couple of other members of the PTCP section. Everything was in place as Kiddie touched down. She was tailed as she took the shuttle bus into central Amsterdam.

The meticulously orchestrated plan started to go wrong as soon as Kiddie arrived at the hotel. She failed to notice the two businessmen finish their meeting and leave, vacating the wired table. Instead, Kiddie took one look at the busy coffee-room, decided that she didn't like what she saw and, calm as you like, walked over to the roped off area, unclipped the rope and sat down in the area which had been 'closed for cleaning'. There must have been a lot of Dutch expletives discreetly spat into a large number of coffee cups that morning. It was an embarassing cock-up for them in front of their MI6 guests. The BVD did their best to remedy the situation. An officer with a briefcase fitted with a directional microphone made his way to a table not too far from Kiddie in the roped-off area. When Fahd arrived and joined her ten minutes later, he managed to get some take, but despite computer enhancement the tape proved inaudible. All we got from the meeting was a couple of surveillance photographs, taken by the briefcase camera of one of the businessmen, of Fahd handing over a thick sheaf of papers.

Fortunately, Badger's frantic couple of days of planning were not entirely unrewarded as the other part of the plan worked far more smoothly. As planned, all the disembarking passengers at Stansted were held up and searched. Kiddie was near the back of the queue, so all the preceding passengers were inconvenienced. Eventually, it was her turn. While one officer diligently searched her carry-on luggage, distracting her by paying particular attention to personal and intimate items, another went through her briefcase. As soon as the officer found Fahd's documents, he slipped them through a photocopier discreetly mounted under the search bench, then quickly replaced the originals in her briefcase. As we'd hoped, they were excellent intelligence and an aid to my efforts to bait Constantine into introducing me directly to Kiddie.

I was at my desk at Vauxhall Cross a couple of days later, studying the documents and trying to understand the technical specifications of the equipment, when my personal line rang. It was Sarah. 'Hello darling, how's Moneypenny?' she laughed. But I knew straightaway that something was wrong. Her voice was weak and strained and she was putting up a brave front.

'Something's the matter, isn't it?' I asked quietly.

'Yes . . .' she replied. 'It's back.'

Sarah had been in for a further check-up that morning. The doctors had found that the cancer had spread into her lymph system and she had been readmitted to hospital immediately for an urgent course of chemotherapy. She didn't say so, but I knew from her voice that the prognosis was very poor. She died two months later.

I put the phone down and held my head in my hands. I felt a numbing sickness and wanted to cry. My work seemed irrelevant and I discarded the papers on my desk with contempt. I needed to get out into some fresh air. It was nearly 12.30 and the office bar would be open any moment. I never normally drank at lunchtime but today would be an exception.

I took a pint of Fosters on to the terrace outside the bar and sat down in the corner on one of the wooden benches overlooking the Thames and the Houses of Parliament. It was a spring day, the sun was out and a freshening breeze was coming in off the river. But thinking of Sarah in hospital, then about the girl blown to bits in Bosnia, it was difficult to stop myself crying and I had to put my head in my hands before I could compose myself. I knew there was no point in staying at my desk that afternoon. Badger was on the balcony with some colleagues and I made my way over to ask permission for the afternoon off. 'Is it anything you can tell me about?' he asked.

'Not at the moment' I replied.

Back at my desk the following morning, I was doing my best to concentrate on the job and was making headway with understanding the plans of the chemical plant. The phone rang. It was personnel department wanting to see me as soon as possible. With a heavy heart, I arranged an appointment for the next day. I didn't know what they wanted but it was never a pleasure seeing them.

Ostensibly, personnel department were responsible for staffing decisions in MI6 and it was they who took the decision to post me to Bosnia. But their manoeuvres, reasons for decisions and policies were always shrouded in intrigue and secrecy, buried in a network of unofficial soundings from line-managers and secret deals over boozy lunches. Because they were career spies with no training in personnel management they operated like a mini secret service within the secret service and could not resist applying their tradecraft to do their temporary job. They treated us like agents, subjecting us to the shallow bluff and false flattery which they were accustomed to use with Nigerian generals and Brazilian governors. Personnel did not even allow us to read or countersign the minutes of our own interviews with them, yet these notes formed an important part of our personal records, upon which key posting decisions were taken. This secrecy gave *carte blanche* for a personnel officer to make or break a fellow officer's career as there was no check against glaring personality clashes, favouritism or cronyism. The general mistrust of personnel department was exacerbated by the rapid turnover of staff in the job; they could post themselves to the best overseas jobs as soon as they became available.

It was therefore with trepidation that I took the lift up to the eighth floor to meet my new personnel officer. Because of his small stature and aggressive self-promotion, his previous department had nicknamed him 'Poison Dwarf', after a character in a popular computer game.

'What were you doing out on the terrace the other day?' PD/2's voice was accusatory, belligerent. He skipped through the normal pleasantries without any conviction and obviously he had carefully planned the ambush. 'You were seen out there, drinking a beer on your own, ignoring everybody. Are you interested in your job? Do you want to work here?' After such a gratuitously unpleasant attack, I could not bring myself to talk to Poison Dwarf about Sarah. Even if he did feign sympathy and understanding, it would not be welcome. 'Is there anything you wish to discuss with me?'

'No, not at all,' I replied disinterestedly.

'Well, I've just got your SAF covering your time in Bosnia. P4 has given you a Box 4, and frankly I am not surprised. Your performance was dismal.' Poison Dwarf tossed the brown manilla staff appraisal form down on to the coffee-table between us. 'Read it, and explain yourself,' he ordered.

Reading the report left me sickened and let down by String Vest. When he visited me in Bosnia, he made no adverse comment about my performance, and his report reeked of a set-up. He went out of his way to find criticisms of my performance and ignored all the good work that I had done, making a great issue about my failure to wear a necktie during the VIP meeting with Karadzic.

'I find it incredible that you didn't wear a tie,' grumbled Poison Dwarf in the background.

I chose to ignore him and pressed on with String Vest's vitriol. He heavily criticised me for failing to visit and debrief DONNE in Sarajevo after a crucial meeting of the Bosnian-Muslim leadership. Undoubtedly DONNE would probably have provided some useful CX on the meeting, but String Vest conveniently ignored the closure of Sarajevo airport and the impossibility of reaching the city overland. I'd had a rough deal by comparison with my IONEC colleagues who were still preparing for their first posts. Spencer was on German language training for assignment to a four-man station in Vienna. Castle, as ever with an eye on his bank balance and living standards, was lined up for a posting to Geneva where even the junior officer received a substantial house with swimming pool and a generous living allowance, and was on a year-long French course. Barking had elected to become an Arab specialist and was on a two-year Arabic course in Cairo. Forton was also learning French in preparation for a post to Brussels, Bart was learning Hungarian and Hare was learning Spanish in preparation for the number two job in Chile. None of them were yet in post, and even when they arrived, they would not be expected to do much more during their first six months than learn the ropes of the local community. The contrast with my own posting was stark but String Vest had not made the slightest concession.

The report reeked of a stitch-up by personnel and had probably been orchestrated by the devious Fowlecrooke, but I could never prove anything. My best response was just to put the incident behind me and work hard in my new job in PTCP section. Badger was an honest and ethical boss and Fowlecrooke would never dare pressure him to mark me down.

I got up and left Poison Dwarf's office, hoping that he would soon thrust his way into a good overseas posting so that I wouldn't have to deal with him again.

On joining PTCP section, I found the number of telephone intercepts they ran eye-opening. Usually there would be two or three FLORIDA reports landing in my in-tray every day and that was just for the projects I worked on. Other officers in the section, working on different projects, received many reports which I did not see. The number of telephone warrants MI6 had could be gauged from the size of UKZ, the section responsible for transcribing the intercepts. Based in an office at 60 Vauxhall Bridge Road, abbreviated to VBR in the service, UKZ numbered around 20 officers in total, of which the buxom Debbie was one. They worked closely with OND, a detachment of vetted British Telecom engineers seconded to MI6 to set up the intercepts. Each UKZ officer was a talented linguist, often the master of five or six difficult languages, and worked at state-of-the-art computers much admired by visiting liaison services. On a good day, they could process 20 or so conversations, though less if the language was difficult or the take quality poor.

Under the terms of the 1975 IOCA (Interception of Communications Act) a warrant should be given only if the target is breaking UK law or if the interception yields intelligence. Under these terms, I felt no compunction about reading the transcripts of an Iranian terrorist or a Russian intelligence officer. But we had many intercepts running which did not fall into either category. Even our intercepts on Kiddie and Constantine were not within its spirit – they would break UK law only if they exported proliferation material from the country, and never once did we issue a CX report as a result of one of their telephone transcriptions. Perhaps what they were doing was slightly amoral but it was not our job to pass judgement on that. Unlike every other country in the western world, warrants for telephone intercepts in Britain are signed not by a judge but by the Home Secretary or Foreign Secretary, explaining why the intelligence services could obtain so many warrants.

MI6 abused the privilege of the IOCA in other ways too. The transcribers in VBR were supposed to ignore personal chit-chat and condense only relevant operational intelligence into the pink FLORIDA reports for distribution to Vauxhall Cross. This obligation enabled MI6 successfully to persuade the Treasury that it was necessary to keep the transcribers isolated in VBR, rather than incorporating them into the new building. Nevertheless, one day a colleague threw a pink FLORIDA report on my desk, chuckling, 'Have a good laugh at this!' The target was a transvestite in his spare time and the FLORIDA reported his intimate conversation, line by line, with his boyfriend. Admittedly, it was an amusing document but it added nothing to our understanding of the operation and was a clear breach of the act.

Meanwhile BELLHOP had just taken a new and interesting twist. Badger, as overall head of the operation, was responsible for its coordination with foreign liaison services. The extent to which information on the operation was shared depended on the perceived trustworthiness of the other intelligence service and the extent to which they could bring to the table useful intelligence of their own. MI6 were always warm and cordial with CIA liaison because the Americans had such fabulous resources. Badger's relationship with the DST on BELLHOP was also good and they cooperated energetically if they were asked to help out. But Badger could never establish the same level of easy cooperation with Mossad. It was always a puzzle why they were so uncooperative, for we expected them to be keenly interested in penetrating the attempts of Iran, their most feared enemy, to obtain chemical weapons. But meetings with them were tense affairs, with little given away by either side. The section suspected that Mossad had another hidden agenda that we were not privy to. This suspicion was reinforced when Badger showed them copies of the weapons plant that we had obtained from the search of Kiddie at Stansted. They feigned interest, but it was not convincing and Badger came away suspicious that the Israelis already had their own copies.

Further clues came from the Warsaw station. Examination of the plans by MOD experts established that the plant was an old Polish design, a relic from their Cold War chemical weapons programme. Badger asked H/WAR to find out how the plans could have fallen into Manbar's hands. The Polish intelligence service was restructuring from a KGB-like secret police into a western-leaning European-style intelligence service, but the rebuilding was not complete. Many old-guard officers were too steeped in the Cold War to trust western intelligence officers and H/WAR had a rocky relationship with them at best. They would not even admit that the plans were of Polish origin, despite H/WAR's assurances that acknowledgement of a defunct chemical weapons programme would not be used as political ammunition by the West.

Polish intelligence did, however, provide an important clue. They made available their surveillance reports on a Polish-Jewish businessman, known to have Mossad links, who had cultivated a close relationship with the senior civil servant in charge of Poland's 'chemical defence programme', double-speak for their chemical weapons programme. Reading between the lines, the implication was that the plans for the plant had been passed from the official to the Jewish businessman, and then to Mossad, with the tacit compliance of Polish intelligence. Now the reason for Mossad's less-than-enthusiastic reception of our copies of the plans was clear. As Badger had suspected, they already had them.

Other interesting parts of a giant jigsaw puzzle were starting to fall into place. We had never been sure where Manbar had obtained the equipment list for the plant – it might have come from Fahd, but transcripts of Manbar's conversations with Fahd suggested that Manbar had them before Fahd. As they used veiled conversation, codewords, and spoke in Farsi, we couldn't be completely sure. At around the same time, Manbar had several discreet meetings with Mossad officers in the Israeli embassy in Paris. The only theory that stitched all the pieces together was that Mossad were, for motives not yet clear to us, using Manbar to deal indirectly with the Iranians. The key to pinning down what was going on was Manbar and we needed to find out a lot more about his movements and activities than we could get from the transcripts provided by the DST.

Badger decided to target Andrea, Manbar's personal secretary. She was an attractive 40-year-old German divorcee who had worked for Manbar for four or five years, and Badger asked the DST to try to recruit her. She was on their territory, so it would be rude not to let them have first crack. MI6 avoids honey-trap approaches, recognising that sexual attraction is too complex to predict or control, but the DST were not so subtle. Andrea had lunch every day in the same bistro, so they sent down a male officer to try to pick her up. That night's telephone transcripts were of her complaining to her mother in Germany about an over-perfumed Frenchman who seemed to think that he was god's gift to women pestering her over lunch. The embarrassed DST gigolo claimed lamely in his contact report that she must be a lesbian.

Meanwhile, I was labouring in my cover job as a clerical worker in the offices of Bari Trading. The work was stifling but my cultivation of Constantine was progressing. Over cups of tea in the office, a lunch or two at the nearby Hilton and the occasional pint, he accepted and trusted me. Nibbling at the bait, at each meeting he asked more and more questions about the extent of my knowledge of chemicals equipment.

We knew from telephone transcripts that Constantine kept a copy of the plans in the locked top drawer of his desk. Once I saw him take them out and refer to them in a conversation with Kiddie. Later that evening, back in the office, I read the transcript and learned that they were trying to figure out the specifications of a glass valve, whose number was obscured on the plans. MOD experts in chemical weapons helped me work out the exact specifications of the part and tracked down the companies – one in Germany and two in Switzerland – that could supply it.

A few days later, doing my best to appear interested in a thick sheaf of bills of lading, I was straining to listen in to a Constantine phone conversation with Kiddie. She was doing most of the talking and when Constantine could get in a word edgeways it was to apologise for the slow progress. Eventually, Constantine blurted out 'Listen Joyce, I've really done my best on the project but I'm stuck. I know somebody who can help us though, and he's sitting right here in this office.' They conferred for a while longer and after he hung up Constantine called me across. 'Hey, Alex, I've a problem you could perhaps help me with.'

'Really?' I replied, trying to sound laconic, and ambled over to his desk where he had laid out the plans.

'What do you make of this?' Constantine asked, eying me hopefully.

They were intimately familiar to me, so I had to feign puzzlement, studying them for a few minutes. 'Seems like they're the plans for some kind of chemicals plant. Something corrosive, because of all the glassware. I'd guess it's for something like an aspirin plant,' I proferred.

Constantine looked delighted. 'Spot on, but do you know what that part is?' he asked, pointing to the mystery valve. I rattled back its specifications and where it could be sourcd. 'You really do know your stuff, don't you?' replied Constantine. 'Listen, I've got a friend who needs some help with this project. Would you like to give her a hand?'

'Sure,' I replied, trying my best to hide my glee.

Within minutes Constantine had rung Kiddie back and introduced me over the phone. After a brief chat she invited me to go up to visit her in Girton.

Walking back into the office later that evening, Badger gave me the thumbs up, having already seen the transcript. 'Good stuff,' he grinned. 'We need to plan the next phase – let's pop out for a breath of fresh air.' This was Badger's euphemism for a cigarette. Smoking was banned in the new office, so smokers were limited to the bar or the fire stairwells.

'If you must,' I sighed with mock exasperation, contemplating the cold, drafty stairwell.

As Badger lit up, we went over the progress made so far. We already had a good idea of what to expect in meeting Kiddie, as we'd been reading her telephone conversations for the past three months and Cambridgeshire SB, one of whose officers was a close friend of her second husband Len Ingles, had provided a helpful report. 'Kiddie really depends on Len,' Badger said. 'She never does anything without first discussing it with him. If you want to win her trust, you'll also have to win his. Build something into your cover story that will pull him in.'

'I'll go up on a motorbike then,' I suggested. 'Len's passionate about bikes: if I turn up on one he'll immediately take an interest.'

My own motorbike: a battered high-mileage Honda Africa Twin, was ruled out by SBO5 as it was registered in my own name, so a few days later I hired a powerful Honda Fireblade from Metropolitan Motorcycles, a dealer opposite Vauxhall Cross in one of the railway viaduct arches that lie under the main south-west line. It was a clear, brisk but sunny February day, and perfect for motorcycling. Speeding up the M11 to Girton, I thought to myself how lucky I was to have such a great job. BELLHOP was going well, Badger was a good boss and the atmosphere in the section was cheerful and friendly, unlike the mistrusting environment of the secretive East European controllerate. The problems in Bosnia were forgotten and I was enjoying socialising more.

Kiddie's personal file was stuffed with SB photographs of her house, so it was easy to find in the pretty village of Girton. She heard my powerful motorbike pull up on her gravel drive and came out of the house to greet me with a friendly handshake. A slightly plump, middle-aged woman, dressed in tight leggings that did not do much for her, she was not a likely person to be the centre of a complicated secret service operation. 'I am so glad you've come up, Alex,' she exhorted jollily, 'Albert has told me all about you! We've been struggling for months on this project.' Her appearance and voice were so familiar from the file and telephone intercepts that it felt strange to meet her personally, like meeting a famous film star. She ushered me into her study and, over a mug of Nesquick, explained her project. The details were intimately familiar, so I had to fake curiosity and surprise as the story unfolded.

Kiddie moved on to her meeting earlier in the year with Fahd in Amsterdam. 'It was so funny, I arrived at the hotel and it was all closed down for cleaning!' she giggled. 'I had to go into the closed off area to wait for Mr Fahd!' She even remembered the inconvenient hold up at Stansted airport on her return. 'They went through all my knickers, the little perverts. But apparently they were only looking for drugs,' she added obliviously. She was completely unsuspicious of me; as we had hoped, Constantine's recommendation was sufficient for her to trust me. And as we suspected from the telephone transcripts, she was unaware that she was being manipulated by Fahd and Manbar into illegal dealings.

Only half an hour or so into the meeting, Kiddie suggested that I should meet Fahd. 'I've been struggling for months with this project, getting nowhere,' she continued. 'I'm also really busy with my charity work and I've had enough of travelling. It would be great if you could help out.'

'Sure,' I replied, trying to sound cautiously enthusiastic. 'How should we proceed?'

'If you like,' Kiddie replied, 'I'll ring him right now and you can talk to him – he told me he would be in Tehran this week.' She reached up to a bookshelf above her desk, pulled out the project file, found Fahd's Tehran number and dialled him up. Unbeknown to her, she was dialling not into Fahd's purported company in Tehran but straight into the headquarters of the Iranian intelligence service, and I couldn't wait to get on the line. Disappointingly, he was not at the office and she just got his ansaphone. 'Never mind, we'll call him next time you're up.'

Kiddie talked enthusiastically about her charitable work. She ran a thrift shop in Cambridge and some of the proceeds went to a project to provide schoolbooks to impoverished children in a favela in Rio de Janeiro. I had been planning a trip to Brazil for some time because PTCP section had an Argentine nuclear scientist on the books, codenamed GELATO, who was overdue for his annual debriefing. Her charity work there presented an opportunity to ingratiate myself further with Kiddie: 'I'm going out to Rio in a couple weeks on business. Is there anything I could do for your project while I am out there?'

'Sure,' she replied, 'there are always things to do.' She described the project enthusiastically and detailed how I could be of assistance. The conversation was interrupted by a popping splutter as an old motorbike pull up outside. 'Ah, that must be my husband, Len. Would you like to meet him?'

We went outside to find Len parking up his leaky Triumph and looking admiringly at my Fireblade. 'They're fearsome machines,' he grinned, holding out his gloved hand in greeting. 'Careful you don't kill yourself.' We chatted for a few minutes about motorcycles while Kiddie busied herself in the kitchen getting a snack together.

We spoke for several more hours in the study over tea and sandwiches, about Fahd, the charity project and motorcycles. By mid-afternoon, Badger's objectives for the first meeting had been met and exceeded. Kiddie and Ingles were taken in by my cover and were keen for me to meet Fahd as soon as possible. We were winding up the meeting when the doorbell rang. Len went out to the hall to answer it and by the hearty greetings the visitors were male. Len poked his head around the door of the living-room where Kiddie and I were sitting. 'It's Paul and Roger,' he hissed.

Kiddie stood up urgently. 'Quick, follow me,' she whispered conspiratorially, ushering me into the kitchen to leave the sitting-room free for Ingles and his guests. 'They're business friends of Len – best you avoid them,' she explained as we bade goodbye at the back door. Unbeknown to her, I knew more about Paul and Roger than she did. They were the SB officers who had been tasked to keep an eye on the family.

Back in London, Badger was delighted that the meeting had gone so well. 'Excellent work. I heard Kiddie trying to ring Fahd, shame she couldn't get hold of him,' Badger chuckled. A few days later he chucked another report on my desk. Paul and Roger described me as a 'suspicious visitor on a motorbike who Kiddie was obviously keen to hide'.

Because the objective of meeting Kiddie had been accomplished, there was no further need for me to cultivate Constantine. One last visit to Bari Trading was enough to say goodbye to Constantine, Patricia and Fazad, with the excuse that for family reasons I had to return urgently to South America.

GELATO was a nuclear scientist who had worked during the 1970s and '80s on Argentina's nascent nuclear weapon's programme. He was recruited in the mid-'80s by one of the station officers in Buenos Aires and was subsequently run by VCOs. Argentina was regarded as having fairly efficient counter-espionage capabilities, so the debriefing meetings took place in Rio de Janeiro and GELATO was paid a couple of thousand pounds per meeting into a secret account in Luxembourg. He provided some good CX over the years but his usefulness dwindled after Argentina abandoned its nuclear weapons programme at the end of the '80s. My task would be to see him one more time and, assuming he had nothing more useful to offer us, discontinue him. I sent a telegram to Buenos Aires asking the station to notify him via the agreed method – a note slipped into his locker at his country club – that he should ring 'David Lindsey', an alias of my predecessor. A couple of days later he rang, the number was patched through to me by the MI6 switchboard and we arranged to meet on the evening of the 12 April 1995 at the Hotel President on Copacabana beach.

The second objective of the trip was to build my credential with Kiddie by visiting the small orphan school in a Rio favela that her charity supported. After several phone calls to Kiddie and to Brazil, I had an appointment for Friday, 21 April, nine days after my meeting with GELATO. 'It's hardly worth coming back, between the meetings, is it?' I asked Badger, hopefully.

He laughed, 'All right, you can stay out there – just don't get yourself into any trouble. You deserve a break as you've done some good work in the section. Here's your SAF.' Badger tossed over the staff appraisal form that he had just completed for submission to personnel department. I read it with satisfaction. It was glowing with praise for the success of BELLHOP and would be a solid basis to request an overseas posting, though this time a normal posting like the rest of my IONEC colleagues.

The meeting with GELATO in Brazil went smoothly. He wasn't upset to be discontinued, and telephone intercepts showed that the head of the favela orphanage reported my visit positively to Kiddie. The time between the meetings provided an opportunity to explore Rio de Janeiro and the surrounding hills, and to lunch with H/RIO, who told me that there was a vacancy in the station. The job sounded interesting, the location agreeable, so I decided to put in a request on my return to Vauxhall Cross.

Monday, 24 April dawned with spring rain. Waiting their turn at the security doors, there was already an impatient and bedraggled queue of people, folding away umbrellas and overcoats. When my turn came, I slipped my swipe-card down the groove, typed in my PIN code, six-nine-two-one, and awaited the familiar green light. But it flashed an angry red. Presuming that I'd mistyped the PIN, I tried again. Same result. The third attempt, and the intruder alarm went off, lights and sirens bleeping in the guards' watch-room. A couple of guards hurried over, glaring at me suspiciously. I showed my pass through the perspex and they manually unlocked the VIP's side-entrance. A queue of muttering colleagues had built up behind me, awaiting their turn to enter the building, and it was a relief to be admitted. 'Are you a member of staff, sir?' asked one of the guards.

'Yes, of course. I'm PTCP/7, staff number 813317.'

The guards led me into their watch-room, tapped my staff number into the computer and studied briefly the resulting message on the screen. 'We're sorry, sir, but your pass has been cancelled. We've been told we have to take you up to personnel department.'

The two security guards escorted me across the lobby in front of a crowd of onlookers. Wheeler, back from Moscow, was waiting to go up the lift and studied his shoelaces rather than greet me. Something must be seriously wrong to get dragged up to personnel department in this way, but I had no idea what it could be. My mind raced desperately. Presumably there must be a mistake and soon all the problems would be cleared up, I reassured myself.

The guards escorted me up to the eighth floor where Poison Dwarf was waiting. He led me into his room and bade me to sit down. He didn't mince his words with any pleasantries. 'As you know, last time we met I gave you a warning that unless your performance improved, you would not be able to stay in the office. It has not improved, so you are fired.'

The words took a moment to sink in. 'How can you make such an absurd claim?' I blurted out when the shock had subsided. 'H/PTCP has just given me a glowing SAF.'

Poison Dwarf talked over me, assuring me that the office would find me alternative employment 'in the City' but I was too dumbstruck, incredulous and devastated to pay much attention. Poison Dwarf's assured manner made it plain that he was acting with the support of officers above him. There was no point in arguing and the atmosphere rapidly became unpleasant. 'My secretary will show you out of the building. Go home and don't come back until we contact you,' Poison Dwarf dismissed me.

Back home, I lay down on my sofa deeply upset and confused. Poison Dwarf had given me no plausible reasons for dismissal and his claim that he had given me a warning was a brazen lie. Badger had just given me a good report, so that could not be the reason. I suspected the devious hand of Fowlecrooke but there was nothing more to do except to wait until personnel department contacted me.

A couple of desperate days later, one of the secretaries from personnel rang up and told me to come in for an interview with the head of the department, Julian Dimmock. I had never previously met HPD, but knew that he was an ex-marine with no work experience outside MI6, and that he still carried a lot of military baggage. He was fond of the city uniform of loud pin-stripe suit and clicky shoes and the office rumour was that he was after a job as personnel manager with one of the banks that employed ex-MI6 officers in return for titbits of economic intelligence. He wasn't an ideal person to be in charge of personnel department, but MI6 often appointed ex-military officers to the post, mistakenly believing that a few years in the army was all the training needed for the job. Still, I supposed that he couldn't be worse than Poison Dwarf and Fowlecrooke.

'So what are your reasons for sacking me?' I asked belligerently as soon as we had shaken hands.

'Why on earth do you want any reasons?' Dimmock replied smoothly as he settled into the low seat behind the coffee-table. 'It won't do you any good, and in any case somebody like you won't have any problems finding a good job in the City.'

'Under UK law, you have to give reasons for a dismissal,' I replied, firmly sticking to my ground. The afternoon spent in Kensington library looking up employment law was not wasted.

'Your personnel officer, PD/2, gave you the reasons for your dismissal at your last meeting,' Dimmock huffed.

'No he didn't, he gave me none at all,' I replied with conviction. Dimmock was cornered, and shifted uncomfortably. 'Give me the reasons, right now,' I pressed home my advantage.

Dimmock thought for a moment. 'You are motivated by challenge.'

I ridiculed his meaningless excuse. 'What does that mean, and why is that bad?'

He couldn't reply. 'You lack commitment,' he claimed.

'Oh yeah, sure,' I replied sarcastically. 'So that's why you posted me to Bosnia.'

Once again he couldn't substantiate it with any evidence or explain why it should be a reason to sack me. He dreamed up another. 'You are not a team player,' he claimed.

'So how come P4 gave me glowing praise for the relationship I built with 602 troop in Bosnia, then?' I replied angrily.

Dimmock squirmed as he dreamed up more excuses, but like the others they were vague, meaningless, easily overturned by me and completely unsubstantiated by any of my line managers' reports. Dimmock's bluster was based on some hearsay from Poison Dwarf or Fowlecrooke and he had not thought through the issues for himself.

'I want these reasons committed to writing, which is my right under employment law,' I demanded.

'You know we can't possibly give you anything on paper, it would break the Official Secrets Act,' Dimmock replied weakly.

But I stood my ground. 'I want them tomorrow.'

'All right, I'll see what I can do,' Dimmock meekly agreed.

But I was not finished. 'And I suggest you do it properly, because you've dismissed me illegally and I intend to take MI6 to an employment tribunal.'

Dimmock looked really appalled. After a moment for the implications to sink in, he replied, 'We really hope you won't do that. It would cause a lot of bad publicity for us. In any case, what would be the point? Even if you won, we wouldn't give you your job back. Nobody can tell the Chief of MI6 what to do.'

This last sentence of Dimmock's was perceptive, though he didn't realise it himself. It was this belief, which he held in common with many other senior officers in MI6, that was the reason behind the patently unfair dismissal and the cause of the long disagreement between me and MI6 that was to follow. Dimmock genuinely believed that MI6 was above the laws of the land. There were mechanisms such as the submissions process that conferred token accountability to the Foreign Secretary and the Prime Minister, but to the likes of Dimmock, these were just minor bureaucratic formalities that needed to be completed in order to carry out important operations. Democratic oversight did not apply to something as trivial as employment law. In his eyes, MI6 had no obligation to give any warning that my job was in jeopardy, or to provide any reasons justifying my dismissal. He expected me to take the sacking on the chin, not complain, not demand any explanation, and meekly accept their offer of help with a stiff upper lip. 'We'll get you a job in the City,' blustered Dimmock feebly as I stood up angrily.

'Keep your feeble ambitions to yourself,' I shouted, storming out.

Dimmock picked the wrong person to impose his arbitrary authority on. There was no way that I would let MI6 get away with such a casual abuse of power and I resolved then and there to fight them to the end. It was not just because I liked my job and had no interest in working in the City. It was also a matter of principle. I knew that if I did not fight them, they would do the same thing to somebody else, then somebody else.

A few days later, personnel department allowed me back into the office for an hour to make a final appeal to the Chief himself, David Spedding. Dimmock assured me that it would be an impartial appeal and that Spedding had not been briefed about the background to my case. But it was clear from the first words of the meeting that this was a lie. Spedding was already fully briefed, the decision was firmly cut and dried, and I had no chance at all of getting it overturned. Spedding dismissed me with a wave of the hand, adding, 'I understand personnel department have already found you some interesting possibilities in the City.'

My perfunctory firing was a classic example of the type of behind-closed-doors MI6 decision that happens regularly in the service due to the ultimate lack of accountability of the Chief. As Dimmock had pompously pointed out, the Chief answers to nobody. He never has to justify a decision, no matter how crass or stupid, to a parliamentary select committee or to the Foreign Secretary or Prime Minister, and so has no incentive to scrutinise recommendations that are passed up to him. His non-existent upwards accountability means he needs only to cultivate the support of power-brokers below him. It is expedient to accept recommendations where they are politically easy, such as the dismissal of a junior officer, so that he has a stronger power base for more difficult internal decisions. Just as in a dictatorship, this shoddy decision-making cascades down the power structure, and explains how the decision to dismiss me had been taken. Poison Dwarf decided he wanted me out, wrote a recommendation to Fowlecrooke, who signed it off and passed it up the chain to Dimmock. He in turn signed it off without bothering to form his own opinion by interviewing me and passed the decision up to the highest levels of the service. Like many ex-military people, Dimmock did not know the difference between 'leadership' and 'rigidity' and by the time he actually met me for himself, he dared not reverse his decision.

I left Spedding's office frustrated and angry, realising that this last chance was just a sham. I waited in the corridor outside his office for the guards who were supposed to escort me out of the building, but after a few minutes I realised they had forgotten. My first instinct was to do my duty and make my way directly home. But rebellion was brewing inside me. 'Bastards,' I thought. They hadn't even let me clear out my desk and say goodbye to Badger. 'Sod 'em, I'll go and see him whatever.' Brazenly walking through the centre of the building to Badger's office was too risky – somebody might collar me. It was nearly 11 a.m., so Badger would be having his morning 'breath of fresh air' on the fire escape. Down on the ground floor by the gym, I dodged into the fire-escape stairwells and made my way through the clammy connecting tunnel to the PTCP fire-escape.

Badger was there having a cigarette and, unusually, was alone. 'Hey, how are you doing?' he greeted me enthusiastically. 'I'm really sorry about what they did to you. As soon as I heard, I rushed up to personnel to persuade Dimmock he was making a mistake, but he wouldn't listen,' Badger explained angrily. 'They've ruined BELLHOP,' Badger continued. 'Without you, we've no choice but to abandon it. And we just had a big breakthrough. Kiddie phoned Fahd yesterday. He wanted you to go to Vienna to meet him.' Badger threw down his cigarette stub with annoyance. 'And Dimmock said something very strange to me,' he added, 'he said that they were very worried about having a potential Aldridge Ames in the service.'

'What?' I asked incredulously. 'What the hell has Ames got to do with me?'

'I really don't know,' replied Badger sympathetically 'he wouldn't elaborate.'

We spoke for a few more minutes, but I was struggling to hold back tears so I bade goodbye to Badger and checked out of the office for the last time.

Ames was a CIA officer who had recently been arrested in America and sentenced to life imprisonment for systematically betraying secrets to Russian intelligence over many years in return for millions of dollars. To this day I don't know whether Dimmock's comment was supposed to imply that I was some form of potential security risk, but it was a deeply unpleasant and unprofessional comment to make, and for which he had absolutely no justification.

Personnel department gave me three months' pay after the sacking. In that time they expected me to come to terms with my dismissal, identify a new career and find a suitable job. I had a mortgage to pay and other financial commitments, and no idea what to do for an alternative career. Even if I were to lamely accept their advice and work in the City, a prospect that appalled me, it would mean starting at the bottom of an unfamiliar and considerably less interesting career, with a much reduced salary. I would accept such misfortune without complaint if my dismissal was merited, but it wasn't.

I went to see Dimmock and made my feelings clear but, secure in the knowledge that his decision was unquestionable, Dimmock had little time for my complaints. 'PD/PROSPECT has already lined up some interviews for you in the City,' he urged, 'but if you really must insist on complaining, here's the Staff Counseller's details.' He handed over me the business card of Sir Christopher France with undisguised exasperation.

The Staff Counsellor was a vetted senior civil servant, supposedly independent, to whom members of MI5, MI6 and GCHQ could take complaints or concerns about the conduct of the services, which he was then empowered to 'investigate'. The mechanism was supposed to allow members of the services to let off steam internally, thus removing the need to go to the courts. In reality, it was little more than window-dressing to fend off criticisms from legislators. Dimmock showed his exasperation because he knew that my complaint could not change the decision but would cause him extra paperwork. Nevertheless, I made an appointment to see France in his Whitehall office the next day, and he listened to my complaint patiently, concernedly noting details. I felt that at least I had a sympathetic ally.

France invited me back to his office a month later to give me the result of his investigation. 'I went to see the Chief,' he announced loftily, 'and Sir David Spedding assured me that his personnel department had done everything they possibly could for you.'

'But didn't you ask to see the papers I told you about? Personnel department's own minutes directly contradict that claim,' I replied with barely contained exasperation.

'Oh, I could not possibly ask to see the papers of the Secret

Intelligence Service!' France replied with horrified surprise. 'And in any case, to do so would be to doubt the word of Sir David,' he added loftily.

I left the meeting close to tears and with anger welling up inside me. It was not that the procedure had proved ineffective: that I had expected. It was just that France, who at the first meeting had appeared genuinely concerned at my mistreatment, had then dismissed my version of events after no more than a quick gin and tonic with the Chief, and had effectively branded me a liar. Unwittingly, France drove the wedge between me and MI6 deeper.

The only way now to seek an independent judgement of the legality of their actions was to go outside the service, and that meant going to an employment tribunal. A quick search of the telephone directory turned up a small law firm in north London, Bahsi and Partners, that specialised in employment disputes and advertised themselves with the banner 'NO WIN, NO FEE'. This pledge was attractive because my small savings were not sufficient to pay lawyers. Satisfyingly, the partners all had Farsi names and I smiled at the thought of Dimmock receiving a disclosure demand from an Iranian lawyer. A quick phone call and we'd arranged a meeting. Two days later they had sent MI6 a preliminary notification letter, requesting copies of all my personnel papers.

My hunch was correct. Dimmock rang me at home. 'We can't possibly have you taking us to court, we'd have the whole of Fleet Street outside the court building,' he whined. 'Why don't you come in to see the outplacement officer, PD/PROSPECT? He's got you a really well-paid possibility in the City.'

'I've told you already I'm not the slightest bit interested in working in the bloody City, so please stop imposing your own career regrets on me,' I replied angrily. 'You bastards sacked me illegally and it is my right to take you to an employment tribunal.' Dimmock rang off impatiently.

Dimmock wrote to me a few days later, now addressing me as 'Mr Tomlinson' instead of 'Richard'. They'd probably already started tapping my phone too, I thought to myself. Dimmock wanted me to change my law firm to something 'more established' and offered to pay my legal fees. On the face of it, it was quite a generous offer but inevitably there was a hidden agenda behind personnel department's uncharacteristic platitude. Another search of the phone book, this time looking for expensive-looking companies with big adverts, turned up the prestigious city firm of Herbert Smiths. The efficient receptionist put me in touch with John Farr, their partner specialising in employment law. Over the next few weeks, we put together a detailed application to an employment tribunal and submitted it to the tribunal centre in Norwich. My last paycheque from the office, for the month of August, arrived a few days later. It would take three or four months for the application to come to courts, so my limited savings would have to support me in the interim. I was not too concerned – my case for unfair dismissal was straightforward and when I inevitably won MI6 would be forced to reinstate me with full back-pay.

My optimism was naïve and I underestimated the deviousness of personnel. Farr called me up at home and asked me to go into his offices near Liverpool Street station to see him.

'There's been an interesting development,' he said, from the other side of his designer desk. 'They've used a Public Interest Immunity certificate to stop your application.'

'What?' I cried angrily. 'How the hell can they justify that?' PII certificates are a legal mechanism – a sort of 'get out of jail free' card – that MI6 occasionally use to get them out of difficult legal situations. They had last used one to cover up their failings in the Matrix Churchill and Astra scandals. The certificates, obtained from the Foreign Secretary via a submission, allow them to block the release to the courts of any documents that they assert could 'damage national security'. Farr explained that he had been visited the previous day by three legal officers from SIS, who had served the PII certificate on him, gravely explaining that any discussion of my case in court, even in closed session with no access to the public gallery, would be 'gravely prejudicial to national security' and that they had been 'reluctantly forced to ask the Foreign Secretary, Malcolm Rifkind, to sign the PII certificate'.

This was a disgraceful and cowardly lie. My personnel papers contained no more secrets than the papers of an employee of the gas board. Discussion of the circumstances of my dismissal by responsible lawyers in a closed court with no journalists or members of the public present could not endanger national security in any way. The real reason MI6 had obtained the PII certificate was that they knew that they would lose their case. The ludicrous reasons that Dimmock had dreamt up for dismissing me, and which I had ambushed him into committing to paper, would have been roundly ridiculed in a court. Poison Dwarf would have been obliged to admit the dishonesty of his claim to have warned me that my job was under threat and MI6 would have been forced into an embarrassing climb down.

I left the meeting with Farr completely disgusted with MI6, my resolve to fight them undiminished but now tinged with growing anger. Moreover, MI6 told Farr that they would no longer pay his fees after he had presented a first interim bill for £19,000, so I would have to find another lawyer.

On the IONEC, a guest-speaker from MI5's counter-subversives branch had lectured us sneeringly about the activities of 'Liberty', a civil rights lobby group based in south-east London. Amongst other issues, they campaigned against excessive state secrecy, lack of accountability of the intelligence services and the misuse of PII certificates to cover up government cock-ups. Their principal lawyer, John Wadham, agreed to see me after a nervous call from a public phonebox. It was with some trepidation that I knocked on the door of their slightly dilapidated premises at 21 Tabard Street.

'There is no legal remedy available to you now except to appeal to the IST (Intelligence Services Tribunal),' Wadham explained over a cup of tea. 'This is a panel of three senior judges who've got the power to examine the legality of actions by MI6.' The tribunal was set up shortly after the avowal process in 1992 in order to give MI6 token public accountability. In theory, any member of the public could make a complaint about illegal activities of MI6 and the tribunal was obliged to investigate. But there were many restrictions on its powers and loopholes that MI6 could exploit, and it was little more than a fig-leaf to give token respectability to the accountability supposedly conferred by avowal. 'They might agree to investigate a case of unfair dismissal,' Wadham advised sceptically, 'but your chances of winning would be nil whatever the merits of your case. They've never once found in favour of a plaintiff.'

It was my only remedy, so I gave it a go depsite Wadham's pessimism. Unusually, the IST requested to interview me personally and appointed a meeting in a committee-room at the Old Bailey towards the end of October. The panel, consisting of appeal court judge Lord Justice Simon Brown, a Scottish Sheriff and a senior solicitor, were seated imposingly at a heavy raised table, with thick dossiers in front of them, presumably the documents that MI6 had submitted to them about me. The court clerk bade me sit down at a desk a dignified distance from the panel. Lord Justice Brown, the chairman, spoke first, explaining their powers of investigation and outlining their understanding of my case. It was several minutes before I was invited to speak. 'Can I be assured that you will take the decision only on papers that I have seen myself?' I asked, aware of Wadham's warning.

Lord Justice Simon Brown paused for reflection before replying. 'There are indeed papers here that you have not seen and will not see,' he gravely admitted, indicating the thick pile of papers on which they were taking their decision. He was clearly uncomfortable with this basic betrayal of a fundamental legal principle. 'I am sorry to say that we cannot be more transparent. We can only work within the terms of the Act.' The huge pile of papers that they were examining, far more than personnel department had ever shown to me, was not encouraging. Personnel had probably rewritten most it, knowing I could not contest its veracity. My prospects of success were non-existent.

In November, I took a short holiday in South Africa to visit my uncle and aunt and to follow some of the England cricket tour of the country. I could scarcely afford the trip but I'd made the commitment before my dismissal. Later I learned that my trip had cost MI6 far more. Concerned that in my disaffected state I might be vulnerable to recruitment by South African counter-intelligence, they pulled my friend Milton out of the country and cancelled the whole undercover operation. In fact, the South Africans made no approach and I wouldn't have cooperated if they had done. But rather than just interviewing me on my return, MI6 wrote off many thousands of pounds of taxpayers' money.

The tribunal were unable to give a date or even a time-frame for their decision. Over the coming months Dimmock wrote several letters urging me to accept help from PD/PROSPECT, but they went straight in the bin. Conceding to their help would be like accepting a set of false teeth from somebody who had just kicked my face in. Besides, even if they dragged me kicking and screaming into one of their tame companies in the City, my previous experience in management consultancy had been so disastrous and unpleasant that I would not last a week.

I had a lot of spare time on my hands and little cash. The little outstanding DIY tasks in my flat and garden were soon completed. Having no money curtailed my enjoyment of London's nightlife, my sacking cut me off from mixing with colleagues in the office, and unemployment left me feeling ostracised from outside friends. I needed to find a new activity to keep myself occupied. By chance, walking down King's Road one afternoon I bumped into a former girlfriend and together we spontaneously bought a set of rollerblades and tried them out in Hyde Park. After an hour of cuts and bruises, she gave up and never used them again. But the sport hooked me and thereafter every waking hour was spent blading around the myriad paths of Hyde Park, Kensington Gardens and Regent's Park. I soon fell in with a gang of hardcore bladers who were also rarely employed, amongst them Shaggy and Winston, two dread-locked black guys who had been blading together since childhood. They were an eclectic bunch, but good fun and a refreshing change from MI6 staff. However, my money could not last forever.

11

THE AGREEMENT

MONDAY, 25 MARCH 1996
LAVENDER CAFÉ, KENNINGTON ROAD,
LONDON

I wasn't surprised that PD/PROSPECT was late. Mike Timpson asked me to meet him at two p.m. in the Lavender Café off the Kennington Road, a stone's throw from my flat in Richborne Terrace. It was Monday, 25 March 1996; the clocks had been put back one hour over the weekend to British Summer Time, and it normally took the office a day or so to change all the wall-clocks. I supposed that Timpson would appear about three, so ordered another coffee and reflected again on the events of the past four months.

It took the IST until 12 March to uphold MI6's dismissal. Although the verdict was not unexpected, nevertheless it was a crushing blow seeing my final chance for legal redress disappear. Until that day, I abstained from accepting MI6's help in finding alternative employment. It was a matter of principle. Accepting their offer would be a concession in the battle against unfair dismissal. I'd had a few interviews – Patrick Jephson, Private Secretary to the Princess of Wales interviewed me to work in her office, but no offer materialised. I went along to some private-sector interviews but my lack of enthusiasm for that sort of career must have been plain. The lack of a regular salary for eight months decimated my savings and even cut-backs on expenditure and some casual work as a motorcycle dispatch rider left me with a big overdraft. Eventually there was no choice except to swallow my pride and accept help from Vauxhall Cross.

Timpson walked into the wine bar at ten to three, imagining himself to be in good time for the meeting. I had met him a couple of times and liked him. He had joined late in his career, after working as an aid worker in Africa. He remained an Africa specialist – unusual in MI6 where specialism is frowned upon – rising eventually to head the Africa controllerate. His career stalled there, perhaps due to his lack of experience outside the dark continent, but probably also because he was no thruster.

'Thank you for agreeing to meet me,' he said cautiously as we sat down with our coffees, careful not to sound sanctimonious that I had not contacted the office sooner or triumphant that I had finally been forced to accept their help. 'I've just finished reading a book which made me think of you. It was about a young chap called Christian Jennings who was in a desperate state like you – broke, no job, lost his home. He went off and joined the French Foreign Legion, then wrote a book about his experience called *A Mouth Full of Rocks*. Anyway, things turned out right for him in the end.'

'What, are you suggesting I join the Foreign Legion?' I asked.

'No, no,' spluttered Timpson. 'I was merely trying to say that things could turn out for you OK in the end.' We spoke for an hour about the outplacement help MI6 could offer but Timpson was as barren of ideas as I was. At least he did not suggest the City. 'I've never had to give career advice to somebody like you who obviously does not want to leave – most people whom personnel department fire are happy to go,' he said.

'That's the first sensible comment I've heard from personnel,' I replied. 'But listen, I need to get some sort of employment urgently. I've been unemployed for months, I'm heavily in debt and can't pay my mortgage next month. If you can't help me find something, even temporarily, can the office help me out with a loan?' Dimmock had implied to Badger that he thought I was a potential security risk: if that's what he thought when I had a regular salary and an interesting job, then surely he would help me stay in my home so I would have a stable base from which to job-search?

'I understand your financial difficulty,' Timpson replied sympathetically, 'but it's out of the question. Julian Dimmock specifically told me that it was not an option to give you a loan. But I will write up your concerns when I get back to the office. Personnel department have obviously made some serious errors of judgement here,' he said cautiously. 'But I have to be frank, I very much doubt they will do anything. They've taken their decision now and it would be too embarrassing to reverse it and admit their mistakes.' All Timpson could do for me was to put me in touch with an external careers adviser who had been vetted by the office.

Walking back to my flat, I reflected on Timpson's advice. Joining the French Foreign Legion was not an option, but the second idea started to grow on me. How about writing a book? It would be totally illegal – even disclosing the colour of the carpets in MI6's headquarters would be a breach of the OSA. But a cloak of secrecy effectively shielded the service from accountability, creating a climate in which arrogant disregard for my rights, as well as those of countless other employees, came naturally. I was coming to believe that these traits tainted MI6's interactions with society at large. What else could I do? If I just forgot the incident, MI6 would carry on mismanaging their people in exactly the same way as they had mismanaged me. There had been victims before me and there would be victims in the future.

The urge to tell my side of the story publicly welled up more firmly in the following weeks. The news of my dispute with MI6 had diffused through Whitehall, and MI6 had covertly used their influence to blacken me and justify their decision. Some friends in Vauxhall Cross had remained in surreptitious contact and they told me that personnel was putting about rumours that they had 'done everything they could' for me. Also, after some of the broadsheets had reported the use of a PII certificate to block my tribunal, the internal weekly newsletter claimed that newspapers had mis-reported the story and that they had been forced to obtain the PII certificate because I was a 'publicity seeker who would use the opportunity of an employment tribunal to blacken the service'. Prior to my dismissal, the idea of breaking ranks with the service and seeking publicity was anathema, but now their actions were driving me into a corner, mentally and financially, and writing a book was looking like my only way out.

Robin Ludlow, the vetted external career counseller, explained how he had spent most of his career in the army, then worked as a personnel officer before becoming an outplacement adviser. His antecedents were not that different from Dimmock and Fowlecrooke, and he seemed to have been briefed by them too. 'You need to think about a career in the City more positively. With your talents you'd soon be earning a fortune.'

'They wouldn't have to pay me a fortune, they'd have to nail my hands to the bloody desk,' I replied. 'I liked my job in MI6 because of the mental stimulation of working on complex team projects with stimulating, intelligent colleagues, because of the opportunity to live and work abroad, learning the languages and immersing myself in the culture of the host country, because of the fascinating and varied people that I would meet, because of the unpredicatbility and variety in the career and because of the fulfilment of working in public service to my country. Now tell me where I'd find any of that in the bloody City?' Ludlow looked baffled. These criteria were out of his scope. 'Listen,' I said, 'this isn't going to be easy for you, but at the very least can you help get me something temporary and urgently? I am really up the wall financially and am about to default on my mortgage.'

Ludlow thought for a moment. 'How about driving minicabs?' he suggested. 'Sign on the dole and get your mortgage paid by the social security, then work as a minicab driver to pay your groceries.' I got up and left. Ludlow's recommendation was illegal; I would end up in prison if caught fiddling social security benefits.

There was one last recourse against MI6. Strictly it would be a breach of the OSA to tell my MP that I was a former MI6 employee, let alone explain the dispute and ask for help to find a resolution. In practice it would be very difficult for MI6 to press charges. A quick phone call from a public callbox to the constituency office of Labour backbencher Kate Hoey established the times and dates of her surgery.

Hoey's offices were just a few streets away from my home but I took my motorbike as Shaggy and Winston wanted me to go rollerblading on Trafalgar Square later that evening. Drawing up outside her surgery, I saw that she was scurrying down the steps towards her car. 'Miss Hoey?' I called, dismounting my motorbike to pursue her on foot. She stopped and turned to face me. 'Could I have a word?' I asked politely and keeping my distance, aware that she might feel intimidated by a six-foot-four man in black motorcycle gear on a dark evening in a dodgy part of London.

'I am terribly sorry, but I am in a real rush to get to an official function – could you see one of my assistants in the surgery?' she replied helpfully.

'I would really rather talk to you directly – it concerns the Official Secrets Act and I'm not sure that I'm allowed to speak legally to one of your assistants.'

'It's OK, go and see one of my assistants,' she insisted. She was pressed, and it would be rude to push.

'OK, I'm sorry to bother you,' I replied with a smile.

Back in her surgery there was a lengthy queue awaiting attention, so I sat down in one of the plastic seats to wait. When my turn came up, the young assistant invited me into an interview cubicle and asked me to explain my problem. 'I have a dispute that I would like Miss Hoey's assistance to resolve. But it would be a breach of the Official Secrets Act if I were to tell you anything more. Would it be possible to make an appointment to see Miss Hoey herself?' I asked.

'Well, this is very unusual,' the assistant replied sceptically, probably wondering why he got all the nutters. 'I think it best that you write to her,' he continued. 'Here's her address.' He gave me a business card with the constituency address and telephone numbers, smiled and indicated that I should leave.

Hoey replied commendably quickly with the news that she had written to the Chief, David Spedding, and that he had invited her out to lunch to discuss the problem. Vauxhall Cross was in her parliamentary constituency, as was Century House, so she had often met the various Chiefs. Spedding even had his London flat just a few houses away from me on Richborne Terrace, so he perhaps he was also a constituent. But my optimism that Hoey might mediate successfully was short-lived. A few days later, she wrote to me again and told me that over lunch Spedding had assured her that I had 'been fairly treated' and that personnel department had 'done everything they could'.

A few weeks later, my ever-expanding overdraft forced me to pack up and vacate my flat. The rental income would be enough to pay the monthly mortgage arrears. After a brief visit to my parents, I loaded up my trusty Honda with as many of my possessions as it could carry and set off for the channel ports. I had no specific destination in mind, I just wanted to go somewhere warm and cheap.

As far as Customs and Excise were concerned, Richard Tomlinson was nowhere in sight as I entered the docks at Portsmouth, glared over the pier at the Fort and handed them the well-worn passport bearing my picture and Alex Huntley's name. I'd been sacked so abruptly after arriving from Rio that there had been no opportunity to return the alias passport, driving licence and other documents to CF. If their absence hadn't been noted yet, it probably never would.

Living under alias would give me the opportunity to write with less possibility of intervention by MI6. Although I'd left the UK countless times using fake identification, this time was different. I hadn't yet violated the OSA since leaving the service but handing over Huntley's passport was crossing the line. Living on fraudulent documentation could be problematic, so as a safeguard before leaving Cumbria I curled up my real passport, driving licence and some money, stuck them in an empty shampoo bottle, weighted it with some old fishing-line weights and slipped it through the filling aperture of the Africa Twin's petrol tank. Even if the Customs officers searched my bike on entry to the ferry, they would be unlikely to find it.

The next two weeks were spent meandering down the back roads of France, camping in coppices and by mountain streams with my bivvy-bag and poncho. Every few days, when I felt the need for a shower and a comfortable bed or had received a soaking from the spring showers, I stopped in a cheap hostel. There was no fixed destination – my turns took me down country roads that looked interesting and avoided those leading to ominous clouds. The random route took me from Calais to the industrial city of Le Mans, down to Poitiers, across the Massif Central to Marseilles, through the Languedoc, then over the Pyrennees into Spain. There the language was easier and it rained less. After drifting down the Mediterranean coast, my journey was brought to a halt in the Andalucian coastal town of Fuengirola when the drive chain jumped the sprocket. The local Honda dealer said it would take several days for a replacement to arrive.

I was as worn out by the long ride as the motorcycle, so when a time-share hustler on the town promenade said he knew of somebody with a flat to rent until the tourist season started, it seemed the right place to stop. On 15 April I moved into the small bedsit, unpacked my few belongings and settled in. The money hidden in the petrol tank was enough to live on frugally for about four months and, if it became necessary, selling the Honda could extend my sojourn. This should be long enough to draft a book. I set up my old laptop and started typing. The injustice of being forced out of my home, and the loss of my steady income and comfortable lifestyle rankled hard: it felt good to start putting the story on paper at last.

Within a week of my disappearance, MI6 started looking for me, alerted by the silence on my telephone. Unaware that I was now Alex Huntley, they looked fruitlessly for Richard Tomlinson. My bank account in the UK was examined by Cumbria SB but yielded no clues because I had paid cash throughout the journey. Tapping my parents' telephone yielded nothing because I rang home using a GSM mobile phone with disposable SIM card, making it impossible to pin me down. Soon friends in London received a phone call from a 'Mr Sturton' of the FCO, MI6 having obtained their names and telephone numbers from intercepts of my home phone. Feigning compassion, 'Sturton' claimed the FCO wished to assure itself of my wellbeing, fearing that I was suicidal. They were naïve to imagine that my friends would fall for the despicable pretence. Without exception, they phoned me to report the approach. Even Shaggy told me he'd been rung up by a 'toff'; he just offered to sell him some dope.

One afternoon, without the courtesy of making an appointment, two female MI6 officers arrived in Cumbria, having travelled from London that morning. My parents were too polite to turn them away after their journey and invited them in for tea. They stayed for over two hours, pretending to be concerned for my safety and trying to trick my parents into revealing my whereabouts. It was a futile exercise. My parents were completely behind me, and the officers left empty-handed.

Joining MI6 was rather like joining a religious cult. The IONEC was the initiation process. We went in wide-eyed and innocent, a blank sheet on which training department imprinted their ideas. The impression that the work was wholesome and justified was reinforced by the carefully nurtured culture within the service. We were reminded constantly and subtly that we carried special responsibilities and the brainwashing process instilled a deep-grained loyalty. Even after the shoddy treatment from personnel, I felt fealty to MI6. It wasn't the same unquestioning loyalty of before, but the embers were still glowing and could easily have been fully rekindled. If, by some amazing twist of fate, they had rung me up, apologised and offered me my job back, I would have gone.

This sense of loyalty was strong enough to make me feel uncomfortable about my writing. Some mornings I woke in my bedist burning with anger and the words flew forth. But more often I felt guilty about violating my lingering loyalty to the service and dreaded the confrontation that publishing would provoke. If there were another solution to resolve the dispute, I would embrace it openly. All I wanted was the chance to take them to an employment tribunal and prove to myself, my friends and family, and to the likes of Kate Hoey and Malcolm Rifkind, that my dismissal was unjustified. There was no possibility of getting my job back but at least I would be able to hold my head high at an interview with a future employer and explain that the dismissal had been proven illegal.

MI6 had the upper hand and felt no pressure to negotiate. They had listened and watched impassively as my personal situation disintegrated in London, so they would not negotiate now. The only way to get them to the table was to switch to terrorist tactics; some juicy titbits in the newspapers would wake them up.

On 12 May, the *Sunday Times* published a small piece about MI6's spying operations against the French. Terry Forton had told me one day over lunch in Vauxhall Cross that he was working under cover as a defence journalist to run a French engineer on the Brest naval base. Forton was paying the witless informer to provide information on a secret French technology to track submarines using satellites to spot the tiny surface wake they left, even when submerged. The information I gave the *Sunday Times* was unsubstantiated and vague, because it had come to me second-hand from Forton, so the newspaper used a bit of journalistic imagination to pad the story. It made a small splash on the back page but no doubt caused a few more ripples in Vauxhall Cross.

Later that week I rode down the coast to Gibraltar and faxed my mobile phone number to the office, asking them to contact me. MI6 would already know my number from intercepting calls to my parents, but they would not dare ring me on it until they had it 'officially' from me.

MI6 did not contact me over the next two weeks, so I rang the *Sunday Times* again. They were very interested in the 'hot potato' story of possible Bosnian-Serb donations to the Tories. This time they ran the story on the front page, with follow up articles inside. It caused a big rumpus in Fleet Street, with the broadsheets running second-day stories on Monday and follow-ups for most of the week. It must have been embarrassing for the Conservatives and I hoped that angry Tory ministers would force MI6 to take action.

A few days later, when the media storm had subsided, a grave-sounding message was left on my mobile phone, asking me to ring a London number. My call was answered by Geoff Morrison, a personnel officer I had met briefly. He was on the verge of retirement and presumably was asked to take on this one last job because there was too much animosity between myself and other members of the department. 'Would you be prepared to meet me?' Morrison asked.

'Of course, that is why I got in touch,' I replied, 'But I first want your word of honour that you will not arrest me and that you will not use surveillance to establish my whereabouts.' Once my base was known, MI6 might ask the Spanish police either to arrest me for talking to the *Sunday Times*, or, worse, to frame me for another crime.

'We will not call the Guardia Civil during the negotiations,' promised Morrison, 'but there is no point in entering discussions if there is not good faith on both sides.' I reluctantly accepted Morrison's vague promises – I had striven hard to get this far.

Morrison insisted that neither John Wadham nor any other lawyer could represent me. 'You know we can't possibly let you have a representative,' he said. 'It would be gravely prejudicial to national security.' It was utter baloney, but there was little option other than to go along with them. Morrison demanded that the meeting take place in Madrid, to enable him to use the embassy as a base to work from, and offered to pay my expenses from Fuengirola.

We met for the first time on Thursday, 14 November 1996, in the Hotel Ambassador, a short walk from the embassy. Waiting for them in the lobby with my hand-luggage, I was surprised when Morrison turned up accompanied by a younger officer whose face was familiar. 'Hello, Richard,' Morrison greeted me cordially. 'This is Andy Watts.

I understand you've met briefly before. I've brought him along as we thought it would be better for you to have another two minds to bounce ideas off.' Round two to MI6 – not content with denying me a lawyer, they had stacked the negotiations further in their favour by bringing a two-man team.

Right from the outset my only request, to be allowed to go to an employment tribunal, was stubbornly rejected by Morrison and Watts. 'You know how prejudicial that would be to national security,' Morrison lectured.

'OK,' I ventured, 'You choose the judge at the tribunal, one that you approve of and have vetted. You choose not only your own lawyer but also mine, so that you can pick one you approve of and have positively vetted. We hold the tribunal *in camera*, at a secret location, and I sign a confidentiality agreement binding me not to talk to the press about the result.'

Morrison shook his head gravely. 'You know perfectly well, Richard, that even in those circumstances it would not be secure.' I held my head in disbelief. How could these people be so obtuse and unreasonable to assert that a hearing held in these circumstances would be less secure than having a highly disaffected former officer on the loose?

As I feared, MI6 tailed me on my return journey. I didn't pick up foot surveillance at Madrid airport or on the plane, but leaving Malaga airport, two cars and possibly a third followed me along the *autopista* to Fuengirola. There was no point in trying to shake them off on the motorway, so I carried on past Fuengirola and pulled off into Marbella. The historic centre of Marbella is a maze of narrow, cobbled passageways and it was easy to use the speed and manoeuvrability of the bike to lose them. I then returned eastwards, along the spectacular winding mountain roads to Fuengirola. They would have to try harder if they wanted to find my hideout.

A few days later they succeeded. They must have passed the number plate and description of my motorbike to the Guardia Civil. A large silver Honda Africa Twin with a distinctive bright yellow British number plate must have been fairly easy to find. Riding home one evening after a day trip to the mountain village of Ronda, two Guardia Civil motorcyclists stopped me a few kilometres outside Fuengirola on the pretext of a routine check of my driving licence. 'Donde vive usted?' the senior officer asked. Guessing that I might be tempted to invent an address, they warned me that they would follow me home. The choice was to abandon my belongings, including the laptop, and ride off to a new address, or tell the truth. Chosing the latter, I led the officers to my bedsit.

A week later, Morrison and Watts invited me to another meeting in Madrid. This time they were armed with several thick dossiers, labelled 'D/813317', my old staff number, which they laid out on the table in front of me. 'We've decided to make a special exception for you,' proudly announced Morrison, peering through his thick glasses. 'We're going to let you look at your own personal files.' It was unprecedented for the secretive personnel department to let their charges see their own papers, though such transparency should have been normal practice. Certainly the mistrust and animosity that had bottled up between the department and me would have been avoided had there been an open reporting system in place.

Morrison hoped that the reasons for my dismissal would become clearer to me once I had read the files and that it would help assuage my anger. His motives were sound but his judgement was flawed. The notes of meetings between myself and the various members of personnel department during my four years in the service were a shoddily inaccurate blend of bias, fantasy, venom and plain incompetence. None of the excellent work that my line-managers had praised was even mentioned, but there were scathing criticisms for the tiniest omission or most trivial error. My failure to wear a tie to meet Karadzic earned pages of abuse. Basic communication failings were repeated throughout. Successive personnel officers had read the reports of their predecessors and, rather than interviewng me to seek their own opinion, found it easier to go with the flow and add more layers of garbage.

The files also explained personnel's obsession that I would find fulfilment in the City. During the recruitment process, 'Mr Halliday' noted that I would be taking a hefty salary cut from Booz Allen & Hamilton. On my IONEC report a few months later, Ball advised personnel department to give me an interesting and challenging post because it would be a shame if such an outstanding candidate were to become bored and leave for more highly paid work. A few years later, these casual comments had snowballed into a firm opinion that I was about to abandon the office for a life in stripy shirt and braces.

At my last meeting with Poison Dwarf, I accused him of failing to give any warning that my job was at risk, as required by law. Poison Dwarf insisted pompously that he personally had given the formal warning. But careful scrutiny of all of his contact reports revealed no mention of even a verbal warning, let alone written notice. 'Do you mind showing me PD/2's warning?' I asked Morrison.

'Oh, you don't want to see that,' obfuscated Morrison.

'Yes, I bloody well do,' I replied angrily, 'Show it to me right now. PD/2 insisted that he had given me one, and I want to see his proof.'

Morrison shuffled through the pile of papers reluctanty, eventually pulling out a one-page document to which he had attached a small post-it note. It took just seconds to read the two short paragraphs. 'But this is not even written by PD/2,' I exclaimed. Morrison was admitting implicitly that Poison Dwarf's claim to have given me a warning was a brazen lie. It was written by PD/1, Fowlecrooke, and referred to his brief visit to Richborne Terrace on my return from Bosnia. 'And how does this constitute a warning?' I asked. 'Fowlecrooke makes no mention of warning me, he just refers to my next posting in PTCP section.'

'I've spoken to Rick,' replied Morrison, 'and he says that he warned you verbally.'

'But he didn't!' I spat. 'I remember the meeting clearly. It concerned entirely my next posting. And if Fowlecrooke warned me, why didn't he record something as fundamental as that?'

'Rick told me that he didn't think it important enough to record in the minute,' Morrison replied, staring awkwardly over his pebble-glasses. Morrison knew that I had been unfairly and illegally sacked, but he would not admit it.

After our third Madrid meeting, in January 1997, it became clear the negotiations weren't progressing. My resolute position was that the only way to settle the dispute satisfactorily was to go to an employment tribunal. Morrison and Watts insisted that this basic human right would 'prejudice national security' and that all that they would offer was help finding another job and a small loan to pay off my debts. With no previous experience at complicated negotiation and without the help of an experienced lawyer, I was at considerable disadvantage.

Our fourth meeting, in February 1997, took place in the British embassy in Madrid. Morrison and Watts had twisted my arm into agreeing to it at the previous meeting, arguing that it was more comfortable and cheaper than hotel suites. Technically the embassy was British soil and so there was a risk that the British police could arrest and hold me there, but I agreed in order to show my trust and faith in them.

Morrison and Watts met me outside the embassy gates and ushered me into a grey-carpeted meeting-room dominated by an ugly modern boardroom table. Once again they were prepared with various papers. 'We've written up our agreement,' Morrison announced proudly, and pushed across a two-page document.

I looked at it bewildered for a second. 'But we haven't even agreed anything yet,' I protested.

'Read it. I am confident that you will be happy with the

agreement,' continued Morrison, firmly. The 'agreement' promised assistance to find another job and offered a loan of £15,000, which would have to be repaid in ten years. In return, MI6 would not seek to prosecute me on my return to the UK for the small breaches of the OSA that I had committed by speaking to the *Sunday Times*; I had to drop my demands for an employment tribunal, hand over my laptop computer for formatting of the hard drive containing the text of the book, and sign over copyright on anything that I subsequently wrote about MI6. It was an absurdly one-sided proposal.

'There is no way you're getting my signature on that,' I protested. 'It does not address my right to an employment tribunal.'

'Oh, but we've got you a fantastic alternative job,' countered Morrison, undeterred. 'It's a great opportunity, in industry.' He emphasised the last word proudly, and paused for a moment as if to let the magnitude of this breakthrough sink in. Personnel were still assuming that they could decide what sort of career would suit me and 'industry' was about as appealing as the City, except with the added pleasure of living in somewhere like Coventry. 'You will be much better paid than you were in the service,' Morrison promised, pushing back the bridge of his spectacles.

There was no way that I would sign the agreement without a concession to an employment tribunal. Even if I did sign, it would be impossible to keep to its terms. 'No, I will not sign,' I insisted. 'We need to negotiate something sensible – it is pointless just coming up with something like this.'

The atmosphere in the meeting grew heated and hostile. Instead of negotiating with my objections, Morrison started to cajole and threaten. 'This is all we'll offer,' he announced. 'There is nothing more to negotiate. If you don't sign today, this agreement will be withdrawn and we will cut off all further negotiation.'

'But that is ridiculous,' I pleaded, 'You haven't even paid lip service to my right to a hearing – this will not work.' My and their patience grew thinner. 'What will you do to me if I don't sign?' I mocked them. 'You could never persuade the Guardia Civil to arrest me just for talking to a newspaper – unlike Britain, Spain has signed up to the European convention on human rights, guaranteeing freedom of expression.'

'I wouldn't be so sure of yourself,' spat Morrison menacingly. Watts joined in the bullying. 'Richard, you know that MI6 is a very powerful organisation, with influence around the world. If you don't sign up, we'll use this influence to harass you for the rest of your life wherever you go. We'll make sure you never get a decent job again and can never settle in any country with friendly relations with

Britain.' I could scarcely believe Watts. He had seemed a decent person until this morning.

Morrison stood up impatiently, paced across the room and spun on his heel to face me. 'If you don't sign this agreement NOW,' he shouted, 'we cannot guarantee your safety.' Morrison looked momentarily embarrassed at his burst of anger before recovering his composure by removing his glasses and polishing the lenses. Slipping them back on, he glared through the thick lenses at me as his words sunk in and I tried to imagine what he meant.

'But you can't arrest me, you promised in writing that you wouldn't,' I retorted feebly.

'That promise stood only for as long as negotiations were in progress,' snapped Morrison. 'If you don't sign, we will end the negotiations . . .'

There was no choice but to sign. Morrison had cornered me: first denying me a lawyer, then bringing Watts as a wingman, then using a soft, concerned approach to build my confidence and trust, and finally, once I had taken the bait, luring me into the safe ground of the embassy. They would not have made empty threats, and no doubt SB officers would be waiting with handcuffs outside, ready to arrest me. Even if they decided that repatriation from the embassy would be legally tricky, they would set me up for an arrest by the Guardia Civil, perhaps with false evidence on trumped-up charges. It didn't take much imagination to think how it could be done – planting drugs in my room or on the Honda wouldn't be difficult.

Grabbing a biro that lay amongst the jumble of papers on the desk, I signed angrily, my normal signature distorted by my fear.

12

THE BREACH

THURSDAY, 20 MARCH 1997
MANCHESTER AIRPORT

As the UK Air flight from Malaga touched down I regretted leaving Spain. Staring out the Airbus's porthole, my mood reflected the weather: dull, cold and raining in the way that only happens in Manchester. It was not impossible that MI6 had tricked me into returning to the UK so it was a relief not to be stopped as I checked through passport control using my real passport, none the worse for its eight months in the petrol tank. Alex Huntley's passport was carefully stitched into the armoured padding of my leather motorcycle jacket – it might still prove useful.

It was good to be back relaxing in Cumbria, enjoying home cooking, walking elderly Jesse along the Eden and on the occasional sunny day taking the windsurfer out on Ullswater. But I could not stay there forever; it was time to think about getting a job and starting a new career. I'd already ruled out the obvious option for someone with a first-class degree and a couple of languages. Returning to the world of stripy shirts and champagne-quaffing hoorays would become overwhelming inside of a week. The new job would have to be as challenging and stimulating as working for MI6. That would not be straightforward.

Morrison told me in Madrid that the service had sorted out a job in 'industry'. It transpired that this was in the marketing department of a motor racing team, owned by former world champion driver Jackie Stewart, in the Buckinghamshire new town of Milton Keynes. It sounded glamorous and interesting but I was not sure whether it would be suitable. Classmates who had gone into marketing from Cambridge were all cloth-headed lower-second geography graduates too thick to get anything better and I doubted that selling anything could match the exhilaration of running agents in Bosnia or the stimulation of matching wits with Iranian terrorists. And no one with two neurons firing would intentionally move from London to Milton Keynes, a sterile planned town that gave new meaning to the word 'boring'.

MI6 arranged an interview with the company and, due to their behind-the-scenes string-pulling rather than the strength of my credentials, I was offered the job. But it was at a salary 25 per cent below my MI6 pay, in direct contradiction to Morrison's promise; MI6 had already reneged on their own 'agreement'. A quick tour of Milton Keynes following the interview confirmed that its reputation was richly deserved. I didn't immediately accept the job, and decided to look around elsewhere. Knowing that it would be easier to forget my dispute with MI6 and settle into a duff job if I had the stimulation of living abroad in an attractive country, I decided to try my luck in Australia. Holidays there had always been barmy, and my New Zealand passport would give me full resident rights.

I took a Qantas 747 to Sydney on 19 April, intending to spend a fortnight looking round the job and housing market. After a week in the bright, vibrant and cosmopolitan city the prospect of returning to Milton Keynes to start on the bottom rung of a career in marketing seemed dire, so I telephoned Stewart Grand Prix declining their offer. They begged me to reconsider, probably at the behest of MI6 rather than any genuine desire to employ me, and told me they would ring back again in a week.

Because it would be a breach of the OSA to reveal my former employment with MI6, personnel ordered me to claim on my CV that I had voluntarily left employment with the FCO. Clearly this wouldn't work. No employer would believe that I had voluntarily resigned from a well-paid and stimulating job in the British FCO in order to start at the bottom on a lower salary in a private-sector job. There was no alternative but to tell the truth about my former employment and the manner of my dismissal. I had nothing to be ashamed of; my dismissal was illegal and there was no reason to lie to a potential future employer just to save blushes for MI6. But nevertheless, the job-search was not easy. The Australian economy was going through a rough patch and companies were laying people off. My CV would hardly be regarded as conventional at the best of economic times. Facing economic uncertainties themselves, companies were not prepared to take a punt on an unknown quantity like myself. As the rejection letters piled up, so did my anger at MI6. The idea of publishing a book reared its head again. Peter Wright had succeeded in getting *Spycatcher* published in Australia, so perhaps that precedent would be helpful to me? Starting with the

'As', I methodically rang all the publishers listed in the Sydney phone directory. The initial response was discouraging, mostly: 'We only deal with literary agents.' But my luck changed when I started on the 'Ts'. The receptionist of Transworld Publishers in Neutral Bay put me straight through to a junior commissioning editor, Jude McGhee. She sounded interested and we agreed to meet the next day at the trendy Verona Café on Sydney's Oxford Street. The meeting went well and McGhee, a young New Zealander, invited me to Transworld's offices the following day to meet her boss.

Thursday, 1 May 1997, was a glorious Sydney autumnal day, bright blue sky, temperature in the low 30s and a pleasant breeze blowing in from the harbour. Disembarking the Cremorne Point ferry to walk the few hundred metres to Transworld's offices on Yeo Street, I hoped that the meeting would result in a contract. It would be a big breach of the OSA, but given the way I'd been treated, it seemed justified. They could hardly expect me to keep my 'lifelong duty of confidentiality' if they couldn't keep to their own 'agreement' for a fortnight. And if I meekly accepted without protest my dismissal, MI6 would carry on casually ruining the lives of its employees and trampling on the freedoms it was supposed to protect.

McGhee greeted me in Transworld's reception and showed me through to Shona Martyn's office. Martyn, also a New Zealander judging by her accent, was in her early 40s and pictures of her young family were displayed on her desk. She introduced herself as the Australasian non-fiction editor for Transworld and related some of her previous career as a journalist first in New Zealand and then with the prestigious *Sydney Morning Herald*. Over the next hour we discussed the bones of my story and I threw in a few anecdotes to highlight interesting points. I was careful to disguise names, dates and operational detail. Martyn didn't make it clear whether she was interested in the project or not. She sparked over some details, but the next moment she seemed as though she wanted to end the meeting. She had an oddly hostile approach for somebody who had been a journalist, and kept asking for proof that I had really worked in MI6.

'Obviously I can't give you that,' I replied impatiently after the third time of asking, 'because if MI6 would not allow my personnel papers to be released to an employment tribunal, they obviously will not give them to you.'

'But you have to understand that under ethical standards of journalism, I need proof that you really did work for MI6,' she replied. 'Besides, why do you want to publish this book?' she asked.

'It is in the public interest to expose bad management within MI6,'

I replied, 'in order to encourage them to correct their faults. If I just let them sweep this failing under the carpet, they will not mend their ways, and in the long run that is potentially far more damaging to national security.' Martyn nodded approvingly to that at least. 'I won't gratuitously damage MI6 – I will not compromise any ongoing operations, I will use aliases for members of staff and I would like to submit a draft of the text to MI6 to allow them to censor any passages whose sensitivity I may have misjudged,' I said.

'Oh, I could not possibly allow that,' Martyn retorted, 'that would be against all my ethics as a journalist and defender of freedom of expression.'

'So you wouldn't be prepared to allow me to submit the manuscript?' I asked again for clarification.

'Absolutely not!' replied Martyn emphatically.

As the discussion seemed to be going nowhere, I gave her an ultimatum. 'Well, are you interested in this project or not?'

Martyn thought for a moment. 'Can you give me what you have written so far, and I'll think about it?'

'No, I can't do that,' I replied, 'because I haven't yet written a draft.' It was too risky to give her a copy of the text, even if I recovered it from its hiding place on the internet.

Martyn thought for a moment. 'I'll tell you what, then, write down a synopsis outlining the contents of each chapter and I'll have a think about it,' she replied.

I was still suspicious and reluctant. It was one thing to break the OSA verbally, as it could never be proved in court, but putting pen to paper was another. If a written synopsis fell into the wrong hands, I'd be vulnerable to legal action. But the former journalist had just vouched for her ethics. It was worth the risk. 'OK, I'll give you a synopsis, but I trust that you will show it to nobody.'

Martyn pointed to the steel filing cabinet in her office. 'It'll be locked up in there. It will go nowhere.' She gave me her card and I left to get the late-afternoon ferry to Fisherman's Wharf.

That evening, back in my rented holiday apartment near Bondi Beach, I typed an anodyne and brief outline. The following day, unsure of my prospects for a book contract but confident that Martyn would honour her word, I dropped a sealed envelope at Transworld's office.

My money was running out and, with no job prospects in sight, my thoughts reluctantly turned to England. There were plenty of drawbacks to returning, but at least there was a job there. It wasn't a great offer but it would provide some marketable work experience for the future. Perhaps it would turn out better than expected. If it didn't, I could come back to Sydney. I rang up Stewart Grand Prix, accepted their offer and was given a starting date.

Back in Milton Keynes, things started brightly enough. I found a small flat in Wavendon, a village a few miles from work. A Carlisle Saab dealer, from whom my mother had recently bought a car, kindly helped out by lending one of their demonstration cars. With a flat, a job and a car, my lot was better than it had been for several years. The first day at work, however, confirmed my worst fears. Contrary to what Morrison had assured me, I was the junior employee in the department with no input into policies and no outlet to use my initiative or develop projects. It amounted to little more than a school-leaver's job; MI6 had reneged on another clause of their 'agreement'. Moreover, I felt the cloud of my dismissal hanging over me, making it hard for me to feel settled and welcome. Over the next few weeks I made an effort to find something better and attended several interviews, but the knotty chestnut of explaining why I had left the FCO always reared its thorny head. After many wasted miles in my loan car, I wrote to PD/PROSPECT asking for his help. The reply arrived a few days later, not from the kindly and sensible Timpson but from another officer whose name was unfamiliar. He wrote, 'The service has discharged all its obligations under the Madrid agreement by finding your current employment and we are therefore not minded to help you further.'

The arrogant reply added to my anger. It would have been easy for them to use their contacts to help find something. 'Stuff their lifelong duty of confidentiality then,' I thought to myself. A book contract could be my ticket out of Milton Keynes. I wrote to MI6 to ask how to submit a draft manuscript with a view to potential publication. By return post, they sent a strongly worded letter saying that it would be illegal even for me to write a draft and demanded an assurance that I had not started work on it. If they were not going to be reasonable, then it would have to be done secretly.

MI6 would be listening to my telephone at home, even though they had promised in their 'agreement' not to intercept my communications. But my work PC had an internet connection and it was unlikely that they could get a warrant for that. One afternoon in early September, I fired off a two-line e-mail to Shona Martyn, asking her to get in touch if she was interested in pursuing the project. After two weeks she had not replied, so presuming that her answer was no, I thought no further of it.

A few days later, on 8 September, my landlady rang me at work in an agitated state. 'I'm afraid your flat's been burgled this morning. I noticed the upstairs window was broken and when I checked through your kitchen window I saw the place had been ransacked.'

I rushed home immediately. A token attempt had been made to disguise the theft as a normal burglary; the contents of the fridge were strewn across the floor and and my bookcase had been overturned. But the identity of the culprits was not hard to guess as the only item of value that had gone was the laptop containing the draft. The TV, stereo, video-recorder and even small valuables had not been touched. The police arrived to have a poke around but they were not interested in taking any forensic evidence.

Contrary to their promise, MI6 intercepted my e-mail and my brief lapse in security sparked not only the burglary but much more significant events thousands of kilometres away. After intercepting the note to Martyn, it wasn't difficult for them to find out who she was. The e-mail address gave them the name of her Australian internet service provider, which in turn gave MI6 her name and street address.

On Friday 24 October 1997, Agent Jackson of the Australian Federal Police arrived at Transworld asking to speak to Shona Martyn. She agreed, granting him a two-hour interview during which she provided a full and detailed account of our meeting, handed over my synopsis and then signed a witness statement.

On Friday, 30 October, having a lunchtime appointment for a haircut in Wavenden, I popped home from work for a quick bite to eat first. As I was putting the kettle on, there was a knock on the door. It was the young constable from Buckinghamshire police, PC Ellis, who had investigated the mysterious theft of my laptop. With him was a burly plainclothes inspector. 'Hello, Mr Tomlinson, there have been some new developments concerning your burglary and we want to ask you a few more questions about it.' Ellis seemed friendly enough, and introduced his colleague as Inspector Garrold of CID. 'Would you mind if we came inside?' Ellis asked.

The same feeling of impending doom came over me that I used to feel when about to be tanned at school for some petty misdemeanour. If they were going to arrest me, they would have a search warrant, so the only thing to be gained by refusing them entry was a broken door. 'Sure, come on in,' I replied, trying to sound indifferent.

'Would you mind taking a seat?' Garrold said in a tone that gave me no option but to sit down on the sofa. He and Ellis stood over me menacingly. 'You are under arrest for breaking section 1 of the 1989 Official Secrets Act,' Garrold announced. He grabbed one wrist, Ellis the other, and I was in handcuffs.

More cars pulled up on the gravel drive outside and quickly my flat was filled with plainclothes officers, their mobile phones bleeping. Two joined Garrold in standing over me, menacingly. I caught glimpses of their gun-holsters under their sports-jackets, a sinister sight in the UK where police officers are rarely armed. The atmosphere became even more threatening when the friendly Ellis bade goodbye, a concerned look on his face. A little moustached Welshman opened up as soon as Ellis had left. 'OK, Tomlinson, where's the fucking gun?' he demanded.

'What gun?' I asked, bemused.

'The gun, don't fuck us around, where's your gun?' he glared. Their insistence that I was armed added to the sense of unreality, as if it were another IONEC mock arrest.

'I haven't got a gun, never have had one, and I'm never likely to want one,' I replied with complete bafflement.

The Welshman detected my bemusement and softened his inquisition. 'We have information that you brought back a gun from your time in Bosnia. We want to know where it is.'

'Ah, now I understand!' I laughed. 'That gun's rusting at the bottom of the Adriatic.' MI6 must have told the police that I had kept it, perhaps in order to persuade them to make the arrest as heavy-handed as possible.

Garrold ordered me to stand, removed the handcuffs, and strip-searched me. Finding nothing of interest, he pushed me back on to the sofa. For the next three hours, forced by the tightly clamped rigid handcuffs to hunch with my wrists by my chin and elbows in my lap like a stuffed chicken, I watched the latex-gloved officers dismantle my flat, checking behind every picture, lifting edges of the carpet, stripping the bed, rummaging through my dirty laundry. Every item of interest was sealed in a plastic bag and deposited in a large white box brought for the purpose. It filled steadily. First was my newly purchased Psion organiser, which I had left on the coffee table. Then all the computer disks. Myriad scraps of paper with innocent phone numbers scribbled on to them. My Spanish–English dictionary. Various home videos. My photo album. I was not at all worried until a bald-headed officer, searching my leather motorcycle jacket, suddenly piped up, 'Got something here, sir.' The others clustered over my jacket. Prodding and pushing at the lining, baldy pulled out a small package, carefully wrapped in masking tape. My morale plummeted when I realised that it was my 'Alex Huntley' passport, driving licence and credit card. I watched latex-gloved fingers carefully insert the package into a plastic bag, seal and add it to the growing pile.

Simultaneously, a search team from Cumbria SB descended on my parents' home in Cumbria and a third team confiscated the desktop

PC at Stewart Grand Prix. My captor's mobile phones were ringing incessantly because the three teams were using them to coordinate the raids.

Just after 5 p.m., as darkness was descending, Garrold announced that it was time to go. My handcuffs were released briefly to allow a visit to the lavatory; then, handcuffed to another officer, I was led out into the courtyard and bundled into the back of one of the waiting dark-green Vauxhall Omegas. Garrold got into the driving seat and we pulled out of the courtyard to start the drive towards the motorway and, presumably, London. The remaining officers carried on working in my flat.

We arrived at Charing Cross police station at around 7 p.m., the journey slowed by the evening rush-hour traffic. We parked up in a central courtyard filled with patrol cars. Still in handcuffs, I was led through heavy doors and up a ramp to the main reception desk where they handed me over to the custody of the duty sergeant. My name, address and charge were logged, then he allowed me to make one personal call and contact a lawyer. Still handcuffed, I rang my father, who already knew what was happening by virtue of his own police raid. He tried to sound upbeat and positive, but I knew he was worried. I hoped that my mother was taking the shock OK. Then I phoned John Wadham and asked for his advice. He cancelled his evening plans so that he could come at once. Two PCs took me down to the cells to await his arrival.

As the cell door slammed shut, I felt calm about my situation. My previous experiences of handcuffs and clanging doorlocks in the TA and on the IONEC lessened the unfamiliarity of imprisonment. Massaging my chafed wrists, I surveyed my new surroundings. The cell was bare except for a dirty lavatory, a concrete bench with a plastic foam mattress and one grubby blanket. I rolled the blanket into a pillow and lay down on the mattress to await Wadham's arrival.

At 8 p.m., the flap in the door slapped open, two eyes briefly checked me, the bolt slammed back and two police officers entered the cell. 'OK, let's have a Full Monty,' they ordered, then escorted me in handcuffs to the interview rooms where Wadham was waiting. We only spoke briefly. There was not much he could do, as we did not yet know what evidence SB had. He gave me a book, a biography of former prime minister Gladstone, and some fresh fruit, which would make the evening pass more easily.

I slept well that night despite the primitive bedding arrangements, aided by a sleeping pill given to me by the police doctor. The next morning, after a stodgy cooked breakfast reminiscent of army food, the duty sergeant escorted me back to the interview rooms where Wadham and two police officers waited. They introduced themselves as Detective Inspectors Ratcliffe and Durn of the Metropolitan Police SB. For the rest of the morning and until late in the afternoon, they grilled me relentlessly, the tape-recorder whirring in the background, gradually revealing their evidence against me. First, the copy of the synopsis I had given to Martyn and the transcript of her interview with the Australian police. Then the transcript of a second interview with her, which Ratcliffe and Durn had flown to Sydney to conduct themselves. Finally, the 'Alex Huntley' documents. Just before 6 p.m. they charged me with breaking section 1 of the 1989 OSA. The duty sergeant refused bail and remanded me in police custody until a magistrate's hearing on Monday.

'At least Ratcliffe did not try to charge you for the Huntley passport and driving licence,' Wadham explained to me sympathetically after the duty sergeant had left us for a moment. 'They could have charged you under the 1911 OSA for that, which carries a maximum sentence of 40 years.' Several months later Wadham learned that MI6 had pressed the police hard to charge me under this act. Thankfully, Ratcliffe argued that the charges would not stick because I had not knowingly stolen the documents.

Although the prospect of prison was unpleasant, I was not unduly worried. Indeed, I felt a sense of relief. By arresting and charging me, MI6 were blatantly exposing their hypocrisy in preventing me taking them to the tribunal. If the courts were 'secure' enough for them to prosecute me for breaking the OSA, then why were they not 'secure' enough for me to take them to an employment tribunal? My arrest would get considerable media coverage and it would be more embarrassing and damaging for MI6 in the long-run than it would be for me. Indeed, there were positive aspects of the arrest: until then I had been referred to as 'Agent T' in newspaper reports because MI6 had used an injunction to suppress publication of my real name. Now my name would be in the public domain and I would be able legally to tell friends, relatives and future employers about my previous career and the shoddy way I had been treated. It was quite a relief to leave the shadows, even if it was via a dark prison cell.

Later that evening the duty sergeant unlocked my cell and took me to the forensic laboratory where police technicians took my fingerprints and photographs and a DNA sample by scraping the inside of my cheek with a spatula. The data would be stored on the police's central computer. 'If you are acquitted of the charge then you can apply to have these records destroyed,' explained the technician, 'but until then, welcome to the criminal fraternity,' he added with a smile.

The remainder of the weekend was spent in the dirty cell with Gladstone for company. I wondered what MI6 hoped to achieve by prosecuting me. Passing the synopsis to Martyn had done no harm – it probably had sat gathering dust in her filing cabinet until Federal Agent Jackson visited. Even if she had shown it to the top dog in the KGB, it was anodyne and innocuous. Prosecuting me would not solve the dispute, it would just exacerbate it. Even if they gave me the maximum sentence of two years, I would be out of jail relatively soon, and then what? On release I would be without a job and a lot more pissed off.

On Sunday afternoon I was permitted a short visit from my father, who had driven down from Cumbria bringing a change of clothing and a wash-kit so that I could be presentable for my bail hearing the following day. Wadham came later that evening to discuss the appearance. 'I've found a good barrister to argue your case,' he announced. 'Owen Davies is a flamboyant character, who has a good reputation for taking on political and human rights cases. He's really keen to take you on – it'll make a change from representing death-row inmates in Jamaica,' John added encouragingly.

Inevitably I/OPS would have been working over the weekend to ensure that Monday's media would report my arrest with favourable spin, so we batted back by drafting a short counter-spinner. It was a prudent move, as the Monday morning early edition broadsheets and the *Today* programme on BBC Radio 4 all initially quoted the MI6 line that I had been arrested for 'selling secrets'. It was only when they received our own release that they moderated their line to report that I had merely shown a short synopsis to an Australian publisher.

On Sunday night, I asked the duty sergeant to open me up early in the morning to give me time to wash and shave. Permission was granted but the request 'forgotten', so the next morning I was handuffed and escorted to Bow Street magistrates court unshaven and unwashed. It was a trivial but demeaning little ploy to ensure that I looked as disreputable as possible.

A Group 4 security van picked me up from the police station and in the cells at Bow Street their officers strip-searched me again. 'You'll be up in the dock in about 15 minutes,' the young guard informed me, 'would you like anything to drink?' I sat down, sipped the sickly sweet tea and tried to read Gladstone.

At last the door clanked open and the Group 4 guards entered the cell to re-handcuff me. My cell was at the end of a long corridor, and as we passed cell after cell captive faces pressed up against the tiny door hatches to see what was going on. 'Cor, he's all right,' screamed one female. 'Put 'im in in here with me, and I'll sort him out for ya'.'

'Shut up, Mary,' the guards chuckled, slamming shut her hatch as we passed.

Wadham was waiting in the corridor outside the court with a begowned barrister. 'Hi, I'm Owen Davies.' He extended a hand to greet me, his tanned wrist adorned with the sort of beaded bracelet favoured by beach bums. 'Why is he handcuffed?' Davies demanded of my guards as he realised I couldn't reciprocate the greeting.

'We've instructions from above that he has to be handcuffed to appear in court,' replied the young guard sheepishly. Making me appear handcuffed, unshaved and in three-day-old clothes would make me appear more villainous to the assembled press gallery than if I was clean scrubbed and in a fresh suit.

'Well, we're not having that,' retorted Davies. He shooed the guards away for a confidential word with me. 'Before you even go in the dock, we'll insist that you appear without handcuffs. They are just trying to swing the magistrate against you.' I had never been in trouble before, had no history of violence and had been arrested for nothing more than writing out a few words on five sheets of paper, yet I was being treated like a master criminal or a terrorist. Davies and Wadham returned to the court to argue that I should not be shackled, and I was led back down to the cells.

Davies won the first skirmish. Twenty minutes later, my handcuffs were removed at the door to the court and I walked to the dock with my dignity. The packed court fell silent. Glancing up to the public gallery, I tried to pick out my father but he was lost in a sea of unfamiliar faces. To my left the press gallery was packed with reporters, their faces familiar from television. A press artist was already starting to map out a sketch of me that would be used to illustrate the story in the following day's newspaper articles. Alongside Wadham and Davies to the right were the prosecution barristers, amongst them one of the MI6 legal representatives. I wondered what satisfaction he could possibly get from bringing this prosecution against a former colleague.

The court clerk asked me to stand to confirm my name and address, then Colin Gibbs of the CPS (Crown Prosecution Service) opened the case, arguing that bail should not be granted because I would certainly attempt to abscond. Although Gibbs admitted that my passports had been confiscated, he launched into a flattering though greatly exaggerated account about my training in the use of disguise and ability to cross borders illegally. After 15 minutes of character assassination, Owen Davies stood up to argue for bail. My father had offered the title deeds to his house as a surety and I had offered my own. It was absurd to imagine that, facing a maximum two-year sentence, I would abscond and have my flat and my parents' home confiscated. But as soon as the examining magistrate started his summing-up speech it was clear that he had decided to remand me in custody. 'I have no doubt that you would be a danger to national security if you were given bail,' he intoned gravely, as if he had already made up his mind before hearing Davies' arguments. The guards indicated for me to come down off the dock and brought me back down to the court cells.

Wadham and Davies came down to see me afterwards to offer their sympathies. Peering through the door hatch, John spoke first. 'It's no surprise, really, that you didn't get bail. Magistrates are scared stiff of the OSA.'

'We'll try again next week,' added Owen, his mischievous eyes twinkling. ' Look on the bright side. You'll be a lot more comfortable on remand in jail than in a police cell – at least there you'll get a shower.'

And so my life was about to take a new twist that just a short while ago would have been inconceivable. As the Group 4 prison van drove me south towards Brixton jail, it passed over Vauxhall Bridge, within sight of my former employer. As I peered out of the porthole window at the building where I had spent happier times, I rued the chain of events which had led to my situation. In just a few years, I had gone from being the holder of an EPV certificate in the most sensitive part of the British government, trusted with secrets denied to all but the highest officials, to becoming a scruffy dishevelled prisoner heading for one of London's dingiest and most notorious jails.

'Oi you, Basildon. Follow me.' I looked up at the tattooed screw who had just entered the smoke-filled cell where I had been held since arrival at Brixton jail an hour earlier. Two other newly remanded prisoners were sharing the cell with me. One was an Italian, clutching a two-day-old *Gazzetto dello Sport*, who spoke not a word of English and was bewildered by what was going on around him; the other, his face puffy, sweaty and cement-grey, sat on his hands and rocked gently backwards and forwards, his silence broken only by the occasional gasp. 'Yeah you,' the guard indicated to me. 'Basildon, that's you, innit? James Bond's brother.' The guard laughed with a hacking smoker's cough at his obscure joke. And so, for the duration of my time in Brixton jail, I was named after a famous brand of writing paper. 'Bring your bag, and don't try any kung fu, or any other 007 stuff.' I picked up the small case containing a few extra clothes which my father had brought down and followed him down the corridor to start the reception process.

My knowledge of prison life was limited to what I'd seen on occasional television dramas and odd snippets of wisdom from Winston and Shaggy, who had done time for cannabis dealing. I decided that the best approach would be to adopt the 'grey man' tactic advised to us on SAS selection. Stay quiet but attentive, do not speak to anybody unless spoken to and cooperate quickly with all instructions. Reception took most of the day, each stage separated by a long wait in a smoke-filled holding-pen with my fellow new inmates. 'Mondays are always busy,' explained one screw as he escorted me through to the search-room, 'because of all the drunks and druggies who've been pulled in over the weekend.' In the search-room there was an airport X-ray machine, photographic equipment and a large rubber mat on which the screws ordered me to stand. 'Right, Basildon, your prison number is BX5126, which you'd better memorise right now,' explained the screw, "cos all your mail has to have that number on or else it goes straight in the bin.' Like my school number and army number, BX5126 soon became indelibly ingrained in my memory. 'Empty your pockets and that bag on the table,' he ordered, 'then get back on the mat.'

My possessions were minutely examined. Wallet, money, credit cards, phone cards, stamps and anything else tradeable were confiscated and recorded in my personal file. My sponge bag was emptied, the razor was confiscated and recorded, but the toothpaste, shampoo and aftershave went straight in the bin. 'We don't know what might be in them. They could be full of crack for all we know,' explained the screw. All the fresh fruit my father had brought for me went the same way. 'Right, let's have a Fully Monty then,' the screw ordered. My pile of clothes was passed through the X-ray machine before they allowed me to dress again. After photographing and finger-printing, the screws escorted me to another holding-pen to await the medical exam.

Many prisoners come into jail in poor mental and physical health. Often they are drug addicts and need a methadone fix to ease withdrawal, or may be suicidal at the start of a long sentence. A medical check is obligatory before they can be assigned to a wing for their own safety and the safety of the other prisoners.

The two officers in the medical centre already knew who I was. 'I can't believe they've nicked you,' commented the orderly as he examined my forearms and wrists for injection scars or suicide attempts. 'They've really shot themselves in the arse putting you in here just for writing a book.' The burly young guard, watching over the examination in case of troublesome prisoners, chuckled in agreement. 'Fuckin' madness. But look on the bright side, at least you'll be able to add another chapter to your book when you get out . . .'

A glance at a wall clock showed that I finally cleared reception at about 1830. Clutching a black bin liner containing the few possessions I'd been allowed to keep, I followed two screws down a long corridor. Judging by the smell of stale cabbages that reminded me of the kitchens at Barnard Castle School, I guessed that they were taking me to the dining area to get something to eat. 'Get yourself some scoff in there, Basildon,' the screw ordered, indicating a dining-room filled with tables and benches. About ten other prisoners were already eating from metal trays. There was silence, apart from the occasional grunted request for the plastic salt cellar or for left-over food. I queued up for my rice, beef stew and buttered white bread, and sat down with my metal tray on my own. Like the other prisoners, I felt subdued and unsociable and ate in silence. The Italian, still with his *Gazzetto*, was staring quizzically at his tray of uneaten food. Next to him a Nigerian, immaculately dressed in a brand new suit, read from his bible, his lips moving to the words. In the corner was a distinguished-looking and smartly dressed guy, perhaps in his late 60s, who judging by the anger written on his face had been given a sentence with which he sharply disagreed.

Nearest to me was the heroin junkie who had been doing cold-turkey in my holding-pen. He smiled weakly at me. 'Have you got a fag?' he begged in a hoarse whisper.

'Sorry, I don't smoke,' I replied quietly, not wanting to disturb the silence.

'Lucky bastard,' he replied. 'You're far better off in jail if you don't smoke. And even better off if you don't do drugs.' His chuckle at his self-deprecation was cut short by a spasm and for a moment I thought he was going to throw up.

'Tomlinson, come here,' the tattoed officer who had first christened me 'Basildon' barked from the exit door. I stood up and made my way to him, leaving my tray on the table. 'All right, Basildon, you've been put on the book, so we have to cuff you to take you down the wing.' Expertly, he grabbed my wrist, handcuffing me to his own wrist, and another burly, bearded screw did the same with the other wrist. As they conveyed me out into the damp air of a foggy London evening for the short walk to the neighbouring block, I wanted to ask what 'the book' was, but decided to play the grey man and kept quiet. As we passed 20-foot wire fences topped with barbed wire, illuminated by the depressing yellow of sodium strip lighting, the guards must have guessed my thoughts. 'Sorry about this,

Basildon, but we 'ave to do it, you're on the book, you see. Do you know what that means?'

'No . . .' I replied, guessing it was something bad.

'Well it means the Governor's decided that you're a Category A prisoner, as opposed to a B, a C or a D, and that means that you are a highly dangerous threat to the state. It's a bit ridiculous making a bloke like you an A-cat, if you ask me,' the tattoo explained.

'But who the fuck ever asks us?' the beard laughed.

The cells in C-wing were arranged on three landings around a central atrium, with metal mesh nets across each storey to prevent suicide or murder attempts, and I was assigned cell 32. The wing had just been refurbished and the paintwork on the cast iron stairs was still bright. 'Make yourself at home,' grinned the guards, as they unlocked my handcuffs in the cell. 'You're lucky being on the book, you won't have to share with some other cunt.' They slammed the door behind me, leaving me on my own for the first time. My new home was tiny, about 11 feet by 7 feet, with two bunks against one wall, a barred window overlooking an exercise yard and a sink and open lavatory against the other wall.

I made myself as comfortable as possible by unpacking the few clothes and books reception had allowed me to keep, and storing them neatly in the small wall-cupboard. My plastic knife, fork and spoon, issued to me in reception, went on the narrow windowsill. The previous occupants had been heavy smokers and the floor was littered with the butts of roll-up cigarettes. There was a mop and bucket in the corner, so I cleaned them up as best I could. Then I had my first wash for three days and made up the top bunk using the clean but frayed bedding. After three nights in a police cell, sheets and a pillow were a blissful luxury and I slept well.

We were unlocked just before 9 a.m. the following day. Not sure what to do next, I watched for a few minutes from my door. The other prisoners were scrambling down the metal stairs to the kitchens on the ground floor, so I joined the rush to queue for a fried breakfast, served on a metal platter, which we took back to our cells to eat. I muddled through the routine of the rest of the day as best I could. Nobody explained the myriad little rules and vocabulary of prison; it was just a matter of watching and learning. We were unlocked again at 10 a.m. for daily exercise, a one-hour walk around the prison yard which my cell overlooked. It was a chance to get a look at my fellow prisoners as they traipsed in small groups around the yard or huddled against the surrounding fences to smoke roll-ups. Some were laughing and joking, others were looking morose and depressed. Some of the prisoners had heard on the radio that I had been remanded to Brixton and came over to talk. None could believe that I had been nicked for a writing a book. 'It's a bleedin' liberty, that is, 'commented one shaven-headed cockney, his forearms covered in the livid scars of suicide attempts.

As the day progressed, I picked up the terminology of prison. I learnt that 'association' was a one-hour free period per day when we were allowed out of our cells to take a shower in the landing shower-blocks, watch television or just chat with the other prisoners. 'Canteen' was not a cooking pot as it had been in the army, but the weekly opportunity we were given to buy fruit, sweets or tobacco from the prison shop. It was necessary to ask permission from the screw in charge of my landing, a cheerful cigar-smoking, whisky-reeking Indian, before moving to another landing. I discovered that we could attend various workshops and courses for up to two hours a day. There was a broad choice and I put my name down to learn to play a musical instrument and started to think that maybe my time might not be too unpleasant.

But the authorities had other ideas. That evening, during evening association, two screws came to my cell and escorted me down to the Governor's office on the ground floor. They stood behind me as the Governor, a surly Scot, addressed me disparagingly from behind his heavy metal desk. 'Tomlinson, as you know, we've made you a Category A prisoner. If that decision is confirmed by the Home Office, then you'll have to move from Brixton jail. We're not equipped to deal with the likes of you in here . . .'

I was confirmed as Category A early the next day, Wednesday, 5 November. Two screws came to my cell, strip-searched me, ordered me to change into a prison-issue tracksuit and handcuffed me. 'Where am I going?' I asked.

'We can't tell you that, Basildon, we'd have to kill you if we did.' I did my best to smile at their joke, though it was one I had heard many times in the past few days.

I spent two long hours waiting in a holding cell in reception until at last the door was opened and my escorts ordered me to stand up to refit my handcuffs. 'Sorry about the delay, there was a problem with the escort helicopter,' one of them explained.

I presumed he was joking, but later I learned that helicopter escort was standard for all A-cat prison transfers. They led me out into the grey autumnal afternoon, to a waiting van – this time from HM Prison Service rather than Group 4 Security.

'In yer get,' the screw ordered, pushing me up the steps and into one of a row of tiny cells barely big enough to sit down in, and closed the door on me, trapping my left arm which was still cuffed to his wrist. When he was sure I was secure, my wrist was released and the door swiftly bolted. A few minutes later, the van's engine rumbled into life and we started to move. Through the tiny porthole of darkened and reinforced glass I watched the South Circular Road unfold eastwards, but gradually lost my bearings as we headed into unfamiliar parts of east London.

13

MAXIMUM SECURITY

WEDNESDAY, 5 NOVEMBER 1997
HMP BELMARSH

'Welcome to HMP Belmarsh,' grinned my escort as he opened the cubicle and slapped handcuffs on my left wrist. 'You'll like it here . . . not,' he chuckled, dragging me out of the vehicle into a grim prison courtyard and through a heavily guarded gate to reception. The process was more elaborate than at Brixton, with strip-searches and X-rays between every stage. More of my possessions were deemed illicit, including a white shirt and a pair of black trousers. 'They're too close to an officer's uniform,' the screw told me curtly. My diary went because it contained a map of the London Underground which 'might be helpful if you escaped'. There was little of the good-natured banter of Brixton and most of the process was done in intimidating silence. At last, they ordered me to sign my personal file and, with me holding a bin liner of my remaining possessions in one hand, escorted me down a labyrinth of bleak and cold corridors to cell 19, Spur 1, Houseblock 4.

HMP Belmarsh was opened in 1991 to house approximately 900 prisoners and is one of only five prisons in Britain equipped to house maximum-security Category A prisoners. Most A-cat's are there on remand, awaiting trial at the secure court complex linked to the prison by tunnel. If convicted they are sent to one of the 'long-termer' A-cat prisons such as Durham, Parkhurst on the Isle of White, or Long Sutton in the Midlands. Belmarsh is also a local jail for south-east London, so it houses some convicted petty offenders serving short sentences. Because of the harshness of the regime and its elaborate security, it is also used to house troublesome prisoners as punishment for misdemeanours committed in more comfortable jails. The prison is built on reclaimed marshland which was deemed unsuitable for normal housing because of the infestations of rats and mosquitoes. The four houseblocks are arranged at the corners of a large quadrangle, along whose sides are all the other areas needed for a functioning prison: reception, visiting-rooms, chapel, gym, hospital, kitchens and workshops. Each houseblock is a secure unit in its own right. A command and control room, known as the 'bubble', controls the only entrance, consisting of two heavy doors, electronically linked so that both can never be open at the same time. Each door has a video-intercom and the controlling officer in the bubble can only release it if he recognises the requesting officer. Inside the houseblock, three spurs lead via video-locked doors from a small central atrium containing the hotplate area where meals are served. There are also exits via walk-through metal detectors and video-locked doors to secure areas for A-cat legal and social visits and out to the exercise yard.

Of all this, though, I knew nothing as I dropped my bag in the corner of the cell just after 2 p.m. and sat down on the stained mattress to survey my new home. It was grim and grubby, though slightly bigger than the cell in Brixton. The heavy steel door, slammed ominously shut behind me, had a small solid perspex window at eye height, covered by a sliding hatch which could only be opened from the outside. A small and heavily barred window overlooked an exercise yard, in which a few prisoners were aimlessly walking, surrounded by 20-foot-high fencing bridged with anti-helicopter cables. Down one wall a metal bed was bolted immovably to the floor, a sturdy cupboard was fixed above it, opposite was a small bolted-down metal table and bench, and in the corner was a filthy toilet with a broken lid. Unlike Brixton, the toilet was situated to give some privacy if a screw were suddenly to open the sliding inspection hatch; but just to ensure that there was no hiding place, there was a smaller additional window over it so that he could inspect you if he wished. Between the toilet and the door was a porcelain sink which looked like it had not been cleaned for months, above it a scratched unbreakable plastic shaving mirror and a buzzer to summon the screws in an emergency. The lugubrious mustard-painted walls were smeared with gobs of butter, splattered mosquitoes, stains of dried snot and blobs of toothpaste which previous occupants had used to stick up posters. There was graffiti scribbled in blue biro above the bed. 'Methadone strips the life out of you,' somebody had scrawled in a shaky hand. Another message was more hopeful: 'Remember, no matter how long you are doing, you'll get out in the end . . .' Under the cupboard was a simple Spanish prayer. High up on all four walls were patterns of crosses and Arabic words, put there by a Muslim occupant as prayer aids. Scribbled above the toilet in large, childish letters was a slogan in Turkish. In such filth, I did not feel like unpacking my belongings. I lay down on the bare mattress listening to the muffled activity of prison life. Inmates hollered to each other between cells, sometimes laughing, sometimes abusive. The sharp clacks of a game of pool rose from the floor of the spur, punctuated by exclamations in a foreign language. From the cell next door came the sound of a manically stirred hot drink, then a contented whistled rendition of Monty Python's 'Always Look on the Bright Side of Life'. Every half-hour the flap covering my door hatch was slapped open, a pair of beady eyes examined me for a second, then the flap slammed shut again. Just before 6 p.m., the level of activity started to increase and the heavy clunking of keys signalled that we were being unlocked. My flap slapped open, eyes checked me, the heavy bolt clunked and the door cracked open. Peering out, the other prisoners I saw rushing to join the dinner queue on the first-floor landing and I grabbed my plastic mug and cutlery to join them.

Locked back in the cell to eat alone and in silence from a metal platter, I found that the meal was not as bad as I feared it would be. Stew, two vegetables and rice, a stodgy pudding and custard, a big pile of buttered bread, a mug of hot water to make tea or coffee, an apple and a small bag containing cereal and milk for the next morning's breakfast. We were briefly unlocked half an hour later to kick the trays out for the cleaners to collect, then a few hours later an urn of hot water was dragged around to fill our mugs. It was Guy Fawkes night, and I lay on the bed sipping cocoa listening to the firework celebrations from the nearby housing estates.

'Oi you, you next door, pass this doon,' a hoarse Geordie voice called out. I sat up, wondering if the call was directed at me. There was a sharp rattle on the heating pipe which ran the length of the landing, passing through each cell. 'Oi you . . . new boy next door, grab this and pass it down.' Paper rustled nearby and I looked over the end of my bed, in a tiny gap between the metal pipe and the reinforced concrete of the dividing wall, to see a sliver of carefully folded newspaper. I pulled it through into my own cell. 'Make sure you pass it doon,' ordered the disembodied voice impatiently. Curiosity got the better of me and I unravelled the package revealing small crystals of a hard white substance, LSD or maybe crack. I wrapped it up, stepped over to the other side of the cell where there was also a small gap and pushed it through. It was ripped from my fingers eagerly. Ten minutes later, as the drugs took their effect, the bangs and thumps of the nearby fireworks were joined by the sound of my other neighbour as he sung along raucously to an Oasis concert blaring from his radio.

'Oi, new-boy,' a close-cropped head thrust around the door after unlock the next morning, 'when I tell yer to pass sommit doon, yer jump, right?' he ordered.

'Sorry, I'm new in jail, I didn't know,' I apologised.

He stared at me hard, suspicious at my educated, middle class accent. 'What you in for then?' he asked. I explained my crime. 'I heard about you on the radio last night!' he exclaimed, his tough-looking face breaking into admiration. 'Mind if I come in for a chat?' Sitting on my bed, he introduced himself as Paul Dobson and explained that he had been remanded in custody for allegedly shooting a rival gang leader during the 'bootleg' liquor-smuggling wars in Dover. We discovered that we had been schooled almost together. He had been at the Deerbolt Young Offenders unit just a mile or so away from Barnard Castle School. He'd previously done a few years in Durham prison, so the six months waiting on remand were a stroll to him. 'I'll get natural life if they convict me, but I'm not guilty,' he claimed optimistically.

My other neighbour emerged from his cell, blinking and red-eyed, to collect a mug of hot water at the lunch unlock. He stuck his shaven, scarred head around my door as I prepared a cup of tea. 'Oi, next door, I'm sorry about all the noise last night. I was off me fuckin' head.' He rubbed his bleary eyes. 'I'm Craggsy,' he said, extending a hand in friendly greeting. But his eyes narrowed as I introduced myself. 'Oi, yer not a nonce, are yer?'

'I don't think so,' I replied, not knowing what he meant but guessing that it was not a good idea to be one.

'Well that's alright then,' he grinned, exposing a row of broken teeth. Craggs had been serving a 12-year sentence for armed robbery, but during a transfer to another prison he and three others had escaped from the van after coshing the driver and guards. He had been on the run for two weeks but was now awaiting another sentencing for the assault, and his escape attempt had earned him his E-list 'stripes', a denim uniform with prominent yellow bands down each side.

Normally new inmates to Belmarsh spend the first week of their sentence on the induction wing, spur 2 of houseblock 1, to learn the prison rules with 'short, sharp shock' tactics. Nicknamed 'Beirut' by the prisoners, the conditions were so dirty, petty and harsh that transferring to another spur was a move into comparative luxury. I had missed the privilege because it was considered insecure for A-cat prisoners. Whilst not a problem for other A-cats, who usually had plenty of prior experience in prison, for me it meant learning the Belmarsh rules by trial and error.

Every morning after first unlock we had 20 minutes before breakfast in which to collect our mail, put our names down for gym and phonecalls or to see the duty doctor, and I used the opportunity to grab a shower in the blocks on the top landing. My second morning dawned heavily overcast and a weak, diffuse light struggled through the shower block's grimy barred window. Needing more light to avoid the worst of the filth and swamp flies, I jabbed the push-button switch by the door. Immediately there was a loud klaxon and a sudden burst of commotion from the screws on the landing below as their belt-alarms wailed. 'Where is it? What's happening?' they shouted, sprinting up the stairs on to the landings. The heavy doors leading from the central atrium sprung open and reinforcements from the neighbouring spurs invaded, their batons drawn. Rushing down the landings they bellowed orders – 'OK lads, back in your cells, NOW' – at the few other prisoners who were out and about, slamming their doors shut. I watched bemused for a second, then hurried back to my cell. Through the door-flap I watched the agitated screws scurry around, anxiously looking for something. Having no idea what was going on, I made a mental note to ask Dobson.

We were re-released ten minutes or so later and life re-started as normal. Back at the shower blocks, with my towel over my shoulder, I looked more carefully at the light-switch. Engraved just under the button were the words 'General Alarm'.

'You daft cunt,' Dobson grinned broadly at me in the lunch queue and explained, 'them buttons is only for when a scrap breaks out or sommit. You'll get a week in the segregation block if they catch you meddlin' with them. On yer own in an empty cell, no mattress except at night, exercise on yer own so no cunt to talk to the whole day, nowt te read 'cept the effin bible, does yer fuckin' head in.'

Every day we were entitled by prison regulations to an hour of 'association' which alternated according to the day between mornings or evenings. Our cell doors had to be locked behind us to prevent prisoners congregating out of sight of the screws and the upper landings were closed down, so all 100 prisoners on the spur crowded on to the tiny lower floor. We could take it in turns to play pool or table-football, queue to use the telephone or sit around on the floor and chat over a cup of tea. There were ten or so comfy chairs in front of the television, so there was a scramble to get a seat and then a fierce debate about which channel to watch. Popular programmes were police dramas such as *The Bill* (called 'training videos' by Craggs) and BBC's *Crimewatch*, watched eagerly to see if any friends were featured. The undisputed favourite, however, was

Top of the Pops, transmitted on Friday evening, though we could only watch it every second-week when the association times coincided with the programme.

On weekends we had the luxury of four hours of association each day, two in the morning and two in the evening. We were entitled to an hour of exercise a day in the bare concrete exercise yard, as long as it was not raining, and on Sundays we got a double-session if the screws were feeling generous. But there were few other opportunities for A-cat prisoners to get out of their cells. Being banged up in a cell for up to 22 hours a day was tedious and unrelenting. Even with a good book it was difficult to forget that even the most basic liberties, such as being able to get up and make a cup of tea, had been taken away. A-cats were restricted even when unlocked from our cells. Every move out of our door, whether to take exercise in the yard, queue for a meal or make a phone call, was noted in a small black book held by Mr Richards, the ever-cheerful senior officer in charge of our spur. We had to put in formal, written requests for trivial things. A haircut, or growing a moustache, required written permission from the Governor. Even trimming toenails required an application for the nail clippers and supervision by a screw. My status as an A-cat prisoner was a mystery and a joke to the other prisoners. Even Mr Richards couldn't understand the logic. 'They're taking the bleedin' piss puttin' you on the book,' he laughed. 'You've never been in jail, no previous record, a white-collar crime and they make you A-cat! Somebody's got it in for you up on high, I reckon.'

The morning of 10 November had been set as the date for my second bail hearing at Bow Street Magistrates court. Two screws woke me at 6 a.m., strip-searched me in the cell, escorted me to reception, ordered me to strip again while they x-rayed my clothes, led me in handcuffs to the prison van and locked me into one of the cubicles. 'We're a bit early for the police escort so you'll have to wait,' the screw said through the grill, belting himself into his seat to watch over me. 'And if you piss in there, you'll do a week in the block when you get back.' The cubicle reeked of urine, so the previous occupant must have been desperate.

I'd only been in the holding-cell at Bow Street Magistrates court for a few minutes before the flap slapped open and a set of eyes peered in. This time, however, they were intelligent and friendly. 'The Crown Prosecution Service want you to appear in the dock handcuffed again,' Davies explained. 'I'm going up to argue that you should appear unshackled.' He won the skirmish again and half an hour later the prison service guards led me to the door of the court in handcuffs, then released me to allow me to make my own way to the dock. Davies presented my case for bail first. A barrister friend had volunteered his flat as surety, so in addition to my own flat and my father's house, he offered property of over £500,000 as a bail condition. After a week in Belmarsh, I was far keener to win it. The CPS barrister, Colin Gibbs, announced that he had an expert witness who would support his case that bail should be denied and asked the magistrate for permission for the hearing to go *in camera*. The request was granted and court ushers cleared the public and press galleries so that only myself, Davies and Wadham, Gibbs for the CPS, his assistant and the presiding magistrate were present. My hearing was now in exactly the same circumstances that MI6 had argued were 'not secure enough' for me to take them to court for unfair dismissal. The expert witness turned out to be the second 'Mr Halliday' who had recruited me. He launched into a gratuitous personal attack on me, inventing fictitious reasons for my dismissal and giving me no opportunity to defend myself. I held my tongue with difficulty, but I knew that there was little chance of getting bail, as any sympathy the magistrate may have had for my situation was gone. And so it proved when he stood up to give his verdict a few minutes later.

Davies and Wadham came down to the court cells to commiserate with me, their eyes gleaming through the tiny-door hatch. 'They're determined that you don't get bail, not because they are afraid that you will abscond but because they want you to plead guilty,' explained Wadham. 'They know that by remanding you in custody, you'll have to spend at least a year awaiting trial because of the backlog of cases. But if you plead guilty you'll get a sentencing hearing after a few weeks because it can be fitted into the court schedule more easily. You'll get a shorter sentence and you'll be down-graded from A-cat.'

'I see,' I replied. 'They've got the Governor of Belmarsh to make me an A-cat and denied me bail so I'll have to waste a year in tough conditions if I want to plead not guilty.'

'Exactly,' Davies chipped in. 'They want to avoid the embarrassment of a jury trial, which you would probably win, so they're making that option as unpalatable as possible. And even if you lost, it would still be embarrassing for them as you would stand out because you would have spent longer on remand than your likely sentence.' The maximum sentence if convicted would be two years, which would be automatically halved to 12 months as long as I behaved myself in jail. I would therefore probably walk out on conviction, as I would already have done the time on remand. 'They're blatantly knobbling the system to persuade you to plead guilty because they know that any jury of right-thinking Englishmen would be sympathetic to you and acquit you,' added Davies.

I had plenty of time to reflect on my choice that afternoon. There were no A-cat prison vans available, meaning a five-hour wait in the spartan court cell, with only a wooden bench to sit on and nothing to read. The thought of spending a year in Belmarsh awaiting my day of glory at a jury trial was not pleasant, as the week I had already done had seemed more like a month. On the other hand, if I were to plead guilty, the judge would automatically cut a third off my sentence, so the most I could spend in jail would be eight months – probably as a lower-category prisoner in an easier jail than Belmarsh. The thought of capitulating to MI6's game was galling, but it would be more pragmatic. Reluctantly, as I returned to now familiar surroundings at Belmarsh with its crew of crooks and lunatics, I concluded that pleading guilty was the most sensible option.

One of the consequences of Mrs Thatcher's decision in the late 1980s to dismantle Britain's mental hospital system was that the country's jails filled up rapidly with former mental patients. Booted out of their long-term health-care centres, many could not cope and turned to crime to survive. In prison there were no mental health-care facilities, so their health worsened. Because other jails used Belmarsh as a dumping ground for troublesome prisoners, we had more than our share of 'fraggles'. Most were harmless and amusing, such as Eric Mockalenny, a chunky young Nigerian whose story was typical. He had been convicted of assaulting a police officer while being arrested for exposing himself outside Buckingham Palace. In prison, his mental health degenerated. After lunch one day he came into my cell to introduce himself. 'Good morning, Mr Tomlinson, I am Mr. Eric Mockalenny. Would you please give me a stamp? I must write to Princess Anne,' he said, showing a row of large white teeth. His request was so polite that I felt obliged to help him out. Mockalenny thanked me graciously and scuttled out, beaming gratefully.

Shortly afterwards, the young screw assigned to keep an eye on him collared me. 'Tomlinson, don't give Mockalenny any more stamps. He's been writing three letters a day to Princess Anne, asking her to go into a joint venture of prawn-farming in Nigeria and sending her visit application forms.'

Most of Mockalenny's antics were tolerated by the prisoners and screws alike, but some of the other 'fraggles' were more trying. Stonley had spent nine years in a psychiatric hospital before being released on to the streets in the 'care in community' initiative. He had no home and ended up in Belmarsh for a series of minor burglaries. He spoke to nobody, never washed or shaved, and never changed his clothes. He spent associations pacing furiously in a small circle on the landing, clutching his beard and muttering to himself. Because he stank so vilely nobody approached him and he was immune from bullying or intimidation.

As for many of the other prisoners, visits to the prison gym were a highlight. On days when there were enough screws to escort A-cats off the spur, those of us who queued at Mr Richard's desk quickly enough at morning unlock to get on the list could go to the gym instead of the yard. In the well-equipped sports hall we could weight-train, play badminton, five-a-side soccer or soft-ball tennis. There was also a Concept-II rowing machine and I embarked on a manic fitness program, alternating 5,000m and 10,000m per session – and 20km on Sunday if we got double-gym. Whittling down my times was the best antidote to my otherwise futile and pointless existence in prison.

We were allowed to buy a daily newspaper and a couple of magazines a week, using private money deposited with reception who ordered the papers in bulk from a nearby newsagent. Only pornography and gun magazines were banned. The eagerly awaited paper delivery arrived just after lunch and then there was an impromptu flea market in the dinner queue to trade them. These papers, together with the small radio permitted in my cell, enabled me to follow events outside prison. My arrest was extensively reported and there were smaller follow-up features about my bail refusal. The press had become much less critical once the hostility whipped up by I/OPS in the aftermath of my arrest had abated and truth about my minor offence had surfaced. The reports became more sympathetic every time bail was refused.

'Hey Rich, I'm more famous than you now!' Onion-head, a cheerful Liverpudlian with a ruddy face and a Tin Tin quiff of blond hair waved a tabloid newspaper at me one morning. 'They've even published me mug shot and number, just like Hugh Grant except better looking, eh!' he exclaimed, kissing his own image. It was considered prestigious to get into the papers and Onion-head proudly showed me an article about himself. He was one of a gang who had carried out a series of armed raids against the homes of wealthy home counties families, robbing them at gunpoint. They had just been sentenced the day before, after spending a year on remand. The *Mirror* published a full double-page spread, which was the source of Onion-head's pride.

'What did you get then?' I asked.

'Sixteen years,' he cheerfully replied, licking the edge of a roll-up. 'Flippin' judge just used his lottery numbers, the bastard. Steve got

25, Neil got 19, Owen 22,' he added. 'Still, looking on the bright side, keep me head down and me lighthouse nicely buffed-up, get parole and there'll only be 418 episodes of *Top of the Pops* before I'm a free man,' Onion-head laughed as he lit his roll-up. His flippant optimism cheered me up; my maximum sentence of two years seemed trivial in comparison.

One morning in November, 8.30 a.m. came and went without the usual sound of clanking keys and opening doors. As the minutes ticked by the prisoners registered their rising impatience by banging their metal bins against cell doors. 'What's up?' I shouted to Dobson through the hole by the pipe.

'Dunno, I'll find out and let you know.' He called through to his neighbour and after a couple of minutes shouted back to me. 'Some laddie on the other spur, Colligan, went and topped hissel' last night, daft cunt. Screws found him this morning.'

'How did he manage that?' I asked. It wasn't easy to kill yourself in Belmarsh; there was nothing sharp to slash wrists, no unprotected balconies to jump off or ropes to hang from.

'Apparently he ripped up a sheet, made a neck-tourniquet, then rolled over and over on his bed till he choked,' Dobson answered quietly. I only knew Colligan, a guy in his early twenties on remand for allegedly murdering the wife of a millionaire, by sight, but it was sad news. Apparently the evidence against him was strong and he expected a life sentence. 'Lads like him, who want to be dead, should have the option of asking for a lethal injection,' Dobson added hoarsely. 'It's not fair, putting somebody through living mental torture that they end up topping themsels' like that.'

We were not unlocked until a doctor examined Colligan and issued a death certificate, photographs and forensic evidence of his body had been taken, and his body had been removed from his cell. The mood on the spur was subdued for the rest of the day.

During my early days in Belmarsh, it concerned me what other prisoners would think of my offence. Former law enforcement personnel, especially police, are usually victimised and have to request segregation under prison regulation 43. Most 'rule 43' prisoners are sex-offenders; the so-called 'nonces' so despised by Craggs. But my fears that I might be considered a 'grass' (slang for an informer) were unfounded. In the prison heirarchy – armed bank robbers at the top and those convicted of street crimes such as muggings at the bottom – most gave me 'respect' for my offence. It was just as well, for one Friday night I saw the treatment dished out to 'nonces' whose crimes were regarded as unacceptable. *Top of the Pops* was on and the spur were congregated in front of the television, cheering Mockalenny who was breakdancing incongruously to a Celine Dion single. A young black guy, fresh from 'Beirut', was sitting quietly on his own, sipping a cup of cocoa. Unobserved in the general commotion, Craggs filled a plastic mug with boiling water from the urn, sidled up behind him and tipped the scalding water over his head. The guy fell to the floor clutching his scalp, screaming in agony. Craggs sprang back, arms aloft, vehemently protesting. 'Sorry, mate, it was an accident, honest.' Other inmates rushed over as the livid victim got to his feet, clutching his head and lunging at his assaulter with blind anger. Somebody pressed the alarm before a fight could break out and we were invaded by the usual hordes and herded back into our cells. Craggs was still protesting his innocence as his door was slammed shut, not with convincing sincerity, but just to let everybody know that this should be the version of events given by witnesses to the screws.

Lying face down on my bed, I asked Dobson through the gap what it was all about. 'He was a fookin' nonce,' he whispered. 'We just got word through from t'other houseblock. He raped some lassie. Should've known better than trying to mix it with us on this spur. I was goona do 'im misself, but Craggsy beat me to it. We'll not see 'im again.'

Another new prisoner called Michaels came in for the Craggs Enhanced Negative Vetting interview a few days later, after he appeared at the back of the lunch queue in a new prison tracksuit, fidgeting with his Cartier watch. 'What are you in for, mate?' Craggs asked with an undertone of belligerence.

Michaels, an elderly and educated fellow, hesitated for a moment, unused to being addressed by a scar-faced skinhead. 'A spot of fraud,' he nervously replied, adjusting his glasses.

'Oh I say, just a spot of fraud,' Craggs mimicked an upper-class accent for his audience. 'What did you get then?' he asked, still suspicious.

'Eighteen months,' replied Michaels cautiously.

'Only 18 months! That's a bleedin' touch that is, a shit and a shave,' Craggs jeered. 'So how much did ya nick then?' he asked.

'The judge said that it amounted to about £600,000 in total, over about ten years or so,' Michaels nervously replied.

Craggs frowned, as his brain made a quick calculation. 'Wot, you swagged six hundred bleedin' grand, and you only got 18 month?' Michaels looked at the floor and fidgeted uncomfortably with his watch. 'I only swagged five bleedin' grand and got 15 years!' exclaimed Craggs indignantly.

'Aye, but you did shoot the bank manager while you were at it,' Onion-head butted in helpfully.

But Craggs was unrepentant. 'Six 'undred bleedin' grand, and only 18 bleedin' month,' he repeated wistfully. 'Fuck me, that's what I'm gettin' into when I'm out o' here. I'll go into fraud. That's gotta be the answer, heh,' he nudged Onion-head jubilantly in the ribs, pleased with his new idea. 'Yeah, that's wot I'll do,' he repeated optimistically, pleased with his brainwave. But a frown slowly crumpled his scarred face, as a dark cloud loomed. 'Fuck, if only I could read 'n' fuckin' write.'

Most of the other prisoners on my spur and the neighbouring spur with whom we shared our hour in the exercise yard knew me because of the media coverage and it was not unusual for a complete stranger to approach me to express his disgust that I was in prison for writing a book. They also sought my perceived expertise in case it might prove useful in the future, erroneously assuming that I would be an expert on firearms, have an insider's knowledge of the workings of every obscure department of the police or customs service and a solid grounding in criminal law. My hour in the exercise yard, where it was possible to talk out of earshot of the screws, was dominated with questions like, 'What's better, an Uzi or a Heckler & Koch?', 'Can SMS messages between mobile phones be intercepted?' and 'How do you spot police surveillance?' The questions broke the ice, enabling me to quiz my colleagues about their own crimes, and gradually the exercise hours evolved into informal symposia on criminal tradecraft. They taught me how to ring cars, where to buy false passports, how to slip out of the UK without documents and the best countries in which to evade recapture and extradition.

Another popular topic of conversation was the relative merits of one prison over another. By universal consensus, Belmarsh was the worst prison anyone had experienced; the lack of freedom and association irksome even to the career criminals. The acknowledged jail connoisseur was Ronnie, a cockney who had been in so many foreign jails that he spoke fluent rhyming slang in several languages. His last stretch had been in a Monaco jail. One afternoon, queuing for dinner with Dobson and Onion-head, he told us how he ended up there. He had just come by some money by virtue of a 'little venture' and decided to treat his mother to a weekend in Monte Carlo. 'I came out of the bleedin' Casino Royale,' he continued, 'all spruced up in me dinner jacket, and there was a bright yellow Lamborghini Diabolo parked outside. I thought to missel', "I'll have that", so I went up to the garçon and told him to get the keys to me macinino pronto. The little con went and fetched the Lambo' from where it was parked and handed it over! I was with me Mam and she was saying, 'No Ronnie, don't do it, don't do it', but I shoved her in the front and told her to shut up. We were halfway to the Costa Brava before the flics nicked us.' Jail in Monaco was, according to Ronnie, a 'piece of pissoir'. Dutch jails too were a breeze. 'They kept payin' me to go on drug-rehab courses, but I was so stoned I kept 'avin to start again.' Swiss jails were 'like bleedin' Hiltons' and Spanish, French and German jails were all 'a touch' compared to British prisons.

Even the experienced Dobson and Craggs were in awe of Ronnie's prison knowledge. 'Which country would you say has the best jails then?' asked Dobson, who was considering a career move abroad if he were acquitted from his current offence.

Ronnie furrowed his brow for a second. 'Ah, there's no fuckin' contest. You wanna get yoursel' in a fackin' Icelandic jail. They're a bleedin' swan. I was getting paid £100 per week to sweep the yard, only I didn't 'ave to do it if it were covered in snow, which was all fackin' year. I came out rich like a bleedin' rag'ead.'

One bitterly cold afternoon I was pacing the exercise yard furiously, trying to keep warm against a biting wind and cursing to myself about the circumstances that had lead to my imprisonment. Other prisoners were huddled in the corners of the yard sheltering from the wind, except Mockalenny who had stripped to the waist and was energetically dancing in a puddle in the middle of singing the Lord's prayer with his arms raised to the sky. Suddenly, a meaty hand clasped my shoulder from behind. I spun round, brushing the assailant's hand away and bracing myself for trouble. It was a relief to see a grin on the gnarled but friendly face of an elderly prisoner from spur two. 'You're that spy fella, aren't you?' he asked. Before I could reply, he introduced himself. 'The name's Henderson, Pat Henderson . . .' (a grin crumpling at the familiar joke). 'I wanted a word with you,' he continued. 'Do you know a bloke called George Blake?'

'I've heard of him,' I replied, 'if we're talking about the same George Blake.' George Blake was the last MI6 officer to go to prison for a breach of the OSA in 1950. After spending six years in prison he escaped and fled to Moscow. 'Yeah, that's the one,' Henderson laughed. 'I was in Wormwood Scrubs with him, years back. A cracking fellow. He went over the wall one night.'

I laughed at the irony of ending up in jail with somebody who knew Blake.

'What's he up to now?' Henderson asked.

'I think he's living in Moscow these days,' I replied.

'Well if ever you get to meet him, make sure you give him my regards,' Henderson beamed.

The screws escorted me back up to Bow Street Magistrate's court on Monday, 17 November for my third and final chance to get bail. They subjected me to the usual Full Monty's, but this time there was no police escort. The authorities presumably realised they didn't have a dangerous prisoner on their hands, despite MI6's claims. By then it mattered little to me whether or not bail was granted as I was resigned to spending more time in jail. My only chance of release lay in the slim possibility that the Attorney General, John Morris, might drop the charges. Breaches of the OSA are not automatically prosecuted: specific authorisation, known as a 'fiat', must be issued by the Attorney General. Ostensibly, it is his decision alone, but in reality the intelligence services decide. They are always the first government agencies to discover breaches of the OSA, so if they do not want a prosecution, as in the case of Melissa Norwood, they keep quiet. But if they want a person prosecuted, as was clear in my case, they swing every axe they can find in Whitehall to ensure that it is carried out with an iron fist. MI6 would lobby Morris hard. But he had not immediately conceded, suggesting that he might at least have some doubts. Like Prime Minister Tony Blair and the rest of the Labour cabinet, Morris had voted against the OSA in 1989. But Owen came to the door-hatch to bring the news. 'Morris has just faxed through the fiat. I am afraid there's no way out now.' It was a blow, but I had taken care not to let my hopes of release get too high. There was now little point in contesting bail. With a fiat issued only a few minutes before the hearing, only a brave magistrate would grant it. Anyway, there were advantages to staying in prison, as time spent on remand would count towards my final sentence.

Three days later, on the BBC radio I heard news that highlighted the political nature of OSA prosecutions. Chris Patten, a former Tory minister and political heavyweight who had lost his seat in the last general election, had been appointed Governor of Hong Kong to oversee the years leading up to the 1999 handover of power to China. As Governor, he signed the OSA and regularly received CX reports. He also authorised the journalist Jonathan Dimbleby to write an official biography glorifying his governorship, entitled *The Last Days*. In order to substantiate aspects of the book, and no doubt also to pump up sales, Patten gave Dimbleby direct copies of many CX reports. This brazen breach of the OSA was more serious than that posed by giving Martyn a heavily disguised synopsis that was never published. The police and the CPS wanted to prosecute but Morris refused to issue the fiat, arguing that there was 'no useful purpose' in prosecuting Patten.

If breaches of secrecy laws are not applied consistently to all offenders, whatever their status, then they are political offences. I wrote to Morris from my prison cell asking him to explain this inconsistency and asked what 'useful purpose' he saw in prosecuting me. He never replied.

One of the many restrictions imposed on A-cat prisoners is close control over visits. We were only permitted visits from immediate family, and then only after they had been approved by the police and prison service. On my first day in Belmarsh, using a special application form, I nominated my mother as my first visitor. This was sent to Cumbria SB and two PCs interviewed her at home. It wasn't until Friday, 21 November, three weeks after my arrest, that she was cleared to make the seven-hour trip to south-east London for a 40-minute visit. There was a thick sheet of perspex between us to prevent any physical contact and we spoke through a recorded intercom. My mother found the visit traumatic and, though she tried to put on a brave face, I could tell that she was close to tears.

A-cat prisoners were allowed to receive up to four letters a day which were censored by the staff and, in my case, copied to MI6. Most of my mail came from family and friends and I could recognise who a letter was from by the handwriting and postmark. One day a letter came bearing unfamiliar handwriting. Even after reading it, it took me several minutes to realise that it was from a former member of staff. She wrote that in a few years time my offence would be regarded as purely political, a morale-boosting fillip from somebody ostensibly from the other side. Shortly after her letter, a second piece of surprise mail arrived, the envelope bearing handwriting that, by the forward slope and cut-down letter 'y's, was that of a native Russian speaker. More mysteriously, it was from prisoner XM2920 in Wormwood Scrubs. It took several scans of the letter to make a mental connection with the name at the bottom. 'Nueman' was the MI6 resettlement name for NORTHSTAR. My last news of him was that he was about to start an MBA and he explained in his letter what had happened next. After finishing the degree, he set up a business organising conferences on western commercial practices for Russian and Ukranian businessmen. Unfortunately, having accepted their substantial up-front registration fees, he forgot to do the rest. When some of the delegates demanded the return of their fees, he fled to Geneva. After a lengthy legal battle, he was extradited back to the UK and received 36 months for fraud. We exchanged a few letters and started a game of correspondence chess which he was soon winning handsomely.

In early December Mr Richards collared me as I was going through the metal detector to the exercise yard. 'Tomlinson, get back here.' he bellowed cheerfully. 'No exercise for you today, you've got a police visit.' My spirits fell. Police normally visited prisoners only to press more charges.

After the strip-search, two screws escorted me to the A-cat legal visits rooms. Waiting for me were DI Ratcliffe and the baldy who had searched my flat at the time of my arrest. He introduced himself as DI Peters and explained that he was a computer expert. Wadham was there to give me assistance. 'Richard, we need your help to crack the encrypted material on your Psion,' Ratcliffe asked sheepishly.

It surprised me that SB, MI6 and GCHQ had not yet cracked the text I wrote in Spain, as the encryption programme was tiny and used only a small key and a simple password.

'We wonder if you could give us the password,' Peters asked.

'You're joking!' I laughed. 'Why would I want to do that?'

'Well have a think about it,' Ratcliffe replied in a manner that indicated that life might be difficult if I didn't.

The police left the room for a moment so that I could confer with Wadham. 'They've got something planned if you don't give them it,' he advised. 'Unless you've really got something to hide, I'd tell them.' There was another copy buried on the internet, so it would not be a problem to lose the files. 'Also,' added Wadham, 'if you cooperate the judge should knock a few months off your sentence.' Ratcliffe and Peters filed back into the room a few minutes later. 'The passphrase is "MI6 are stupid tossers",' I told them.

'We should have thought of that one,' Peters grinned.

Even A-cat prisoners have the right to speak confidentially to their lawyers, enshrined in 'rule 37' of the prison regulations. If I needed to telephone Wadham, informing Mr Richards beforehand supposedly ensured that the automatic recorder would be turned off. Likewise, if an envelope was marked 'rule 37', supposedly the censors would not open it. But like most of the other prisoners, I had little confidence that this rule would be respected, especially in the lead up to my committal. MI6 would be keen to learn how I would plead because it would allow them to use I/OPS to ensure favourable spin in the press. I later learned that my efforts at discretion were futile and that MI6 always knew in advance of my intentions. Over on spur 1 were three Algerian students who had been on remand for nearly a year under the Prevention of Terrorism Act. Ironically I first came across their files while in PTCP section. The DST asked MI5 to arrest them because of their alleged links to the FIS, the Algerian Islamic Fundamentalist group, but MI5 had been reluctant to deploy their limited A4 surveillance resources. In retaliation the DST withdrew their cooperation with us on operations such as BELLHOP, so with some internal politicking, MI5 were persuaded to take an interest in the students. Their telephones were bugged, they were put under foot surveillance and were eventually arrested for allegedly conspiring to obtain explosive materials. The evidence was weak and the three were adamant that they were not guilty. They came up for trial at the Old Bailey shortly before my committal. But the CPS made a basic error in their opening statements by revealing knowledge that the Algerians had disclosed only to their defence lawyers in the Belmarsh legal visits rooms. The defence realised that these visits had been bugged and challenged the CPS. When the CPS refused to explain their source, the judge dismissed the case and the defendants were released. Suspiciously, whenever Wadham or Davies met me in Belmarsh, we were always allocated the same room that was used by the Algerians.

Our cells were regularly searched by the screws. Without warning, specially trained three-man search teams with sniffer dogs would enter the spur and choose one or two prisoners. The inmate was strip-searched, then ejected from his home. Anything illicit in the cell was confiscated and the prisoner punished with a spell in the block. They took silver foil because it could be used to melt heroin before injection, matches as the heads could be used for incendiary devices, polythene bottles because they could be filled with chopped fruit and sugar to brew into 'hooch'. The search teams also took two large, heavy-duty black suitcases into each cell. Nobody knew what was in them but the rumour was that they contained portable photocopiers. 'You just see,' Dobson told me. 'They'll be round your cell with those suitcases a few days before you go up in court.' And he was right; I was subjected to a lengthy search just two days before committal. So even if they had not already learnt of my intended 'guilty' plea by bugging my discussions with Wadham and Davies, they would have known from copying the 'rule 37' papers in my cell.

Two screws escorted me back up to Bow Street Magistrates on Monday, 24 November. Up in the dock, the magistrate asked me to confirm my identity, then read the charges against me. 'What is your plea?' he finally asked.

The court was hushed in anticipation and in the press gallery I could see the hacks with pens poised to record the plea of the first MI6 officer charged with violating the OSA since Blake. 'Guilty,' I replied, keeping my voice as steady as I could. The press gallery scrabbled out of court to broadcast the news. But there was not a flicker of reaction from Colin Gibbs or the SIS legal representative.

In the prison van going back to Belmarsh my guilt was reported in sensational fashion on the radio news bulletins every half hour. The next day it was on the front page of most of the broadsheets. *The Times* accused me of having 'attempted to sell secrets' to an Australian publisher. The *Telegraph* lamely repeated the MI6 line that I had 'endangered the lives of agents'. I/OPS must have been pleased with the results. The sensational coverage would strengthen the mythical status in which MI6 are revered in some quarters and deepen the mysterious importance of their work. But a more direct consequence for me was that there was a danger of the media coverage 'hyping' my sentence and that on sentencing day on 18 December the judge would give me a longer stretch than I would otherwise have received.

'You look like a bleedin' hippy,' Onion-head laughed in the lunch queue a few days before my sentencing.

'I'd get it cut if I were you,' advised Dobson. 'The joodge'll give yer three months more with yer hair like that.'

They were right – a haircut was already overdue when my appointment in Wavendon had been peremptorily interrupted by my arrest. That evening's association I filled in the application form to the Governor and Mr Richards advised me the next day that permission had been granted.

'You can be our new barber's first client,' he grinned. 'Clarke! Come here,' he shouted across the spur, 'your services are required!'

The new barber, a Jamaican armed robber who had just been remanded the previous day, ambled out of his cell, pulling up the drawstring of his trousers. He suffered from a severe nervous twitch which had caused his shotgun to accidentally discharge while he was holding up a bank in Southall. Luckily the shot hadn't hit anybody but nevertheless he was facing a longer sentence as a result of the negligent discharge. He had never cut hair in his life but Mr Richards had appointed him spur barber because he shared his name with Nicky Clarke, a celebrity London hairdresser. 'Here's the clippers,' Mr Richards bellowed cheerfully, passing a small wooden box to the bemused Clarke. 'Get one of those chairs and set up shop under the stairs.'

'Can you just tidy it up a bit?' I asked Clarke as soon as a chair had been positioned and the clippers had been plugged in. 'I'm up in the dock for sentencing tomorrow.'

Clarke muttered something back to me in an unintelligible Jamaican accent, checked that the clippers were plugged into the wall, switched them on and paused for a moment, studying the buzzing blades quizzically as if weighing up their potential for robbing banks. He muttered some more. Thinking it impolite to ask him to repeat himself I just smiled encouragingly. Tentatively, he leant over me and began clipping the right side of my head but suddenly and painfully, the clippers dug hard into my ear. 'Bollocks!' Clarke muttered, taking a step back to recompose himself after the twitch. Bending over, he tried again. But he was siezed by another twitch. 'Shite!' Clarke muttered, as a large clump of hair fell to the ground. Frowning in concentration, he studied the right side of my head, then the left, then the right, and began to trim again.

There were no mirrors on the spur so there was no way to check progress. 'Are you sure you know what you are doing?' I asked politely.

Clarke muttered something back and started fiddling with the clipper blades. He looked a bit hurt and I thought it better not to press him. But judging by the ever increasing pile of hair on the floor, he was a quick learner and he finished off with a flourish just as Mr Richards bellowed the familiar order, 'Spur 1, get your dinner.' Clarke hurriedly unplugged the clippers and returned them to Mr Richards as the spur clamoured into a disorderly queue.

Dobson and Onion-head were, as usual, at the back, maximising the time out of their cells, and I joined them as soon as I had collected my plastic mug and cutlery from my cell. 'You look like a bleedin' convict,' Onion-head laughed as he saw my new crop.

'Yer daft booger,' added Dobson. 'The joodge'll give yer three months more with yer 'air like that.'

I woke shortly after 5 a.m. the next day, shaved, washed, polished my scalp, dressed and sat on my bed reading until the screws arrived at about 7 a.m. to escort me to the Old Bailey. Having put in a request form the previous evening's association, my suit and best shoes were brought out of storage in reception for me to change into. We left at 9 a.m. for the familiar drive across east London to the Old Bailey. It was an evil, blustery, overcast day and through the darkened glass porthole of my cubicle it appeared almost night outside. As we were crossing Tower Bridge in heavy traffic, an elderly man on the pavement stopped in his stride and stared impassively into my porthole. Probably an ex-con, I thought to myself, reflecting how lucky he was to be on the outside.

The dock in court 13 of the Old Bailey was oddly positioned high above the court, like a projectionist's booth in a cinema, giving me a panoramic view of the sentencing judge, Recorder of London Sir Lawrence Verney, his two court assistants, the CPS, my defence team and various court clerks and stenographers. To the right the press gallery was packed with the usual faces. High up to the left was the public gallery, also full, and curiously there were two strangers with their fingers crossed for me. To their right was another smaller gallery, less full. Ratcliffe and Peters were there, so perhaps it was a gallery for members of the CPS who had been working on the case. Ratcliffe and Peters seemed decent on the occasions that we had met and I wondered if they really got any satisfaction from prosecuting me. It was intimidating to be the centre of so much attention and I felt more distressed than at the other court appearances.

The CPS spoke first, arguing that my actions 'greatly damaged national security', without ever attempting to define 'national security' or explain how it had been harmed. Emotion welled up inside me at the stupidity and injustice of the allegations and I held my head in my hands. Gibbs wanted to bring another expert witness and Verney granted permission to take the court temporarily *in camera*. Redd, former H/MOS, took the stand to bleat that my synopsis had 'endangered the lives of officers'. Davies spoke well in my defence, pointing out that there was nothing of substance in the synopsis, that it had not left a locked filing cabinet and that my 'guilty' plea and cooperation with the police deserved consideration. A glance at my wristwatch showed that the arguments went on for 53 minutes, until Judge Verney called a recess to consider his verdict. The screws slipped my handcuffs back on to take me down to the dungeons, but I only had to wait in the cell for a few minutes before the door opened and they dragged me back up to the dock.

Verney's opening words described the 'seriousness of the offence', immediately dashing my hope to be out in time for Christmas. He took into account my guilty plea and that it was my first ever offence, but gave no consideration for my cooperation with the police. 'I therefore have no alternative but to sentence you to 12 months imprisonment,' he announced gravely. My release date would be 1 May, only four-and-a-half months away on a calendar but a long time in Belmarsh.

Davies and Wadham came down to the dungeons to commiserate. 'You know that you have the right to appeal against the sentence,' Wadham explained, 'and you might get a few weeks less.' But I declined the offer. Wadham and Davies were acting for me *pro bono* and it would be an abuse of their generosity to ask them to mount an appeal. Ratcliffe and Peters also wanted to see me for more help in decrypting my Psion, but I declined. Judge Verney hadn't given me any consideration for my previous cooperation, so there was no reason to help them now.

Unusually, there was another inmate in the prison van on the way back to Belmarsh. The reason was clear once back on the spur. 'Tomlinson, you're off the book,' announced Mr Richards cheerfully. 'You'll be on work as soon as Christmas is over.' The Governor had downgraded my security status from A-cat to B-cat, meaning I could visit the gym more frequently and people other than immediate family would be able to visit.

For the Christmas break, the prison staff made an effort to bring some spirit to the spur with a small tree and tinsel above Mr Richards's desk. On Christmas day, we had a half-hour lie-in and a cooked breakfast, then all-day association. We were only briefly locked back into our cells to eat lunch of a chicken leg, roast potatoes and sprouts, Christmas pudding and a real treat of a Cornetto ice-cream. In the afternoon the staff arranged a pool tournament (won convincingly by Dobson) and then a young female screw whom we had not seen before organised a bingo game with first prize of a £5 phone card, won by Onion-head with some blatant cheating.

'You've got to give the screws some credit,' Dobson muttered as Onion-head cavorted up to the pretty screw to collect his prize, giving her a cheeky kiss, 'they've had to give up their own Christmas day at home and spend it in here with us bastards.' Dobson was right that the Belmarsh staff did an excellent job, and not just on Christmas day. Relations between staff and prisoners were generally cordial and there was little of the confrontational 'them and us' management style that existed in other prisons. And it couldn't be easy spending all day confined in a pressure cooker with a brewing mixture of depressed, psychopathic or violent criminals. They regularly got abused verbally and attacked physically by angry prisoners, and were at risk of being taken hostage or even murdered. The dangers they faced on a daily basis were far higher than those ever faced by the bleating Redd, the MI6 officer who had whined at my sentencing that my synopsis had 'endangered the lives of agents'. And then at the end of what amounted to a very stressful day the screws had to go home to try and live on a salary a fraction of Redd's, in one of the world's most expensive cities.

'You'll not believe yer ears tonight, Rich,' Dobson told me enthusiastically on New Year's Eve. 'We're gonna have a reet party!' A few prisoners had got themselves a joint prepared and there were rumours that there was some hooch about.

It was customary for prisoners to see in the New Year by banging any hard object against the heating pipes, cell doors and window bars. It seemed pointless to me. 'You'll not catch me joining in with that nonsense,' I replied. 'I'll be tucked up in bed.' I consoled myself that for once I would wake up in the New Year without a hangover.

'Nah, yer big wuss,' jeered Dobson, 'you'll be up bangin' wi' the rest of us.'

The first sporadic clatter and whooping started at about 11.30 p.m., gathering in intensity until it became pointless trying to concentrate on my book. I had just put out the light when somebody attacked the heating pipe with their waste-paper bin, jolting me upright. Soon somebody else joined in and, as midnight approached, the din became a cacaphony as every inmate released a year's frustration in wild fits of banging, screaming and hollering. The joyful spirit was too infectious to ignore and I got out of bed, picked up my bin and hurled it against the door, then again and again, and whooped and shouted with the rest.

The only advantage of being an A-cat prisoner was automatic assignation to a single-cell on security grounds. Since my downgrading to B-cat, that privilege had gone and my days in such comparative luxury were numbered. Sunday morning associations, when we were issued with a clean sheet, pillow case and Bic razor, were when the screws also reallocated cells. On the first Sunday in January, Mr Richards bellowed out from his desk on the spur floor, 'Tomlinson, get your stuff.' My time had come and resignedly I tipped my belongings into my bin liner, rolled up the mattress, sheets, pillow and blanket into a bundle and presented myself to his desk. 'Over there,' he indicated, pointing to the double cell right by his desk, grinning as ever.

'You bastard,' I muttered. The words were meant to be unheard, but they slipped out too loud. 'Tomlinson, I'll have you down the block if you say that again!' Mr Richards threatened without menace. Cell 2 was right next to his desk and he reserved it for troublesome 'fraggles' or suicidal 'toppers' so he could keep a close eye on them. Two fraggles or toppers could not be together in the same cell, so a well-behaved prisoner had to take the other bed. I'd been selected as the spur's psychiatric nurse. 'You'll get your new cellmate tomorrow afternoon,' Mr Richards grinned mischievously.

Dumping my foam mattress and bedding on the metal straps of the hard iron bed, I surveyed my new cell. It had just been vacated by Parker, an untidy, overweight, chain-smoking gun-freak. Before Belmarsh, he had lived at home in Essex with his mother and weapon collection. One day he drank too much beer and fell sound asleep on his bed. His doting mother found him and, fearing he was dead, called an ambulance. The paramedics arrived, realised he was just drunk, but also found a shotgun under his bed. They called the police who arrested him and he was sentenced to two years imprisonment for illegal possession of firearms. His other hobby was lying in bed smoking and eating jaffa cakes, so jail was a Butlin's activity camp for him. The cell stank of bad hygiene, the floor had not been swept for weeks and even a bluebottle would have thrown up at the toilet. The rest of that Sunday was spent cleaning with the tiny strip of pot-scrubber and miniature bar of soap which we were allowed in our cells. That night, lying on my bed listening to a violent storm battering the prison, I prayed that my new cellmate, whether, a fraggle or a topper, would at least be clean.

As a newly demoted B-cat, I was now eligible for 'work' and my first day in my new job was the next morning. Work gave me the opportunity to get out of the cell more often and my daily prison allowance went up from £1.26 per day to £1.76, making it possible to buy extra fruit, food and toiletries from the prison canteen. Somewhat surprisingly, given my crime, the Governor assigned me to the computer room, down in the basement of the workshop area. Mike, the patient and kindly course instructor, quickly realised that I already knew how to use a PC so allowed me to do as I liked rather than follow the basic computer literacy course.

Shortly after returning to the cell from my first day in the lab, the door-flap slapped back, Mr Richards's narrow eyes checked me, and the heavy door locks clunked. 'Tomlinson, here's your new cellmate,' Mr Richards announced with a devilish grin as he flung the door open. I put down my pocket-computer chess game and stood, ready to greet my new cellmate. Holding open the door, Mr Richards impatiently beckoned in the new arrival, but the smell announced Stonley's presence even before he was visible. Mr Richards instinctively recoiled back into the fresher air of the spur and slammed the door shut on us.

Stonley walked over to the spare bed, put his only possessions, a plastic mug and cutlery, on the bedside locker and began angrily pacing the cell in tiny circles, clutching his beard, oblivious to my presence. I watched for a couple of minutes, and realised that he was not going to stop. 'Hey Stonley,' I said warmly, 'would you mind giving it a break?' Stonley stopped in his tracks and stared in surprise at me as if I were a talking flowerpot. 'Have a sit-down,' I suggested. Stonley obliged immediately, as if used to being bullied around, and once perched on the edge of his bed stared angrily out of the window, still clutching his beard. 'I'm Richard, what's your name?'

Stonley made no eye contact but after a short pause, spat out, 'Stonley.'

'No, I mean what's your first name?'

Stonley turned from the window, flashed an angry glare and replied, 'Dunno', before returning his anger to the window. I tried again, but got the same response, this time more angrily. Although Stonley was sitting motionless on the edge of his bed, his stench had wafted over to me and I had to move to the other end of my bed.

The door-flap slapped open and Onion-head, who had just been appointed a spur cleaner and was outside collecting the lunch-trays, leered in. 'Arright, Rich?' he laughed, gooning his face into an exaggerated imitation of Stonley. 'Wait till he starts playin' his pink oboe!' I gave him the finger and he slapped the flap back with another laugh.

I had to find a way of getting out of sharing the cell with Stonley, but my options were limited. The staff were usually reasonable about putting compatible cellmates together as it caused them less bother if they got along. But they would not let me off the hook with Stonley so easily; nobody was compatible with him and the screws accurately guessed it was not in my nature to start a fight, a tactic his previous cellmate had used to engineer a separation.

At unlock for evening association, I made a beeline for Mr Richards. 'You've got to get me out of there. Stonley should be in hospital, not in prison. You'll turn me into a fraggle too if I have to share with him much longer,' I pleaded.

Mr Richards laughed, 'You're going nowhere, Tomlinson. Doctor's orders. Stonley has to be in a double cell so that he learns to interact with other prisoners.'

'Well, if I have to share with him, will you please tell him to wash his clothes and get a shower?' Mr Richards obliged and ordered Stonley to take a shower and hand in his filthy clothing to the unfortunate Turkish laundryman for washing.

Locked back in after association, I found that Stonley had used the toilet and badly missed. He would never clean it up, so there was no choice but to do it myself. He was still perched on the edge of his bed, staring angrily out of the window, twiddling with his beard, as I finished and junked my last strip of pot-scrubber in the bin. As there had been cases of fraggles attacking sleeping cellmates, I didn't dare go to sleep before him and stayed up playing chess on my pocket set. At about 1 a.m., Stonley briefly went to the toilet, lay down on his bed, pulled a sheet over himself and started masturbating.

After a fitful night's sleep, inspiration struck in the morning. 'Stonley, do you smoke?' I asked as soon as he was awake.

'Dunno,' he replied angrily.

'You must know the answer to that, surely?' I replied.

'Dunno,' he shouted back.

As soon as we were unlocked, I grabbed my half-full phone card, two Twixes, and a tube of custard creams, and dashed over to Onion-head's cell, where he was having a cup of tea with Dobson. 'Arright, Rich?' he asked. 'How's the fraggle, did he burp his worm last night?'

'Shut up, you bastard,' I replied with a smile. 'Onion-head, you got any tobacco?'

'What's up, Rich?' jeered Dobson. 'You tekkin' up smokin', it's that bad is it?'

I dumped the phone card, Twixes and custard creams on Onion-head's bed. 'I'll swap you all that for an ounce of tobacco and five Rizlas.' Onion-head's eyes lit up – it was a good swap – and he handed me the remains of a pouch of Golden Virginia with a few papers.

Back in the cell after breakfast I asked Stonley if he would like a smoke. He glared at me suspiciously. It was perhaps the first time anybody had offered him anything since coming into prison. I produced the pouch and papers, and pushed them over to him. 'They're yours, I don't smoke.'

He studied them suspiciously for a few seconds, like a stray cat who has been given a tempting morsel by a stranger, then pounced, expertly crafting a rollie and lighting up. As soon as the cell was nicely full of smoke, I got up and pushed the 'room service' bell to call a screw. It was supposed only to be used in emergencies and I risked getting a day down the block for its abuse. Mr Richards arrived a few minutes later to investigate. 'Tomlinson, what do you want?' he asked impatiently through the perspex window.

'Mr Richards, you never told me Stonley was a smoker.'

Mr Richards looked at me quizzically. 'So what?' he asked.

'Prison regulation 12a,' I replied, 'A non-smoking prisoner cannot be forced to share a cell with a smoking prisoner against his wishes.'

Mr Richards glared back at me for a moment. 'Tomlinson, I'll 'ave you one day,' he replied, exasperated. But he knew he was beaten. Most prisoners didn't know about the rule, but my study of the prison regulation book during associations had paid off. 'OK, get your stuff, cell 8 on the first landing is free.' Mr Richards held the door open while I bundled my stuff back together and escorted me up to my new home, a single cell.

Early in January, Belmarsh received a visit from the 'Health and Safety at Work' inspection teams. When we were unlocked to queue for lunch the spur and hotplate area had been plastered with signs warning us of dangers. By the stairs was a neat sign announcing, 'Caution: Steep Stairs'. Around the hotplate notices warned us, 'Caution: Hot Surfaces'. It was absurd to pretend that these presented serious hazards to our wellbeing, when we were cooped up in such confines with some of the most violent men in the country. 'What a bleedin' liberty,' laughed Onion-head, scornfully eyeing the warning on the stairs. 'They lock up an ordinary, decent armed robber like me with dangerous, book-writing ex-secret agents like you,' he said to me, 'and then they warn us about steep bleedin' stairs.' With a quick glance around to ensure no screws were watching, he drew heavily on his roll-up until the tip glowed red, and lit the corner of the sign. As flames leapt up the paper laying long, black soot streaks up the wall, Onion-head chuckled mischievously, 'That's that fixed then, eh? They should put up another sign saying "Caution: Inflammable Signs".'

Shortly after the next computer workshop session a few additional notices appeared, written on identical paper with the same typeface. Above each toilet appeared the notice, 'Caution: this toilet is fucking filthy'. On the wall behind Mr Richards' desk appeared another, 'Caution: this screw is bloody thick'. It took Mr Richards a few days to notice and then we never saw any more of the 'Health and Safety at Work' notices.

Even though Belmarsh was a maximum security prison and elaborate precautions were taken to prevent prisoners smuggling contraband on to the spurs, there was still a fair amount of drugs about. For several prisoners, especially those facing long sentences, getting high was their only relief from the numbing boredom and lack of challenge in prison life. Drugs were smuggled in by two routes. One was by a crooked screw who had been recruited by a former inmate. The other was via the visiting-rooms. Now that I was a B-cat prisoner, I could attend open visits and saw for myself how it was done.

Open visits took place in a large hall, filled with six rows of visiting-booths. There were 20 booths on each row, separated by low dividing partitions. Around the edge of the room was a raised gantry where the screws could observe the visits. We waited in a large, smoke-filled holding-cell for our turn to go forward, be briefly searched and to receive a coloured, lettered bib to wear. The colour and letter corresponded to a particular booth. When all the prisoners were seated, the visitors were permitted to enter. They had been checked for drugs with a sniffer dog, but it was not legal for the prison staff to search them physically. Wives and girlfriends of the prisoners defeated the dog without too much difficulty by wrapping the drugs in cling-film and secreting the package in their bodies. Prisoners were allowed to kiss their partners briefly at the beginning and end of the visit, and the package was transferred. We were searched on leaving the visits hall, but prisoners who were seen kissing suspiciously were searched more thoroughly, including inside their mouths. Smugglers therefore had no option but to swallow their package, which was potentially fatal should it burst. They later retrieved the package, as Ronnie explained, 'from one orifice or the other'.

Prisoners were regularly tested for drugs. Those suspected of drug-taking were called up more often to give urine samples. I had my first mandatory test on 2 February. As I was preparing to go to work, a screw came to my cell. 'No work for you today, Tomlinson. Drink that tea down fast and don't have a piss.' He escorted me down unfamiliar corridors to the drug testing centre, and put me in a holding-cell with couple of other prisoners. Amongst them was the Italian guy I had briefly met when first remanded to Brixton, his cockney English now fluent.

When my turn came I was asked to confirm that I was not on any medication. 'No bad back, then?' the screw asked suspiciously. Most of the dope-using prisoners had permanent 'bad backs' and queued every day to get a dose from the doctor of Brufen pain-reliever which masked traces of marijuana in their blood, rendering the test worthless. Indeed, Ronnie's bad back was so 'bad' the doctor had ordered him to have an extra mattress in his cell. The screw lead me over to a urinal, gave me a small receptacle and told me to fill it. 'Tomlinson, if you hear of any drug use, you'll give us a nod, won't you?' he asked lamely afterwards. 'You'll have to do better than that to recruit me,' I laughed.

The probation service summoned me on 29 March, and I went to the legal visits rooms to find a young female officer waiting for me. 'There is something very odd about your case,' she frowned. 'Normally we have a first appointment with a prisoner three months before they are released, but we were only told about you by the Home Office two days ago and the Governor wants to talk to me about you after this meeting.' I suspected the meddlesome hand of MI6, but said nothing. She explained that I would be on probation for three months after my release, and during that time I could be re-imprisoned for breaching any probation conditions. 'But frankly, for somebody like you who is a first-time, non-violent offender, there won't be any conditions and we probably won't bother you much.' She made an appointment to see me three days before my release, and wished me luck for the rest of my sentence.

The mood on the spur varied from day to day, depending on which screws were on duty. If the good-natured and cheerful Mr Richards was in charge, associations were quiet and generally trouble-free. But when Mr Richards was on leave, senior screws from other spurs stood in and their different management style, or unfamiliarity with the foibles of a troublesome prisoner, could quickly antagonise the whole spur. In early April the atmosphere became so tense that even Mr Richards was losing his cool. First, a bottle of hooch was found brewing behind the washing machine and because nobody would own up association was cancelled for the day. Then the local newsagent went bankrupt and all the prisoners, myself included, lost the money paid in advance for the deliveries. Then we lost another association because most of the screws took leave to attend the funeral of a colleague who had hung himself. With missed associations and trivial annoyances, the spur was in a tetchy mood and there were some minor scuffles in the lunch queue. That afternoon association was late starting because a screw had fallen ill and a replacement could not be found immediately. We were late getting to the gym, so our session was shorter than usual. 'Spur 1, in your cells, no shower, no water.' Mr Richards bellowed as soon as we were back, the timetable disruption forcing him to cut the ten minutes we normally had to get a shower and hot water. A cup of tea at every bang-up was an important part of the daily routine, and having it denied was demoralising.

'Mr Richards, yer a fat, fat bastard,' hollered Onion-head from the balcony, ducking into his cell before Mr Richards could identify him. A few prisoners tried to make a dash for the urn, but Mr Richards collared them and emptied the mugs of those who had succeeded in filling them. Other screws starting banging-up prisoners like me who had reluctantly gone into their cells, and the spur resounded with the clunking of the heavy locks and the slapping of the flaps. One irritated prisoner banged his metal waste-paper bin against the cell door and soon everybody joined in. I lost my temper too, and kicked my cell door so hard that I bruised my toe, making me madder still.

A few prisoners who had not yet gone into their cells were putting up a protest, Craggs the most vociferous. I heard Mr Richards hollering at Craggs, 'In your cell, Craggs!' even his good humour tested to the limit.

'I'm havin' my fucking mug of water,' screamed back Craggs.

'Craggs, get in your cell NOW!'

The argument was hotting up and I hopped over to my flap. The screw had slammed it shut with such haste that it had bounced back open slightly and the spur floor was just visible. Mr Richards was standing in front of the hot water urn, blocking the furious Craggs. 'Craggs, if you take one step closer, you're down the block.'

Craggs glared at Mr Richards and then rushed, leaping for his throat. Mr Richards just had time to press his belt alarm before the angry inmate was on top of him. Craggs' moment of vengeance and glory was short-lived. He was quickly overpowered by screws bursting in from the other spurs and was hauled off down to the segregation block, never to be seen again.

The tension of the day's events was too much for Mockalenny.

That evening at unlock for dinner he emerged from his cell wearing nothing but his underpants, singing 'God save our Princess Anne' to the tune of the British national anthem. He had painted his face with toothpaste for tribal war paint, had fashioned a head-band out of threads from his blanket and was brandishing a pool-cue like a spear. The screws allowed him get his dinner, still singing and waving his spear. When he had eaten his meal and we were all banged-up once more, he was escorted from the spur and we never saw him again either.

A few days before release, Mr Richards called me up for another probation visit. Making my way over to the legal visits rooms, I was expecting to see the pretty young officer again. But this time it was a senior male officer who didn't smile or shake hands in greeting. 'Tomlinson, here's your probation conditions.' He handed me a two-page sheet. 'You will not be allowed to leave the country after you are released and you will have to hand both your British and New Zealand passports to the Metropolitan police SB. You will not be allowed to speak to any journalists or any members of the media. If you do you will be immediately reimprisoned. Do you understand?' I nodded, though I found it difficult to believe that they could impose such Stalinist conditions. 'And finally, you will not be allowed to use the internet or e-mail.'

'You're not serious,' I laughed. 'Don't tell me, I am not allowed to use a telephone either, or read a newspaper, I suppose?'

The probation officer glared humourlessly at me, and didn't reply.

Dobson kept telling me that the last few days before release would be the longest of my life but they were little different from any of the others. Even when the remaining days of incarceration could be counted on my fingers, the intense feeling of anger at my imprisonment never left me. The manner in which MI6 had dismissed me, abused their powers to block my right to expose their malpractice with the argument that the courts were 'not secure,' and then hypocritically and glibly used the same courts to sentence me still rankled deeply. Unable to come to terms with my fate like the other prisoners, even one day of incarceration was too much. All the six months of boring frustration had succeeded in doing was to increase my resolve to publish this book.

14

ON THE RUN

FRIDAY, 1 MAY 1998
LONDON

'Morning, Tomlinson, you're out and about early,' Mr Richards greeted me cheerfully as he pushed open my door at 7 a.m. He must have unlocked many other prisoners on their release days, but he still got pleasure from it. The previous evening I gave my spare food, magazines and books away, leaving only a few items to stuff into a bin liner while Mr Richards held the cell door open. He gave me a moment to bang up Dobson and Onion-head to say goodbye through their flaps.

'Good luck wi' yer book. If ye' need a hand smugglin' it into Britain, yer know who to call,' shouted Dobson, already up and reading at his desk.

'Tell 'em I'm an innocent man!' yelled Onion-head from his pit. Mr Richards then escorted me down the now-familiar corridors to reception. 'And I hope I never see you again,' Mr Richards said with a smile as he handed me over to the reception staff.

Even though my release was imminent, there were still the familiar strip-searches, X-rays and long waits in smoke-filled holding-pens. 'You might be nicking something for all we know,' explained one reception screw. 'Them prison shirts are all the rage at the Ministry of Sound these days.'

The process had dragged on for three hours when a screw stuck his head around the door of the holding-cell. 'Which one of you's Tomlinson, then?' he asked, glaring around at us. I stuck up my hand. 'You're wanted down at Scotland Yard this afternoon, 3 p.m.,' he announced seriously, 'and you've to take your passports.' The releasees waiting with me whistled and cheered. 'You'll be back in 'ere Monday morning then,' laughed one black guy. 'They'll charge you with somfin' new tonight, hold you in the police cells over the weekend, then nick yer back 'ere Monday sharp.' It was gut-wrenching to know he was probably right. If MI6 were planning on bringing new charges, they would do it on a Friday afternoon, meaning a long weekend in the police cells until a Monday court appearance.

Stepping through the heavy gate of HMP Belmarsh clutching my bin liner, brought no feeling of jubilation, just a quiet sense of relief that it was over and pleasure at seeing my mother waiting for me. Thankfully there were no journalists, just a couple of police in a Mini Metro who watched as I walked to greet her. She drove me to Richborne Terrace for my first decent shower in six months and a quick lunch before my appointment at Scotland Yard.

A WPC met me in the lobby and took me upstairs, where Ratcliffe and Peters were waiting in an interview room. A pile of polythene specimen bags were spread out on a table. 'To put your mind at rest, Richard,' announced Ratcliffe, 'we are not about to charge you with anything new – we just want to give you your stuff back.' One by one, Peters opened the bags and gave back my possessions. It was like opening Christmas presents, the items were so unfamiliar after months locked in a bare cell – my Psion (from which they had 'accidentally' erased all the data), video camera, various books and videos.

'There are some items you can't have back, unfortunately,' Peters said when the items were all displayed on the table. 'MI6 have told us the photographs and videos that you took in Bosnia could damage national security,' he said with a hint of sarcasm. The photos and video footage of burned out Bosnian villages and the Balkan countryside were completely unconnected with my work and could have been taken by any of the soldiers on duty there, and Peters was clearly sceptical of MI6's claim.

'One other thing,' interjected Ratcliffe. 'Have you brought your passports?'

'Sorry, I forgot,' I lied, using my MI6 training to sound vaguely convincing.

Ratcliffe looked annoyed. 'OK, since you've just got out of jail, we'll give you a break, but we'll make an appointment with your local police station for you to hand them in there first thing tomorrow morning.'

'OK, I'll give them my British passport,' I replied superciliously. 'You've the legal right to take that, but you're not having my New Zealand passport.' My probation terms were so unreasonable and irksome that I was determined to be awkward. Ratcliffe said nothing, but looked nonplussed, so I continued. 'My New Zealand passport belongs to the New Zealand government and it is against international law for a foreign police force to confiscate it.' I wasn't sure that my claim was correct but I said it with conviction and Ratcliffe, who probably didn't know himself, seemed to believe me.

'Well in that case, you'll be in breach of your probation and we'll have no choice but to re-arrest you,' he replied.

'Ok then,' I replied defiantly, 'I'll ring the New Zealand High Commission right now and tell them that you want to arrest me for refusing to surrender my passport.' I picked up my mobile phone that Peters had just returned, and started dialling an imaginary number.

'OK, forget surrendering your New Zealand passport to us. How about if you surrender it to the New Zealand High Commission until your probation is over?' suggested Ratcliffe resignedly. It was a fair compromise and my point was made. We agreed that I would post it to the High Commission first thing the following morning.

Ratcliffe, his duty done, got up and left, leaving me with Peters who escorted me to the exit with my things in a bin liner. 'Richard,' he said guardedly in the lobby, 'I just want to let you know I agree with what you've done. They were bastards to you, and they should be held accountable. But if you are going to carry on your campaign, just make sure you do it abroad. It causes us too much work here . . .' Unfortunately I was not to come across Peters again.

Leaving my flat the following morning with my mother, it was evident that we were under surveillance. A green Vauxhall Astra with two male occupants was parked facing my flat only a few metres away at the junction of Richborne Terrace and Palfrey Place. It was the only 'trigger' position that would enable them to watch both the front door and side entrance. There were no obvious followers as we walked the few hundred metres to the Oval Underground station, but once my mother was on her way back home I was alone and had the opportunity to do a few basic anti-surveillance moves. Walking down Kennington Road towards Kennington police station, I picked up a possible watcher, a young, slightly plump female. There were probably others but it would take more rigorous anti-surveillance to be sure. MI6, anxious to ensure that I stayed in Britain, would be watching to check that my New Zealand passport was posted to the High Commission. I was equally determined to mess them around as much as possible and decided to hang on to the passport as long as I dared, to see what would happen.

The police station was almost within the shadow of Century House, now unoccupied and boarded up. It was Saturday morning, so there were half a dozen other people awaiting attention to enquire about relatives locked up the night before, or to present driving licences after the usual Friday evening drink-drive controls. I sat down on the bench in front of the duty sergeant's counter, picked up a copy of the local newspaper and prepared for a long and tedious wait. I was getting into a good article about a gang who had just been remanded to Belmarsh for holding up a Securicor van when there was a sharp rap on the window of the interview counter. The elderly duty sergeant peered at me over his bifocal glasses. 'Mr Tomlinson, step this way. Inspector Ratcliffe is waiting for you.'

'How do you know my name?' I mischievously called back.

The sergeant looked sheepish; he shouldn't have let on that he already knew me, as it revealed that they had followed me to the station. 'Never mind, just get in there,' he replied impatiently, indicating one of the interview rooms.

'There you are, just as you asked,' I announced sarcastically, slapping my British passport on the desk.

'And have you posted your New Zealand passport to the High Commission?' asked Ratcliffe.

'Oh yes, indeed I have,' I lied brazenly. 'When and where,' asked Ratcliffe suspiciously. 'In the postbox by the Oval tube station, just after I said goodbye to my mother this morning,' I replied, stifling a smirk. Ratcliffe knew I was lying, because the watchers had not reported me posting anything. Ratcliffe could not admit that he had me under surveillance, so he had to accept my false assurance.

With my New Zealand passport still in my top pocket, MI6 had no choice but to keep me under surveillance. That afternoon would give the opportunity to make them earn their living. On the IONEC we practised anti-surveillance against teams from MI5's A4 and the Met SB in London on a couple of exercises, and recced two routes. The first, from Waterloo station across the Thames to the Barbican centre, was a beginner's route, full of easy and obvious surveillance traps, and there was no obvious cover reason for me to go to the City. Taking that route would make it obvious that I was surveillance-aware and they would possibly back off. The second, more complicated and advanced, was down Oxford Street. The crowds made it more difficult for both dogs and hare, but there were some really good anti-surveillance traps. Also, there was a plausible cover reason for me to go there: I badly needed some new clothes.

That afternoon was spent trudging up and down the famous shopping street, feigning interest in clothes and taking advantage of surveillance traps. In Debenham's department store, the switch-back escalators allowed me to scan the shop floor below and I picked up one watcher. At the tube station, a little-used short-cut forced another follower to expose himself as he exited the side entrance like a rabbit from a hole, anxious not to lose my trail. Browsing aimlessly in the labyrinthine bookshelves of Foyles bookstore at Charing Cross Road forced two others to do the same. By the end of the afternoon, I had confirmed repeat sightings on three watchers and had picked up a possible fourth.

Sunday dawned with clear blue skies and a refreshing wind. It was a perfect day to skate in the park and that would provide an opportunity to bait my surveillance. Most surveillance teams train only against targets on foot or in a motor vehicle, and they are ill-prepared to follow targets who choose unusual modes of transport. Skating was ideal; too fast to follow on foot, and followers would be reluctant to expose themselves in a slow-moving car. About 11 a.m., I strapped on my K2s, grabbed a Walkman and burst out of the side entrance of my flat. Some rapid skating took me down Palfrey Place, Fentiman Road and towards Vauxhall Cross. It was a gorgeous, upliftiing morning and it was exhilarating to be on skates again. Passing Vauxhall Cross, I gave the surveillance cameras an exuberant one-fingered salute. Skating backwards over the smooth pavement of Vauxhall Bridge gave me an opportunity to confirm that there was no obvious surveillance behind. Arriving at Hyde Park 20 minutes later, I was feeling buoyant, confident that I had escaped.

'Hey, yo," a familiar voice called out. 'Where yo'been?' I spun around to see Winston and Shaggy, weaving towards me through the strollers and joggers on the broad asphalt path in front of Kensington Palace. 'Where the hell yo' been these last months, fella?' Shaggy grinned, pulling aside his heavy-duty stereo headphones so that he could hear my reply.

'I've just done a stretch down in Belmarsh,' I replied, smiling coyly.

Both Shaggy and Winston had done short stretches in Brixton for peddling in Notting Hill and so they would know Belmarsh. Winston looked at me disbelievingly. 'Like fuck, fella, educated white-boys like you don't get bird!'

I explained how I'd ended up in Belmarsh, but they were still disbelieving.

'Nah, yo's pullin' my arse,' laughed Winston scornfully. 'Yo can't get locked up in 'dis country for writin' no book.' Winston skated off, laughing mockingly.

'Right fella,' Shaggy addressed me, suspicious but prepared to believe me, 'if yo's really done bird, what d'ya call a fella like Winston?' he asked.

'A fraggle?' I answered.

Shaggy laughed, 'Hey Winston, git back here, you fraggle, dis fella really has done bird!'

Winston skated back over. 'If yo's really done bird in Belmarsh, that takes respect!' I held out the palms of my hand and Winston slapped them enthusiastically, delighted to find that the educated white-boy really was an ex-con.

'Shit man, dat helicopter is pissin' me right off,' Winston exclaimed a few minutes later, glaring at a Metropolitan police helicopter that was droning a thousand feet above us. 'Let's get some quiet by d'lake, see what's happenin' there,' he suggested.

Dodging through the ambling pedestrians, we skated over to the Serpentine, on the other side of the park. There were half a dozen of the regulars already there and we joined in the banter. But the helicopter followed us over, the buzzing noise intrusive. 'Hey, Winston, yo' been dealin' again?' shouted Shaggy. 'Dat bleedin' 'copter is followin' yo',' he laughed. Winston came over to join us, looking nervously at the helicopter. 'What yo' bin doin' den, badboy?' laughed Shaggy.

'I bin good dees days,' answered Winston. 'He ain't followin' me, no fuckin' way man, but he's gettin' right on my tits.'

They had used a helicopter to escort me on my prison transfer from Brixton to Belmarsh, but that was because it was a standard operating procedure for A-cats. It would be difficult to keep me under surveillance while I was on my skates, but surely they wouldn't go to the expense of using the police helicopter to follow me? There was only one way to find out. 'Let's go down to Trafalgar Square,' I ventured. 'See what's up over there.' We took off through the heavy Piccadilly traffic, Winston blowing his whistle, skating backwards just in front of any taxi-driver who dared get in his way, giving abuse or the finger, and Shaggy, ghetto blaster balanced on his shoulder, hopping on and off moving buses or grabbing the back-rack of passing motorcyclists. The trip only took a few minutes but it was long enough for the helicopter to appear over our heads again.

Winston was now even more agitated. 'Dat bastard, he followin' me!' he glared skywards indignantly, frowning hard as he planned how to deal with this unwanted intrusion on his day's skating. 'Hey, Shaggy, wot you say, we go back over the lake, if he follows us, den we give 'im somfin' interestin' to look at?' We skated back up Piccadilly, around Hyde Park Corner and back over to the Serpentine. The helicopter droned over a few minutes later. Shaggy and Winston glared hard at the intruder. 'Right, 'dem nosey bastards are asking what for,' announced Winston. Without a further word, they turned around, bent over and dropped their shorts. 'Stick your fuckin' lense up my fuckin' arse!' yelled Winston gleefully.

The helicopter surveillance that afternoon made me realise that MI6 were serious about keeping me under watch and persuaded me that it would be prudent not to play around any more. That evening I posted my passport to the New Zealand High Commission on Haymarket. A few months later, a probation officer told me that SB, under instructions from MI6, put in a warrant to re-arrest me after I failed to post it on Saturday morning. The magistrate threw out the application, pointing out that warrants for breach of probation must be requested by the probation service and not the police. MI6 were not deterred and on Monday morning ordered probation to put in another application. But by then my passport was safely in the post and they couldn't justify an arrest.

After my New Zealand passport was out of my hands there was no more obvious physical surveillance. But MI6 were tapping my home and mobile phones and it was irksome knowing that people I knew in UKZ would be listening to me. Whenever I heard a good joke down the pub, I rang my home ansaphone and repeated it so the transcribers would at least have something to liven up their day. I confirmed that my mail was under surveillance by posting a couple of letters to myself, building into them the anti-tamper tricks we learnt on the IONEC. Any letters posted at the nearest postbox to my house on Richborne Terrace were also intercepted.

In early June I saw a television documentary about the death of the Princess of Wales and Dodi Al Fayed in the Alma tunnel in Paris in August of the previous year. It revealed that the chauffeur, Henri Paul, who also died, worked normally as the Ritz security manager. Mysteriously, a large sum of cash was found on his body. It dawned on me that he was the same Ritz security manager I had come across while reading BATTLE's file in SOV/OPS section in 1992. Realising that this information would be important to the imminent inquest into the deaths, but knowing that going to the British police would see me immediately re-arrested, I wrote to the father of Dodi Al Fayed, Mr Mohamed Al Fayed, the owner of Harrods department store. There was no reply from Harrods, so, presuming that he was not interested in the information, I thought nothing more of it. Six months later, after casually mentioning this to a journalist who immediately recognised its significance, a representative of Mr Al Fayed contacted me. He assured me categorically that the letter had never arrived.

Getting out of jail was a relief, but living in the real world meant working to pay for a roof over my head. My flat was mortgaged commensurate with my MI6 salary, so a new job would have to be as well paid if I wanted to stay there. My experience in MI6 had already proven difficult to market, and to add to my difficulties MI6 said that they would not use their contacts to help me. I didn't want another soul-destroying descent into debt, so I chose to sell my flat. It was in central London, had a small but well-kept garden, a garage and was in good condition, so it sold quickly. It was gut-wrenching to move out for the last time in mid-June and load up my possessions for the drive up the motorway to my parents' home in Cumbria, where I could stay until the probation was over. When my travel restrictions were lifted, I planned to move to Australia or New Zealand where it would be easier to start afresh at the bottom of a new career without the millstone of a mortgage. I bought a laptop computer and hooked up the internet so I could research job opportunities there. It was in direct breach of my probation conditions, but MI6 would have to admit that they were tapping my parents' telephone if they wanted to re-arrest me. In any case, it gave me pleasure to break an absurd and technophobic condition. The internet proved fruitful and soon my Psion was filling with contacts in Auckland and Sydney. One career that interested me was telejournalism and I made contacts with TV companies in both cities. Among them was Australia's Channel 9 TV and their young London correspondent, Kathryn Bonella, met me a couple of times in London. These meetings had to be discreet, because although I was just looking for a job, MI6 would view them as a breach of probation and would try to have me re-arrested.

As the end of my probation neared, I started to fear that MI6's reluctance to provide any resettlement help was an ominous sign. If they believed that I was such a threat that it was necessary to confiscate my passports, ban me from the internet, prevent me talking to journalists and oblige me to rigidly check in with a probation officer every week until 31 July, how were they planning to control me from 1 August? From that date onwards, I would be legally free to talk to journalists, use the internet and travel abroad. It was too suspicious that they would use the stick until the end of probation but then not offer even a whiff of a carrot thereafter.

There was only one conclusion to draw. MI6 must have an elaborate, possibly sinister, plan in place, to control me after 31 July. I feared that they planned to frame me for a crime with a lengthy prison sentence. They had examples of my fingerprints and genetic signature and it would not be difficult to use this as evidence in, say, a drug-smuggling prosecution. I concluded that it was better not to stay in the UK to find out. It would mean going before the end of my probation and without a passport. But how? Luckily there was my training in HMP Belmarsh to fall back on.

Dobson advised me that one way to slip out was to take a ferry from Liverpool to Belfast, then the train to Dublin. A passport was not required to travel to Northern Ireland because it was part of the United Kingdom, nor was one required to travel between the two Irish capitals because that would antagonise the Irish Republicans. Once in Dublin, I could apply for another New Zealand passport from the High Commission and fly out. But the security forces had such an obvious loophole swamped with surveillance, including CCTV cameras that could identify a face in a crowded station, and it was ground I did not know. Dobson also gave me some of his Dover tobacco-smuggling contacts who had fast boats. But getting caught up in a smuggling racket would play into MI6's hands. After reviewing the options, the best was the most brazen – just blag my way on to one of the cross-channel ferries to France. Dobson told me he had succeeded a couple of times when the check-in staff were too busy with other passengers to pay him much attention.

I chose Monday, 27 July for my abscondment because it was the school holiday season, so the ports would be busier than usual. MI6 would be particularly vigilant during the last week of my probation, meaning subterfuge was needed. On 12 July I telephoned a travel agent and booked a Qantas flight from Manchester airport to Sydney for 2 August, the day after the end of my probation and just when MI6 would anticipate my departure. Friends who rang me were informed that the last week in July was to be spent on a cycling tour of Scotland. This would all be picked up by the UKZ telephone transcribers and relayed through the corridors of Vauxhall Cross.

On 22 July an unexpected visit forced me to bring my plans forward. At about 11 a.m., as I was upstairs in my bedroom working on the internet, I heard the crunch of two sets of heavy footsteps on the gravel drive. Spying from behind a curtain, their odd and inappropriate clothing revealed they were from SB. The elder was in a dark pin-stripe suit and heavy brogues, the younger in jeans and a blue fleece top; they looked like *The Professionals* with Bodie off sick.

Presumably they wanted to question me, though about what I didn't know. I had not committed any new offence and SB had no business inquiring about breaches of my probation conditions. I paid no attention when they rang the front door bell and ignored their banging on the back door. They must have known I was at home through surveillance, for they did not give up easily and rang and banged until Jesse, now nearly stone deaf, heard the noise and started barking. Luckily I had locked all the doors so they could not enter without using force. They would have brought a bigger team if they had a warrant, so as long as I lay low, they would give up and go away. After a poke around the garden and outbuildings, as if recceing the lie of the land for a later arrest, they trudged back up the drive some 40 minutes after their arrival.

They would be back with a warrant and a bigger team, so there was no choice but to leave. It took half an hour to pack. I had time for a quick lunch once my parents were back, said a fond goodbye to Jesse, knowing that I would never see her again, and put my two cases on the back seat of my mother's Saab. In case SB had posted surveillance, I hid in the boot like Gordievsky until clear of the village. We arrived 20 minutes later at Penrith railway station, from where the picturesque west country line took me to the southern port city of Poole.

The morning of 24 July broke cloudy and dull, like so many others during the summer of 1998. As planned, the terminal was thronging with families and children, off to France on the first day of the school holidays. Flourishing my birth certificate, driving licence and credit cards at the harassed check-in girl at the 'Truckline' counter, I explained that my passport had been stolen a few days earlier and, after some cursory questioning and a quick but nerve-wracking phone call to her superior, she issued a boarding pass for the 1245 Cherbourg ferry.

With my luggage stowed, I went up on the promenade deck to catch my last view of England and watched the myriad windsurfers and jetskiers flitting across our bows as we pulled out of Poole harbour. Just as when I left the country two years earlier on my way to Spain, it gave me no jubilation or triumph to slip from under the nose of MI6, just sadness that the dispute had ever arisen and that it was still not resolved.

I hung back from the other foot-passengers as we disembarked at Cherbourg and joined the back of the queue, thinking that if the French customs officers stopped me it would be better not to hold up a line of grumbling holidaymakers. My caution was prudent because French customs were having one of their periodic clampdowns. As soon as I presented my limited documentation and caught the sceptical glare of the French Douane, it was evident that getting into France without a passport would be harder than getting out of England. In rusty French, I explained to the first Douane my cover story; I had left my New Zealand passport in Paris and travelled to England on my British passport, which had subsequently been stolen, and so needed to get back to Paris to pick up the New Zealand one. He called his boss over, who asked me to explain again. We were then joined by a third officer and my cover story was starting to sound very thin even to my own ears. 'C'est impossible,' the first Douane told me repeatedly. 'You must go back on the next boat.' But after much discussion, grumbling and criticism of the English authorities for permitting me to travel, the senior officer allowed me to proceed. Grabbing my bags, I made a dash for the Cherbourg train station, eager to get away before they changed their minds. By 11 p.m., I was lodged in a cheap hotel on the Rue d'Amsterdam by the Gare St Lazare in Paris. The first part of my return to New Zealand had gone reasonably smoothly. Now, all that remained was to persuade the New Zealand High Commission in London to send my passport to Paris.

The switchboards of the New Zealand embassy in Paris opened at 9 a.m. on the Monday morning and the receptionist put me through to Kevin Bonici, the second secretary in the consular section. He agreed to ring the High Commission in London and request that my passport be sent over in the next diplomatic bag. It was a relief that he saw no objection to returning it immediately. 'Sure you can have it back. You've broken no New Zealand law, and no French law,' he assured me. This sensible attitude was encouraging, but a couple of hours later he rang me back again. 'We have new instructions from Wellington not to return your passport until the expiry of your licence on 1 August,' he explained. It was astonishing that Wellington had taken an interest in such a trivial incident – the MI6 liaison officer there must have swung his axe. Was not New Zealand a sovereign country with complete independence from the United Kingdom? Wellington had no legal justification to refuse to return my passport, as my breach of the OSA was not illegal in New Zealand or France. Guessing that Wellington's capitulation to pressure from MI6 would be of interest to the New Zealand media, I rang a few journalists there.

Their inquiries must have caused a bit of uneasiness in Wellington, for the following morning, shortly after 10 a.m., Mary Oliver, the consul in Paris and Kevin Bonici's boss rang me. 'Sure you can have your passport back,' she enthused. 'Wellington have now issued a fresh instruction. You can collect it as soon as it arrives from London on Friday morning. Come round here at noon. I look forward to meeting you.'

I spent the next two days enjoying Paris in glorious weather, though fears about MI6's next move were never far from my mind. Drinking a beer on the Champs Elysée in the summer evening sunshine, the possibility that the French police would arrest me at the request of MI6 seemed mere fantasy. MI6 would be reluctant to give the DST the opportunity to question me about their operations against France. Even if they did arrest me, what would be the charge? Skipping a few days of probation was not an extraditable offence. But that gnawing feeling that re-arrest was imminent never totally disappeared. Realising that the best defence against MI6's excesses was to ally myself with journalists, I rang the *Sunday Times*, and told them the story of my abscondment. David Leppard of their 'Insight' team was already in Paris covering another story and we arranged to go together to the New Zealand embassy.

The following morning was warm and humid, and it was a relief to step into the air-conditioned lobby of Leppard's hotel on Avenue Lafayette. After a couple of calls to his room from reception, Leppard ambled down. 'Bloody phone's playing up. I'm sure it's bugged.' I let his comment pass. It amused me that even experienced journalists imagined that a few crackles on the line were signs that their telephone was intercepted.

We took a taxi round to the embassy on the Avenue Leonardo da Vinci near the Place Victor Hugo. To take some photographs for the accompanying article, a *Sunday Times* photographer, Alastair Miller, was waiting outside as we pulled up. Even the heavy-handed DST would shy away from arresting me in front of a journalist and photographer. My suspicions about the New Zealand embassy staff were well-founded. Now they had changed their tune for the third time. 'We've had new instructions from Wellington,' explained Mary Oliver, 'You can't have your passport back until tomorrow.'

The embassy's capitulation to MI6 pressure over my passport was disappointing, and Oliver's farewell pleasantries fell on deaf ears as I stormed out. On the street outside I felt guilty about my rudeness and considered going back in to apologise, but Miller was impatient to get on with the photo-shoot. We walked over to the Trocadero, five minutes away, where the Eiffel tower would make a suitable backdrop, had a light lunch in an outdoor bistro, then Miller set to work. Soon we had a small crowd around us, presuming that I was a rock star or a football player.

We finished at around 1430 and since we were going the same way hailed a taxi together from the Place Victor Hugo. I kept an eye out for surveillance as we ploughed through the slow-moving Paris traffic, but saw nothing obvious. I asked the taxi-driver to drop me at the Gare St Lazare, as it was easier than giving directions to my hotel. The station was being refurbished and heavy polythene dust sheets and scaffolding obscured the familiar facade, disorientating me. Glancing around to find another landmark, I noticed a dark grey VW Passat pulling up 150 metres away. A similar car had been waiting near the taxi rank at the Trocadero. I didn't note the number so I couldn't be sure they were the same, but it added to my unease. I walked up the Rue d'Amsterdam, past the entrance to my hotel and bought a bottle of Evian from a Lebanese delicatessen. Doubling back to my lodgings, there was nobody obviously following.

No sooner had I locked the door of my room behind me and sat down on the narrow bed than there was a knock at the door. It was the sharp, aggressive knock of somebody in authority, not the soft apologetic knock of a hotel maid. 'Oui, qu'est ce-que vous desirez?' I asked, unable to hide the suspicion in my voice.

'C'est la réception.' The voice was too belligerent and in any case reception would have used the internal phone if they needed to speak to me. I stood up, took a deep breath and turned the key in the door. It burst in as though there was a gas explosion outside. Three heavily built men catapulted through the door, screaming, 'Police, Police!', cartwheeling me backwards, smashing my head on the desk and crushing me to the floor. Resistance would have been futile, even if I was so inclined. My arms were wrestled behind my back and handcuffs snapped into place, biting into the flesh. I was helpless, but blows still rained down on the back of my head until a well-aimed kick in the ribs sucked the breath out of me. Only when I fell completely motionless did the assault stop. I was hauled upright, then thrown on to the bed. Three heavies stood over me, their glowers relaxing into triumphant, toothless grins. One was sucking a knuckle that had split during the assault. Behind them stood two more officers, their revolvers pointed at my chest. The taller of the two appeared to be in charge. A wave of the barrel and the three heavies started searching the room.

'L'ordinateur, où est l'ordinateur?' he snapped at me. I pointed at the overturned desk where my laptop lay on the floor, face down, open at the hinge, but seemingly still in one piece. A heavy picked it up, dusted it down, slammed it shut and rammed it into a specimen bag. 'Et le Psion?' continued the gun. I nodded at the bedside table and the bloody knuckle slung it in another bag. Working in silence, they gathered my other possessions and clothes together, crushed them untidily into my suitcase, struggled to close the zip, gave up and strapped it together with my belt, leaving my suit trouser-leg and a shirt-tail hanging out.

Silently they dragged me out of the room and down the narrow corridor to the lift. The commander stabbed the button but then muttered an order and decided on the stairs. There were five steep flights of them and for a moment it crossed my mind that they might give me a shove. As the five police led me past the front desk of the hotel, my hair dishevelled, shirt splattered with blood, shirt-tail hanging out, I smiled apologetically at the receptionist. He glared back, presuming I must be guilty of some villainous offence.

Outside, a small group of onlookers had already gathered. Two plain clothes police cars waited with an ambulance behind them, suggesting that they expected me to put up a fight. 'Why did you smash me up?' I asked one of the officers in French as he pushed me into the back seat of the first car. He grunted menacingly and I shut up.

Sitting impassively in the back of the car, handcuffed to a *flic* on each side, we made our way westwards and then along the south bank of the Seine. It was a sickening feeling to lose control of my freedom again and dull helpless resignation set in, like a rabbit caught in a snare knowing its time is up. MI6 had got me again on a Friday afternoon, meaning a whole weekend in an uncomfortable police cell before a court hearing. Still, on the bright side, French handcuffs were a lot more comfortable than British ones, and Ronnie had told me that French jails were not too bad.

The traffic became more fluid as we left central Paris and we picked up speed down the southern embankment. Turning suddenly left, we passed under an elevated section of the metro and then abruptly right down a steep ramp into an underground compound.

My captors hauled me out of the car, led me through a few dimly lit corridors and shoved me into a custody cell. I gave it two stars: no toilet, no window, only a wooden bench with a dirty blanket and no mattress or pillow. British police cells were a category above. The front wall of the cell was entirely reinforced glass, allowing the guards to watch my every move. My handcuffs snapped off and the heavies ordered me to strip, then handed back my clothes, minus my belt and wristwatch. Wordlessly, they left and locked me in. I sat down on the bench and put my head in my hands. I had no idea how long they would hold me, so prepared myself mentally for the worst.

Perhaps an hour later they returned, handcuffed me again and escorted me down a short corridor into a windowless and stuffy interview room, lit by flickering neon lights. There was a long desk, behind which five police officers sat, Ratcliffe amongst them, smiling triumphantly as the heavies pushed me into a chair. Ratcliffe caught me glaring and spoke first. 'You can't be surprised to see me here, Richard.'

I knew that Ratcliffe was only doing his job and following orders from on high, but it was difficult not to feel hostility towards him as the executor of this inconvenience. I ignored him and turned to the French officer who had overseen my arrest. 'Je suis desolé, mais je ne veux pas répondre à l'Inspector en anglais ici sans votre permis.' There was no better way for an Englishman to annoy a Frenchman than by speaking English on his territory, as Ratcliffe had done. If I spoke French, it could only be helpful to my cause. His stern face cracked into a half smile and he introduced himself as Commandant Broisniard of the DST. Alongside him was Captain Gruignard, a new face who had not been present at the arrest. He had a small laptop computer in front of him, used by the French police to record interviews instead of a tape recorder. Another SB officer, Inspector Mark Whaley, sat alongside Ratcliffe and between the British and French officers sat an interpreter. In front of them, scattered across the desk, were my laptop, Psion, mobile phone and various papers and faxes.

'You have been arrested under the Mutual Assistance Act,' explained Broisniard in French. This agreement obliges a foreign police service to arrest a person at the request of another police force, whatever the reason. It was a piece of legislation that was open to abuse and SB were testing its spirit. 'I am sorry', he explained, 'but we are obliged to arrest you.' He advised me to cooperate fully with the questioning, assured me that Ratcliffe and Whaley were not entitled to question me directly and explained that the only language permitted in the interrogation would be French. The SB officers could propose questions via the interpreter but only he and Gruignard could directly question me on French soil.

As Broisniard explained this, every now and again the interpreter paraphrased a few sentences into English for the benefit of Ratcliffe and Whaley. They tired of listening to the French, and in a lull, Ratcliffe interjected impatiently, 'We think you may have used the internet in breach of your probation conditions.' I ignored him, and replied to Broisniard in French.

'What did he say?' I asked, innocently.

Broisniard's smile broadened. The interpreter translated Ratcliffe's question into French and Gruignard opened up the laptop and started typing. He seemed unfamiliar with a keyboard and typed using his two index fingers, pausing occasionally while he searched for a key, his lower lip mouthing the letters as he tapped them in. 'Voilà', announced Gruignard finally, evidently pleased with his work. 'Est ce-que vous avez utilisé l'internet,' he read out aloud, checking his handiwork.

Broisniard put on his glasses and leant over to read the computer screen. 'Est ce-que vous avez utilisé l'internet,' he repeated to me sternly.

'Jamais,' I lied emphatically.

Ratcliffe remembered enough schoolboy French to understand and, eager to get on with the interview, started to ask another question. But Broisniard cut him off. 'Attendez, attendez un moment,' he said, holding up his hand, and leant over the laptop to watch Gruignard type in my reply.

Gruignard's lower lip quivered as he tapped out the letters J – A – M – A – I – S, his eyes scanning the keyboard for each key. 'Et voilà,' he triumphantly announced as he completed the word and hit the 'Enter' key.

Ratcliffe tried again to get in his question, but Broisniard cut him off with a movement of his hand. It was the interpreter's turn to speak next. He sat up from his slump with a jolt. 'Never!' he translated.

Broisniard looked satisfied and at last Ratcliffe could begin his next question. 'We believe you may have spoken to an Australian journalist, Kathryn Bonella, in breach of your probation terms.'

I waited while the interpreter rephrased the question in French, Gruignard labouriously tapped it into the PC and Broisniard finally put the question to me in his own language, all of which provided at least five minutes to think of a good answer. 'Bien sûr, j'ai parlé à Mademoiselle Bonella quelquefois.'

My response went back through the recording and interpretation process, while Ratciffe fidgeted impatiently. He sensed that he had got me when the English translation finally arrived. 'What did you speak to her about?' he demanded urgently. Again, the interpreter translated the question, Gruignard slowly typed the question into the PC and Broisniard put the question to me.

'Un emploi.' I replied and the process started again. Broisniard was starting to look irritated. Not with his officer's amateur typing or my facetiousness, but with Ratcliffe's irrelevant questions. They had arrested me at gunpoint, as if I were a terrorist, and now Ratcliffe just wanted to know about my job interviews and whether I had used the internet.

The Janet and John style of the interrogation was leaving me plenty of time to think, and I went through a mental list of everything on my computer and Psion. I was not confident they would find nothing incriminating. Files on my laptop were encrypted with PGP and the hard disk had recently been defragmented so there was no danger there. But although everything in my Psion was also encrypted, I feared that they might succeed in breaking the small encryption program. Moreover, they would probably keep the computers, and the Psion contained important information including all my contacts and research on the job market, my bank account details and PIN numbers. I would be crippled without it. The Psion sat temptingly close on the desk between Broisniard and myself; if only I could get hold of it without being seen.

I asked Broisniard for a drink, as the adrenaline rush of the arrest had made me thirsty and it was hot in the interview room. Broisniard barked an order into the internal phone and one of the guards came back a few minutes later with a bottle of Evian and put it on the desk. I picked it up with both handcuffed hands, took a swig and replaced it close to the Psion. Ratcliffe wanted to know the password to my encrypted files and while his question was being translated and typed, I took another swig and replaced the bottle even closer. The question was put to me in French by Broisniard.

'The password is "Inspector Ratcliffe is a nonce",' I lied.

'C'est quoi, un "nonce"?' Broisniard asked seriously. After my explanation, the smirking Broisniard repeated the phrase to Gruignard to tap it into the laptop and the interpreter leaned over to help with the spelling. Out of the corner of my eye, I could see Ratcliffe and Whaley conferring, heads down. This was my chance. I reached for the bottle of Evian, took a swig, replaced it next to the Psion, slipped my hands down from the bottle, and grabbed the pocket-sized computer. With it under the table and out of their sight, I slipped out the stamp-sized memory disk, stuffed it down my boot and replaced the Psion. None of the five police officers noticed anything and I couldn't stop myself grinning.

The first interrogation session lasted about an hour but Ratcliffe got nowhere. The heavies took me back to my cell and gave me a baguette, a piece of cheese and a cup of coffee. One sat down at the desk outside and switched on a soap opera on the portable TV. Once he was no longer paying me any attention, I pulled my boot off and slipped the Psion disk under the sole-lining. It was a tight fit around the toe but I could walk without showing a limp.

Ratcliffe and Whaley were not present at the second interrogation. 'Où sont les anglais?' I asked politely.

'Pah,' Broisniard flicked his wrist dismissively. He explained that he was holding me 'garde en vue', meaning he could hold me for up to 48 hours without pressing charges, without allowing me to make a phone call and without allowing me a lawyer. Only a police lawyer could visit me after 20 hours to explain my legal rights. He then continued the interview disinterestedly, running through a list of questons Ratcliffe had given him while Gruignard slowly tapped my banal responses into the laptop.

The increasingly bored Broisniard interviewed me once more that evening before putting me back in a cell at about 11 p.m. with another bottle of Evian and a greasy bacon sandwich. Sleep would be difficult enough in normal circumstances on a hard bench with no pillow, with the strip lights on and a guard watching, but as soon as I lay down, I realised that the police had cracked a rib during their assault. The pain prevented me lying on my left-hand side, and even lying on my back the rib hurt every time I inhaled. It would be a long, sleepless night, giving me plenty of time to reflect on the events of the day. The sheer stupidity of MI6! What did they hope to achieve by arresting me? They would get a whole load more bad publicity once the details got out. Even if GCHQ set one of their Cray computers churning and six months later cracked the PGP files on my laptop, what would that prove? The French would never extradite me for having encrypted files that were shown to nobody, whatever the contents. I consoled myself with the message they would find if they did crack the book-sized decoy file on my laptop; 'MI6, you are a bunch of sad fraggles and are wasting your time and taxpayers' money,' repeated thousands of times. The real text was snuggled up under my big toe.

Broisniard came to my cell at about 9 a.m. with a plastic cup of instant coffee, syrupy with sugar. It was Saturday morning and he was probably not happy about having his weekend wasted on a pointless arrest. As I held out my wrists for the usual handcuffs, he shrugged dismissively. 'No handcuffs this morning,' he replied in French. 'But if you fuck around, we'll beat you up,' he added, waving a finger at me sternly. I had a sneaking admiration for the DST – they didn't pussyfoot around.

Fortunately, the mood in the interrogation room lightened. Broisniard was relaxed and even irreverent. He asked a few more of Ratcliffe's questions, but with me repeating the same rubbish as yesterday he soon got bored and his questioning took another direction, which at first left me unsure how to respond. 'How many times did you come to France on operations?' he asked, with a sly grin. It was not a straightforward question. I had indeed been to France a few times on operations which were not declared to them. Was Broisniard really expecting me to cooperate, or was he leading me into a trap? Revealing details of MI6 operations against France would breach the very law for which the DST arrested me.

I decided to play it safe. 'I'm sorry, I can't tell you about that.' 'Why not?' asked Broisniard, slightly disappointed.

'The British might ask you to arrest me,' I replied gravely.

Broisniard gave up around lunchtime. Back in my cell, the guards bought me another sandwich and a bottle of water and then, as I had been in custody for more than 20 hours, a young police lawyer visited to explain my legal rights. 'By lunchtime,' he explained, 'you will have been in custody for 24 hours, and so a judge will decide whether to extend the *garde en vue*. You will probably be released as you have broken no French law.' I kept my fingers crossed.

Gruignard came to my cell an hour later to say that the judge had given them permission to hold me for a further 24 hours. My spirits had been reasonably high until then, but the news that they would not release me hit hard. Gruignard told me that they still had not been able to decrypt the files in my computer and they would not release me until they were cracked. 'But it is impossible to crack PGP encryption,' I retorted in French. 'Breaking it would take a Cray supercomputer at least six months!'

'Alors, donnez-nous le mot de passe,' replied Gruignard. They were blackmailing me: no password, no release.

Fortunately, Gruignard was bluffing. At about 2200, Broisniard and Gruignard had had enough and came to my cell with broad smiles. 'You are free,' Broisniard announced. 'You have broken no French law.'

'So if I broke no French law, why did you arrest me?' I asked furiously.

'The English asked,' shrugged Broisniard. 'They said that you were a terrorist and dangerous. That is why we beat you up,' he continued, matter-of-factly.

'Can I see the warrant?' I demanded.

'You're free without charges, why do you want to see that?' he retorted.

'The English want your computers,' Gruignard said, changing the subject. He showed me my Psion and brand new laptop, smothered in red sealing wax and string, ready to be sent off to London for examination. (I did not see them again for five months, despite energetic recovery attempts by Anne-Sophie Levy, a young Parisian lawyer who volunteered to represent me. It wasn't until Christmas 1998 that she rang me to tell me that SB had finally agreed to return them. They did not find anything illegal on either computer and did not charge me with any offence. SB posted them back to me, but although my laptop came back unharmed, exasperatingly, my Psion, containing most of my important personal information, never arrived. SB claimed that it must have been 'lost in the post'.)

'Je veux parler avec les anglais cons,' I demanded to Broisniard, intent on giving Ratcliffe and Whaley a piece of my mind.

'They've gone down the Pigalle,' he replied with a smirk. I considered going to the notorious red-light district with a camera to look for them, but settled for a good night's sleep. Broisniard and Groignard led me out to the car, at last without handcuffs, and drove me round to a nearby cheap hotel. They handed over my NZ passport with the explanation that the British had picked it up from the embassy for me and even shook hands as they left me in the lobby.

With little sleep the whole weekend, my instinct was to crash out but there was work to be done. Adverse publicity for MI6 would be the best weapon to dissuade them from trying the same tactic again and I got to work ringing London. Most of the British papers carried the story prominently the following morning, portraying MI6 adversely.

SB had been busy in London the same weekend. At 6 a.m. on the day of my arrest, they burst into the south London flat of Kathryn Bonella, pulled her out of bed and took her down to Charing Cross police station for questioning about her meetings with me. She was eventually released without charge, but not before SB threatened to cancel her UK work permit.

After a few hours sleep, I got up early the next morning, packed my bags and checked out. MI6 would be disappointed they had not been able to detain me and they would be working overtime on the computers. If they realised that the Psion disk was missing, there was no point in hanging around waiting for another chat with the DST. I took the Paris metro to the Gare du Nord, where there was a small independent travel agent who specialised in cheap tickets to Australasia. They sold me a ticket for a Nippon Airways flight which left from Charles De Gaulle airport late that evening to Tokyo, where I changed for the New Zealand leg.

'Are you Richard Tomlinson?' a spotty, callow young man in a cheap suit addressed me with a Kiwi accent.

'No,' I replied dismissively, thrusting my trolley through the airport crowd. He looked like he might be trouble, and having just stepped off the long flight from Paris I was not in a mood to do an interview.

'You are Richard Tomlinson, aren't you?' he persisted, impatiently strutting alongside my trolley.

'I most definitely am not,' I replied in a Pythonesque French accent, 'I am Mr Napoleon Bonaparte. And who are you?'

But the stranger was undeterred. 'You are Richard Tomlinson, and I hereby serve you with this injunction,' he announced pompously, thrusting a thick sheaf of official-looking papers on to my trolley, and scuttled off anonymously into the crowds.

Thumbing through the 85 pages of legal jargon intended to stop me speaking to the media in New Zealand, it mystified me what MI6 were so afraid of. I learnt nothing in MI6 that would be of interest to the New Zealand media. The gagging order, taken out at considerable expense to the British public, was intended only to stop me criticising the way MI6 had treated me. Sitting in the back of the cab on my way to the Copthorne hotel on the Auckland waterfront, the thought of all those civil servants slaving away over their weekend putting together the injunction against me made me smile.

MI6 could not have used a more stupid tactic, as everybody wanted to know why they had gagged me. The next few days were a hectic whirlwind of interviews with New Zealand television and newspapers. The news soon crossed the Tasman Sea to Australia, and the Australian media wanted interviews with me. Even *Time* magazine picked up the story and ran a full-page article covering my arrest in Paris, the injunction and the stupid obstinacy of MI6 in refusing to admit that the root cause of the whole problem was their own glaring management faults.

The injunction meant that NZSIS (New Zealand Security & Intelligence Service) would take an interest in me. Although New Zealand has some of the most liberal laws governing individual freedoms anywhere in the world, their actions in injuncting me had shown that they were prepared to drop all these laws without hesitation if asked by MI6. NZSIS maintains very close links to MI6, to the extent that every year one of their new-entry officers is sent to the UK to attend the IONEC and spend a few years working as a UK desk officer. Dual-nationality holders of New Zealand passports, such as myself, were not automatically barred from working in NZSIS, unlike dual-nationality citizens of other closely allied countries such as Australia or Canada, and there is at least one fully fledged New Zealander working full-time in MI6. It irked me that NZSIS would be intercepting my phone and following me, and made me feel unwelcome in the country of my birth.

Moreover, without my Psion all the job leads in New Zealand that I had researched back in the UK were lost. I decided to give up my thoughts of settling in New Zealand and try Australia instead. I had a good network of friends in Sydney and had a job offer there with a company whose name was still in my head.

With the New Zealand authorities watching my every move, it would require some subterfuge to get to Australia unobserved. I laid a false trail, telling journalists that I was going to spend the weekend up on the Coramandel peninsula, a well-known beauty spot on New Zealand's north island. The message would get back to the authorities one way or another, whether through the bugging of my hotel telephone or through word of mouth from one of the journalists.

Late on the afternoon of Friday 7 August, I packed my suitcase, checked out of the Copthorne and took a taxi to Auckland airport. The Qantas sales desk sold me a one way ticket to Sydney for a flight that would be leaving an hour later. From the moment I checked out of the hotel until the aircraft took off, there would be just over two hours. Even if NZSIS had seen me leaving the Copthorne, they would not have much time to react and stop me leaving New Zealand. Hopefully, it would allow me to sneak into Australia unnoticed. But I had greatly underestimated the determination of MI6 to cause me as much bother as they could.

'Mr Tomlinson?' I looked up from my seat, into which I had just settled on the packed Qantas MD-11, to see two of the stewards standing over me. 'Would you mind stepping off the plane please, Mr Tomlinson,' continued the senior of the two men. 'And bring your bag,' he added, to underline that I would not be going to Australia. At least there was no sign of the police, so I hoped that I wasn't about to be arrested.

The two stewards led me off the plane and escorted me back through customs to a Qantas administrative office. There a more senior official explained what had happened. 'We have had a fax from our head office in Canberra saying that you have not been given an Australian visa,' he said apologetically. 'We're holding the plane back while we get your suitcase out of the hold – I am really sorry about this.' He had seen me on the television and knew who I was.

'Can I see the fax?' I asked, suspecting that there was some foul play. The Australian authorites could only have learnt of my intention to go to Sydney a few hours earlier and the fax probably didn't really exist.

'Sorry, we're under strict instructions not to show it to you. If you phone Marien Smith at the Australian consulate in Auckland, she will explain everything.' The fax was probably just an invention to buy them more time to find an official reason to pull me off the plane. I rang Marien Smith immediately and my suspicions were confirmed when she admitted knowing nothing about the visa refusal. I felt really let down by the New Zealand and Australian authorities' attitude to me. They were joining in with MI6's bullying and harassment without examining the issues for themselves and making their own minds up based on their own laws. It was far easier for them just to bow to political pressure from MI6 than stand up for the rights of one individual.

Back at the Copthorne, the receptionist insisted that as the hotel was full, he would have to give me the main suite at the price of a normal room. The hotel lobby and dining area were deserted and the hotel didn't appear full to me, but I shrugged my shoulders and took the key. As soon as I was up in the suite, the telephone rang. TVNZ had heard the news of my removal from the plane and wanted to come over with a camera crew to do an interview for that evening's late news slot. I agreed to let them come over and in the meantime started to unpack my suitcase which had been packed only a few hours earlier. They arrived at 8 p.m. and shot a short interview, during which I protested at the harassment I was receiving at the hands of the New Zealand authorities, then they rushed back to edit it for the main news at 9 p.m.

Alone at last, I grabbed a Steinlager from the minibar and sat down on the bed to decide what to do next. It was disappointing to be banned from Australia. Although as an New Zealand citizen a visa was not normally required, there was a clause in their agreement that allowed each country to ban nationals of the other if they were of 'character concern'. The clause was drafted to allow each country to ban the other's serious criminals such as rapists and murderers, but Australia had invoked it to keep me out. The Australian authorities had nothing against me but just like the New Zealand authorities, they had been asked by MI6 to make life difficult for me and so had obliged.

Lying on the bed, I dialled a friend in Sydney to tell him that my trip was off. No sooner had he answered than there was a soft knock on the door. I told him to hang on for a minute, put the phone down on the bedside table, and got up to answer. My previous arrests made me suspicious of unexpected visitors. 'Who is it?' I asked cautiously, without opening the door.

'It's Susan. Is Caroline there?' a female voice answered.

'Sorry, wrong room,' I answered, and went back to the phone. But there was another more impatient knock. Somewhat irritated, I got back up to answer the door again.

'It's Susan here, I think I may have left something in the room.'

There was no spyhole so I slipped on the security chain and turned the key. The door smashed to its limit against the chain, then again and again. 'Police, police, open the fucking door,' shouted an irritated male voice. 'All right, all right, calm down,' I replied, slipping the chain to avoid a big bill from the Copthorne.

A pugnacious-looking Maori led the charge. 'Get back over there, in the corner,' he yelled, shoving me backwards away from my half-unpacked suitcase. Two more officers followed him up.

Once the room was secured and they had me under control – not that I was resisting – a fourth entered. 'I'm Detective Inspector

Whitham, Auckland Threat Assessment Unit,' he announced, flashing his ID at me. He introduced the glowering Maori, who looked disappointed I had not hit him, as Constable Waihanari.

'We have a warrant to search you and your belongings,' announced Waihanari, waving a sheet of paper at me. 'Strip,' he ordered. While my clothes were being searched, a female officer and a portly fourth officer pulled on latex gloves and started a careful search of my belongings. The telephone was still off the hook, with my friend listening in from Sydney, so the female slammed down the receiver and for good measure pulled the telephone lead out of the wall socket.

'Can I see the warrant?' I demanded after Waihanari had allowed me to get dressed again. I checked it for accuracy – any discrepancy would make it invalid and I could force the police to leave – but every detail was correct. They even had the correct hotel room number, explaining why the receptionist insisted I took the suite.

I heard other voices lurking outside in the corridor and as I finished reading the warrant they entered. To my surprise, one was Ratcliffe. 'What the hell are you doing here?' I shouted, leaping to my feet and causing Waihanari's eyes to light up. Ratcliffe had flown all the way to New Zealand at the British taxpayer's expense (and I later learnt that Whaley had accompanied him) for this latest episode of petty harassment. 'Get out of this room now!' I shouted. Waihanari was limbering up with a gentle haka and I turned to him. 'If he doesn't get out of here right now, you can have your fun.' Ratcliffe held up his hands to calm me down, and backed out of the room. He knew this latest piece of harassment would be relayed to the press the next day and he did not want a repeat of the bad publicity of the Paris.

The New Zealand police searched my hotel room more professionally and thoroughly than the French. Anything unscrewable was unscrewed – all the light fittings, electrical sockets and desk fittings, and they dismantled all my personal belongings. They found the Psion disk after an hour and a half, hidden inside a clunky British adaptor plug. The porky officer smiled with delight when he opened it up and pulled it out. I smiled too, as I had backed a copy up on the internet that morning in an Auckland internet café.

Just after 11 p.m. the police left with the disk and a few other pieces of paper that they decreed were evidence that I was 'endangering New Zealand security'. Feeling bloody annoyed, I went out into downtown Auckland to get drunk. The second pub I stumbled into had a promotion evening for a canned vodka cocktail called 'KGB'. When I was halfway through my first can, a young man came up to me and clapped me on the shoulder. 'I know you, mate, I've seen you on telly every night this week. You're that fella those pommy bastards have been chasing around the world,' he grinned. 'Here, have a KGB on me.' He waved over the waiter and got me another can.

Soon all his mates joined in and I knew I was in for a long night and a rough tomorrow. 'Stick at it and put one over the bastard poms,' they urged me. Their fighting spirit and irreverent attitude to state authority was a refreshing contrast to the attitude of many people in England who limply advised me to give in to MI6.

Despite the support from the drinkers that night in the pub, and from many other ordinary Auckland folk who approached me on the street during the next few days, one even asking for an autograph, I reluctantly decided that it was not advisable to stay in New Zealand. If MI6 had twisted the arms of the New Zealand authorities into the confiscation of my property, then it was inevitable that sooner or later they would try to press charges against me. I decided to go back to Europe, and chose Switzerland because of its reputation for neutrality.

But first I had to find myself a lawyer who could help me get back my confiscated property, as once back in Europe it would be impossible to act for myself. One of MI6's objectives in continually having me detained was to force me to spend my savings on lawyers to recover property that they confiscated from me. Whilst they had unlimited legal resources at their disposal, they knew that my reserves were finite. I was therefore pleased to find a lawyer who was prepared to represent me *pro bono*. Warren Templeton, a diligent and independent barrister from Auckland, had seen coverage of my case on TVNZ and tracked me down to the Copthorne Hotel. I accepted his kind offer gladly and he has worked ceaselessly ever since to put an end to MI6's treatment of me, not only in New Zealand but also elsewhere around the world.

15

SINISTER CIRCLES

SUNDAY, 30 AUGUST 1998
JOHN F. KENNEDY AIRPORT, NEW YORK

'Good evening, ladies and gentlemen. For security reasons would all passengers kindly return to their seats.' There was a collective groan as passengers replaced their coats and hand-luggage in the overhead lockers while the Swissair captain repeated the message in French. I hadn't stood up to join the rush to the exits and paid little attention to the delay as I buried my nose back in *The Economist*. My neighbour in the aisle seat sat down impatiently. 'JFK's a goddarn disgrace,' he drawled grumpily to nobody in particular.

I took a circuitous route from Auckland to Munich via Singapore and Bangkok, hoping MI6 would lose my trail somewhere along the way. After two days in Munich, rollerblading in the English gardens to keep any surveillance on their toes, I took the train to Zurich then Geneva, where I found some digs. There lawyers for Mr Al Fayed contacted me, inquiring about my knowledge of Henri Paul's relationship with MI6. I had not given it any thought since posting the letter to Harrods a year earlier, but after a casual comment to a journalist who realised its significance, his lawyers wanted a full statement. Judge Hervé Stephan, the magistrate in charge of the inquest into the crash that killed the Princess of Wales, Dodi Al Fayed and Henri Paul himself, invited me to Paris shortly afterwards to give evidence. It was a breach of the OSA for me to do so, but I felt entirely justified, given the significance of the tragedy. I told Stephan about Paul's MI6 file, the notes I saw of his meetings in 1992 with his MI6 case officer, Fish's plan to assassinate President Milosevic in a tunnel car-crash and about the *paparazzi* photographer who worked for UKN. I do not know anything more about the fatal crash, but I am convinced that there is information in MI6 files that would be useful to the enquiry, in particular concerning the movements of

Henri Paul on the evening of his death. For despite thorough police inquiries, his whereabouts for an hour have not been accounted for. I suspect that he was having a drink with his MI6 handler, as a large sum of cash was found on his body later that evening. Examination of his MI6 file would clarify this and might shed light on the mysteriously high levels of alcohol and carbon monoxide found in his blood. Disappointingly, Stephan did not request the files from the British government.

NBC wanted to interview me live on their *Today* news programme on Monday, 31 August about this evidence and MI6's pursuit of me around the world, hence my flight to New York. But, watching a group of uniformed, armed men methodically counting down the seat rows of the MD-11, I feared MI6 had other ideas.

'Can I see your passport please, sir?' the badly overweight INS (Immigration and Naturalization Service) officer asked politely as he and three colleagues stopped at my row. I handed over my passport, open at the page with the multiple-entry indefinite visa issued while a student at MIT. The official flipped to the photograph and glanced at me to verify the resemblance. 'Come with us please, sir,' he ordered.

My grumbling neighbour stood to allow me out and as I stepped into the aisle, two INS men grabbed my wrists and slapped on handcuffs. 'Where's your hand luggage?' one snapped, and picked out my canvas shoulder bag from the locker I nodded towards. I smiled back at the hostile glares from the plane's passengers as they frogmarched me off the plane, two in front, two behind, through the docking gantry into the crowded arrivals area, then down into the bowels of the airport.

The INS detention centre was dominated by a substantial desk on a raised plinth, behind which two officials surveyed the detainees sitting in a row on a bench against the opposite wall. My captors uncuffed me, sat me down between a snoozing Mexican in a sombrero and a greasy-haired Russian in a tight T-shirt, and manacled me to the bench with leg-irons. 'I thought you gave up leg-irons for new arrivals 200 years ago,' I quipped.

'We've been ordered not to let you into the United States,' a marginally slimmer officer replied humourlessly. 'Wait your turn here, and you'll find out why.'

Fortunately my turn for an interview came quickly. 'Sit down over there,' the INS officer indicated a plastic chair in the corner of a small interview room containing a desk and computer. 'Right, Mr Tomlinson,' he announced as he fired up the PC and took his seat. 'We've got here a standard list of questions that we put to every alien who has been denied entrance to the USA. First, I expect you'll be wanting to know why you've been denied entry?'

'I already know,' I replied. 'The CIA told you not to let me in.'

'How did you know that?' he asked, confirming my guess. He pushed over a directive from the State Department denying me entry at the request of a 'friendly government'.

'But what reasons are you giving me?' I asked, knowing that a request from another government, no matter how friendly, would not be sufficient legal reason to expel me.

'We haven't got to that yet,' he replied, tapping my passport details into the PC. 'Right, first question. Have you ever been convicted of any offences relating to the supply or smuggling of drugs?'

'Nope,' I replied confidently and waited while he tapped in my answer.

'Have you ever been convicted of any firearms offences?'

'Nope.'

'Have you ever been convicted of any serious offence carrying with it a jail sentence of more than one year?'

'Nope,' I replied truthfully.

'Have you ever used any alias names?'

'Oh yes, indeed,' I replied cheerfully.

'Well let's have them,' he ordered.

'Daniel Noonan, Richard Harwin, Richard Ledbury, Ben Presley, Tom Paine, Alex Huntley,' I rattled off. One by one he tapped them into his computer, asking me to spell them out. The last must have flashed up an INS record because he examined the screen for several minutes when it went in.

'OK, have you ever been involved in any espionage or terrorism?' he eventually asked.

I hesitated for a moment. Under British law it was illegal to admit membership of MI6, but lying to the INS would be grounds for denying entry to the USA. 'Yes, I used to work for British intelligence,' I admitted.

He looked round his PC at me sceptically. 'OK, between what dates and where?' He grilled me for 20 minutes about my work and operations. I replied fully and cooperated completely. At the end of the interview, he picked up an ink stamp from his desk and stamped my passport. 'Mr Tomlinson, you are a former intelligence officer, and under regulations 217.4(b), 212(a) and 212(c) of US immigration policy you are banned from entering the territory of the United States of America.'

He led me back to the holding-pen and manacled me to the

bench, this time in a row of Chinese labourers wearing identical dark-blue 'Chairman Mao' suits. 'You'll be going back to Switzerland on the next available flight, in about seven hours. We'll get you a Big Mac and fries.'

'Great!' I replied with exaggerated enthusiasm. When it arrived, I gave it to my Chinese companions, who jabbered with excitement as they opened up the evil-smelling carton. He did not even allow me to ring the NBC producer who was waiting for me in the arrivals hall.

As the INS officer admitted, the CIA were behind my entry refusal, banning me for life from entering 'the land of the free and the home of the brave', just for criticising a foreign intelligence service. MI6, however, unwittingly saved my life. If all had gone according to plan, I would have boarded Swissair flight SR-111 on Wednesday, 2 September to return to Geneva. The MD-11 took off as scheduled at 8.19 p.m. from JFK and crashed into the Atlantic ocean at 9.40 p.m, killing all 229 passengers and crew.

'I'd like to make it clear that you are not under arrest,' Commandant Jourdain assured me smoothly, 'but we think that you may be able to help us safeguard the security of Switzerland.'

His colleague, Inspector Brandt, nodded enthusiastically in agreement. 'We'd like you to tell us all about illegal British espionage operations against Switzerland,' he added.

Jourdain of the Swiss Federal police, and Brandt of the Geneva Cantonal Special Investigations department, sent me a *convoqué*, a compulsory interview request, a few days after my return from the USA, ordering me to report to the Geneva police headquarters on Monday, 21 September 1998. 'The British asked us to put you under surveillance when you came to this country because you were a dangerous terrorist who could jeopardise Swiss security,' Jourdain explained, nudging a copy of MI6's letter towards me on the desk. 'We watched you for the first couple of weeks. Did you spot anything?' Jourdain asked.

'No, nothing,' I replied truthfully. I hadn't been looking, but in any case I knew that Swiss surveillance was among the best in the world.

'Good,' replied Jourdain, pleased that his teams hadn't been compromised. 'We saw you arrive at Zurich Hauptbahnhof at 1225 on 17 August, then you stayed at the Hotel Berne for the night.'

If they picked me up arriving at Zurich railway station, they must have been tipped off that I was arriving from Munich. MI6 must have put in a massive operation to follow me from New Zealand.

'We then followed you until 31 August, when you tried to go to New York,' continued Brandt. 'But when we realised that you were not presenting any danger to Swiss interests, we decided to invite you here, to see if you could help us.'

Jourdain and Brandt were putting me into an awkward position. They wanted me to break the OSA by telling them about Britain's operations in Switzerland, which could lead to prosecution in Britain. On the other hand, since MI6's undeclared operations in Switzerland were illegal under Swiss law, refusal to help the police in a criminal investigation would be an offence for which I could potentially be imprisoned, and it would certainly scupper any chance of getting Swiss residency. Jourdain appeared to read my thoughts. 'Failing to help us will not help your application for a residency permit,' he added menacingly.

I had to think of my long-term future. MI6 had used their influence to prevent me making a fresh start in New Zealand and Australia, despite Warren Templeton's and John Wadham's strenuous efforts to persuade them to negotiate an end to the pyrrhic dispute. I would have settled just for the return of my computer and for an Australian visa, but MI6 were set resolutely on a Thatcheresque, no-compromise, no-turning-back policy. Given their intransigence, I decided to pledge my future to Switzerland in the hope that I could get permanent residence status, a work permit, then find constructive and permanent employment.

'OK, how can I help?' I replied cautiously.

Over the next three months, the Swiss police *convoqué*'d me four times. Each time, I cooperated fully with their enquiries and I built up a good personal relationship with Jourdain and Brandt who even showed me MI6's increasingly irate requests to have me arrested and deported to Britain, or at least expelled from Switzerland. Jourdain assured me that they had ignored the letters, as I had done nothing against Swiss law.

'C'est vraiment vous?' laughed the French Douane incredulously, pointing out my description, which had flashed up on the screen in the border kiosk after he had tapped my passport details into the computer. In French, under my police mugshot, was written:

Name:	TOMLINSON Richard John Charles
Nationality:	British and New Zealand
Born:	Hamilton, New Zealand, 13/01/63

Resident:	No fixed abode
Details:	Subject is former member of British Special Forces and Special Services, trained in firearms, explosives, unarmed combat, scuba-diving, pilots licence, parachutist, expert in cryptography. Subject is a menace to the security of France.

'Ridiculous,' I laughed. 'It's a joke. The British are pulling your leg.'

'Sit down there,' the Douane replied, ignoring my protests. 'Wait until the police arrive.' He indicated a chair in the corner of the kiosk

For the sixth time in a year, I was being detained at the request of MI6. It was late on the evening of Wednesday 6 January, and I had just picked up my parents in a hire car from Geneva airport. We were heading to a rented chalet in the French Alps, an hour's drive over the border, for a week's skiing holiday. But MI6 had learnt about the arrangements through their tap on my parents' phone and decided to spoil our holiday. They alerted the DST of my intended movements and DST notified the Douanes to stop us at the Swiss–French border. I now had to wait until the DST turned up from their regional headquarters in Grenoble. It was a bitterly cold evening, and although I was warm enough in the customs kiosk, my parents were waiting outside in the freezing car.

Four DST officers turned up at 10.30 p.m. Although the French Douanes had been happy to leave me unattended in their kiosk, confident I was not a troublemaker, the DST slapped on handcuffs the moment they arrived. 'Alors, we have some questions for you, Monsieur Tomlinson,' announced the senior officer. They escorted me out of the kiosk into the main police building at the frontier, sat me down in an office and interviewed me for 90 minutes. They asked no questions relating to any form of criminal activity and all they were interested in were details of an MI6 officer who owned a chalet in the Haut-Savoie, on their home turf around Grenoble. I refused to help, so at the end of the interview they served me with papers banning me for life from entering French territory. Just like the US immigration officials, the DST had to find a reason under their regulations to justify the ban. On the standard entry-refusal proforma, there were four possible justifications. He could not tick the 'lack of correct papers' box because my British passport entitled me automatically to entry. I could demonstrate that I had the funds to support myself in France, so that option was denied. I was not the bearer of any infectious diseases, so he could not select that. All that remained was 'threat to the security of France'. He ticked the box with a flourish, stamped the document and handed it over to me. 'You must go back to Switzerland,' he ordered. 'If we find you in France, we will imprison you immediately for six months, no questions asked.'

Back in the hire car, two stern-faced officers stood blocking the route south just to ensure that I didn't try to dash for it. There was no choice but to turn around and return to my digs. It was too late for my parents to go to the chalet that evening, so they had to stay in a hotel in Geneva.

The DST were in blatant breach of European law by stopping a British passport holder entering France. MI6 and the DST were gambling that I would not have the legal backing to mount a challenge via the European courts, and if I did try, that it would take many years for my appeal to be heard. Two days before the first stage of my appeal came before the Grenoble district court on 5 May 2000, already over a year after the illegal order was served on me, the DST served an injunction to delay the hearing. I cannot take my case to the European courts in Strasbourg until all domestic remedies have been pursued, so I have no alternative but to spend more money on lawyers and wait.

Although I was enjoying life in Switzerland, had made some good friends and was earning some money with casual work, getting a work permit and permanent job was difficult. I therefore mounted an appeal against the Australian ban, using a firm of lawyers in Canberra. I suspected that MI6 had used their influence with ASIO (Australian Security and Intelligence Organisation) to get me banned, though MI6 denied this, improbably claiming in a letter to me that they 'would not interfere in the policies of another country'. A few months later, via the Australian Freedom of Information Act, my lawyers got proof that MI6 were lying. They obtained a copy of a telegram sent by MI6 to ASIO on 2 November 1998. Although many paragraphs were blacked out with the censor's ink, it was clear that it was a request for a ban, to which the Australians had complied limply. Moreover, the date of the request was two days after my arrest, but long before I was convicted of a crime; MI6 were not content to see me receive only the punishment deemed fit by British law and had decided to add to it by stopping me from emigrating to Australia. Getting an Australian visa became a major preoccupation but after spending thousands of dollars of my savings on legal fees, I realised that I was falling into the financial trap MI6 had laid for me.

Reasoning with MI6 was not working either, and the energetic efforts of Warren Templeton and John Wadham were futile. My only remedy was to use publicity again to bring them to the table. At the end of April, I bought some web-design software and learnt how to build internet pages. My first site was an amateurish and jokey affair and appeared on the Geocities server late on the evening of Saturday, 1 May. The pages contained nothing secret and were just a light-hearted poke at MI6. On the front page, there was a photograph of me in a silly hat superimposed against Vauxhall Cross, with the Monty Python theme tune playing in parody of MI6's absurd pursuit of me, and on the inside pages were copies of the documents served by the Australian, American and French authorities banning me from their countries at MI6's request. Nevertheless, on Monday morning the Geocities security officer, Mr Bruce Zanca, e-mailed me to say that they had received a complaint about my website from a 'third party' and were therefore closing down the site. By late morning my pages had disappeared. I found another empty space on the Geocities server and re-posted them, including Zanca's e-mail. A few hours later I got another, more irate, e-mail from Zanca telling me they had removed my new pages, and ordering me not to post anything else onto their server. I copied this e-mail into my pages and posted everything back. That came down a few hours later and Zanca got badly annoyed and threatened legal action. Fortunately, I didn't need to put them up again because word spread around the internet of the preposterous way that MI6 and Geocities were censoring me, and numerous 'mirrors' of my site sprang up.

On 13 May, another site about MI6 appeared on Lyndon Larouche's website, publishing a list of 115 names purporting to be of serving and former MI6 officers. This news exploded onto the front pages of newspapers worldwide. Because of the publicity about my first site, I was immediately assumed to be the author.

To this day, I do not know who published the famous list, but it was not me. I have my suspicions, however, that it was MI6 themselves. They had a motive – to incriminate and blacken me. They had the means to make the list and the knowledge to post it onto the internet without leaving a trace. And, despite their protestations to the contrary, the list was not particularly damaging to them. Later I got the chance to study it for myself. I did not recognise most of the names and so cannot comment as to whether they were from MI6 or from the FCO. Of the names that I did recognise, all were retired from the service or were already widely blown. If MI6 had set out to produce a list that caused me the maximum incrimination, but caused them the minimum damage, they could not have done a better job.

The way the existence of the list was publicised to the world's press was also odd. The first announcement was made when the British government's official censor, Rear-Admiral David Pulvertaft, issued a 'D-notice' to stop UK newspapers publishing the web address of the list or any of the names. There was no better way to generate publicity because immediately every journalist in Britain wanted to know what the D-notice was censoring, and foreign newspapers the world over, to whom the D-notice was irrelevant, published the web address and even the entire list. The next peculiarity was the manner in which the FCO announced the incident. If MI6 really wanted to limit the damage, they would have used a junior spokesperson to dismiss the list as a hoax. Instead, British Foreign Secretary Robin Cook announced at a packed news conference that not only was the list accurate but, without presenting a shred of evidence, named me as the culprit. Both these tactics can only be explained by a plan to incriminate and discredit me.

They certainly succeeded if it was their intention. Until the list was produced, the press had been fairly sympathetic to me. But after Cook's accusation, the media turned on me with vitriol. In Britain, the *Sunday Telegraph* led the charge. They accused me of being a traitor who had recklessly endangered the lives of MI6 officers in a selfish pursuit of an employment tribunal and printed the I/OPS propaganda that MI6 sacked me for being 'unreliable' and 'going on frolics'. Their columnist Andrew Roberts, a contemporary at Cambridge but now an establishment toady and friend of MI6, wrote a petty personal attack on me, making absurd claims such as that I cheated to gain admission to MIT. The tabloid newsapers were equally hostile. The *Sun* tracked down Tosh, now out of 602 Troop and working in the City, and paid him £500 to claim that I took the troop to a brothel in Split on his birthday. He e-mailed me afterwards to apologise and at least he had the guts to give the newspaper his name, unlike some of the anonymous worms they also dug up from my old TA regiment. The *Sun* also published my e-mail address and encouraged its readers to send me hatemail. I received over ten thousand e-mails over the next week, some of them amounting to death threats. Interestingly, however, by no means all of the e-mails were hostile, perhaps indicating the lack of judgement of the *Sun*'s editor and the lack of public support for MI6. The majority of readers who e-mailed me thought that it was a good thing to publish the names of MI6 officers, one writing that I deserved an OBE for services to humanity and another stating that taking Tosh to a brothel was a good use of MI6 money.

The publication of the list had all the hallmarks of a classic I/OPS operation to winkle me out of fortress Switzerland, an objective that was accomplished three weeks later. On Monday, 7 June, Inspector

Brandt rang to summon me to the Geneva police headquarters at Chemin de la Gravière for a meeting at 2 p.m. I arrived to find a stone-faced Commandant Jourdain, in no mood for small talk. 'You must leave Switzerland immediately,' he told me. 'You are banned from entering Swiss territory until 7 June 2004, and must be out of the country by 1800 this evening.' My protests that this was an unreasonably short period of notice fell on deaf ears. It would scarcely give me time to pack my suitcase. 'And we don't want any publicity in the press,' continued Jourdain. 'If you talk to the newspapers about this, we will increase the ban to ten years.'

'So where do you want to go to?' asked Brandt. 'We will book the ticket for you.'

'I really don't know,' I replied angrily. Just about every reasonable option was closed off. All of the anglophone countries were out of the question and I feared that I would have legal problems if I stayed in Europe. 'OK,' I replied, after some consideration, 'get me a ticket to Moscow.' I didn't really want to go there, but I knew that Jourdain would be uncomfortable with expelling me from Switzerland at the request of the British only for me to seek refuge in Moscow.

Jourdain stared at me for a moment while the implication sunk in. 'You don't want to go there,' he replied. 'It's cold and you don't speak Russian.'

'OK, then I'll go to Havana. It's warm and I speak Spanish.'

From Jourdain's point of view this was no better, and he needed to seek advice from his superiors. 'Wait here while I call Berne,' he announced. 'All right,' announced Jourdain on his return a few minutes later. 'Berne have given you an extension until 1800 tomorrow, so that you have more time to find a place to go,' he smiled weakly. 'Telephone Inspector Brandt before 1200 tomorrow with your decision.'

I was very disappointed by the attitude of the Swiss authorities. They had a reputation as a neutral country who were prepared to shelter individuals harassed by foreign powers, and I had helped them a lot over the past six months. Now they were blatantly siding with MI6 and were expelling me for the publication of the list without any evidence that I was the culprit. Even with the extension, there was not much time to sort out my plans. I had become quite established in Switzerland, even though I did not yet have a resident's permit. My French was fluent, I had made some good friends and I was getting some serious job interviews and felt that it would only be a matter of time before one materialised into a job. The Swiss had dealt me a low blow in forcing me to start again from scratch somewhere else (I later discovered the full extent of their double standards: every time I went for a job interview, Jourdain rang the company afterwards and told them not to employ me). My threats to go to Havana or Moscow had bought me some extra time, but I did not really want to go to either of these cities. I would not be able to work there and guessed that after a few months I would be bored. Also, I was in no mood for a long journey. I rang up Geneva station and asked for a rail ticket to the nearest town not in France or Switzerland. They booked me onto a train leaving at 1735 the following evening, 25 minutes before my deadline, arriving at Konstanz in southern Germany at 2235.

'Herr Tomlinson?' The voice behind me was friendly, but still my anger flashed within. It was late in the evening, I had arrived in a strange town in a country I hardly knew and whose language I hardly spoke, it was raining outside, I had nowhere to stay and I had only struggled a few yards off the station platform with my two heavy suitcases, yet already somebody – presumably an official – wanted a word with me. I spun around, scowling with hostility. 'Nein, Ich bin nicht Herr Tomlinson.' It was about the limit of my German.

A stone-faced uniformed police officer and two civilians, one male in his mid-40s, one a blonde female, stood before me. 'Ausweis, bitte,' ordered the uniformed officer.

'What?' I replied impatiently and rudely.

'Your papers, please,' interpreted the civilian male.

'Oh fuck off,' I replied and picked up my luggage. I couldn't help my language. The Swiss must have tipped off the Germans and now, I presumed, I was about to be arrested. If they wanted to arrest me, I would not make it easy for them.

'No, no, wait, you're not under arrest, Herr Tomlinson.' The civilian grabbed me by the shoulder, as if to get my attention rather than to restrain me. 'We just want to talk to you, Richard,' the female spoke for the first time, smiling sweetly.

I shifted to face my interlocutors squarely, still suspicious. 'I am Herr Kugel, from the BfV (Bundesamt für Verfassungsschutz), and this is my colleague, Fräulein Gajabski.'

'We guess you must be tired after your journey, and as it's so late, we've booked you into a hotel for the night,' Gajabski said in flawless English.

'We'll help you with your luggage,' added Kugel. He dismissed the uniformed police officer with a short command and whistled up a railway porter who scuttled over with a baggage trolley.

'Don't worry, you are not in any trouble,' Gajabski assured me. 'We'll just have a quick drink tonight, then if it is OK with you, we'll have lunch tomorrow.'

Kugel and Gajabski escorted me in the drizzle over to the Halm Hotel opposite the station, the porter struggling behind with my heavy luggage. Kugel checked me in, paying the bill in advance, while Gajabski tipped and dismissed the porter. 'We guess you'll want to go up to your room for a few minutes. We'll meet you at the bar at 11 p.m.,' Kugel said. It was more of a firm request than a direct order, but in any case I was intrigued to know what they wanted. Also, I needed a beer.

'Fräulein Gajabski and myself are from the BfV,' explained Kugel once three bottles of Becks had been served, with glasses. 'Our duty is to protect the German constitution, particularly against the activities of foreign intelligence services. We've read about your case in the newspapers, and we think that you may be able to help us with our investigations into British and American operations against Germany.'

The Swiss Federal police must have tipped them off about my arrival in Konstanz. Jourdain had previously questioned me about ORCADA, the spy in the German ministry of finance that Markham had run in Bonn, even offering me money for his identity. The Swiss Federal police work closely with their counterparts in Germany, particularly on the banking and finance sectors, and it was inevitable that Jourdain would tip off the Germans. The two BfV officers did not push me hard at the first meeting, but they asked me to reflect on their request overnight and insisted that I take lunch with them the next day.

'So, have you decided if you are going to help us?' asked Kugel hopefully. We were nearing the end of a long lunch in the Seerestaurant of the Steigenberger Inselhotel overlooking Lake Constance. Kugel and Gajabski used all the cultivation tricks on me that I learnt on the IONEC. They were sympathetic to my situation, flattered me on my very limited German, assured me that any information that I gave them would be treated with the utmost confidentiality and offered me help in settling in Germany. Now, as the meal was ending, they were putting to me their final recruitment pitch. I could imagine how eagerly anticipated my reply would be and how they must already be mentally writing up their contact report.

'No, I am sorry, I really can't help you,' I replied. I could see the disappointment in their eyes. They would have to report back negatively to their line-manager, and would not get the pat on the back they were hoping for. 'I could go to jail for 40 years in Britain under their Official Secrets Act, and it is just not worth it.' The 1911 OSA, which stops Britons 'collaborating with a potential enemy', was enacted just before the First World War to stop British naval engineers helping the Germans to rebuild their navy. I could just imagine 'expert witnesses' like Redd taking the witness stand to argue that Germany was still a potential enemy.

'But we can assure you, Richard, that your identity will never go beyond the two of us at the table,' Gajabski argued.

It was just what we had been trained to say to potential informers too, and I knew that it was not true. 'But even if I do help you,' I argued, 'how do I know that you will help me? I helped the Swiss police with their enquiries and where did that get me?'

Kugel and Gajabski had no reply.

Though I had arrived in Konstanz with the intention of quickly moving on elsewhere, the meeting with the BfV persuaded me that I was better off staying put in Germany. They would be unlikely to bother me at MI6's request after they had tried to recruit me. As there was a language school in Konstanz, I decided to study until my German was good enough to look for a job. I found a bedsit and started an intensive four hours per day language course. Living in a European Union country had other advantages. Unlike Switzerland, I needed no work permit or residence permit because my British passport automatically gave me those rights. I registered as a resident, opened a bank account, obtained a phone-line in my own name and even bought a car. The little second-hand BMW I got from a dealer in Hamburg gave me mobility and so if I had to move again suddenly, I would not have to throw away most of my possessions as I had done in Switzerland.

Kugel and Gajabski contacted me several times over the next few months and took me out to two further lunches at the Tolle Knolle restaurant on the Bodanplatz in Konstanz to persuade me to talk about ORCADA or other aspects of British and American operations against Germany, but finally they realised that I would not cooperate with them and told me that our meeting in September would be the last. I was relieved when they assured me that I could stay in Germany and that they would not bother me again.

Driving back to Konstanz from a day out in Austria one Sunday in late September, I accidentally strayed into a Swiss border post near Bregenz. Before I realised my mistake, the guard tapped on my window demanding my documents. I lowered the window, 'Nein, nichts,' I replied honestly, and tried to reverse away from the control post.

But that just made the guard suspicious and he blocked me off. 'Ausweis,' he snapped, holding out his hands for my passport. Realising that there was no way out I handed over my papers and he took them into his kiosk to check them. Two guards came out five minutes later, hauled me out of the car and threw me into a holding cell. The police arrived two hours later, strip-searched me, handcuffed me and took me to the police station. A day in a Swiss police cell was not much hardship – it was really very comfortable with clean bedding, a spotless toilet and sink and even a welcoming bar of soap and a towel, neatly folded on the bed, just like in a Hilton – but nevertheless the inconvenience was annoying and did not endear either the Swiss or MI6 to me.

By October my German was fairly fluent and I found a job as a private mathematics coach for a wealthy German family in a town in southern Bavaria. I moved to Oberstdorf, a small village nearby, nestled in the foothills of the German Alps. I only had to teach for a couple of hours per evening, so as soon as the snow started to fall I bought a new snowboard and got a day-job teaching snowboarding on the nearby Fellhorn range. Things were starting to look up for me – I was earning enough to make ends meet, was making a few friends in Oberstdorf and MI6 appeared to be leaving me alone. But I was wrong on that last count.

Since arriving in Germany, I had avoided talking to journalists and there had been scarcely an article about me in the British press. Warren Templeton meanwhile was energetically seeking to open dialogue with MI6 to put an end to the dispute. But despite my ceasefire and genuine attempts at conciliation, MI6 were determined to cause me as much inconvenience, cost and hassle as they could.

In February 2000, Patrick, a friend from Geneva, invited me to his chalet in Chamonix, at the foot of Mont Blanc, for a fortnight of skiing and snowboarding. Strictly, I was not allowed in France but I gambled that the DST would not realise I was on their patch. I'd not been there long when my landlord in Oberstdorf rang me. 'What have you done?' he asked me accusingly, 'the police are here.' He explained that at 6 a.m. he had been awoken by a sharp knock on the door. On opening it, he had been bowled over by four uniformed police and two civilians. The latter turned out to be my friends Herr Kugel and Fräulein Gajabski. They were searching the flat as we spoke with a warrant to confiscate my computer.

Presumably the BfV bowed to MI6's pressure and sided with them once they realised that I would not help them. Whether Kugel intended to arrest me or not, there was now no way that I could go back to Germany. MI6 had ratcheted down on me again, cutting me off from another potential opportunity to put the dispute behind me. Luckily I had my computer and other valuables with me.

I was in France illegally and could not stay there for long. I needed to find another home, and was running out of options. The only sensible choice was Italy, and an internet search found a language school in Rimini, a holiday resort on the Adriatic coast. On 2 March I packed up my car again, said goodbye to Patrick and moved out of Chamonix.

I found a little holiday apartment a block away from the beach in Rimini without problem – being the off-season still there was plenty of empty tourist accommodation. Having previously learnt French and Spanish, Italian was relatively straightforward and I made rapid progress in the classes. I found the lifestyle in Italy agreeable too, and started to think about building a long-term future in the country. But before I could make any firm commitments to an employer or a long-term rental contract, I needed to sort out my dispute with MI6. Despite everything that they had done to me, I still felt some perverse loyalty to them and wanted to find an amicable solution. I had more or less given up any hope of getting them to an employment tribunal – the only fair settlement – and I would have settled just for an assurance that they would lift their surveillance on me, let me travel freely and allow me to get on with my life. But all my letters to this effect to them were ignored and Warren Templeton's attempts to mediate were firmly dismissed. They seemed absolutely determined to break me both financially and mentally, and once again my only option was to pressure them to mediation. After I had been settled in Rimini for a couple of months, I wrote to MI6 to inform them that a Swiss literary agent was negotiating on my behalf with a publisher who was interested in publishing my story, and asked them how I could submit my manuscript for clearance. I hoped that MI6 would agree to mediate, in which case I was prepared to withdraw completely from the publication deal. But MI6 reacted a week later with their customary vindictive stupidity.

'Emergenza, Emergenza!' cried the overweight and sweating figure, perched on the tip of a ladder swaying just below the balcony of my apartment. 'There's a gas leak!' he shouted urgently in Italian. 'Gas leak, get out of your apartment immediately!'

The police had been knocking on the door of my third-floor apartment for the past two hours. They must have watched me arrive home on my bike from my Italian class shortly after 1 p.m., as they started knocking as soon as I put the kettle on. I wasn't expecting anybody and, peeping through the spyhole, I realised from the training videos in Belmarsh that they were plain clothes police – they all had large moustaches and bad haircuts. The door was heavy duty, so I let them exercise their knuckles. I realised that MI6 must have used my letter admitting that I had a book manuscript as an excuse to raid me yet again and confiscate my computers. Quickly, I encrypted everything important on my laptop, defragmented the hard disk for good measure and hid the tiny but crucial Psion memory disk inside the apartment's television set. With everything secure, I went out onto the balcony to escape the increasingly impatient banging, lay on my sun-lounger and opened up a book. They eventually admitted defeat to two-inches of dead-locked oak and called out the fire brigade. Now the police chief was peering up at me from his wobbly perch, sweating profusely in the midday sun, pretending that there was a gas leak in the hope that this would trick me into opening the door.

'You've got the wrong building,' I replied mockingly from my sun-lounger. 'This building is electricity only! Try that building over there,' I pointed out the neighbouring block. 'Yes, I can smell the gas from over there!' I said with an exaggerated gesticulation.

'Open the door,' he ordered back impatiently, pulling out from his top pocket a heavily chromed police ID badge and thrusting it at me, the gesticulation sending the ladder into a worrying sway. 'Police, open the door.'

'OK,' I smiled, 'but why didn't you just come up the stairs and knock on the door? It's a lot easier than coming up a ladder.' I ducked back into the apartment before I could see his reaction. It was Wednesday, 17 May, the same day that Mrs Stella Rimington, the former head of MI5, announced that she intended to publish her memoirs about MI5, and was negotiating a huge advance with a British publisher. Unlike me, she had not been arrested or had her computer confiscated and the British authorities were happy to let her publish. As in the Patten case, it was one rule for the people at the top and another for the little guy like me. Britain's 24-hour news channel, *Sky News*, had booked me for a live telephone interview at 1530 to discuss this jaw-dropping hypocrisy. The phone started ringing as the Italian police burst into my flat.

'Up against the wall,' screamed the two heavies who led the charge, their pistols drawn and pointing at my chest.

'All right, calm down,' I urged them. It was my tenth police bust and I had my hands up against the wall and feet apart before they'd even recovered their breath. Five other officers entered the room and one put the lights on. 'Hey, turn them off,' I ordered, remembering a tip given me by Onion-head. 'You might have a warrant to search my room, but you haven't got one to steal my electricity.' The irritated officer flicked them off and went over to raise the blinds. The sweaty chief arrived a few minutes later, introduced himself as Inspector Verrando of Rimini DIGOS, the Italian special investigations police, and presented two British SB officers who had come along for a day's outing on the Italian seaside. Whereas Peters and Ratcliffe had some human decency and intelligence, these were a couple of jobsworths, selected to follow MI6 orders unquestioningly.

The search of my flat took about two hours. The jobsworths waved a vaguely worded warrant that empowered them under the Mutual Assistance Act to confiscate anything they wanted. My computer and Psion were first in the pile. Then my whole CD collection, both music and software. 'I'm not competent to examine them for hidden files,' announced Jobsworth One.

'Are you competent to do anything?' I replied helpfully.

Next all my legal papers. Then my mobile phone. 'So that we can see who you've been calling,' explained Jobsworth Two.

Then the television remote control. 'So you can see what I've been watching on telly?' I asked.

Finally they helped themselves to one of my suitcases, loaded it up and announced they were ready to interview me at the Rimini police station. Glancing behind as they escorted me out, I realised they had cleared my room of everything of value. The only thing they couldn't get in my suitcase was the television containing the precious disk.

Verrando interviewed me for six hours before he realised that I had done nothing illegal and that the British police had abused the powers of the Mutual Assistance Act. But by then it was too late. The jobsworths were on their way back to London with all my belongings. They returned my suitcase a few days later when I faxed the head of SB in London with a description of their incompetence, but I never saw my computers, software, CDs, mobile phone or TV remote control again.

A few days later, Verrando wrote asking me to go back to the police station. I ignored his request, thinking it meant trouble. I had just applied for registration in Rimini, which I needed in order to legitimise my presence in Italy, and presumed that Verrando wanted to tell me that I couldn't have it and order me to leave Italy. If they wanted me urgently, they would come and get me, I reasoned. I heard nothing more until I bumped into an off-duty Verrando browsing the top shelf of a newsagent's in the town centre. 'Why didn't you come to see us the other day?' he enquired politely, hurriedly grabbing a photography magazine from a lower shelf. 'Your permit is ready. The British embassy in Rome rang us and asked us not to give you one, so we decided to give you it immediately so that they would not be able to take the decision up to the Interior Ministry.'

But I was underestimating their capacity for spite. MI6 might have lost the support of the Italian police, but that didn't deter them. Driving up the *autostrada* to Milan to see an Italian lawyer about the confiscations, I found that I was under surveillance. It started off discreetly just outside Rimini, but by Bologna I had made repeat sightings and noted the number plates of three cars – a white Fiat Punto, a silver Volkswagen Golf and a grey Fiat Bravo. The Golf got so close on several occasions that I could clearly make out the driver, a swarthy character dressed in a red vest. I rang the lawyer in Milan for advice, and he called the police. They told me to pull into the Stradale Nord service station, just outside Piacenza, and I watched in my rear-view mirror as the Punto and Golf followed me off the motorway and parked up behind the service station complex, partially shielded by some bushes. The Fiat Bravo continued up the motorway, no doubt to park up in a lay-by to watch for when I left the service station. The Italian police arrived 20 minutes later in a Fiat patrol car, and I explained the situation to them. They were sceptical at first and I had to stretch my Italian vocabulary to persuade them that I was not completely mad. They realised I was not a crank when they eventually approached the two vehicles. The four occupants promptly abandoned their cars, scattering into the nearby woods. 'Go on, shoot, shoot!' I urged the police, pointing at the machine-guns hanging from their waists, but disappointingly they were not too enthused by the idea.

The police poked around the vehicles to see if the occupants had left any traces of their identity, but there was nothing except empty coke cans and hamburger wrappers. 'They're not police surveillance,' they assured me. I had already guessed as much. The surveillance was far too amateurish to be from the Italian authorities, and the occupants would not have run away if they were officials. The only explanation was that MI6 had hired an amateur surveillance team to watch me once the Italians had refused to help them any more. When the patrol car left, I bought a Stanley knife in the service station and slashed their tyres. Back in my car, I faxed the British ambassador in Rome using my newly purchased replacement Psion and mobile phone and asked him to send me the bill. Not surprisingly, he didn't send me the bill – I would have sent it straight to my lawyer.

A few days later, my stay in Rimini was over. The landlady of my apartment did not like the embarrassment of the police visit and she told me that the apartment had been 'booked by some Germans last year'. She asked me to leave with a week's notice. I was without a home and with the holiday season approaching fast it was impossible to find other accommodation in Rimini. But perhaps that was a blessing in disguise. I moved north and after a few weeks roughing it in various hostels I found an apartment in Riva del Garda, a far more pleasant town on the northern edge of Lake Garda. It was a sportsman's paradise, with fantastic cycling, windsurfing and walking opportunities for the summer, and with good skiing nearby in the winter. I decided to settle there for a while, MI6 permitting.

But my optimism was short-lived. A few days later, on a trip to Monte Carlo for a job interview, MI6 had me arrested again by the Monaco Special Investigations Unit, who threw me into the cells of their station, by the harbour front. Sitting on a hard bench for a few hours, I rued that I was becoming even more of a connoisseur of police cells than Ronnie from Belmarsh. MI6 asked the Monaco police to confiscate my new Psion and mobile phone, but fortunately they rang for advice from the DST, who advised them to let me go. After six hours of detention they released me on condition I went straight back to Italy.

Shortly after returning home to Riva del Garda, I found that MI6 had been busy again in my absence. The estate agency with whom I had found my flat rang me up and called me into their office on the pretext of requiring a copy of my passport. 'Richard,' announced Betty, the elder of the two sisters who ran the agency, 'while you were away, we had a visit from two men who said that they were from the police.' Anger welled up inside me at this latest intervention from MI6, but worse was to come as Betty explained. 'But we realised straight away that they were not really from the police because they asked such unprofessional questions about you.'

'Like what?' I asked.

'They wanted to know how much you were paying in rent for your flat, and whether you had a telephone line – the real police would not be interested in that.'

'Did they say anything else?' I asked.

'Yes,' Betty hesitated for a moment before continuing. 'They told me that you were a paedophile and warned me to keep you away from my daughter.'

I left Betty's office scarcely able to contain my despair and anger at the depths to which MI6 seemed prepared to stoop in order to wreck my chances of settling anywhere. For although Betty realised immediately what was going on, Riva del Garda is a small town and I knew that she would not have been the only person whom MI6's hired goons approached. I soon detected hostility from other acquaintances who had presumably been fed the same line, then after a month or two my new landlady got cold feet and told me to leave my new flat. Once again I was without a home, and yet MI6 still had not finished with me.

Another trip to Milan was necessary, but more surveillance immediately appeared, this time a white Volkswagon Polo. The same fat bloke in a red vest was behind the wheel, with a long-haired, scruffy companion alongside. This time they made no pretence at discretion and sat glued to my bumper. If I stopped in an *autostrada* lay-by to check my map, they stopped right behind me. On the roads leading into Milan, if I indicated left, but turned right, they did the same. I dived on to a roundabout near the central station in the city centre and drove around it, indicating at every turn-off, but swerving back on at the last moment. They did the same, right on my bumper. I drove around again, this time a bit faster. They did the same, the narrow tyres on their Polo squealing. I accelerated, my BMW gripped firmly and I pulled away a car length from them. Once more around the roundabout and I had pulled out half a lap lead on him. Two more sinister circles and I was right on his tail. The fat bloke was grimacing in his rear view mirror, unsure how to react, and his companion was shouting down his mobile phone for advice from his controller. I flashed my lights and gave them a friendly wave. 'Where will this end?' I thought to myself, unsure whether the story was farce or tragedy.

EPILOGUE

MI6 have spent a substantial amount of British taxpayers' money on preventing me from taking them to an employment tribunal or informing the public of the toll that their lack of accountability has had on my life – a toll that mirrors the harm the unaccountable agency inflicts on other individuals whose civil liberties are violated. MI6 prosecuted and imprisoned me under laws which on 20 July 2000 were scathingly condemned by a UN report into Britain's human rights record. They took expensive injunctions out against me in the UK, Switzerland, Germany, the USA and New Zealand, all in disregard for laws governing freedom of speech, guessing correctly that I did not have the funds to appeal through the courts. They have had me arrested or detained a total of 11 times in the UK, France, New Zealand, the USA, Switzerland, Germany, Monaco and Italy and have used these detentions as excuses to confiscate valuable personal property which has not been returned, and which Special Branch have spent thousands of man-hours examining. MI6 senior managers have used their leverage with friendly intelligence services to have me banned from France, the USA, Switzerland and Australia, again guessing correctly that I would have limited funds to appeal.

MI6 have never justified to the government why this expenditure is necessary; MI6 is not accountable so it need not do so. They need only make a vague claim that my attempts to seek an employment tribunal 'damage national security' and other government agencies or foreign intelligence services spring to their assistance. No attempt is ever made to substantiate their claim, or explain exactly how 'national security' has been damaged (though ironically, when one of their officers recently got drunk in a tapas bar and lost his laptop, and another fell asleep on a train and mislaid his briefcase, on both occasions they gravely assured the nation that the loss of secret documents had 'not in any way prejudiced national security').

MI6's actions against me, purportedly to safeguard 'national security', have had the opposite effect. By using their contacts with foreign intelligence services to pursue me so relentlessly, they have notified them as to my whereabouts. Several foreign services have promptly taken advantage of my captivity or dislocation to ask me to reveal information about MI6 to them. MI6 have thereby confirmed that they regard it as more important to harass, imprison or inconvenience me than to keep secret whatever it is that I am supposed to know.

MI6 cannot justify all this expenditure for any genuine motive to protect national security. During the cold war, the stakes were high enough that perhaps they could make a legitimate case for the prerogative for absolute security transcending the rights and freedoms of individuals. But the cold war has been over for two decades. MI6 has moved into new pastures, mainly nuclear and biological weapon proliferation, organised crime, money-laundering and drug-trafficking. All these are sources of possible danger to Britain, but they are problems that have been efficiently dealt with for years by the police, the customs service and open diplomacy. MI6 has attempted to grab these new areas from other perfectly competent government agencies, but in doing so has not shed its cold war culture. MI6 managers have retained all the baggage that accompanies excessive secrecy and lack of accountability: inefficiency, poor decision making, arrogant management. They have got away with it because, despite all their cock-ups over the years, MI6 is still eulogised by powerful parts of British society and wields disproportionate power in Whitehall. The reason that MI6 has spent so much money suppressing this book is not because it contains anything damaging, but because they fear it may undermine their quasi-mythical status.

Through my lawyers, Warren Templeton in New Zealand, Anne-Sophie Levy in France, John Wadham and latterly Madeleine Abas in the UK, I have attempted to negotiate with MI6 throughout this pyrrhic battle. All I have ever asked for is an independent judgement on the legality and fairness of my dismissal. MI6 could have diffused this dispute at any time over the past five years by picking up a phone and opening an honest dialogue to achieve this basic human right. Instead, they have teased and played me on a line, encouraging me to negotiate, not with any genuine intention of finding a solution, but simply and cynically as a means to gather intelligence on my intentions and whereabouts. They have then used this information, which I have given them in good faith, to persuade foreign police forces to take punitive actions against me or confiscate my possessions.

All MI6 has accomplished with its expensive strategy is to drive me into a corner, forcing me to fight back. They have forced me to flee from the UK and live abroad, then obliged me to hop from one country to another, never living at the same address for more than a few months. They have made it difficult for me to get fulfilling employment and have actively sought to disrupt my career plans. This ceaseless harassment has ironically left me with no choice except to publish this book. Once my story is in the open, MI6 will find it difficult to exaggerate the threat posed by me and thereby persuade allied police and intelligence services to act against a 'terrorist'. I hope that it may put an end to the dispute and allow me to move forward in life.

I chose to publish first on the internet, because it is the only means to circumvent MI6's gagging orders or other persuasive methods. Shortly after I sent my manuscript to a UK publisher, Fourth Estate, their premises were raided by special branch police and their computers confiscated. Fourth Estate declined to publish this book and other UK publishers were put on notice that they would face serious legal and illegal action if they attempted to do so. An American publisher I approached quickly received a menacing visit by the FBI, acting on behalf of MI6, and was persuaded to drop the project. The FBI then recruited an American literary agent to gather intelligence on my intentions and waste my time and money. Publishers I spoke to in Australia and New Zealand also received threatening visits from their respective security services. Even the Swiss literary agent who initially brokered a publishing deal was hit by a swingeing injunction and was forced to withdraw his services. I have also offered on three occasions to submit the manuscript of this book for vetting but MI6 has merely responded with menacing letters threatening me with imprisonment or used my admission of having a text as justification to confiscate my computers.

This waste of time, money and resources would have been avoided in the first instance if MI6 were properly accountable to the government. The belief amongst senior MI6 officers that they are above the law, encapsulated in the head of personnel's claim that 'nobody can tell the Chief what to do', was the cause of this debacle. If the Chief were accountable, he would have ensured that personnel officers were trained in employment law and that professional personnel management practices were in place within the service. (Ironically, the *Spycatcher* débâcle of the 1980s was also caused by shoddy personnel management; MI5 refused to allow Peter Wright to transfer pension credits from his previous employment in another branch of the civil service, resulting in his disaffection.) The way to stop a repeat of similar farces in the future is not to spend large amounts of public money wielding a big stick to punish miscreants, but to prevent disputes in the first place by implementing sympathetic and fair management practices. This will only happen when the Chief, and the entire service, is really accountable to democratically elected government.

A step towards greater democratic accountability was taken when the Parliamentary Intelligence and Security Committee, chaired by Tom King MP, was given limited powers to examine the activities of the intelligence services. But its role remains entirely advisory, and attempts by King to extend its powers have been resisted by MI6, who pay only lip service to his recommendations. In his 1998 annual report to the Prime Minister, amongst several other criticisms of MI6, King made an indirect reference to me, writing, 'recent experiences on both sides of the Atlantic underline the importance of having a range of effective measures for dealing with staff problems as they arise'. King was also referring to the case of Edward Lee Howard, a CIA officer who was peremptorily sacked, then forced to seek refuge in Moscow when his former employer vindictively stifled his protests at his treatment. But MI6 paid no attention to King's recommendation, did not learn from the CIA's mistake and continued to employ the same counterproductive tactics against me throughout 1999. In his 1999 report, Mr King repeated more strongly his recommendation, made a direct reference to me, and wrote in bold text, 'We strongly support the right to have access to an employment tribunal.' Still MI6 paid no attention to this criticism, or many of his other recommendations, and refused to grant me a tribunal. MI6 will continue to ignore King's recommendations until there is a radical shake-up of the Official Secrets Act and the way the intelligence services are run.

The Official Secrets Act should be abolished immediately and replaced with a Freedom of Information Act, similar to the laws that exist in Australia and New Zealand. 'National Security' should be clearly defined in the act. The Chiefs of both MI5 and MI6 should be replaced by a single Intelligence Tsar from outside the services who is not indoctrinated with the existing cover-up secrecy culture, and who is fully answerable to a Parliamentary Select Committee. Only then will there be full democratic control over the intelligence services. The new head should moreover oversee the merging of the two services into a single entity, perhaps renamed the United

Kingdom Security and Intelligence Service. Expensively maintaining separate overseas and domestic intelligence services makes no more sense than having separate health services for men and women.

National security will not in any way be compromised by the merging of the two services into a single accountable entity – similar procedures work fine in the USA, Canada and New Zealand – and indeed security will be greatly enhanced as an answerable service will rapidly review its management procedures and there will be no repeat of the numerous intelligence fiascos which the country has suffered in the past five years.

I am not sure how MI6 will react when this book is published. I hope that they will react positively by reforming their obvious shortcomings to ensure that no other employee is driven down the same route. Unfortunately, past experience suggests that they will not be so prudent. In reality, their vindictive efforts to stop me telling this story are not to protect anything that is still sensitive – I left MI6 six years ago, and even then knew nothing of major sensitivity – but just to cover up exposure of their unreasonable mismanagement of my dismissal and their incompetent attempts to stop me having a fair hearing. Every time they have taken a punitive action against me, they have been forced to dig yet deeper to cover up each new piece of unreasonable vindictiveness.

Yet MI6 could save themselves all these efforts, legal battles and the British taxpayer considerable expense if they were to accept this simple pledge from me. I will come back to the UK voluntarily, hand over to charity all my personal profits from this book, accept whatever legal charges MI6 wish to bring against me, and if necessary go to prison again, on one simple condition: that I first be allowed to take them to an employment tribunal. If MI6 were a noble and fair organisation, genuinely interested in protecting national security and accountable for the public money that they spend, then they would accept this offer with alacrity. But having worked both for, and been targeted by, them for nearly a decade, I doubt that they will.